WISDOM
— IN —
LEADERSHIP DEVELOPMENT

CREATING A PIPELINE TO GROW LEADERS
AND MAKE MORE DISCIPLES

CRAIG HAMILTON

SYDNEY · YOUNGSTOWN

Wisdom in Leadership Development
© Craig Hamilton 2021

All rights reserved. Except as may be permitted by the Copyright Act, no part of this publication may be reproduced in any form or by any means without prior permission from the publisher. Please direct all copyright enquiries and permission requests to the publisher.

Matthias Media
(St Matthias Press Ltd ACN 067 558 365)
Email: info@matthiasmedia.com.au
Internet: www.matthiasmedia.com.au
Please visit our website for current postal and telephone contact information.

Matthias Media (USA)
Email: sales@matthiasmedia.com
Internet: www.matthiasmedia.com
Please visit our website for current postal and telephone contact information.

Unless otherwise indicated, all Scripture quotations are from the Holy Bible, English Standard Version® (ESV®), copyright © 2001 by Crossway, a publishing ministry of Good News Publishers. Used by permission. All rights reserved.

Scripture marked 'NIV' taken from the Holy Bible, NEW INTERNATIONAL VERSION®, NIV®. Copyright © 1973, 1978, 1984, 2011 by Biblica, Inc. All rights reserved worldwide. Used by permission.

ISBN 978 1 875245 80 2

Cover design and typesetting by Lankshear Design.

For Lyle Schaller
1923-2015

Acknowledgements

A book may seem like the singular effort of an individual hammering away at a keyboard, but writing a book is actually a team effort. This book is the product of the leadership input from the many people who have helped, rebuked, instructed, critiqued and given input into my leadership over the last 20-odd years.

Thanks, first and foremost, to Jesus of Nazareth, who is the leader *par excellence*. If I could be the slightest fraction of the leader he is I'd be satisfied.

To my wife, Nix, who believed in my leadership before anyone else did.

To Avalon, Willow and Ezekiel, the first and best team that I lead. And of course, special thanks to my favourite child. You know who you are.

To the leaders, students and students-who-became-leaders at Velocity who partnered with me to work out what developing leaders at every layer actually looks like and how it works in practice. Particular thanks to Mark McKeown, Matt Bennett and Miles Stepniewski for each playing his part in pioneering the unit leader layer.

To Lyle Schaller, whose creativity, specificity, contrarianism and insight are continually inspiring. Although we never met, his influence stands behind all my leadership activity—not just in the parish but also down to how I've written this book—through his example of the competent composite Don Johnson.

To Walter Mahler for his career-crossroads model that helped lay the intellectual foundations for what became pipeline architecture.

To Dr Sarah Irving-Stonebraker for being the most ridiculously overqualified research assistant in the history of the world.

To Ian Carmichael, Emma Thornett and the whole Matthias Media team for all the behind-the-scenes effort and energy it takes to make a book happen. Especially when you have to do a whole bunch of it one and a half times over! Thanks especially to Rachel Macdonald for editing the manuscript to make me much more succinct, ordered and articulate than I am in real life.

Over the years there have been many people who read parts of this book and helped me make it better: Joel A'Bell, Ray Galea, Craig Glassock, Steve Jeffery, Ken Kamau, Col Marshall, Tom Melbourne, Tony Payne, Gav Poole and Dominic Steele. Thanks to each of you for your encouragement, feedback, pushback and clarifications. If there are any mistakes or weaknesses in this book then presume that at least one of these people warned me against it or recommended that I change it, and that I then ignored their sage advice.

Contents

NB	Pipeline planning meetings have been highlighted with grey shading throughout the book so that they are easier to find.	

Introduction   9

Section one

1.	Setting the scene	17
2.	Discipleship	29
3.	Wrestling with clarity	37
	Pipeline planning meeting 1	53
4.	An overview of the framework	57
5.	A cultural foundation	77
6.	The challenge of becoming a team leader	87
7.	Pipeline 101	97
	Pipeline planning meeting 2	105
8.	The key impediments to starting a pipeline	109
9.	The ten pipeline commandments	117
10.	Common experiences in the pipeline	131
11.	Before you install	141
	Pipeline planning meeting 3	145

Section two

12.	Culture and leadership development	151
13.	Navigating the culture	163
	Pipeline planning meeting 4	171
14.	Ministry grouping	175

15.	How to group ministries	189
	Pipeline planning meeting 5	201
16.	Full outline of the pipeline: leader	205
17.	Full outline of the pipeline: team leader	223
18.	Full outline of the pipeline: ministry area leader	241
19.	Full outline of the pipeline: senior leader	255
	Pipeline planning meeting 6	270
	Layer summary	272
20.	Leader recruitment	275
	Pipeline planning meeting 7	293
21.	Leader recruitment: selecting team leaders	295
22.	Leader recruitment: hiring staff	305
	Pipeline planning meeting 8	315
23.	Leader assessment	317
	Pipeline planning meeting 9	328
24.	Ministry monitoring	331
	Pipeline planning meeting 10	348
25.	Training and coaching	351
	Pipeline planning meeting 11	363
	Core skills summary	365
26.	Ongoing challenges	367
	Pipeline planning meeting 12	369
Appendix:	Unit leader layer	373
	Layer summary (with unit leader layer)	382

Introduction

Maybe some people pop out of the womb as leaders and it comes naturally. Effortlessly, even.

I was born middle of the pack, though towards the back, and you'd be lucky to find me facing the right way. If you were looking for leadership qualities, there were precious little to find. Everything about leadership was hard. If there's a fountain of crystal-clear leadership brilliance that gets dispensed into gifted individuals at birth, then my leadership brilliance was decanted from a brackish swamp.

I wasn't a born leader. I was helped. Forged. Developed.

Not a natural

When I was studying at theological college, the institution set a somewhat unrealistic amount of required reading. Every student knew it was physically impossible for a normal human to read what was 'required'. Many still made heroic efforts in the face of the unfeasible, while others gave up in frustration and despair.

In my second year there, I read a quote from John Stott where he said that a full-time church leader needs to read for an hour a day, a day a month and a week a year. Minimum.[1] Perhaps the college was trying to instil the same discipline, but at the time, putting aside those immense readings, it would have been a miracle if I read for an hour a month, let alone per day.

Now, I write hefty books, but I'm not a 'good' reader. I'm slow with a short attention span—however, I *am* consistent. So I decided, along with a custom of only sporadically turning up to lectures, to read a grand total

---

[1] John Stott, *Between Two Worlds,* Eerdmans, Grand Rapids, MI, 1982, p. 204.

of zero required readings and instead try the John Stott approach. I never asked permission or told anyone; I just did it. No-one seemed to notice, and it didn't make any discernible difference—except now I had more time both for other activities and to allocate towards different reading.[2]

Around this same time, it also dawned on me that when I started working as an Anglican minister, I wouldn't be spending all day reading the Bible and teaching it; I would also have to deal with people in groups and help resolve conflicts. I would need to organize them, roster them, plan things with them, for them and around them. I'd need to do hospital visits, funerals and staff meetings, as well as deal with financial reports and budgets—none of which I felt even remotely prepared for or competent to be involved in, let alone to lead and drive.

This was no-one's fault. My church had trained and equipped me fantastically. The college was rightly focused on developing me theologically. But it was still a deficiency that existed. If it was going to be solved, I was going to have to figure it out myself.

So I decided to use the John Stott approach for this too, despite my slow pace and always-impending boredom. I resolved to read between 30 and 40 non-fiction books a year, a mixture of theology and leadership. And I did it. And again in third year. Then again in fourth year. By the time I finished college, I'd read 30 leadership books. Combined with all my mistakes made at the churches I worked at both before and during college, I thought "Surely I've got a leg up on this whole 'doing ministry' thing". And perhaps I had, but boy it didn't feel like it when I arrived in an actual parish as an actual minister in an actual church.

My first job out of theological college was at a growing church in western Sydney as the youth minister. I inherited an existing youth ministry and a team of amazing leaders. They were fun and faithful; they loved Jesus and loved the students. They welcomed me and my wife along with our six-week-old daughter, and we became friends and fellow workers in the ministry.

When I arrived, the youth ministry had three small teams of leaders

---

[2] I'm not actually recommending this as a study plan for college students. Take it as descriptive rather than prescriptive.

each led by a team leader. I had a feeling deep in the cockles of my heart that I wanted these team leaders to do more than just organize and coordinate the team—but I couldn't put my finger on what exactly I needed them to do. They were all doing precisely and well what I had asked them to do, so I sensed I wasn't asking them to do the right things. But what were those things supposed to be?

By my third year there, I knew I needed to figure this team leader thing out. Developing leaders was going okay, but not great. My training wasn't intentional and predictable. I didn't really know *what* to do or *who* to do it with. I had an idea of some basics I wanted people to learn about—character as king and some specific ministry skills—but besides that, I was at a bit of a loss. I'd continued reading 30-odd non-fiction books a year, so I began looking for books on developing leaders. Then I stumbled upon *The Leadership Pipeline* by Charan, Drotter and Noel.

The Leadership Pipeline

The Leadership Pipeline was first published in 2001, but that wasn't where the concept started.

In the 1970s, Walter Mahler worked closely with the business juggernaut General Electric (GE) to understand and develop plans and practices for the replacement of key executives. This became known as 'succession planning', but what Mahler was doing at GE was actually an approach to leadership development that was spread throughout the whole organization, a series of feeder groups up and down the organization that focused on succession planning at every level.

Mahler, with William Wrightnour, first published his framework in 1973 as *Executive Continuity: how to build and retain an effective management team*, outlining what he called the "four critical career crossroads".[3] Thirteen years later Mahler published another book, this time with Stephen Drotter, called *The Succession Planning Handbook for the Chief Executive*.[4]

---

3   Walter Mahler and William Wrightnour, Executive Continuity: How to Build and Retain an Effective Management Team, Dow Jones-Irwin, Homewood, IL, 1973, pp. 64-66.
4   Walter Mahler and Stephen Drotter, The Succession Planning Handbook for the Chief Executive, Mahler Publishing Co, Midland Park, NJ, 1986.

In this book Mahler and Drotter expanded the framework from four crossroads, or passages, to six.

This further-refined framework was then implemented in over 80 companies across the US. Drotter, along with fellow business consultants Ram Charan—who was heavily influenced by leadership guru Noel Tichy of the University of Michigan and former head of GE's Crotonville Leadership Development Center[5]—and Jim Noel, then wrote the first version of *The Leadership Pipeline* in 2001. They'd taken Mahler's framework and added their own insights gleaned from helping all those companies implement it. Ten years later they revised the book further, after observing both the changing global business landscape and the continual challenges companies encountered in implementing. It was at this point that I then stumbled upon the book.

How we got from there to here

The Leadership Pipeline is insightful but nigh impenetrable. If you've read and finished it: congratulations. I completed it due mostly to my borderline-pathological need to finish every book I start without skipping a word. The other challenge with the book is that it's written for multinational business conglomerates, which is a vastly different context to the average local church. But I knew the pipeline framework was a crucial part of the answer to my leader development problem, so I started the work of transposing it to the world of church ministry.

In 2012 I began implementing version one in the ministries I led. As the years rolled on, I began to oversee more and more ministries and I kept on refining the pipeline architecture. As I taught and discussed the concept with hundreds of pastors across Australia and internationally I learned new things, made subtle tweaks to how it applied and should be implemented in various ministry contexts, made changes as I thought through the ways our theological assumptions impacted things and saw nuances that I hadn't seen before. What you have here in this book is now version eight!

---

5   Noel M Tichy and Eli Cohen, *The Leadership Engine*, HarperCollins, New York, 1997.

In 2015 I published *Wisdom in Leadership*, which helps set the groundwork for leadership in the church context. Even clocking in at almost 500 pages, that book is still only about getting the fundamentals into place. This book you're reading now is about putting in place the next step, putting those pieces together into a broader system for developing leaders. Throughout this book, you'll notice plenty of footnotes linking back to various chapters in *Wisdom in Leadership* because these two books dovetail into each other. If you haven't read *Wisdom in Leadership* yet, you'll still be able to read this book on its own with no problems, however reading both will deepen your understanding.

How the book works

This book is split into two sections. Section one outlines the overall problem we face, in one form or another, in our churches and how the leadership development framework helps us to solve it. Section two then digs into the details, stepping through each piece of the framework up close to fully grasp it.

Elements like 'ministry grouping' and 'pipeline architecture' are discussed over multiple chapters since for many they will be the most foreign. Aspects like recruitment or assessment are covered more briefly, adding shading or a new perspective to practices that we are already familiar with and implementing to some extent. There were many companies who tried to superficially emulate GE and ended up as shallow copies; gaining a deep understanding will allow you to avoid some common mistakes.

The book also includes several narrative chapters. These aren't gripping stories with three-dimensional characters—I'm not expecting to see *Wisdom in Leadership Development: the movie* any time soon—but they will help us see the issues from a slightly different angle.

Leadership development is too broad and complicated for even a book this size to completely canvas, which is why I've also created a companion website: **revcraighamilton.com**. There you'll find plenty of free resources to download and use, such as role description templates, quizzes to help you find the right place to start, and training courses to help get you developing your leaders at every layer.

Section one

1
Setting the scene

"I just don't have enough leaders", Phil sighed as he sipped his coffee. "Maybe you're doing things you shouldn't really be doing, and you need to close some ministries and redeploy some leaders", Luke said, half-teasing, half-serious.

Luke was the senior minister at St Luke's—the church down the road from St Philip's. Luke and Phil often sat at the local café to talk about life, God and ministry. They'd been friends for years, and since Luke was older and had been in ministry longer, Phil often went to him for help and advice. Neither church was the largest in the area, but Phil had watched St Luke's grow healthier and bigger than St Philip's. Phil was curious as to what had been happening there and what he could learn from Luke—although sometimes, deep down, Phil was also frustrated that his church wasn't growing as fast.

"Oh, we probably do some things we shouldn't or don't need to", Phil replied. "But it's more than that. People are happy to serve, and when we call for helpers some step up. Not as many as we'd like, but there's certainly people willing to be involved in ministry. But we can't seem to develop those people into leaders—certainly not leaders who can lead other leaders."

"Well, leading followers is one thing, and it's tough enough, even if by definition they're meant to be led. Leading leaders is even harder."

"But at St Luke's you guys seem to have figured it out", Phil interrupted. "You have leaders everywhere. It looks like they sprout out of the ground like weeds: it just happens. What did you do to make it like that?"

Luke laughed. "Oh no, it doesn't just happen, and it sure isn't easy. In fact, it's extraordinarily hard and takes relentless effort and attention. It's not what *I did*, it's what *we're doing* that makes it happen. But just to clarify:

why do you think you should be growing the people of your church into higher-level leaders?"

"Why?" is always an important question and is often an excellent place to start. Going all the way back to first principles can feel difficult, but the resulting clarity is often hard to come by any other way. And Luke's question of *why* we might think to grow and develop leaders in a church can be answered in several ways.

One answer is: "So I can get other people to do the things I don't like doing". This may indicate a selfishness and a 'wrong fit' of the person to the role, but it doesn't *have* to be a negative indicator. We don't all enjoy the same things and no matter how much we love a particular job, there will always be aspects we like and do better than others.

Another answer might be "It's what the big churches are doing", or at least "It's what other churches are doing". This isn't a particularly strong reason for wanting to improve leadership development in a church. My mum taught me that just because the cool kids are doing it doesn't mean you should do it too. Big churches do lots of things, but that doesn't mean anything about whether or not they should be done. And other churches might be building and developing leaders, and that is *definitely* a good thing to do, but it's not good *because* other churches are doing it. Plus, are you *sure* the big churches are doing this?

A third answer is the problem that Phil raised with Luke: "We don't have enough leaders to staff the ministries we want to run and therefore we need more". Like the first answer, there is something in this that is good and right. Raising more leaders means you can implement the plans that you have to reach more people with the message of Jesus and serve and love people. But raising more leaders to fill existing ministry positions might mask some issues at the foundational level of how you're thinking about ministry.

'Filling spots' might indicate a bare minimum view of leadership, where what you're after is really helpers, doers. Now there's nothing wrong with wanting helpers, but it's not the same thing as wanting to build leaders.

Needing more people to staff the current ministries might also mean that, once all the current positions have been filled (and hence that presenting problem has been solved), the drive for leadership development will be over. There's no more motivation to pursue leadership development—until a new shortage occurs. It's an inherently reactive mode of engagement that will be unlikely to sustain leadership development long-term.

Lastly, the call for more leaders may also be masking a more subtle problem: we don't need more leaders; the leaders we have need to be developed so that more ministry can be done by the same, or sometimes even fewer, effective people. That is, *more* leaders may not be the solution because *not enough* leaders may not have been the actual problem. This could be a training and development challenge, though it may equally be a systems and structure issue.

Needing more leaders isn't always (or even often) a wrong motivation, but this need can sometimes mask more profound issues. As this book progresses, we'll come back to some of these issues and how to go about solving them, or at the very least minimize their impact.

Phil's answer

"I've thought a lot about *why* I want to grow the leadership of my people", Phil answered slowly, carefully organizing his thoughts, "and the answer is fundamentally theological. I'm a firm believer in the priesthood of all believers. While different people have different roles, and some of those roles are different offices—like the office of pastor—there is still a common status among all Christians. Every one of us, ordained or not, are equal in Christ by the Spirit. And while I may have the work of preaching and proclaiming as a pastor-teacher, we all have the responsibility to speak the word of God to one another and to those we meet.

"But more than that," Phil continued, "in 1 Corinthians 12, every piece of the body has a part to play and if people don't do theirs, not only are they impoverished but so are the rest of us. The body only grows and matures as every part does its work. It's not my job as 'the minister' to do all the work of ministry myself. Our job as a staff team is to equip and prepare the rest of God's people to do the ministry, their own works of mutual service, so that we all reach unity in Christ. Ephesians 4 is the model to emulate, I think. And this is the fundamental reason I have for wanting to build leaders at St Philip's. I want to help them to use their gifts amongst the body because that's what God has designed them to do—expects them to do. It's my job to equip and prepare them for that; that's what God expects *me* to be doing."

Luke sat quietly for several moments, then finished his last sip of coffee. "I don't think I could have said it better even with a week to prepare. So what do you do to equip and prepare them?"

Now it was Phil's turn to pause. He'd never thought much about that question and he was a bit embarrassed. He knew Luke wasn't trying to trap him, but he felt a little flustered because he was about to be much less impressive. "I preach the word of God as well and as clearly as I can, and I challenge people with and spell out its implications for their life. And I model, as best I can, what it looks like to serve with enthusiasm and humility."

"And how's that working out for your church?"

"Well, people are being converted and growing in their knowledge and maturity as disciples", Phil began, somewhat defensively. But then he slumped back in his chair and admitted, "But obviously it's not working out as well as I thought it would because here we are and I'm lamenting the lack of real leadership, even among those we'd call 'leaders'. People are happy to help, but there's a dearth of initiative and drive, and it's getting exhausting having to think of everything and solve every problem."

"Just because you label a person a leader doesn't make them one", Luke said. "Preaching and modelling are necessary components of discipleship, but they're not sufficient for the task by themselves. It's the same for building and growing leaders—preaching and modelling are vital but insufficient. There's more you need to do."

When Phil heard "more you need to do", he sank even lower in his chair. Phil hated those words.

Across town

"I just don't know what went wrong", Andrew sighed from the passenger seat. "Dan is one of the best youth leaders I've ever seen. He's faithful and reliable, loves Jesus and the students, and has good character. He's not perfect, but he's certainly above reproach. He's got energy and enthusiasm; he really connects with the students; he's a great Bible teacher; and there's no-one better at running fun, creative games."

"I'm almost tempted to try and steal him to join my kids' ministry team", Matt grinned behind the steering wheel. "Why is he such a problem?"

"Oh, there's no problem with *him*. The problem is all the other leaders. I really hoped they'd follow his lead and become more like him. I know classroom training is of some value, but on-the-job training is much more powerful. I figured if I made Dan the team leader for the ministry team leading the 12-to-15-year-olds, those leaders would flourish under his leadership, seeing it up close and all that. But it's just not happening."

Andrew was the youth minister at St Philip's. He and Matt, the children's minister from St Luke's, were on their way to a children's and youth gathering.

"What am I doing wrong? It's not just that the leaders aren't getting better with Dan as a team leader… They're getting worse!"

"Getting worse?"

Andrew explained, "Yeah, they're getting worse. I thought Dan would inspire them to be a little more reliable, enthusiastic, to get better at running games and small discussion groups. But all the leaders on his team are *worse* at all those things than they were before!"

"And how long has Dan been the team leader?"

"Not even five months!"

"Yeah, that is the power of leadership: the right person can help everyone improve, while the wrong one can make even good leaders perform less well", Matt said, pretty sure it wasn't going to get a good reception.

"But Dan is the best leader we have! It was you who taught me the five C's—character, convictions, chemistry, competencies and capacity. Dan's a five-C leader, so how can he be the wrong choice?"

Matt replied, "Well, the five C's are a good conceptual grid for thinking about people in terms of general recruitment onto a team, for ongoing development, and as a way to think about each leader as an individual. But when it comes to the move to being a leader who leads the team, there are other things to take into account." He paused for a few seconds. "But first, can you describe how you saw the leaders on Dan's team getting worse? Worse in what way?"

"Well, I guess they just got worse as leaders. They're late more often, sometimes not even turning up at all. I mean, everyone's lives are full, and things come up unexpectedly, but before they were basically reliable or communicated if they couldn't come. And now they put less effort into running games, too. They're only semi-prepared. The rules are confusing and sometimes they don't even bring all the props they need. But you know what else?" Andrew continued, "I was talking to Dan about how his leaders are going, and he mentioned that they're hard to work with during group time."

"What does that mean?" asked Matt.

"I asked the same thing, and Dan said that sometimes he has to tell the leaders to be quiet just as much as he does the students. They're disruptive! He also said when the leaders turn up underprepared he then has to step in to salvage the game and make it work, or explain the rules again, or even actually run the game for the struggling leader. He said sometimes it feels like he's the only leader and the others are just older high schoolers."

"This is all very familiar", Matt sympathized. "This used to happen to me almost every time a new team leader took on the role. I was so frustrated and discouraged. I thought seriously about just giving up as a children's minister and going and doing something else. But there is an explanation for why this happens and a way to solve the problem as well. And it's a simple solution."

"Great! A simple and easy solution is my favourite kind of solution!"

Matt laughed at the enthusiasm of his friend. "Oh, no. The solution is definitely simple, but it's not easy. It's hard to implement consistently and takes a lot of skill and focus. Like a lot of simple things, it's actually quite hard to do."

Phil and Luke

"I hate those words, Luke. I hate having to do more. I already work way too many hours a week. I just don't have room for *more*."

"Yeah, I know what you mean. About five years ago, I was doing too much and not resting properly—but also not leading properly. I asked a friend of mine pretty much the same questions you're asking me, for the same reasons. I needed to relearn leadership—though in some areas, learn it for the first time."

"I thought I was the only one who struggled", sighed Phil, somewhat relieved.

Luke laughed. "Oh, I've lost count of the number of ministers who I've had this exact conversation with, almost word-for-word. But back to the time issue... When I said you had to do more, I didn't mean there's a whole truckload of things to do *on top of* what you're already doing. I meant there are some different things you should do *instead of* what you're currently doing. In a lot of cases, you'll need to view what you already do differently and make some adjustments. But, yes, there will be some additional things, and that'll mean making hard decisions about what you're going to stop doing so that you can start these new things. But I guarantee you, down the track you'll get back more time than you ever knew you had. The hardest part is starting."

"Okay, I think I'm up for that. What do I need to do?" Phil said, sitting up straighter.

"First", Luke smiled, leaning back in his own chair, "we're probably both going to need another coffee."

After they'd each ordered, Luke turned back to Phil and said, "Let me paint a picture, and you tell me if this basically describes you and your church or not. This is what my church was like before, and it's the kind of story I hear from other ministers.

"You want to see people come to know Jesus as their Lord and Saviour. You want to see people grow in their trust and obedience, and, among a host of other things, for them to engage in ministry—whether formal or informal, within or outside the church—with genuine acts of love and care for others and by speaking the word of God in various forms and fashions. There are some ministries at your church that do these things better and more clearly than others, but that's basically what you want to see happen. Right so far?" Phil nodded, not yet particularly impressed by Luke's insight.

"As a church", Luke continued, "you're doing okay at recruiting volunteers for ministry. There're probably gaps, and you could do with more workers for the harvest, but there still are many people serving in your church, both in official and unofficial positions. And you're doing okay at equipping the saints for this first layer of ministry, but it's a struggle to build leaders who can lead teams or perhaps shoulder even more responsibility. You may send one or two outstanding candidates on for some kind of full-time ministry training, but on the whole, it's harder to build high-level leaders. Still sound right?" Luke asked.

The waitress brought over their coffees and quietly set them down on the table. Phil replied, "Basically. My church has many people who are reliable and faithful in their ministries, and some who give an extraordinary amount of time serving. It's just that they don't seem willing or able to step up to lead. Help, yes; lead, not really. I suspect it might be either because they're just not wired that way, or because I haven't given them a vision for what could be."

"Yes, they may be factors, but it's highly unlikely that all the born non-leaders just happened to gravitate to your church. And yes, vision could be one component, but it's almost always one among many, and rarely the primary one. I think there are at least three other factors that make equipping leaders so hard, and they each feed into the others to create a negative spiral.

"The first factor is that everything tends towards complexity. Churches often start simple—say one minister, one service, one small group—and then over time they become two services, then three. They get an extra minister or two. New ministries start up and before you know it, you're organizing the roster for the ministry to left-handed men aged 34-36 who have yet to master frisbee throwing and have every second Tuesday off. Once that's where you're up to, your church has become very complex before you've even noticed.

"The second factor is that there is always more to do. Work creates work. Tasks create tasks. This feeds into the first factor, so the more things there are to do, the more complicated things get—and the spiral begins to emerge."

"That's happened in many areas of my life over the years," reflected Phil, "but I definitely see it happening around church as well. What's the third factor?"

"The third factor", said Luke between sips, "is that equipping people for works of ministry *is* really hard. It takes a long time, and it's not always obvious what we should be training people to be doing or what that training would look like. It takes great care and intentionality to conceptualize teams and team leaders and what they would all do within a broader area of ministry, say across a men's ministry.

"There are basically two ways that people have gone about trying to deal with these feedback-looping factors. The first is to just keep working harder, both paid staff and the volunteers. The main problem with this solution is that it works! At least initially. You work harder and longer and you get the things done. But that doesn't last forever, or even for very long, because the work continues to increase and grow in complexity, and also because you only have so much energy and so many hours until things begin to start collapsing on the inside and you're staring into exhaustion and depression. Solution one is burning leaders.[6]

"And so then we try the other solution: hire another person to do some of it, perhaps an assistant minister or a youth minister. But we don't hire them to multiply and train the saints: we hire them to do the work of ministry. Maybe we *think* that we're hiring them to multiply ministry, but really what often happens is we just ask them to do stuff. And it also works, initially. But then that new hire will also be maxed out, and we'll need to either buy another leader or switch back to burning.

"Obviously, I don't like these two approaches. Instead of burning or buying, I like to *build* leaders."

Phil reflected on his own church over the past few years. "I think this is where I'm up to", he quietly admitted, sheepish that he had fallen into a trap that seemed so obvious when Luke laid it out. "We burned some people, then we bought some, but now we don't have enough money to buy anyone else. Perhaps people have realized we're back to burning leaders and are keeping their distance. But yes... I'm supposed to be equipping the saints for works of ministry. I knew that before we started talking. But I don't really know how to do it. How do I build leaders?"

---

6   Obviously this cycle is often far more complicated than this. A good place to start if you want to think more about it is *Zeal Without Burnout* by Christopher Ash (The Good Book Company, Surrey, 2016).

Matt's opening salvo

"The thing that a lot of people don't realize", Matt began as he changed lanes on the motorway, "is that the transition from being a leader to being a team leader is actually the most difficult leadership role transition there is. Nothing is as challenging or paradigm-shifting as the move from being a *part of* the team to being *responsible for* it.

"Even when leaders are aware that it's a tough transition," Matt continued, "they still often don't understand just how profoundly hard it is, and they don't do enough to help another person make it successfully. I can't count the number of times I have seen someone be asked to lead a team, agree, be thanked and then the person who asked them says, 'If you get stuck or need help, let me know'. They're left to fail frantically and quietly. It's cruel to that leader, but it's also cruel to all those in the team who are then subjected to the new team leader's flailing."

Andrew felt guilty as he remembered saying something similar to Dan. Matt noticed Andrew shift uncomfortably. "Don't feel too bad. I know lots of people who haven't been taught situational leadership. But my heart goes out to the people they lead. Leading people is all about loving them, and one of the best ways to love people is to lead them well.

"But back to that leader to team leader transition. There are three elements that need close attention when a person makes any leadership transition, but especially the team leader transition. The first is the specific skills a team leader needs to be trained in so they can fulfil the requirements of that role. They won't instinctively know how to do it. They might have seen it done well before; equally, they may have seen it done badly. But seeing isn't enough for them to now be able to do it well themselves. They need some critical moves scripted for them. Like learning anything, we start out bad and we get better. This is normal."[7]

"I did neglect to train Dan in the beginning", Andrew admitted. "I was busy and it slipped off my to-do list. But then I realized I'd been neglecting him, so Dan and I started to meet up for training in some of the skills he'd need to function as a team leader."

---

[7] See Craig Hamilton, 'Anything worth doing is worth doing badly', in *Wisdom in Leadership*, Matthias Media, Sydney, 2015, pp. 179-181; 'Fail forwards', pp. 209-217; and 'Treat them like children', pp. 303-306.

"That's great to hear!" Matt replied. "What kind of things did you train him in?"

"Hmm, in changing his default leadership style and understanding the life cycle of a team. We talked about delegation and the importance of communicating with a team. Oh, we also began talking about vision and strategy and using these to inspire and focus the team. Next, I plan on talking through things like coaching and performance monitoring, then we'll move on to running a productive meeting and some introductory conflict resolution skills. That's the plan anyway.

"But I'm no closer to figuring this out. Yes, team leaders need to be taught the skills they need, and if I wasn't doing that then it would make sense of why Dan's team isn't working. But he has been learning those skills, and yet his team is still going backwards. Now that I think about it, when I started training him it actually made the problem worse."

"Yes, that's exactly what I would've expected", Matt said cryptically.

"Well, yeah, I know I'm not the world's greatest leader or trainer," Andrew defended, caught a little off-guard, "but I don't think I've done that bad a job".

"That's not what I meant", Matt said. "I'm sure your training is grade-A. If the content was even vaguely what you listed, it was spot-on. The problem is much more likely to be that he *did* understand than that he *didn't*. What's happening with Dan is textbook.

"Remember how I said there are three elements to think about when someone makes a leadership transition? Skills are one of them, and they're vital. But the other two elements are even more important. What we need to talk about next is really the 11 secret herbs and spices of any leadership transition and they're what people often overlook. But here we are at the conference, so they'll have to wait. I know you're getting a lift back home from one of the others, so let's make a time in the next week or so to catch up, and I can share with you the next piece of the puzzle."

Determined to hear more, Andrew got out his phone and the two worked out a time to meet up while they walked across the car park and stood in line to register and get their nametags. After parting from Matt and as he sat down in the auditorium, Andrew sent a quick text message to his boss before the first session got underway.

Luke's way forward

"What you need is a leadership pipeline", began Luke, but at that moment the phone alarm he'd set to remind him to leave for his next appointment started buzzing. "But we'll have to talk about that some other time. I need to head off to the next thing." He quickly finished the dregs of his coffee and began packing up his diary and notebook. "I'll tell you what though," Luke said, "the common mistake that people make at this point—the mistake that I made!—is that as soon as they realize they need to clarify and implement a leadership pipeline, immediately they start working on implementing a leadership pipeline."

"I don't even know what a leadership pipeline is!" said Phil.

"Well, it's something that only works if it's one part of a larger leadership development system, and a leadership development system is only worth having if you've got the right people to begin with and if you know what you want your leaders to be making. Which means we need to start with discipleship: What are disciples? How do you make them? What are you doing to build them, and how does all that relate to leadership development—or as you put it, equipping them for works of ministry? That's the place to start. I'll pay the bill on the way out; let's talk more in a couple of weeks."

The two senior ministers shook hands, and once Luke was gone, Phil took out his notebook and scribbled down some reflections and questions. At the top of his page he wrote: FIRST STEP = DISCIPLESHIP. Just then his phone pinged with a message from one of his staff members, Andrew, who was at a conference a couple of suburbs away. The message read:

> Just had the best conversation with one of the ministers from St Luke's. Lots to talk and think about! Will update you tomorrow.

Phil texted back:

> Me too.

2
Discipleship

It may seem surprising—for some, disappointing—that the starting point for leadership development is discipleship. This book isn't outlining the case for discipleship, or making disciples, or that every disciple is a disciple-maker; I'm going to assume that we're all on board with the Great Commission.[8] But I am going to outline why, when it comes to leadership development in the church, discipleship is the place to start, and then tease out the relationship between discipleship and leadership development.

First, so we're all on the same page, when I talk about a disciple I mean a sinner who has turned back to Jesus as Saviour and Lord and is learning to treasure him and live Christlike by the power of the Spirit. A disciple is someone who is learning "to obey everything I [Jesus] have commanded you" (Matt 28:20, NIV). This is more than merely intellectual learning, since Jesus doesn't say disciples need to be *taught* "everything I have commanded you". Instead he says they need to be taught "to *obey* everything I have commanded you". This is transformational learning where you *become* different and *act* different.

There are four reasons it's essential to start your thinking about leadership development with discipleship.

Discipleship is what your church is doing

The first reason is that making disciples is the end goal you're praying for and working towards, both with the people in your church and with those who aren't yet a part of your church. You may or may not think that you're

---

[8] Two of my favourite books on this topic are Tony Payne and Col Marshall's *The Trellis and the Vine* (Matthias Media, Sydney, 2009) and Tim Hawkins's *Disciples Who Will Last* (Hawkins Ministry Resources, Sydney, 2007).

doing an outstanding job at one or both of those goals, but to some degree your church will be trying to get on with making new disciples and strengthening, encouraging and growing existing disciples.

If you think about discipleship narrowly as only the activities of explicit evangelism and encouragement, you might object and say that your church is doing more than just those two activities, like caring for the poor. But if we conceive of discipleship more broadly, we see that activities of compassion are actually essential parts of expressing a true and lively discipleship maturity.

Your involvement in, and responsibility for, this task of discipleship within the church will vary depending on whether you're the senior leader, another member of the paid staff team, or a keen member of the church who is passionate to see the kingdom expand in the lives of those around you. But whoever you are, discipleship needs to be the beginning of leadership development for the simple reason that discipleship is what your church is doing. If discipleship is what your church is on about, then every ministry and every leader will be connected into that primary purpose in some way and at some level.

Since leadership belongs in the category of wisdom—it's stitched into creation as the way God has designed the world to work—it doesn't belong solely to the church or solely to Christians. Leadership development isn't 'special revelation' that requires the Lord to unveil the mystery. That might be super-obvious but it's still worth saying. The basic framework in this book would help people make leaders in any enterprise—Christian or non-Christian, profit or not-for-profit, even criminal—for the simple fact that leaders exist anywhere and everywhere. Leadership isn't a *business* idea; it's a *people* idea. This is why the emphasis on discipleship is so vitally important: the goal in the church isn't just to build leaders but to build *Christian* leaders who will seek to lead *Christianly* in all places but specifically in *Christian* activities and ministries.

Discipleship is what you want your leaders to be doing

Second, if making and growing disciples is what your church is doing, then you'll want every single one of your leaders to know how to do it.

Disciples are made as people hear the word of God and put it into practice in their lives by the power of the indwelling Spirit—that is, they learn to obey everything Jesus commanded—and one main way that people hear the word of God is through sermons. But there are also a myriad of other times and places that people will hear the word of God, from explicit teaching in a church service to podcasts, from small group studies to conversations between friends with perhaps no explicit mention of Bible verses. Hearing the word of God is a broad phenomenon, and thus so is *speaking* the word of God. It's something that *every* disciple is engaged in.

So if your church is making disciples, and if disciples are made as people hear the word of God, and if your leaders are leading to enable more people to become and grow as disciples, then all your leaders will need to be speaking the word of God to the people around them—which includes the people they lead.

It's important to underline here that every disciple is *already* involved in disciple-making. That is, being involved in disciple-making isn't what makes someone a leader in the church. Disciple-making is something that every Christian does as they seek to speak the word of God to one another in the power of the Spirit. A disciple *is* a disciple-maker. The point is that leaders will be seeking to grow others as disciples by speaking the word of God not because they're *leaders* but because they're *disciples*. Being a leader means they have different levels of responsibility and authority in that broader disciple-making enterprise that the whole church is doing—and that these leaders themselves are a part of a team with someone leading *them*. We'll discuss this in more detail in section two when we outline the leadership pipeline architecture.

Not every leader will play the same role, have the same responsibilities or make disciples in the same way. The small group leader has the idea of speaking the word of God built into the role itself, whereas the person whose ministry is the church sound desk has fewer opportunities *formally*. But every leader in every role can be looking for opportunities to speak the word of God into the lives of the people around them.

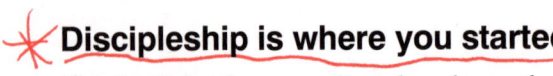
Discipleship is where you started

Third, all leaders are disciples themselves. At least, that's the ideal. Perhaps one or two of your leaders believe they are Christians right now, but in six months they'll discover they weren't and so will turn and put their trust in Jesus. Perhaps others walked away from Jesus some time ago and are continuing with the façade because they like the position and being looked up to. These things happen, and no-one can truly know anyone else's heart—it's hard enough to get a handle on your own—but as much as it's up to you, you want the leaders in your church to be disciples of Jesus themselves.

As an aside, there probably are some *roles* around your church where the line isn't as clear. Say your church asks small groups to provide morning tea after the service on a roster basis. Could Mary, who isn't converted but is keen to learn and is growing in her understanding, bring a packet of biscuits? We may decide it will be okay and even a good thing for her to serve along with her group. But for the most part, leadership in ministry means being a disciple first. Most of us wouldn't want Mary *leading* a small group just yet.

This means that one way to grow more leaders is to first grow more disciples. You need to increase the size of the pond you're drawing from. You can do this by seeing more people converted, or you can mature people in your church to the point where they are keen to serve. If your church is like my church, then there'll be people who are converted followers of the Lord Jesus but who, for whatever reasons, aren't interested in serving in a ministry. But if they could be helped to see that serving is a fundamental part of discipleship and that God has gifted them to strengthen those around them, then they would be keen to find a place where they could do that.

It's not only immaturity that holds people back from serving, though. There could be a whole range of factors in play, from health and mobility to family commitments and work hours. We have to consider someone's whole life, not view them in one narrow, monochrome slice. And *your* systems and processes might hinder more than help. For some people, it's not that they need the right recruitment pitch—they need someone to love them. Having said that, it is still true that discipleship will be the first step towards leadership. For leadership to be occurring and increasing, discipleship needs to be happening.

Discipleship is what your leaders must be growing in

The fourth reason discipleship is the place to start when it comes to leadership development is that the most essential reality in the life of any leader, no matter which layer they lead at, is that they are continuing as a disciple. Knowing God and having sins forgiven are the most critical concerns for every human on the planet, and this is the central work that we are involved in as God's people.

Whatever else your leaders might be growing in—leadership skills, technical skills, relational skills, nunchuck skills—the most important thing for them to be growing in is their discipleship, which means it should be the most important thing in your mind for them. And your leaders' *ongoing discipleship* matters because your *leaders* matter. They're not just tools, where if one breaks you just get another one and keep going. They're not just fuel for the machine, to be poured in, burned up and replaced with the next batch. They're individual humans, precious to God, who purchased them with his own blood.

These four reasons may all be the most obvious thing you've heard today, but it's easy for them to slip out of view. If your leadership development doesn't include a focus on discipleship, then it's both brittle and dangerous because you're ignoring the most important underlying factor. Your leaders are disciples and they need to continue as disciples for their own eternal sake, for the sake of the glory of Jesus and, as a distant third, for the sake of the ministry they serve in.

What's the relationship between growth as a disciple and development as a leader?

So, if discipleship is the *first* step in leader development, what about *after* that? How do the two relate? If someone is growing as a leader, does that tell us anything about their discipleship—and if so, what? Are they two different ways to say the same thing, or are they completely separate from each other?

Same

If every leader is a disciple and every leader should be growing as a disciple, then it seems natural to think that growth in leadership will be growth in discipleship and vice versa. They're both happening at the same time to the same person anyway, right?

In an ideal world they'll both be happening, but this doesn't make them the same thing and we don't live there. People will likely be growing in these two areas at different rates.

There's no guarantee that a leader growing in their leadership skills is also growing as a disciple. There's no obvious correlation between getting better at planning/running meetings/delegating and growing as a disciple. Equally, there's no necessary connection between a leader's growth in faith in Jesus/increased personal Bible reading and their ability to engage in wise strategic planning.

The other problem if we conceive of these two arenas as the same is that then we'll communicate that growth as a disciple means that you also need to move up the chain as a leader, or that moving up layers in leadership means that you are growing as a disciple. If a person in my kids' ministry team grows as a disciple, moving them up into a higher leadership position might be an utterly undesirable outcome. In my kids' ministry I want faithful and mature disciples on the frontlines, hanging out with the kids directly and teaching them the Bible and how to live as a disciple.

I would also hate for people to assume that being asked to lead the kids' ministry team means that they are growing and maturing as a disciple. You need to look elsewhere to discern that information. Just because someone is leading at a higher leadership layer doesn't mean that they are more mature than everyone below them. The senior minister of a church may not, in fact, be the most mature disciple in that church; it could well be one of the welcomers at the door.

Separate

Okay, since development in one area is no guarantee that you'll be developing in the other, then are the two completely separate?

Well, no. We've already noted that we want our leaders to be converted, as best as we can tell. The two overlap at least at this point.

Furthermore, it's usually unwise to have immature disciples overseeing and making decisions that impact large groups of people. We wouldn't want an immature disciple overseeing everything that happened on Sundays in the services, no matter how highly skilled their leadership was or how experienced they were in their day job of running large teams putting on events. Paul counsels Timothy that overseers in the church "must not be a recent convert, or he may become puffed up with conceit and fall into the condemnation of the devil" (1 Tim 3:6). Now, in a church plant of 30 recent converts you need to work with who you have—but as a rule, discipleship maturity is an important factor in leadership recruitment.

There's no easy way to quantify precisely a person's position on the maturity/immaturity discipleship spectrum, but the principle is clear: there is some degree of connection between discipleship and leadership. They're not two separate, hermetically sealed concerns, but they're also not corresponding. So how then should we think about the relationship between the two?

Symbiotic

Leadership and discipleship are best seen as symbiotic: they strengthen and reinforce each other. They are two different things that exist together in an interdependent relationship, like fungus and the tree that it grows on, or certain bacteria and human beings. Leadership and discipleship can be distinguished, and you can talk about them separately, but they are like two organisms in a mutually beneficial relationship.

When people grow as disciples, it will make them better leaders. For example, pride results in leaders treating their people poorly, but if a person grows in humility, love and patience as a result of their ongoing discipleship, this will overflow into how they lead. And the stronger and more mature someone is as a disciple, the more people will naturally look to them for leadership and model themselves after that person. Discipleship *will lead* to leadership, whether the person realizes it or not, whether they want it or not, and whether it's formal or not. Ultimately, we need Christian maturity at every layer of leadership in every corner of the church.

At the same time, you don't grow in patience by sitting on a mountaintop reflecting on patience. Patience grows as you encounter circumstances—or more often, people—where you need to exercise patience. Leadership wonderfully provides a myriad of opportunities to implement and improve this discipleship quality. For a church to be healthy it needs both these organisms to be healthy—and this book is focused on dealing with the health of the leadership organism, without neglecting that it is symbiotically connected to the discipleship organism.

3
Wrestling with clarity

When someone yells "Stop!" I can tell by their face that they think they've been clear and that I know what to do. But I need more information: In the name of love? Hammer time? Collaborate and listen? Bringing clarity is one of the most critical responsibilities of a leader, but it's harder to provide than it first seems. You may feel that you've communicated in 4K ultra-high definition but for everyone else it seems low-res and pixelated. It takes a disproportionate amount of effort.

Clarity is essential to leadership development because leadership is about working *with others*, which means helping everyone to work together. The leader provides the direction for everyone to head in. Everyone on a sporting team needs to know what game they're playing, which way they need to be facing and how they score points. These are the baseline requirements. If a team doesn't have clarity, people will make up their own rules, get in each other's way and achieve far less than they could have.

If you don't fight for clarity at the start, you'll just be doing it later on. It's better to pause and think it through without the pressure of needing to implement something today, immediately, get it done, is this even what we think, too late I've already printed it!

In this chapter, we'll talk through the seven questions that everyone on the team, top to bottom, needs to be able to answer in order to gain shared clarity.

1. Why do we exist?

The first question you need to get clear on is why your church or ministry exists. You can press back as far as you can and come to an ultimate answer like "to glorify God". This is why everything exists, so yes, it's also why your ministry exists. Or you can stop somewhere earlier with "to help people love God and love others" or "to help local churches understand their community" or whatever the appropriate answer is.

This is not "What do you do?" (That's the next question.) You might be the catering team at church and you oversee morning tea. *What* you do is make sure there's food after church, but that's not *why* you exist. The way you might articulate why you exist is "to help people build lasting relationships". The way you do that is by making sure there is food to function as a social lubricant, but providing food isn't *why* you exist.

What your small groups ministry might do is create small groups so people can understand God's word and serve one another, but maybe they exist "to provide comfort and companionship for hurting people". Perhaps it's "to educate people in biblical concepts". Maybe it's "to train people to head out into the world as God's ambassadors".

The point is not to find the single correct answer. There are lots of right answers, and it depends on how far back you want your answer to go and what you will emphasize by articulating it. Your ministry to the poor might exist "to bring the hope of the gospel to the marginalized through sharing practical help"—which is explicitly evangelistic—or it could be "living God's love to the marginalized"—a broader view that may include evangelism but not as the explicit goal. These are quite different ministry emphases. You may lean towards one over the other or consider one more helpful. But is either of them *wrong*? I'm not sure that's a thing here.

My preference for answering "Why do we exist?" is to go big and back to end up somewhere near "glorifying God". This helps articulate that you don't exist for your own sake or for merely human reasons and to remind you that your ministry is God-centred. Not an absolute requirement, but I recommend it.

It's critical to have an answer that you all concur on and can agree that it generally points in the right direction. Exactly how you articulate it is secondary.

2. What's the main thing we're trying to achieve?

The next piece of clarity you need is on what you're actually seeking to do. Handily for churches, God has left us with the main thing we're trying to achieve: we call it the Great Commission, and it's to make disciples of all nations. Now your church might have a favourite string of vocabulary to describe this, but the general answer has already been given to us.

But as you drill down into specific ministry areas, or if you are a parachurch organization, it can become less clear. Thinking about catering again, this ministry will be connected to disciple-making—since that's the main thing your church is doing—but catering isn't *itself* a disciple-making ministry. Maybe you're "creating an environment around food and drink where disciple-making conversations can happen".

There are many examples like this where a specific ministry area seeks to achieve only one part of the broader goal, or something that helps or connects to disciple-making but isn't itself disciple-making. The ministry done by those on the sound desk isn't directly making disciples, but it does relate to disciple-making. You need to communicate what exactly you're trying to achieve and how it plugs into the broader aim of making disciples.

We're still not yet at what you *specifically* do; the answer for catering isn't "put out the biscuits and put the jug on". It's a higher, more abstract level than that. What is the *purpose* of putting out the biscuits and making tea and coffee? What are we hoping to accomplish?

3. What's the overall plan?

Okay, you know why you exist and the one thing that you're trying to achieve above all else. Now you need to clarify what you're going to do to make that happen. This is still not the detailed plans you'll put in place; this is the big plan, the overall plan, what some people call the strategy.

Strategy is just your general plan of attack.[9] Jocko Willink and Leif Babin outline in *Extreme Ownership* the strategy used in the post-9/11

---

9   See Hamilton, 'The point is clarity, not labels', pp. 337-344.

'Battle of Ramadi' in Iraq: seize, clear, hold, build.[10] They would infiltrate and *seize* an area. They would *clear* the enemy soldiers, then *hold* that area and *build* a base from which they could launch their next round of the strategy. That was the overall plan. The tactics would be which platoons would do what at what time. Tactics are the on-the-ground specifics of the overall strategic plan.

Here's one way to figure out what your strategy is: write down everything you can think of that you do and then group things together and start collapsing it all down to the minimum number of items. Once you get it down to three to five things, you've probably found your overall plan. Then you can decide whether you like it or not.

Strategy can be hard to get your head around. If your goal is to read 100 books in the next year, then your *strategy* might be to read two books every week. That's the big, overall plan. Then you'll need to make a number of smaller, tactical decisions, like which books, whether you'll choose books that are all under 100 pages, and whether you'll read for an hour a day or in a weekly seven-hour block. But the strategy is "two books a week". If you do this, you'll hit 100 books. But it's not the only possible strategy that you could go with to achieve that goal. You can choose a different strategy.

If your kids' ministry is "seeking to see kids grow as disciples", then is the overall plan that the kids' leaders will be the primary disciple-makers, or is it that the kids' ministry will partner with parents to disciple their kids? The difference between those two options makes a significant impact on how the ministry operates and on other smaller tactical decisions. Is your youth ministry a place that *Christian* students love to come to, a place that *non-Christian* students love to come to, or a place that non-Christian students love to come to *to hear about Jesus*? Each will create a vastly different youth group.

The clarity brought by these first three questions helps everyone to pull in the same direction and creates a set of boundary markers that help decision-making, since it provides something to evaluate a specific opportunity against. Something may be a great idea, but does it fit what

---

10 Jocko Willink and Leif Babin, *Extreme Ownership*, St. Martin's Press, New York, 2017, p. 226.

we are specifically trying to do? Everyone is able to evaluate the ministry using the same criteria. This clarity also enables individual leaders to connect what they personally do to what the overall ministry is seeking to do—which we'll talk more about with question five.

4. What's our flavour?

What makes your church or ministry distinctively *yours*? What separates it from the church down the road? This is about how you do what you do and the values that underpin your culture. We'll look at the question of values in depth when we talk about the culture that underpins the development framework later. For now, what are the values and behaviours we exhibit—or aspire to exhibit—that will result in us achieving our goal and that set us apart from others?

Let's say your goal was to make your hunger go away, and your plan for achieving this was to eat some chicken. The specific, tactical plan was to cook the chicken in a pan on the stovetop. What makes this chicken in the pan different and distinctive from other cooked chicken? Are you going to use a pinch of salt? A lot of salt? Pepper? Herbs and spices (maybe 11)? The flavour is what makes this chicken *this* chicken. In the same way, your flavour makes your ministry distinctive.

People often like to call these things values or 'core' values. That way of thinking works in the business world to a certain extent because values aren't often at the core of the *actual business itself*. But for churches, our values *are* our business. Things like "Jesus is number one", "the Bible is central" and Christlikeness are things we value centrally as well as the content of our 'business'. But while flavour includes those things, it's also broader than that. Flavour includes things that are still important but aren't as crucial as those core values. They reflect "how things are done around here".

Your flavour is a mixture of core beliefs that define and drive you—what you're willing to die for—and characteristic features that differentiate you from other similar groups. It's the personality of your church or ministry. We'll come back to this flavour idea and how it relates to the various elements of culture in chapter 12.

5. Who's doing what?

By now you know why you exist, what you're seeking to achieve, what the overall plan is, how you're going to behave, and what makes you unique. Now you need to clarify what exactly people will be doing to execute that plan. This means you also need to clarify for each individual leader precisely what you want from them. What are *they* supposed to be doing? You want them to know what a good job looks like before they begin so that they can assess their performance for themselves.

This question might be the most involved and take the longest to answer out of the seven. You'll find that there's actually a lot to clarify, more than you might at first think.

The first step towards clarifying who is doing what is to work out what each ministry as a whole is currently doing. The best approach is to break the ministry down into the big pieces that must be covered for it to do what it's meant to. What needs to happen for the ministry to do an excellent job? What are all the facets that go into running it? What does it take for it to operate? These are its fundamental operations.

On a sheet of paper, break the ministry down into four fundamental operations that completely encapsulate it. If one seems too broad, split it into two more specific areas. You're aiming to have between four and eight fundamental operations that need to be attended to for the ministry to function, depending on how complicated the ministry is.

Once you've broken down the ministry into these top-level fundamental operations, go through and break down each different layer or role into *its* own fundamental operations. The purpose is, again, clarity. What are the basic things that need to be attended to?

Here's an example of how this might look for a small groups ministry. (This isn't how it *must* look—remember, flavour!)

First the top-level fundamental operations:

Overall
What we do

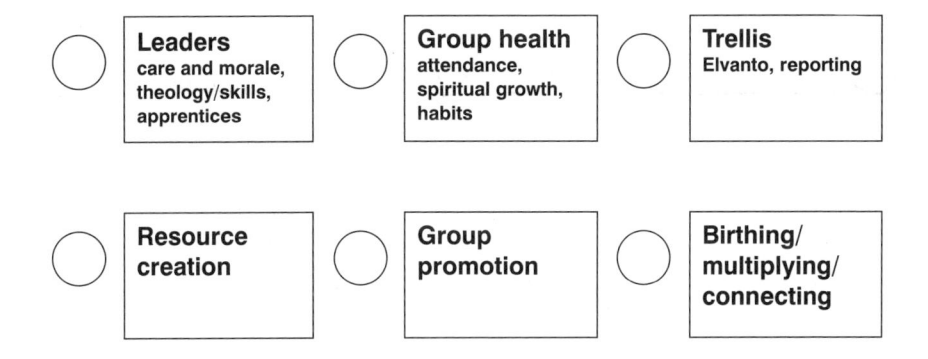

- **Leaders** — care and morale, theology/skills, apprentices
- **Group health** — attendance, spiritual growth, habits
- **Trellis** — Elvanto, reporting
- **Resource creation**
- **Group promotion**
- **Birthing/ multiplying/ connecting**

Then at the team leader layer:

Team Leaders
What we do

- **Leaders** — personal care, morale
- **Leaders** — development, theology, skills
- **Leadership pipeline**
- **Birthing/ multiplying/ connecting**
- **Reporting**

These fundamental operations are the beginnings of a role description for the team leaders.

You might be thinking this is useless busywork that creates documents that live in a drawer or on someone's hard drive and are never used. I can understand that hesitation; this does have the familiar scent of over-articulation. But people need to know what they are supposed to be doing. If clarity is a high priority, then we'll need to come up with a way of embedding it into a system that helps us benefit from all this work. We'll come back to fundamental operations and what you'll do with them in the chapter 'Ministry monitoring', but just consider them as the first step towards answering the "Who's doing what?" question for now.

6. What authority do we have?

The next piece of clarity to bring to the surface is the decision-making of the people in your team. Let's say you are the kids' minister and you have on your team a leader responsible for overseeing the mid-week afternoon kids' group. You both need to know which decisions that team leader has the authority to make and which they don't. Leadership is about *both* responsibility and authority. You shouldn't have one without the other, and the levels should roughly match.

If you give someone no authority and no responsibility, then they're a follower, not a leader.

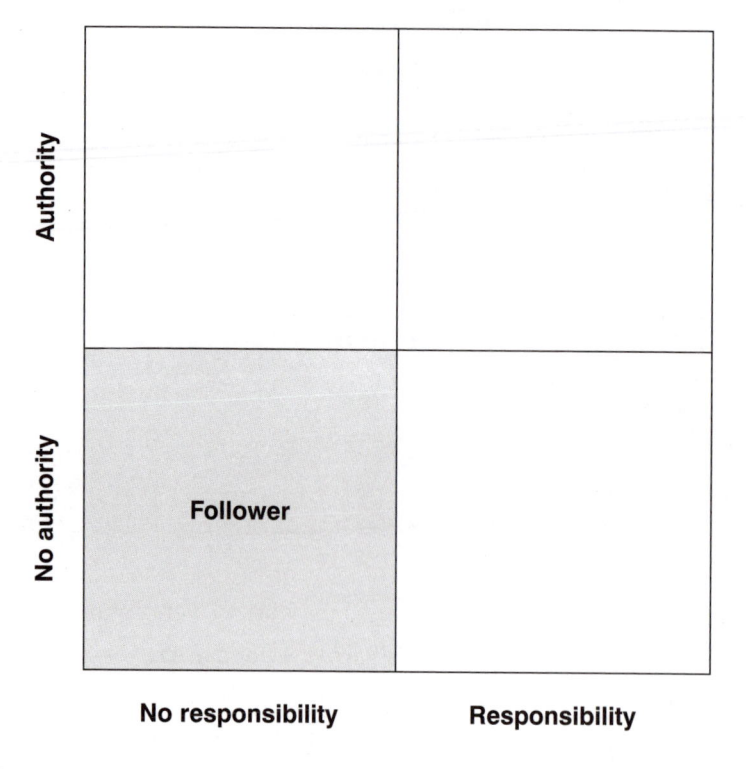

[Diagram: A 2x2 matrix with vertical axis labeled "Authority" (top) to "No authority" (bottom), and horizontal axis labeled "No responsibility" (left) to "Responsibility" (right). The bottom-left quadrant is shaded and labeled "Follower".]

If we give people responsibility and hold them accountable for what happens, but don't also give them the authority to own and improve what's being done, then we've set them up for failure. It's like giving someone the responsibility to start a campfire but then not giving them any wood or matches plus placing them underwater. Responsibility without authority doesn't build leaders; it builds scapegoats.

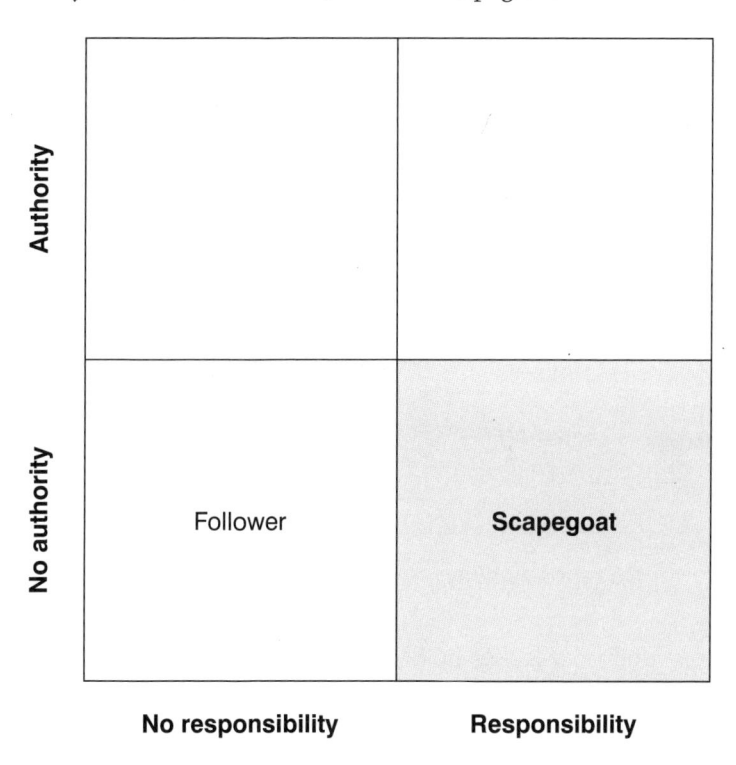

	No responsibility	Responsibility
Authority		
No authority	Follower	**Scapegoat**

On the other hand, giving someone authority without responsibility is equally problematic. It's hard to imagine this happening on purpose, but it does happen by accident when the leader higher up is inexperienced at ministry distribution. They put someone in charge but then don't meet up with them and hold them accountable for what they're doing (or not). Someone with authority can make calls and change things, but if no-one—or someone else—is held responsible, what you're producing is a tyrant and a bully.

	No responsibility	**Responsibility**
Authority	Tyrant	
No authority	Follower	Scapegoat

Clearly you produce a leader by distributing *both* authority and responsibility. Allow them the space to come up with new ideas; give them the resources they need; let them figure out *their* way of doing things—and then make them liable for achieving what needs to be accomplished. If their tweaks improve things, praise them. If their changes make matters worse, hold them accountable and help them figure out how to fix it.

	No responsibility	**Responsibility**
Authority	Tyrant	**Leader**
No authority	Follower	Scapegoat

This means you need to clarify not just what exactly every person and position in your ministry are responsible for, but also the scope of their authority. If the people you lead don't know which decisions are theirs to make, they'll either keep coming to you to ask what they should do at every point or they'll just not do things because they don't want to do the *wrong* thing.

Them coming to you for everything is bad because:

a) it'll be very annoying
b) if everything needs to go through you, the ministry will move slowly
c) sometimes you won't have all the information needed to make a good decision, especially compared with that team leader, which means you'll make decisions that don't actually solve the problem
d) if you're making every decision there's very little point in even having a team leader.

And actually, even if at first people come to ask you at every point, eventually they'll intuitively feel there's something wrong with the arrangement. Then they'll stop coming, either because you're annoyed at them for asking, they *assume* it annoys you, or they're annoyed. And they usually won't miraculously start making their own decisions. They'll just stop doing anything.

For a lot of people, not being wrong is better than being right. If a question is asked in a group, most people won't put up their hands in case they're wrong in front of everyone. This is the same with team leaders who don't know what they have the authority to decide. What might look like resistance is just a lack of clarity.

Ah, now we have a problem. You agree that people need responsibility *and* authority, but it doesn't feel right to give people *complete* authority—especially if they're new to the role or to leading at this layer. Giving someone no authority to make decisions seems like a bad leadership move, but giving someone inexperienced *carte blanche* to do whatever they want doesn't feel like good leadership either.

The solution is to give people clear but *incremental* authority. This helps them build the confidence they need to do something and make a few decisions. This is best done as a conversation, but here's the basic framework.

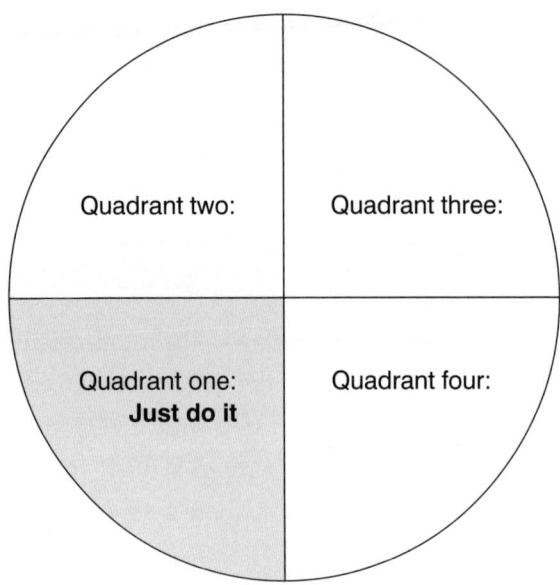

```
        Quadrant two:      Quadrant three:

        Quadrant one:      Quadrant four:
        Just do it
```

Remember that you're the kids' minister working with the leader of the mid-week group? In quadrant one, write down all the things that the kids' group team leader can do without checking with you. They can ask you if they'd like, but they don't *need* to. They can just go ahead.

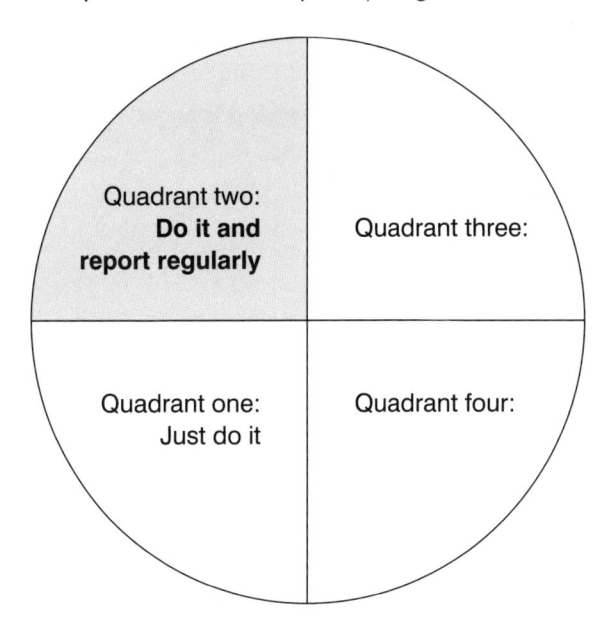

```
           Quadrant two:       Quadrant three:
           **Do it and**
           **report regularly**

           Quadrant one:       Quadrant four:
           Just do it
```

In quadrant two, write down all the decisions that they can make but need to report to you about regularly, whether through a monthly meeting, a weekly email or an online form.

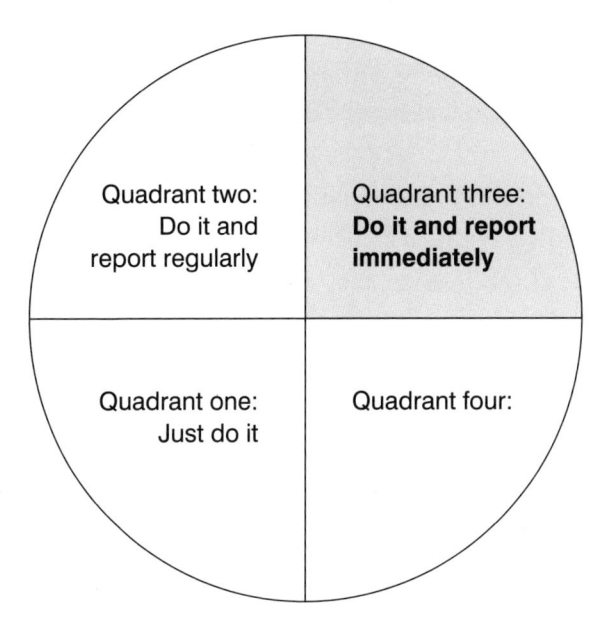

```
           Quadrant two:       Quadrant three:
           Do it and           **Do it and report**
           report regularly    **immediately**

           Quadrant one:       Quadrant four:
           Just do it
```

3 // WRESTLING WITH CLARITY | 49

The third quadrant is for the items that they can do and decide, but they need to contact you immediately afterwards. This could be something like when an injury occurs. If a child gets injured, that leader doesn't need to ask your permission to administer first aid, call the ambulance, or make whatever decision is needed. But they need to let you know what happened straight away.

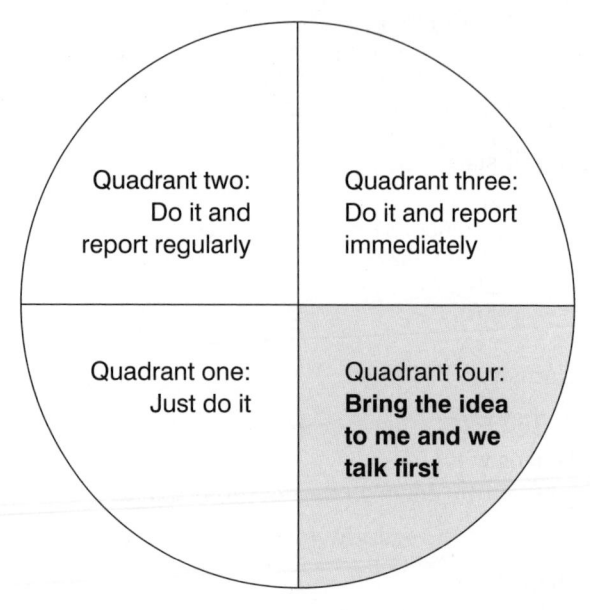

Quadrant two: Do it and report regularly	Quadrant three: Do it and report immediately
Quadrant one: Just do it	**Quadrant four: Bring the idea to me and we talk first**

Lastly are the decisions you don't want them to make on their own. These are all the things you will need to discuss together before any decision is made.

Now you've clarified the authority that you think is appropriate for this person *and* you've outlined something of a roadmap for the future. These decisions aren't set in stone; they can change in the future as the leader and your confidence in them grows. You'll need to schedule conversations to check in and see if anything in the quadrants needs to be moved around—maybe every six months. There'll always be things that live in the fourth quadrant, but what you're wanting is to move as many items as you can up to quadrant three, over to quadrant two, and down to quadrant one.

By the way, this also functions as a diagnostic tool. If everything is moving from the left-hand side back over to the right and pooling in the "we talk first" box, that's a sign that something is going wrong. Either you are leading this person in a way that hinders their development or you might have the wrong person in this role.

7. What's top priority right now?

Our final question to answer clarifies the priorities you want people to be focusing on. The ministry probably has lots of things that are important to do or to improve, but out of all those things, which first?

If you don't communicate what the priority right now is for the ministry, then leaders will start to do whatever they think it is. Maybe this will be nice and helpful, but maybe it won't. Maybe your team leader will decide to focus on developing the people in the team—probably good—but maybe they'll decide to teach the kids modern art theory—an essential piece of cultural instruction that 5-year-olds need, but perhaps not the priority for your kids' ministry in this specific season. More likely, every leader will pursue what they each think is the priority and you'll end up with a lot of activity and chaos with very little progress or sustained momentum.

If *you* think the priority for the welcoming team is getting newcomer contact details, then that's something *you* need to tell them—and then come up with a plan, probably with their input, taking into account what's holding them back and what they need to do to see it happen.

There's no sure-fire way to determine what your priorities should be or how often you should change them, but as a general rule your big priorities will come from three broad categories: quantity, operational processes and discipleship perception.

Quantity will be things like ten new converts this year, 80% of people in small groups, or a 60% retention rate of newcomers. It's about doing or having more of something.

Operational processes are things like improving the music quality of Sunday services, clarifying the pathways into serving, or improving the welcoming systems. This is about doing things better.

Discipleship perception will be things to do with how people self-identify in their discipleship, such as people saying they have experienced "much growth" as a disciple or being "confident to share my faith". This is people making and noticing changes in their own life.

If you're struggling to think of what your priority might be for this next timeframe, these three categories are a good place to spark ideas from.

You might focus on improving weaknesses. This isn't bad or wrong—often problems need focused energy to fix—but this shouldn't be the only way you decide on priorities. You should also look for strengths and bright spots, areas or ministries that are thriving where you might invest time and energy to see even more results. Fixing a weakness *may* be the best thing to focus on, but think carefully and include the possibility of prioritizing an already flourishing area.

You might want to have one or two things you're focusing on across the whole year, or you might want to work in 90-day cycles. Some priorities lend themselves to shorter bursts, while others will make more sense to tackle across 12 months. Different churches and ministries in different circumstances will do different things. The point isn't that you set a priority the right way, but that you *have* a sensible priority or two that everyone knows and rallies around.

It's also important to make sure the priorities really are priorities. If everything is a priority, nothing is. What are the one, two or maximum three things that matter right now? If you have more than three, then you don't yet have any. If you move ahead with more than three priorities, you'll find you will realistically only be able to work on three or less. Then you will unconsciously pick the priorities, and you'll likely pick the easiest or the most fun, not necessarily the most important.

These, then, are the seven questions you need to get clarified at every layer of your church:

1. Why do we exist?
2. What's the main thing we're trying to achieve?
3. What's the overall plan?
4. What's our flavour?
5. Who's doing what?
6. What authority do we have?
7. What's top priority right now?

You need to wrestle these questions to the ground. When you and your people have clarity, when you all agree and are trying to go the same way, then not only will there be less stress, anxiety, wasted energy and unnecessary conflict, you'll also get more done. More people loved, helped, taught, evangelized, cared for and ministered to. Clarity is the first key to focusing the ministry on making these happen.

Pipeline planning meeting 1

Buying this book is one thing; reading it is another. Good job so far! But what you've read needs to be implemented. That's challenging because it can be hard to know how—and *definitely* hard to know how to find the time to do so.

That's where having a pipeline planning meeting comes in. In these meetings you put aside the day-to-day issues and instead you and your team discuss and plan longer term.

Making meetings happen

These general ground rules will get your meetings off the ground and make them useful and enjoyable.

First decide who will be involved. This should be your key leadership team, which may be staff, elders or parish council, a board or some other group. Figure out who you need in the room to have 'big picture' conversations. Try not to have more than 12 people—fewer than eight would be even better—or there won't be enough time for everyone to present their ideas and ask their questions. Take note: these meetings will help your collection of individuals who are sometimes in the same room grow into an actual team. They'll get to know each other while learning to care for and trust each other.

Second, you'll be having pipeline planning meetings regularly as you go through this book, so decide how often you're going to meet. It shouldn't be too frequent—weekly would be a bad idea—because you'll have homework to be done in and around all the other pressing ministry you do. However, if they're too far apart it'll be hard to maintain momentum. Somewhere between every three to six weeks will generally work well.

Third, once you've worked out how often you're going to have these pipeline planning meetings, put the dates into the calendar now. This helps make sure the meetings actually happen. If you organize them one at a time, it's more likely that you'll run out of steam and stop after six months or so. You'll get distracted and the crisis of the month will prevent you from taking time out for a pipeline planning meeting. Book them all in one go.

Fourth, figure out the food situation. Pipeline planning meetings are where big things are discussed and big steps are taken, so do what you can to make them meetings people look forward to and feel good about being at. Good food does this. Maybe you get takeaway or delivery, or some great cook from your church volunteers to provide for you. Maybe each time you meet someone brings their favourite dessert—we can all agree that any meeting is made better by chocolate cake, cheesecake, apple pie, pavlova, profiteroles or a croquembouche. Take turns choosing the restaurant or think up a theme and have everyone bring snacks that match (made with fruit, from your country of origin, on a stick, etc.).

Fifth, figure out where you'll meet. Don't be in the same old room you have your normal meetings in. You want the participants to feel that these are different to the regular meetings you have because you don't want them to unthinkingly bring up the things you normally talk about. Maybe a church nearby has a meeting space you can use for free, or perhaps someone owns a holiday house they'll let you use. But it doesn't have to be extravagant; someone else's lounge room is fine.

Sixth, be clear on how you'll make decisions. Are you going for consensus? Are you gathering everyone's wisdom and then you'll make the final call? It needs to be clear to everyone how this will work so that there's no confusion or frustration.

Objective

At this first pipeline planning meeting you're going to tackle the first three key clarity questions:

1. Why do we exist?
2. What's the main thing we're trying to achieve?
3. What's the overall plan?

The main objective of this meeting is to get everyone on the same page about the answers. You don't need to end up with the exact same words, but you must all be pointing in the same direction.

Meeting plan

In these meetings you're focusing on important things, so wrap them in prayer. Pray for them beforehand, as you start, during, after. Explicitly relying on God and asking him for help is always a good idea.

Make sure every person coming to the meeting has read this chapter and brings their own answers to these questions using vocabulary that your specific church uses. If they like they can also bring answers using language that your church doesn't typically use but that they themselves would like to see *become* the way your church talks. For example, your church might not use the language of *family* or *home* or *joy* or *treasuring Jesus* but you might like to introduce that.

What if you've previously clarified the answers to these questions and everyone can write them out word perfectly? In that case, have people come prepared to explain each of them *in their own words* and discuss which parts resonate the most with them and why. This will not only increase people's clarity but will help deepen the team's understanding of those answers and of each other.

Each person presents their answers and explains why they've said things the way they have. The senior leader should present last.

By the end of this meeting, you'll have many preliminary answers. You or the senior leader need to know what you're going to do with everyone's work. Don't promise to include some or all of everyone's words in the 'official' version. Take all those answers away and see how you feel about them in two weeks. Pray about them. Include as many bits and pieces from each set of answers as you think is best.

These are *preliminary*. Cancel that order to update all your stationery. Don't get the craft ladies cross-stitching these answers onto a new church quilt. You're not trying to publicly launch a new vision statement; you're ensuring that your key team members are all on the same page.

4
An overview of the framework

One part of the whole

At the end of chapter 1, Luke ended his conversation with Phil by saying the missing piece was a leadership pipeline. That pipeline is one part of a multi-piece leadership development system. But before we go hiking through each individual element of leadership development, let's get our bearings. From here until chapter 11 we'll step through the entire framework and get ready to implement it in your church. Then in section two—chapter 12 onwards—we'll unpack each piece and talk concrete specifics.

This leadership development system, with its six interdependent component elements, is cradled within a broader church culture. This culture can itself be split into several key subcultures. We talked already about one of those subcultures in the previous chapter: a culture of discipleship and disciple-making. Both the culture and the six pieces of the leadership development system combine to create the full leadership development framework, and every component requires care and attention.

The surrounding culture helps guide the type of leaders the leadership development system is building, as well as giving shape to what those leaders are themselves doing and producing. The purpose of developing leaders is to help disciples to glorify God, love their neighbours and multiply ministry so that more people can know Jesus and grow as disciples. Another way to say it is that disciples are both the input and the output of the church's leadership development.

It's important also to note that disciple-making isn't the only cultural stratum impacting leadership development in a church. While there are lots of different ways to break down a church culture—and all of them will affect, to some extent, the leadership development in your church—there are two cultural flavours that, combined with disciple-making, will have the most direct influence. Those are the *leadership culture* and the *convictional culture.*

Let's see the whole leadership development framework in a single diagram:

Leadership development framework

- Ministry grouping
- Training and coaching
- Pipeline architecture
- **Leader development**
- Ministry monitoring
- Leader recruitment
- Leader assessment

Leadership culture
Discipleship culture
Convictional culture

58 | WISDOM IN LEADERSHIP DEVELOPMENT

The six leadership development pieces sit on top of, and function within, a broader church culture. If the convictional culture, the discipleship culture and the existing leadership culture aren't reasonably healthy, then the six leadership development elements will not survive. The culture is like soil that the leadership development system is planted in. Without a healthy culture, leadership development will never have the nutrients it needs to grow and thrive. This is the power and importance of culture.

We'll address culture and these specific subcultures in the next chapter, but right now let's look at the six elements that make up the leadership development framework. You'll get a feel for how all the pieces fit together so that you're ready to unpack each of them in detail as the book progresses.

Leadership development framework

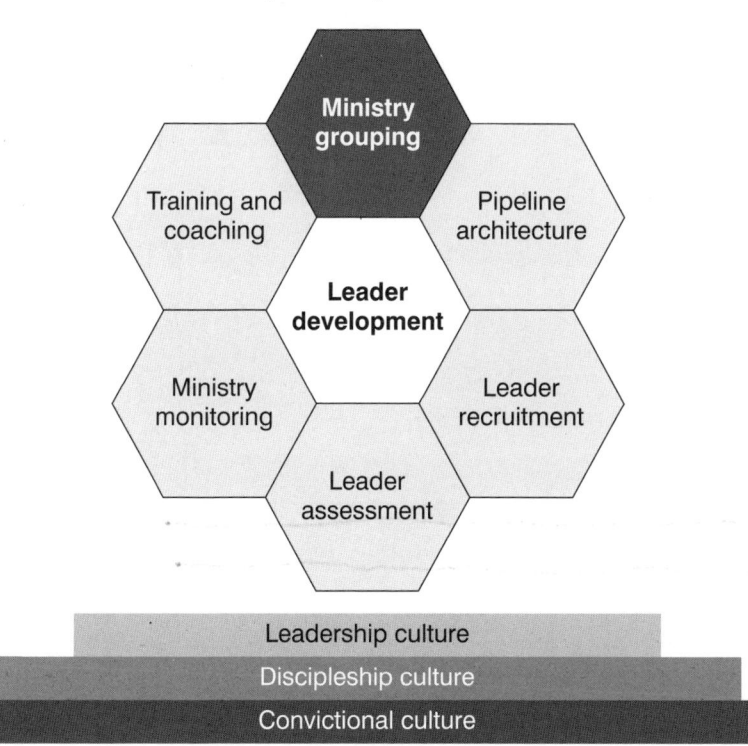

- Ministry grouping
- Training and coaching
- Pipeline architecture
- Leader development
- Ministry monitoring
- Leader recruitment
- Leader assessment

Leadership culture
Discipleship culture
Convictional culture

Element one: ministry grouping

Before you can work out *how* you're going to develop leaders and *what* you need to develop them in, you need to know what ministries you have, who's responsible for them, the formal relationships involved and whether those relationships are realistic. That is, ministries need to be grouped together in a way that makes sense.

Here's an example of ministry grouping in one church:

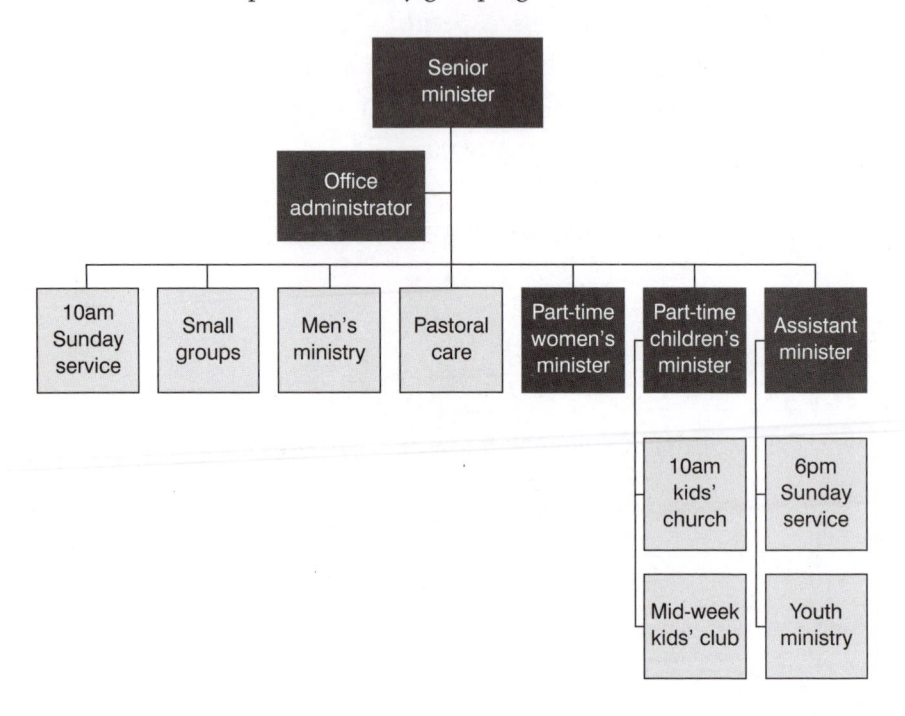

```
                        Senior
                        minister
                           |
                    Office administrator
                           |
   ┌─────────┬─────────┬───────┬─────────┬──────────────┬──────────────┬──────────┐
  10am      Small     Men's  Pastoral  Part-time      Part-time      Assistant
  Sunday    groups    ministry care    women's        children's     minister
  service                              minister       minister
                                                         |              |
                                                    ┌────┴────┐    ┌────┴────┐
                                                   10am       Mid-week  6pm     Youth
                                                   kids'      kids'     Sunday  ministry
                                                   church     club      service
```

This is essentially creating an organizational chart: a two-dimensional drawing of authority and reporting relationships. These charts are polarizing. Some people put too much weight on them and think that drawing one up completes the job of organizational design, strategic planning and leadership development. Others undervalue them because, well, they don't 'do' anything, after all. While organizational charts aren't everything, they still are *something* that adds clarity—so why not try out an opinion in the middle!

Grouping ministries visually will help you do two things. Firstly, it will help you see the shape and design of your church. This is a valuable piece of insight because it's tough to get an idea of what exactly a church does.

WISDOM IN LEADERSHIP DEVELOPMENT

While the ministries and activities are all physically tangible things—in that they involve people and venues—they aren't physically tangible in the sense that if a drone took an aerial photo of your church, it couldn't show you all the church ministries and where they sit in the organization. All you'd learn is that the ministries aren't on the roof.

Secondly, a chart will help you see how *realistic* the responsibilities and oversight relationships are in your church. Sometimes you don't realize that there are too many people reporting to one person, or too many ministry area responsibilities under one person, until you visualize it and draw it out. For example, this ministry grouping should trigger red flags:

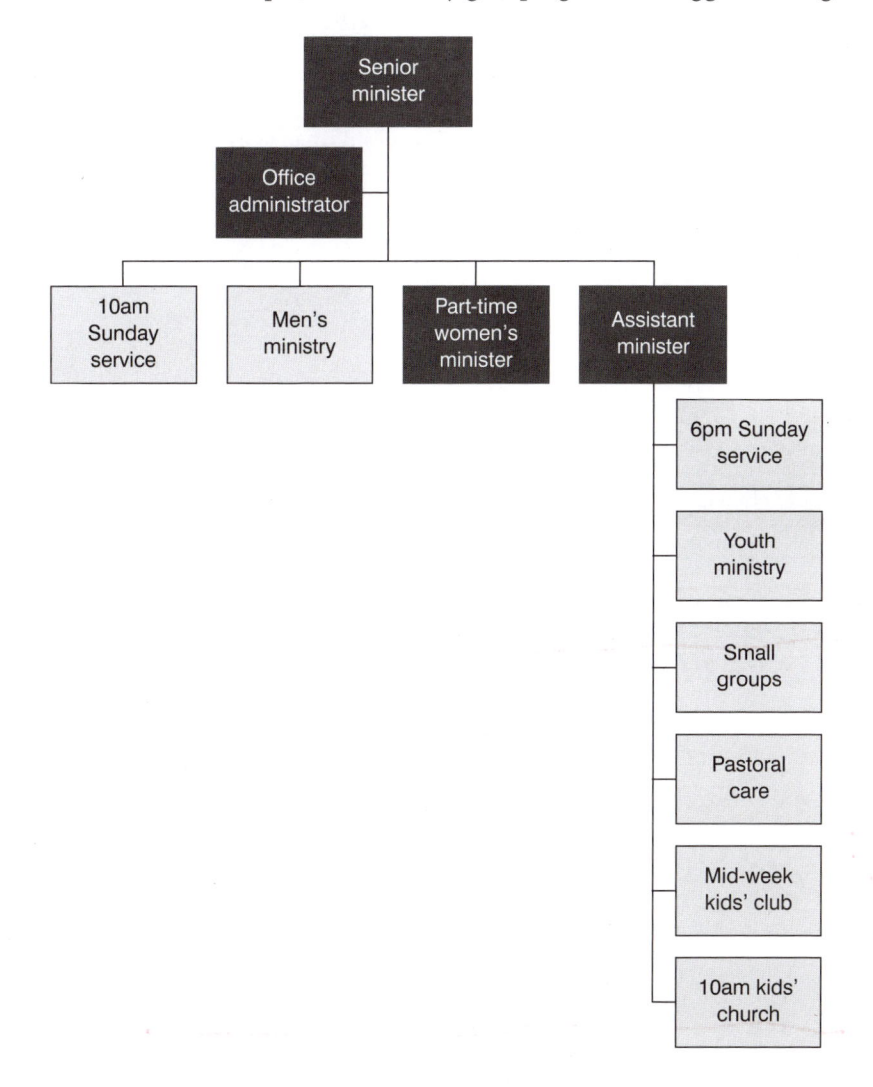

```
                    Senior
                   minister
                      |
         Office ------|
      administrator   |
            ----------+----------+----------
            |         |          |         |
          10am      Men's    Part-time  Assistant
         Sunday   ministry   women's    minister
         service              minister      |
                                            |---- 6pm Sunday service
                                            |---- Youth ministry
                                            |---- Small groups
                                            |---- Pastoral care
                                            |---- Mid-week kids' club
                                            |---- 10am kids' church
```

Someone needs to help that assistant minister! No matter how competent he is, these ministries have been grouped in a way that sets him up to fail.

We'll cover the practicalities of ministry grouping in chapter 14.

Leadership development framework

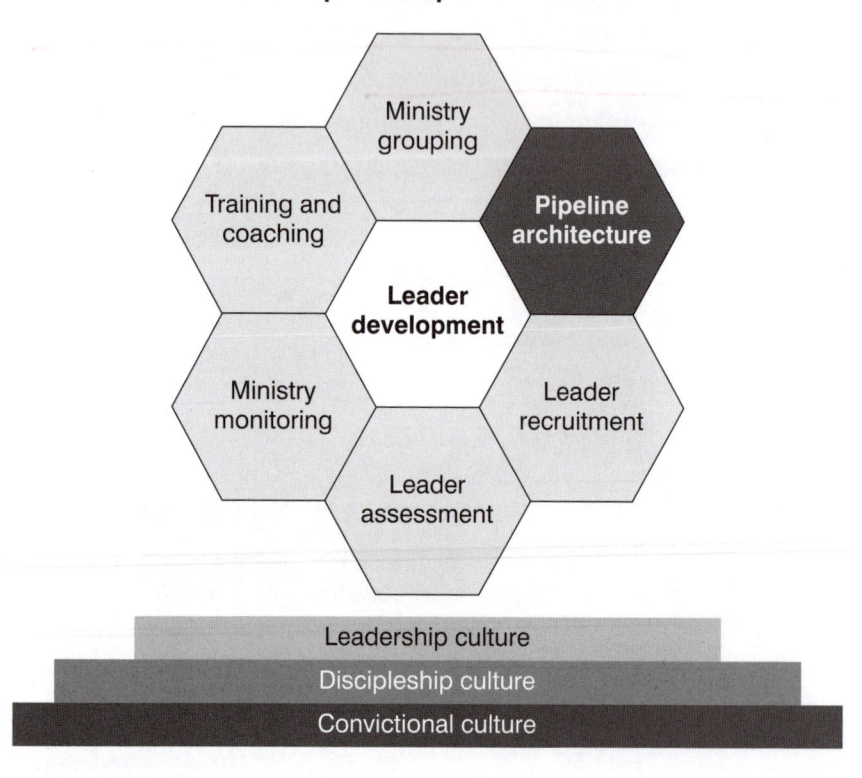

- Ministry grouping
- Training and coaching
- Pipeline architecture
- Leader development
- Ministry monitoring
- Leader recruitment
- Leader assessment

Leadership culture
Discipleship culture
Convictional culture

Element two: pipeline architecture

Once you've worked out your ministry grouping then you can move on to the pipeline architecture of your church—what Luke was talking to Phil about. You might never have heard the phrase 'leadership pipeline' before, but you probably began imagining something like this:

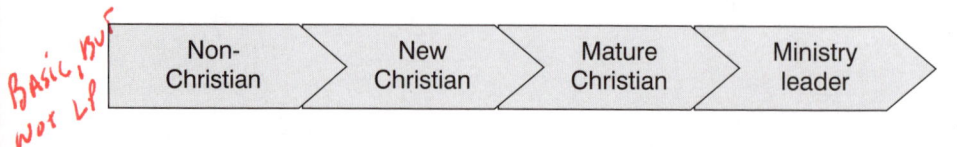

Non-Christian → New Christian → Mature Christian → Ministry leader

BASIC, but not LP

This isn't a leadership pipeline. This is a discipleship pathway. It's helpful as a general overall framework for what we pray and work towards in

62 | WISDOM IN LEADERSHIP DEVELOPMENT

helping people 'move to the right', but it's not what we're talking about.

So if it's not *that*, people then think maybe it's like *this*:

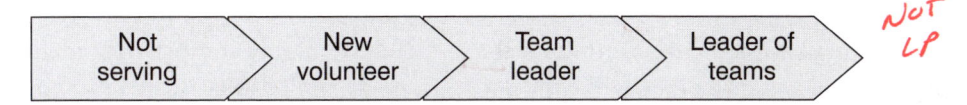

| Not serving | → | New volunteer | → | Team leader | → | Leader of teams | NOT LP |

This is on the right track, but it isn't a leadership pipeline either. This is a leadership progression, since yes, if people are going to progress in leadership, this is usually the way they do it. But the issue with this kind of diagram and mental model is that each of these movements is not just a simple and natural next step.

The leadership pipeline is a philosophy for intentionally developing people in leadership. In particular, it's a framework for thinking about and developing people for different *layers* of leadership. It's a way of viewing different roles and layers of leadership so that there's clarity around what each role and layer is supposed to be doing and what differentiates it from other layers. In a leadership pipeline, leadership progression, role definition and skill development all overlap.

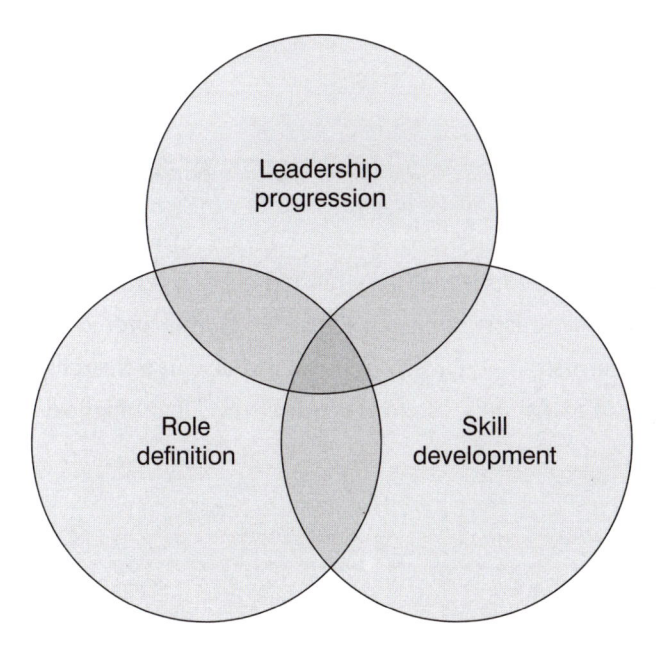

[Venn diagram with three overlapping circles labeled: Leadership progression, Role definition, Skill development]

4 // AN OVERVIEW OF THE FRAMEWORK | 63

If you have leadership progression and role definition without skill development, then you'll have high-level leaders who are incompetent and demoralized. If you have leadership progression and skill development without role definition, then you'll have highly competent leaders with no clarity on what you want from them and so high levels of angst. If you have role definition and skill development without leadership progression, then you'll have an army of overqualified helpers who are highly frustrated by their lack of opportunities to lead. All three parts need to be in play, and that happens when you design a leadership pipeline.

Here's what a leadership pipeline looks like:

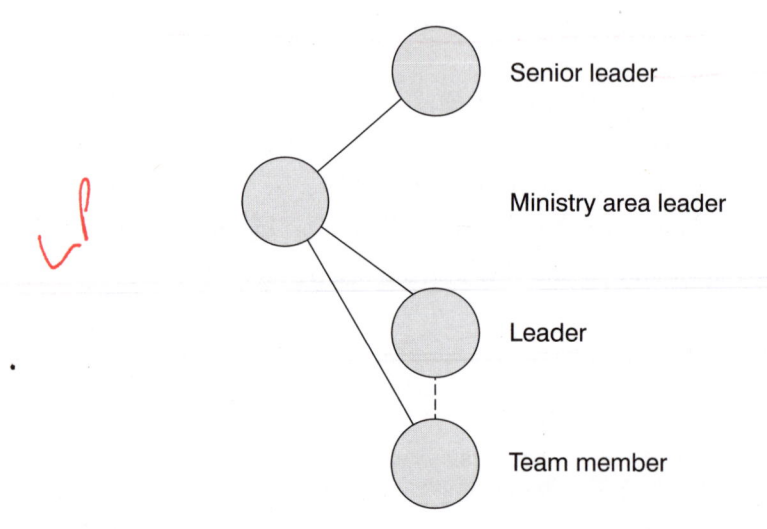

○ Senior leader

○ Ministry area leader

○ Leader

○ Team member

Some churches or ministries may have another layer between the leader layer and the ministry area layer due to complexity or size or both. Children's ministry is typically the first ministry in a church to need this extra layer of leadership due to its complexity. That pipeline would look like this:

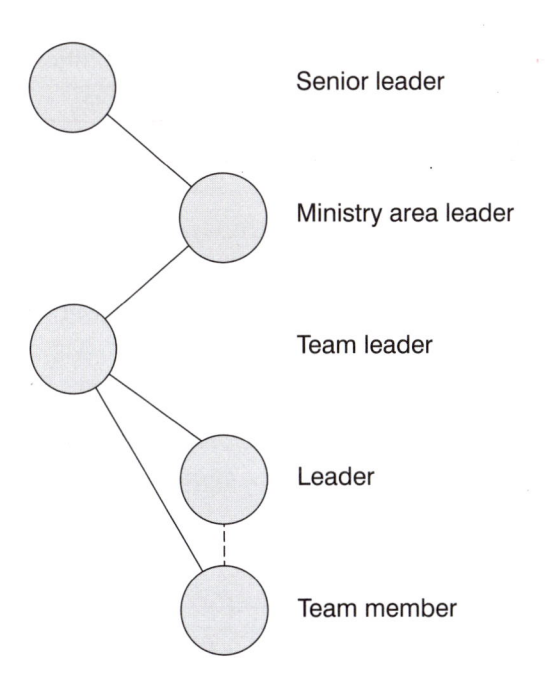

- Senior leader
- Ministry area leader
- Team leader
- Leader
- Team member

There may be churches who need another layer or two due to size or complexity, so I've included an extended pipeline in the appendix for those who are interested. But needing that extended pipeline is rare, and once you get to needing the extended pipeline, you won't need any more leadership layers after that. If you are wise in your ministry grouping, the extended pipeline will suffice in a church of tens of thousands. The leadership pipeline is a potent tool!

The reason we display the pipeline with zigzags rather than as a straight line is that the sharp turns symbolize both how mentally hard it is to transition from one layer to another and also that each layer does vastly different work. A revolution needs to occur within a person when they transition from one layer to another, and it's not easy.

Since pipeline architecture is probably the newest and most complicated idea out of the six leadership development framework elements, we'll spend some extra time unpacking this before we move on to the others. First, let's go through the layers.

4 // AN OVERVIEW OF THE FRAMEWORK | 65

Team member

In most churches, this is a person on a roster. Their service is focused on performing a task that doesn't directly involve *leading* another person. This isn't to imply that the task isn't necessary or that they don't interact with other people or have people as their task's target and end goal. The distinction here is that they are not *directly leading* them.

An example of this layer is those on the Bible reading roster. Bible reading is about more than merely saying the words written in the Bible aloud; reading so that *people* hear the word of God as the *word of God* is a central part of our gatherings. But while they are speaking to people and leading them *through* the reading of the Scriptures, they are not focused on *directly leading* them.

Leader

A leader is someone whose primary role is to lead people at the frontlines of the ministry area. This is the kids' leader, the youth group leader, the Bible study group leader, and so on. This is the main factor that distinguishes them from team members. Team members lead people indirectly, while mainly focusing on performing an important task, whereas leaders lead people directly. Leaders may also, in the course of leading in their role, perform important tasks like running a game during youth group, or explaining a craft to children. The critical point is that their role is primarily directly leading people along with performing various tasks, while team members primarily perform an important task.

This distinction between these two roles doesn't impact what they need to learn. The team member and the leader are functioning within the same leadership layer as each other.

Senior leader

Ministry area leader

Team leader

Leader

Same layer

Team member

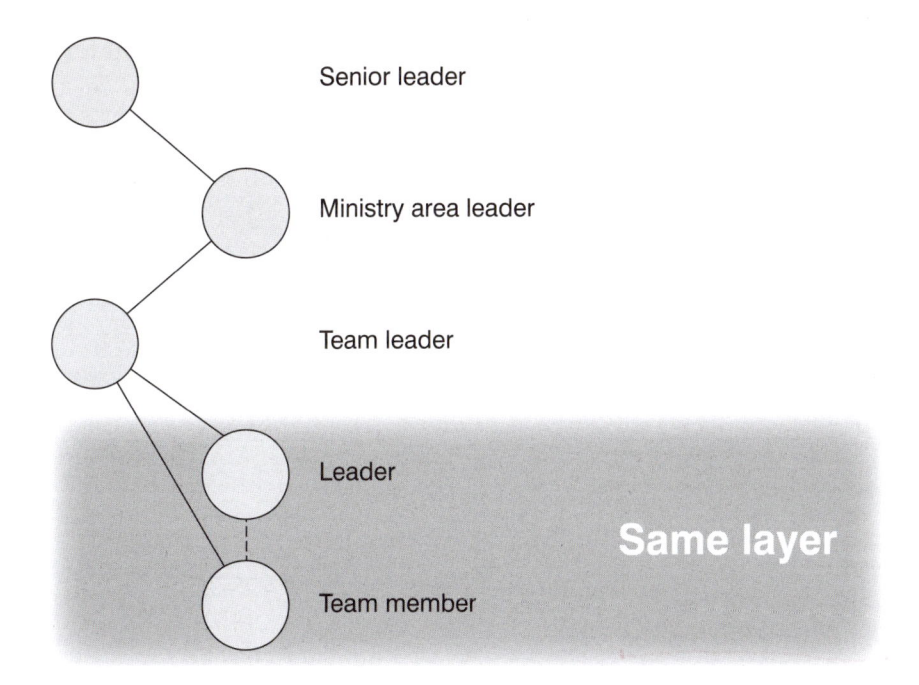

Slightly pulling the team member layer away from the leader layer is more about clarifying the level of expectation and time commitment involved rather than anything to do with the mechanics of leadership. They have the same cluster of competencies to master, but you may expect the leader to be leading every week, while the team member is on a roster and may serve once a term. We'll talk more about the competencies, levels of expectation and time commitments of each layer when we come back to pipeline architecture in later chapters.

Your mileage may vary on the value of this distinction between team member and leader, and you could decide to collapse them into one layer—though I would advise that you keep this conceptual distinction between those who read the Bible once a term and those who, say, lead the children in kids' church every week.

Team leader

The team leader, perhaps obviously, leads a team of leaders or a team of team members. This is the person who leads the youth leaders or who leads the team of people who hand out brochures and seek to talk to people about Jesus at the local train station. They lead a team of leaders.

A team leader isn't just anyone who leads a group of people: they lead leaders. A small group leader is a leader at the frontline of the small groups ministry, but they aren't leading a group of leaders (we'll cover this more in chapter 17). A team leader leads a team of leaders or team members who are all involved in the same ministry. Here are two team leaders leading two teams of four small group leaders each:

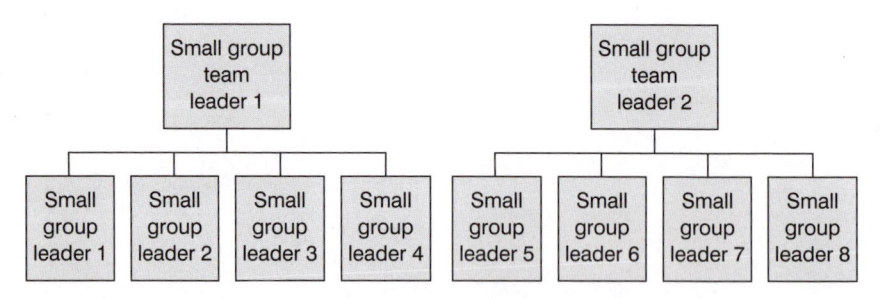

```
        Small group                          Small group
           team                                 team
         leader 1                             leader 2
    ┌────┬────┬────┐                     ┌────┬────┬────┐
 Small  Small Small Small              Small Small Small Small
 group  group group group              group group group group
leader 1 leader 2 leader 3 leader 4    leader 5 leader 6 leader 7 leader 8
```

Ministry area leader

This is the person who oversees an entire ministry area, like children's ministry, small groups ministry or men's ministry. The children's ministry area leader leads and is responsible for the *whole* children's ministry at the church. Usually a ministry area leader would be a paid member of staff, but this isn't absolutely necessary.

Senior leader/s

This is the senior leadership of the church. In many churches this is the senior minister/senior pastor/rector. Some churches are led by a plurality of elders, or have split the senior leadership into multiple roles, in which case *the members of that group* are the senior leaders.

If you skipped to here, go back

Ministry grouping and pipeline architecture are about the space and structure that people minister within in your church. It's abstract and conceptual. It's about systems, structures, overarching philosophy and mindset; it's lines, boxes, ideal ministry distribution, roles and responsibilities. And I can imagine for the highly relational reader this will all sound boring and skippable. I can almost hear you organizing the next coffee catch up with your people.

But these first two elements are 100% necessary and compulsory because they're about making your leadership development smart. No matter how much of a gregarious social butterfly you are, or no matter how much you hate documents, spreadsheets and planning, you know that dumb systems will hurt people. And you love people.

Getting the culture right was about making the system healthy. Getting these first two elements right is about clarity and intentionality.

Ministry grouping helps you see what ministry goes with what and the structure of the whole church. Pipeline architecture helps you diagnose what kinds of leadership pipelines you already have, while at the same time designing what you want them to look like. Pipeline architecture applies the leadership pipeline philosophy to your ministry grouping structure and creates layers of leadership that have clear roles and responsibilities. This is one of the most important and powerful ideas to get your mind around when it comes to leadership development.

Leadership development framework

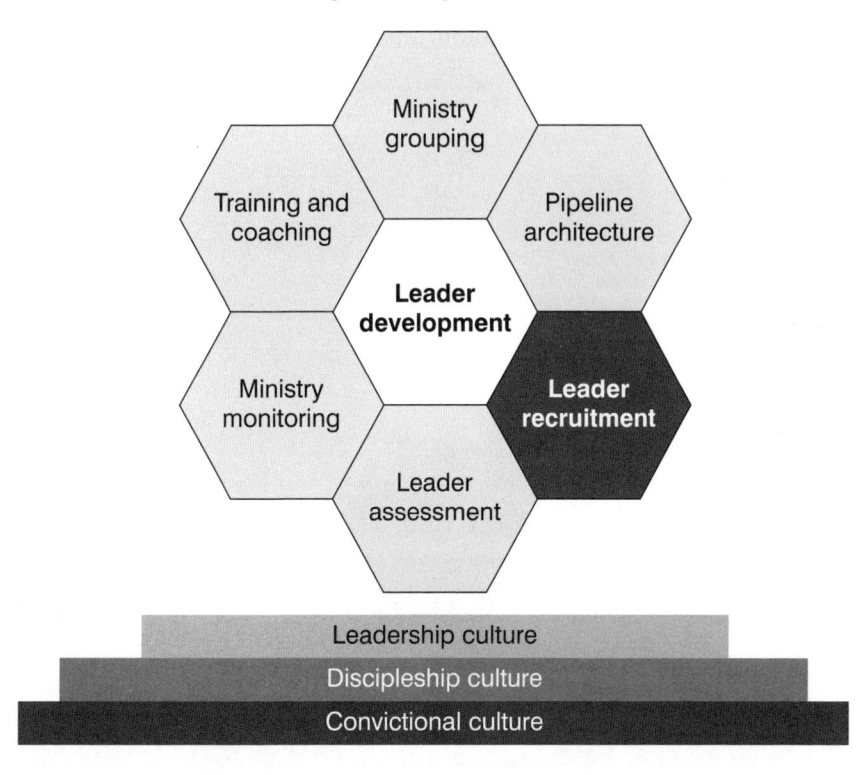

- Ministry grouping
- Training and coaching
- Pipeline architecture
- Leader development
- Ministry monitoring
- Leader recruitment
- Leader assessment

Leadership culture
Discipleship culture
Convictional culture

Element three: leader recruitment

The final four elements of the leadership development framework are about making the system effective. Someone can be healthy and smart and still not do much—we all know that razor-sharp person who just can't get their life together and make things happen. The same thing can happen in leadership development. If you have a healthy and conducive church culture, and you've designed a smart structure and clarified a pipeline architecture framework, don't be too tired to actually implement it.

If you're going to get serious about developing leaders, then you need some leaders to develop. Not only will you be recruiting new leaders into that first layer of ministry service, you'll also want to find the right people to move into layers with more oversight and responsibility. But how do you know *who* to recruit in both of those circumstances? What are you looking for in a person that would signal to you that they should be brought into a new ministry role? How do you get the right people in the right roles? We'll get into this in chapter 20.

Leadership development framework

- Ministry grouping
- Training and coaching
- Pipeline architecture
- Leader development
- Ministry monitoring
- Leader recruitment
- Leader assessment

Leadership culture
Discipleship culture
Convictional culture

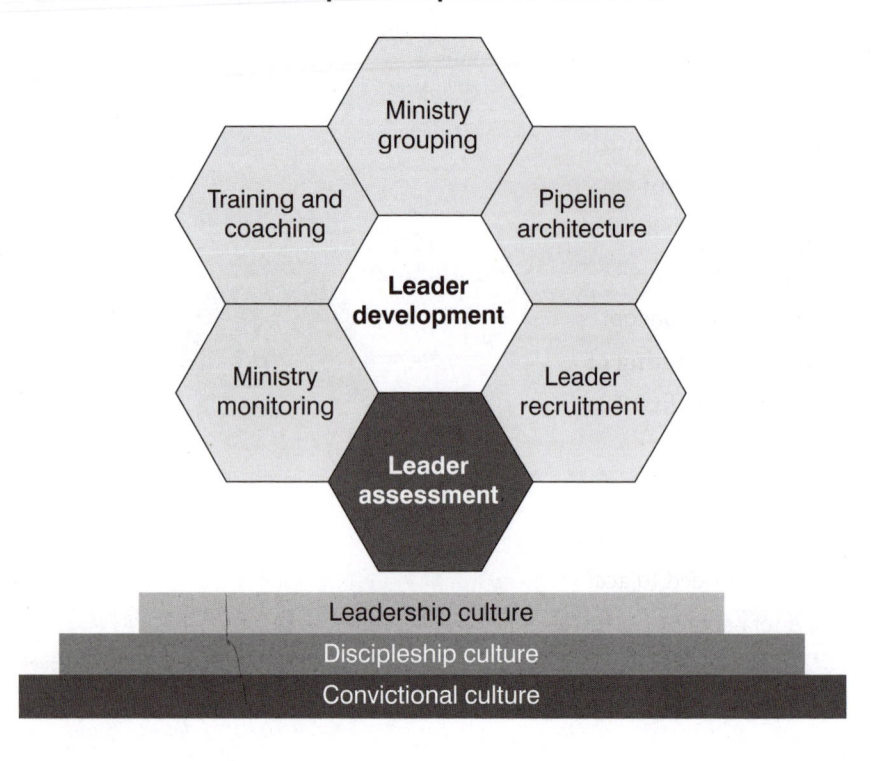

Element four: leader assessment

To recruit the right people to the right roles means being able to assess where those leaders are up to and determining their next steps. Assessment links strongly with leader recruitment—and also with the next element, ministry monitoring—because it helps you to unearth performance issues *before* they happen as well as find possible explanations *once* they've surfaced.

To do a consistently excellent job at developing leaders, you need to assess where they're up to: what their strengths are; what skills and abilities they've mastered and which they've yet to learn; whether they are leading at the level of their pipeline layer or still leading with the mindset and skill set they needed at the layer below. This then helps you to know what they need to learn, experience or leave behind.

My guess is we're all on board with the assessment of leaders. We're already doing it to some extent—some will be doing it formally and intentionally, while others will be doing it informally in their own heads and often when people are being really frustrating. Informally is absolutely fine for now. The point is that we're already assessing people in some form or fashion.

The problem is that humans are terrible at assessing other humans. We might try to rate the people on our teams in terms of servanthood, teamwork or potential, and we might give a rating on a scale of 1 to 5, even just mentally. But what does a '3 in potential' even mean? Is *my* 3 the same as *your* 3? And potential in what? Height? Punctuality? Tracing?

Or teamwork. What is a '4 in teamwork'? Teamwork is an umbrella term: a meta-concept made up of lots of smaller attitudes and behaviours. This is why a rating of '4 in teamwork' is so unreliable. To score a person on teamwork, first I need to dissect that concept down into as many of its components as I can—already not many of us would be able to do this with any significant level of success—then I need to rate the person on each of those component factors (the ratings becoming almost arbitrary), and *then* I need to accurately weight and aggregate those scores back into the meta-score of '4 for teamwork'.

It is highly unlikely I'm going to be able to do this precisely, which means the enterprise is doomed from the start. That's a bit irritating really, since we've established that assessment is critical for leader development, and that we already do it all the time, whether formally or informally. Oh dear.

It's tempting, but don't give up, because there is a way that's easier and more useful, plus more accurate. Admittedly, aiming for 'more accurate' over 'largely inaccurate' might seem like a low bar, but at least it faces the fact that our assessments are always going to be imperfect due to the simple fact that every one of us is flawed. Crooked sticks are never going to give perfectly straight lines, but there is a way to make our assessment lines straighter than they otherwise would be. And that's a noble achievement. We'll get into it in chapter 23.

Leadership development framework

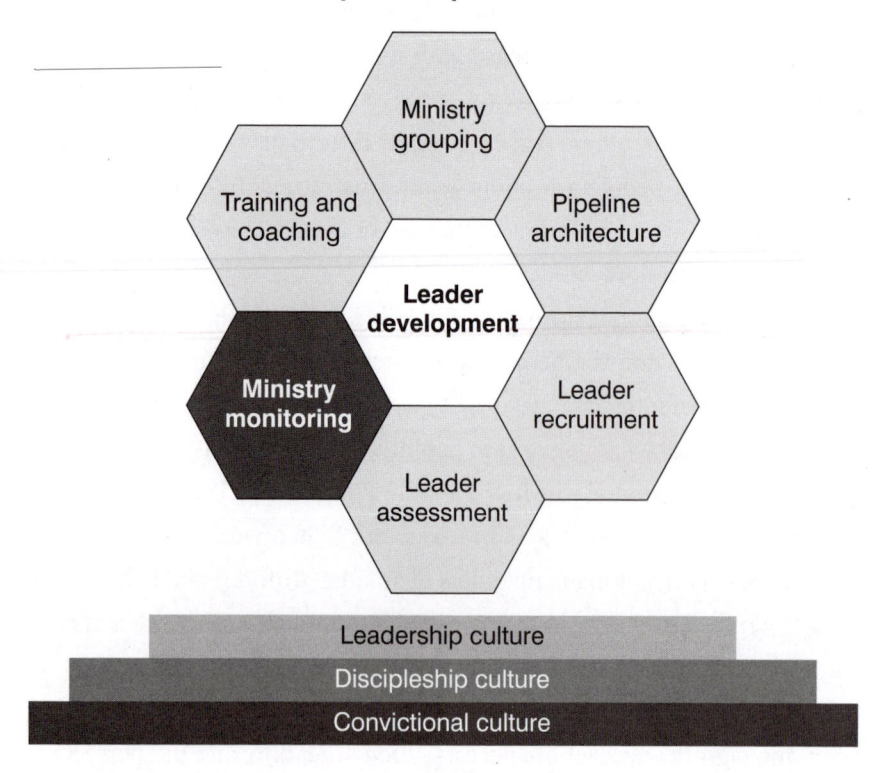

- Ministry grouping
- Training and coaching
- Pipeline architecture
- **Leader development**
- Ministry monitoring
- Leader recruitment
- Leader assessment

Leadership culture
Discipleship culture
Convictional culture

Element five: ministry monitoring

No matter what layer of the pipeline a leader is in, they shouldn't be left alone to go about their work with no regard for how they're doing personally as a disciple or how they're going with their role's work.

72 | WISDOM IN LEADERSHIP DEVELOPMENT

Ministry is always relational, and it's always done in relationships and through conversations. Ministry monitoring is about making sure those relationships are maintained and those conversations had.

For most leaders that I talk with, this ongoing ministry monitoring is the second-most overlooked element in the entire framework (after pipeline architecture). People either don't meet with those they lead (unless there's a crisis) or, when they do meet up, they aren't having the conversations they need to be having.

Along with leader assessment, ministry monitoring is necessary to be able to do well at the final element in the leadership development framework: training and coaching. Without it, any training you run will only be accidentally useful, since you don't know what your leaders need. And your coaching will only be minimally and randomly effective, because again you don't know what they've done, how they've done it, or whether it achieved what they thought it would.

Leadership development framework

- Ministry grouping
- Pipeline architecture
- Training and coaching
- Leader development
- Ministry monitoring
- Leader recruitment
- Leader assessment

Leadership culture
Discipleship culture
Conviction culture

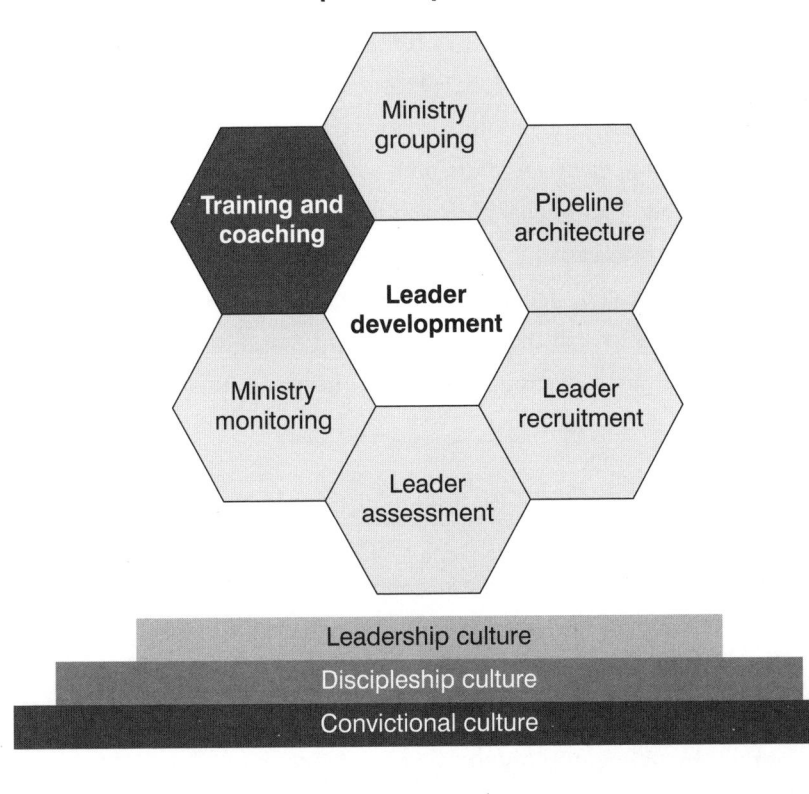

4 // AN OVERVIEW OF THE FRAMEWORK | 73

Element six: training and coaching

If you know people's leadership ability gaps and where they are struggling in their ministry, then the final step in the system enables those leaders to close the gaps and solve their problems. This is the purpose of training and coaching.

When we think 'training', most of us probably think of classroom training: notes and lectures and minimal usefulness. This may just be a bias because of classroom training done poorly; at its best, classroom training is beneficial and necessary. It's a chance to think about overall principles, to tease out ideal processes and to discuss the reasons behind *why* things work the way they do.

But at the same time, classroom training isn't the only kind of training required, because there is also on-the-job training where we are paired up with a teacher and learn by doing. In a ministry context, the majority of learning is done like this. If there's someone along for the ride to help us reflect well and ask the right questions, we can learn far more from our experiences, successes, failures and near-misses.

Almost inherent in the idea of on-the-job training—at least the kind that is most useful—is the idea of coaching. A leader alongside you coaches you by modelling, helping, giving advice and teasing apart results to help us see more clearly and deeply.

Unfortunately, a lot of coaching and feedback is done poorly—and it's often done poorly because it was modelled poorly, and those bad habits have been perpetuated. When we come back in chapter 25 to dive in to this element, we'll look at the fundamentals of coaching—care and maximizing—as well as the discipline of asking questions and giving feedback.

These final four elements of the leadership development framework are about directly caring for and working with the actual people who lead the ministries and inhabit the structure and systems from the first two elements. These final four are concrete and personal; they are where lives are touching lives. These elements make sure the system is faithful in caring for people and effective in growing them into high-functioning, high-level leaders in your church.

Hopefully you now have a feel for how these six elements interlock and rely on each other for the entire framework to be as useful as it can be. Ministry grouping is needed for thinking through pipeline architecture. Pipeline architecture helps you clarify each leader's role, which you need in order to assess where they're up to. Assessment, along with ministry monitoring, helps you to train and coach intelligently. And everything is fed and sustained by a healthy culture.

This signals that building leaders instead of burning or buying them is a complicated and challenging process. These complications arise because leadership development is the product of interweaving elements that each have their own issues, weaknesses and pressure-points, all needing constant monitoring and managing. Since they're all connected, it affects the entire leadership development system when one element is ignored or lacking. There is no going halfway.

5
A cultural foundation

Leadership development framework

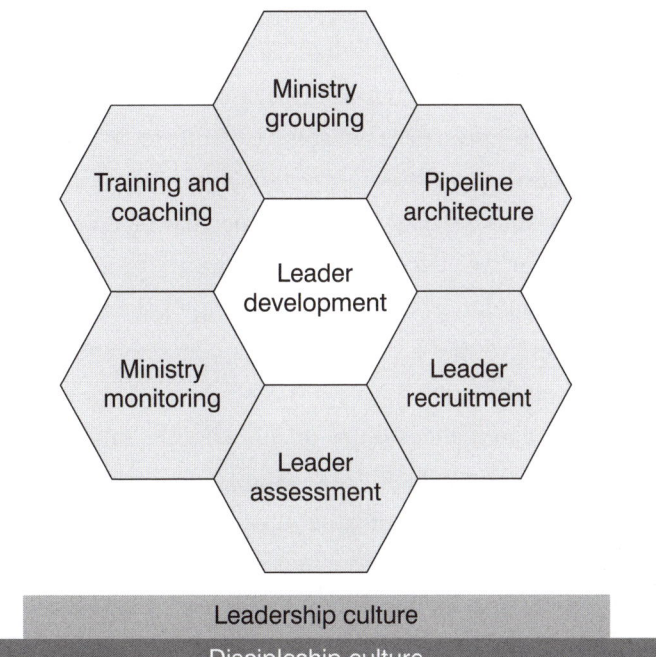

- Ministry grouping
- Training and coaching
- Pipeline architecture
- Leader development
- Ministry monitoring
- Leader recruitment
- Leader assessment

Leadership culture
Discipleship culture
Convictional culture

If we don't get the culture right, we'll have a much harder time developing leaders than we otherwise might. Culture itself doesn't develop leaders, but it will either undermine or multiply our efforts.

Every church has a certain way things are done. Churches with the same theology from the same denomination with the same liturgical practices will still be different. It's often intangible and rarely written or formal; it's not easily defined or measured. It's the culture of the church.

As we said in the previous chapter, the culture is like the soil that the leadership development system is planted in and draws the nutrients it needs from. Everything that happens in your church grows out of the culture.

What is culture and what does it do?

A church needs two things to do well: smart processes and a healthy culture. Processes are things like Bible teaching, financial systems, organization and ministry grouping, and strategy and recruitment. These processes *should* be smart (faithful Bible teaching, transparent financial systems), but they can also be dumb (false Bible teaching, sloppy financial systems). Chronic inconsistency in these areas is a recipe for mediocrity.

Alongside these processes is culture. Culture is an often underappreciated leadership reality—understandable, since it is so notoriously difficult to define and describe. Culture is also hard—if not impossible—to measure. When we place it alongside the more easily quantifiable phenomena of attendance, conversions, giving or the number of people involved in small groups, it's not nearly as concrete and so it's hard to devote much thought to it.

But thinking about the culture of our church, ministry or team is vitally important (along with all those other more measurable processes) because culture is the air you breathe. It will either multiply the power of our smart processes or undermine their effectiveness. The cherry on top is that it's virtually free and any leader has access to it.

A function of organization

Every group of people who spend enough time together will form their own unique culture. In that sense, culture is a by-product of a group of people; it's a function of organization. Countries have a discernible culture, as do regions, schools, businesses and families. Churches, too, will each have their own unique culture.

Culture is the set of assumptions, attitudes, values, beliefs and behaviours that govern and guide *what* an organization does and *how* they do it.

When someone says, "That's just how we do it around here" or "That's just what we do", they're probably talking about their culture—and if you're able to scratch just a bit beneath what they're referring to, there's a good chance you'll unearth an aspect of *your* culture.

It's generally agreed that culture and language are intertwined.[11] If culture is the expression of values and beliefs, then it follows that language would be one of the primary vehicles for that expression. Culture is transmitted and encoded in language and is itself shaped and moulded by language. Another way to define culture then is that it is the common verbal and non-verbal language of a specific group or organization.

Furthermore, since culture is a function of groups of people, shaped by and expressed in language, this means that it will also always be, to some degree, an expression of sin and disunity while at the same time an expression of faith and unity. We need to analyse and understand our church culture, but we also need to repent of it occasionally, while refining and strengthening it too.

It's the nature of culture being the air and soil we're in that makes it so hard to discern your own, especially if you've been in it for a while and in particular if you're the senior leader who has been there for a long time. The fish discovers water last. It's like how sometimes in your house you'll have a strange piece of furniture in a strange place, but it's been like that for so long it doesn't seem strange to you any more. But if someone visits for the first time and they ask why you have a statue in the bathroom of a little boy urinating on a surprised dog—which has been there ever since you moved in and you just never got around to binning it—it's almost like you see it again for the first time. Culture is like that. Humans are so good at pattern recognition and behavioural adaptation that what was once foreign and jarring quickly becomes absorbed, adopted and assumed. So if you don't know what your church culture is, ask those who are new.

---

11 Alfred Louis Kroeber: "In short, culture can probably function only on the basis of abstractions, and these in turn seem to be possible only through speech, or through a secondary substitute for spoken language such as writing, numeration, mathematical and chemical notation, and the like. Culture, then, began when speech was present, and from then on, the enrichment of either means the further development of the other." *Anthropology: culture patterns and processes,* Harcourt, Brace & World, New York, 1923, p. 102.

They'll more quickly detect and describe it for you.

We'll talk more about how to assess and navigate a culture later in section two.

Multi-subcultural

Thinking of your church's culture as a single block is a helpful exercise, but another useful way to conceptualize it is to think of the various subcultures that make up that broader culture. Of all the subcultures that could and probably do make up your culture, there are three in particular that heavily influence the viability and sustainability of your efforts to develop a leadership development system. And when I say subcultures, I don't mean ethnic subcultures or demographics or surfers and goths. I mean your convictional culture, your discipleship culture and your leadership culture. These protect and promote the health of the framework, just as a healthy church culture protects and promotes a healthy church.

Convictional culture

All churches have a set of convictions that they cherish, hold to and teach, such as the Anglican 39 Articles or the Westminster Confession of Faith. But that's not what I'm referring to when I talk about your church's convictional culture. Convictional culture isn't those convictions that you hold; it's the culture that has been created as a result of convictions that have made it deep into the heart of the church and its behaviour.

In one sense, convictional culture is just culture, since culture is itself simply the beliefs and values that flow from convictions and get codified into behaviour. But in churches, where teaching and convictions play a central role, it's useful to tease apart convictions *as taught* and the convictions that have been *entrenched*. The distinction matters.

For example, sometimes a church will believe that God loves and welcomes all people, that the gospel is for all people, and that they as a church are called to welcome anyone and everyone. That's what they believe and are taught. But then when someone who looks or acts differently arrives, the church may struggle to enact and live out its convictions. In this instance, those beliefs about the imperative to welcome others don't

80 | WISDOM IN LEADERSHIP DEVELOPMENT

actually drive the behaviours of the church at the *cultural* level. Those convictions haven't influenced the convictional culture.

You might be tempted to simply diagnose that this hypothetical church doesn't *really* hold this set of convictions like they say they do, because if they did it would then impact their behaviour. Maybe you'd be right. But it may also be that they do think these convictions are true, but they are struggling to press them down deep into the values and assumptions that govern how they behave—that is, into their culture. The process of convictions making their way from the head to the heart and then out into instinctive behaviour is complicated even for the individual, let alone an entire church made up of individuals.

The convictional culture is often foundational in forming other subcultures, like a welcoming culture, an evangelistic culture, an encouraging culture and so on. It is possible to have a church where the convictional culture is at odds with one or more of the subcultures, however this kind of dissonance won't stay forever. Over time, one will yield to the other.

The reason convictional culture matters for developing leaders is that it influences the strength and longevity of leadership development efforts. Some specific values and assumptions organically foster leadership development; certain cultural elements will predictably make leadership development harder as you work against the grain. These cultural elements may be obvious, but it's important to spell them out nonetheless.

Some of the most potent values and assumptions that impact leadership development are:

- **Who does the ministry?** Does the congregation believe that the ministers do the ministry or do they believe it's the role of the minister to equip *others* for the work of ministry? The answer to this question will significantly impact the likelihood that they will embrace leadership development. Now remember, this is not the same as asking what *you* think on this particular issue—although what you believe will have a profound impact on the culture of the church if you have any influence. What does the church *as a whole* think? And has that conviction made its way into the church's culture as an assumption and value that drives behaviour?

5 // A CULTURAL FOUNDATION | 81

- **What is pastoral ministry?** Does the congregation picture the senior church leader doing hospital visits and having scones and tea with members of the church? Or do they think about the multiplication of people involved in ministry through the proclamation of the Word, which may or may not include hospital and home visits that may or may not be made by the minister?
- **Who is gifted?** Does the church deeply believe that every Christian is gifted by God for the strengthening of the body, and that each gift should be discovered, encouraged and developed?

You'll be able to think of other aspects of a church's convictional culture that will impact the viability of leadership development in a church, but these three questions highlight some of the most significant ones.

Discipleship culture

We touched on discipleship back in chapter 2, but it's important to hone it here. In some ways, a discipleship culture is a subset of convictional culture, but it's worth its own space. Discipleship culture is about what you think you're doing at every layer of your organization. What is the church on about? It's obvious, and I've said it already: leadership development will develop whatever kind of leaders you want to develop. If you're a church and you think growing disciples is *the* core activity of your church, then this will need to be embedded in the culture if it's going to be embedded in your leadership development.

The leadership development framework will help you embed and expand an existing discipleship culture, but it will not *create* a discipleship culture within an existing culture that is hostile to the idea, especially one that is hostile in its conviction. A leadership development framework will strengthen, reinforce and quicken an existing—even embryonic—discipleship culture by creating an upward spiral of discipleship, but the framework is not designed to create a discipleship culture *ex nihilo*.

If you want to develop leaders who *are* disciples and who *make* disciples, that discipleship culture needs to be built separately or exist already.

Leadership culture

If you, as a church, don't value leadership then it'll be near impossible to consistently develop quality leaders.

Do *you* value leadership? You probably value your own leadership—most leaders do. But do you value leadership in others at your church? And what kind of leadership do you value? Do you value the leadership where you have direct input and final say, or do you value giving away decision-making authority? Do you want to grow the number of actual leaders, or are you just looking for more helpers?

You also need to model a certain degree of leadership competence. If you are not exercising good, basic leadership then you will constantly be dismantling the leadership development framework you're trying to construct. The values, assumptions and behaviours that I unpack in *Wisdom in Leadership* need to be reflected in your leadership if you want to grow a leadership culture. That's not to say that you need to have mastered or implemented everything in *Wisdom in Leadership*, but you have to have made a real start in actively growing in your leadership—and people need to have noticed. If the church can see that leadership development is important to you as an individual, they'll be much more likely to come with you when you start trying to make it important to the whole church.

Culture is continuously in flux

Since culture *impacts* everything you do while also being impacted *by* everything you do, it will be continuously in flux. Everything you do—every decision you make, every hire you bring on board, every time someone is promoted to a higher responsibility—will either reinforce your culture or undermine it.

If you have a culture of conscientiousness but you promote Mildred to a higher responsibility, who is known to be last-minute and close-enough-is-good-enough, by giving her more responsibility you've signalled to everyone that the culture of conscientiousness isn't as influential as they thought. You are, unwittingly, undermining that positive culture.

If that happens often enough, the culture will change. But fear not:

5 // A CULTURAL FOUNDATION

making one decision won't destroy your culture. Culture change, which we'll come back to in chapter 12, is a slow process the vast majority of the time.

All is not lost when a mistake is made, but we need to be able to spot that a mistake *has* been made. If you are not aware of what your specific church culture is and that everything you do either reinforces or undermines it, then you won't realize that promoting a non-conscientious person in a culture of conscientiousness is a mistake. When you know what your culture is, you can be more alert to the moments when it's being undermined. You'll also be more intentional about guarding and reinforcing your culture through every other decision you make, plus able to help others reinforce it through their choices as well.

Of champions

The temptation for most leaders will be to move quickly past all this wishy-washy and clearly long-term culture stuff and just get right to the nuts and bolts of the framework itself. I totally understand. I hate it when books say, "Now stop here and make some notes on what you need to do next. I'll wait for you right here… You're back! I hope that proved as useful and fruitful as I knew it would be!" I have never once stopped while reading a book and done any exercises, or for that matter even read the end-of-chapter discussion questions to help me process what I've learned. I turn the page and have zero guilt about doing so.

If you do happen to be a 'pause and reflect' person, then may the Lord bless you! But if you're like me, you desperately want to skip straight to the framework itself—but I'm begging you not to. If your culture is not healthy and nutrient-rich for leadership development, you're just setting yourself up for slow, frustrating and inevitable failure. In 18 months you'll be worn out and discouraged and this book will go up on the shelf as a fad that you got suckered into but that doesn't work.

If growing and developing leaders is not already going well at your church, then there's a good chance there's something in the culture that's dysfunctional. Whatever is currently growing is growing because your church culture is perfectly designed to encourage and support it. If leadership development is weak or non-existent, it's probably because your culture has the exact cocktail of nutrients to grow leadership weeds. You need to take a soil sample. You need to assess your culture.

"Culture eats strategy for breakfast" is a saying apocryphally attributed to management guru Peter Drucker. Whether or not Drucker ever said it is entirely unimportant, because it's true. If you try to introduce a strategy—like the leadership development framework—that is at odds with your culture, then your culture will always win. If your culture is hostile to leadership development then your efforts to implement what I'm talking about in this book will be doomed. It is in your absolute best interests to double-check that your culture is conducive to leadership development before you begin to implement the framework.

Now you don't need to put the book down immediately and go fix your culture and then and only then come back and keep reading. But you should start to evaluate your culture *while* you continue reading, and *then*, once you finish the book, return to the culture chapters and double-check that things are progressing well before you implement any of the rest. Get those culture thoughts bubbling away in the back of your mind. Trust me, we will return to them.

6
The challenge of becoming a team leader

Leadership development framework

- Ministry grouping
- Training and coaching
- **Pipeline architecture**
- Leader development
- Ministry monitoring
- Leader recruitment
- Leader assessment

Leadership culture
Discipleship culture
Convictional culture

The second and third elements

Andrew and Matt sat down after placing their orders at the gourmet burger restaurant that had recently opened up near Andrew's church, St Philip's. Andrew had been waiting for what seemed like weeks to continue the conversation he'd had with Matt on the way to the conference.

In the meantime, Andrew had been discussing things with his boss, Phil, and trying to absorb all that Phil had learned from Matt's boss, Luke. Now that they'd ordered their burgers, it was finally time.

"So," Andrew began eagerly, "what are the 11 herbs and spices?"

Matt glanced around, confused. "That's not the restaurant we're in."

"Oh, no," replied Andrew, "I meant what you said in the car that time on the way to the conference. You said something about the 11 secret herbs and spices of any leadership transition—the thing that people often overlook. And then you left it on a cliffhanger! I've brought my notebook. I'm ready. Why isn't Dan working out as a team leader? What did I do wrong?"

Matt laughed. "Oh yeah, that's really important. Remind me where we got up to?"

"Well, you said that the transition from leader to team leader is the most difficult leadership role transition there is—which really surprised me. I mean, once you're involved in a ministry, wouldn't the leader to team leader transition be the most common transition?" Matt nodded in agreement as he poured them both a glass of water. "So once you're a leader," Andrew continued, "the first transition is also the hardest! That blew my mind. Then you said there were three elements needed for a successful transition.

"You said the first element is the skills you need to do the role. And that these abilities require specific training. But *then* you said that training Dan in leadership concepts was probably what made things worse, which I don't understand."

"Well, kind of", replied Matt, carefully. "It's more that training *only* in skills without dealing with the other two elements often means that a new team leader is even more accidently corrosive to the proper functioning of their team. When you train them in those skills, you're giving them bigger weapons but no training on how to use them safely. In that kind of scenario, the chances of inadvertent injury are very high."

"So then what are these other two elements?" Andrew asked.

"The second element that needs to change when a person transitions from one leadership layer to another is how they think about and use their time. When you're a leader or a team member, you're basically thinking short-term, mainly week-to-week. That's pretty normal. My kids' ministry leaders are thinking, 'Am I on games this week? Am I teaching this week?' Maybe sometimes they'll think a few weeks ahead, like when we have our big school holiday extravaganza. But generally they're thinking about arriving on time and organizing their stuff for this week. With a team leader, on the other hand, their thoughts need to be term-by-term. They need to make sure things are humming and getting organized further into the future."

"But they still need to think about this week and arriving on time, don't they?" Andrew interrupted.

"Of course," Matt replied, "they'll shift into weekly thinking to make sure the people who are *supposed* to be thinking weekly actually are. But that's not their default timeframe any more. But the *more important* change the new team leader needs to make is in who they think their time is for."

"What does that mean?"

"When you're a frontline leader, your time is about *you* and it's *for* you. I mean, of course it's about and for Jesus and the people you're serving, but *you* serve by doing *your* things. You use *your* time to prepare *your* stuff for the week: game, talk, small group material, whatever. And that's pretty much it.

"When you're a team leader, you need to start making your time available for the people on your *team*. If a team member asks you a question, you don't think about it as being interrupted. The interruption *is* the work. The role is to invest time in the members of your team."

Andrew furrowed his brow. "You're right that I'd never considered this! But it makes total sense. That's what I want Dan to be doing for the people on his team. So, the third element?"

"Yes!" Matt's eyes lit up. "This is the most significant factor in why team leaders fail. A team leader needs to change their feelings and focus—their heart. This is the most dramatic shift.

"At the leader layer," Matt continued, "when the leader focuses on doing a good job they focus on the tasks they're responsible for. Talking to the kids, registering new families, all that. The leader is an individual contributor primarily responsible for themselves and their own duties and attitude. A good leader is reliable, well-prepared, encouraging, loving, kind. They do good ministry.

"But this focus on being an individual contributor needs to change when they move to be a team leader. Now they need to focus on getting ministry done *through others*."

Andrew blinked. "The leader's job is to think about themselves, and a team leader's job is to think about others? I don't agree. Everyone should be a servant."

"Yeah, all leadership—well, all true leadership—is servant leadership. My kids' leaders are there to serve the kids, and your youth leaders are there to serve the youth. But as you think about those leaders and whether they're doing a good job, the question being asked is: how did *you* go serving those youth? It's not quite like that for the team leader. Their job is to get ministry done *through* their leaders. The team leader doesn't do a good job when they themselves talk to all the youth; they do a good job when they help and enable *their leaders* to talk to all the youth. The question for them is more like: how did you go *leading your team* to serve these youth?"

"Okay", Andrew said. "So the summary for a leader is: I do a good job when I do a good job. I succeed when I succeed. For a team leader, the summary is: I do a good job when *you* do a good job. I succeed when *you* succeed."

"That's a great way of putting it", Matt said, smiling. "And the team leader needs to know that this move to 'through others' is legitimate ministry. It's not laziness or abdication of responsibility. It's never anyone's responsibility to personally minister to an entire group of people; the responsibility is to make sure your group of people *is personally ministered to*.

"Working through others is a revolution that needs to take place in the heart and mind of the team leader—and like most revolutions, there will be blood. It is *so* personally hard to let go. This is why a lot of people don't make the transition well. Some don't know about it, and others do but just can't make it. But when the revolution doesn't happen, it cripples the team."

"Why is that?" Andrew asked. "How does it cripple the team? This is all pretty much what's been happening with Dan. He hasn't made any of these shifts, and I haven't helped him well. But how is it that not doing these things caused all these other problems?"

The gist of it

Luke was sitting in his office when the phone rang. A familiar voice was on the other end. "Hey, it's Phil from St Philip's. How's life been treating you?"

"Phil! Great to hear from you. Life is good; how are things going in your world?"

"Good, good", Phil replied. "Look, this is just a quick call to follow up on our conversation a month ago. You mentioned the leadership pipeline. From speaking to other people, I've gathered that the pipeline is a philosophy where you think very intentionally about what kind of ministry work is being done by people at each layer of leadership. I've also heard that *you've* done some work that fills out what should be happening at each layer of leadership. Would it be possible for you to briefly step me through the basic shape of the framework?" Phil asked.

"Sure thing!" said Luke. "Here's the gist. Every layer of the leadership pipeline is made of up three essential elements. First, each layer has a collection of things that leaders at that layer simply need to learn. Sometimes these things are hands-on, practical skills. Other times it's a way to think or a concept.

"Then secondly, there's how the leader uses their time. Time is one of the most (if not *the* most) precious resources a leader has. If you cannot get your use of time under control, then you will get nothing else under control.

"And thirdly is the heart of the leader. I don't mean their character, although character is obviously crucial. I mean how the leader goes with being able to change their relationship to the hands-on, in-the-trenches ministry. Can they adjust to focus on enabling others to do the frontline work?

"These three pieces are the basic framework of the pipeline. We have a one-page summary that we use; you can have that if it'd be helpful."

"Yes please—that'd be great!" said Phil.

"That summary also helps you break the 'things to learn' element down further. Each layer has a particular set of skills, abilities and concepts that help the person to serve well at *that specific layer*. The team who makes phone calls and writes emails to welcome and follow up visitors to the Sunday service will be mainly doing different work to the person who leads and oversees them. Their team leader might make some phone calls and write some emails to some visitors, but their role is mainly about making sure others in that team know what they're doing, how to do it and why they're doing it. They'll also troubleshoot tricky situations as they come up. We call these 'layer-specific abilities'.

"Then there are also 'ministry-specific abilities'—the skills and abilities needed to do that specific ministry—and 'core abilities': vision, strategy, development and financial stewardship. They're core in that they're always relevant, but they do manifest themselves differently depending on the leadership layer."

"I'm not sure I really get what you mean", Phil admitted.

"Fair enough", Luke said. "It'll be clearer once you've got the summary sheet in front of you. I'll send it through now, and then we can talk more another day."

"Thanks! And thanks for your time too. You've been really helpful. I'll let you get back to it."

"No worries! Speak to you soon." After Luke hung up, he quickly emailed the summary to Phil before turning his mind back to writing Sunday's sermon.

A successful revolution

"Here's why the lack of a heart revolution cripples the team", Matt continued, pausing as their food was placed in front of them. "On the time side, if the team leader sees the questions and concerns of their team as a distraction, then that's a sign that the team leader isn't valuing the development of their team. It means they don't think it's important to help the leaders on their team get better as leaders. So they won't, and their team won't improve very much or very fast."

Andrew chewed a mouthful of burger and felt some of the pieces falling into place. "So if I'm not developing you then you might still be getting better if you're a self-reflective person, or you look for help elsewhere... But most people aren't like that, so their development will be much slower than it could be. That all makes sense. But what're the dynamics behind Dan's team getting worse?"

"If I'm the team leader", said Matt, "and I don't think my job is to help you, then what do I think my job is? Where will I be spending my time as a team leader?"

Matt ate a couple of chips while Andrew thought. "Well," started Andrew, "I think he spent his time on administration: rosters, reminders, that sort of thing."

"Yep", said Matt. "What else?"

"I suppose nothing much else. Apart from that, Dan just did what every other leader did."

"Bingo!" said Matt, quickly swallowing. "He focused on being an individual contributor. If I'm being an individual contributor, not just to help out in a crunch but all the time, then I'm a team leader competing with the people on my team. Not consciously, but I'm doing the same things, and probably better. Now, if I do your work and I do it better than you, instead of you, and more of it than you can, then what am I communicating to you?"

"That I'm not needed."

"Exactly. I think my boss was telling yours about the image of a pipeline? Imagine I went up a pipeline when I became a team leader, but now I'm trying to come back down to do the ministry of a leader. That pushes *you* back down the pipeline too. You go from being a leader of ministry to *not* being a leader, even though you still have that official title."

"Oh man." Andrew sighed as it suddenly became clear what had happened with Dan. "So I start to take less and less responsibility, show less and less initiative, and I begin acting like a big high-schooler in the youth ministry." Matt nodded as he finished off his burger. Andrew continued, energized and food forgotten. "The more the team leader does the leader's ministry for them, even if it's with noble intentions, the more the team leader pushes everyone else out and ends up creating more work for themselves."

"Exactly."

But there was something that still didn't quite make sense. "I guess this happens because team leaders don't understand their roles or haven't had their roles explained to them properly," Andrew said, "but I did explain the role to Dan. I guess not in terms of a pipeline and time considerations, but certainly in terms of being responsible for leading the leaders. I could've been clearer, and will be now, but we had training on some of these team leader skills. What went wrong there?"

"Well, as is often the case when it comes to people, the deeper problem isn't so much in the head as it is in the heart", Matt began. "I can know all the changes that need to happen as a new team leader, but it can be tough to actually *do* them. Implementation is often harder than information.

"So I find these new ways of operating difficult, and I know I'm not doing a good job because I'm still learning. But I want to feel like I'm doing a good job—and I know I can do a good job of the things that leaders have to do. So I'll go back and do that job, since it makes me feel more in control."

"People do this without realizing it, right?" Andrew clarified.

"For sure. People slip into the path of least resistance. This is why the focus and feelings element of each layer is the secret ingredient and the most important shift. If people learn all the things they need to learn and change how they use and conceive of their time, but refuse to make this heart-shift, then it's almost guaranteed that they'll slide back down the pipeline before too long. They need to make that gear-change so they get just as excited and satisfied when someone on their team succeeds as they did back when it was them personally who succeeded. As a team leader, I need to have that same sense of 'I did it!' when it's you who did it."

Andrew had another question: "Are you saying that the leader doing frontline ministry is focused on caring for those they are leading—say the youth or kids—but when they move to a team leader role their focus changes to caring about the leaders?"

"Not quite", Matt replied as he finished his fries. "A team leader must still be focused on whoever the ministry is designed to serve, but they do it *by caring for the leaders*. The primary concern is the same, but the *method* has changed."

"It sounds like the idea is that everyone is concerned for, caring about and serving *everyone* under them: for leaders, that's the kids, and for the team leaders it's the kids *and* the leaders."

"So long as you don't mean that it's the team leader's job to care for the kids *in the same way* as the leaders. The team leaders should still talk to the kids and get to know them and minister to them, but even then they should do it in a way that helps and enables the leaders to get better at it themselves."

"Yes," Andrew said, "that makes sense. I get what you mean about it being a revolution! It makes so much sense of what happened with Dan and his team. It's like I've gone behind the curtain at a magic show! Does this mean that the shift between a leader and a team leader doing their ministry is essentially a shift in prioritization? They learn new skills and concepts, but they need to reprioritize their time and their focus and their feelings of success. They need to reprioritize how they go about seeing all the people under them cared for and discipled."

"That's right", said Matt. "And reprioritization is painful. When it comes to personal discipleship and Christian character, your fruit grows on your own tree. But when it comes to leadership, your fruit starts to grow on other people's trees. As you move to the team leader layer and beyond, other people's trees will grow more and more fruit while your tree will look more and more sparse. They'll get extra praise and you'll get less, because most people won't be able to tell that much of the fruit on your leaders' trees actually belongs to you. Some team leaders can't handle this. They'll want to start taking some of that fruit and putting it back on their own tree. The negative effects of that are always huge.

"That change from 'success is what *I do*' to 'success is what *you do*' is extremely challenging. But we've got to help team leaders get it right, because otherwise it will undermine every leader in the team, make the team less effective than it could be and seriously hinder any further development instead of helping people grow as much as they could."

Suddenly, both Matt and Andrew's phone alarms started buzzing to remind them to wrap the meeting up.

When Andrew got back to his office and put the cold remains of his lunch on his desk, he noticed an email from Phil. It said:

I got this document from Luke at St Luke's today. Let's look it over together soon.

Phil

Andrew replied:

Sure. I've got more to share too.

Andrew

Then he opened the attachment Phil had forwarded. This is what he saw:

General overview

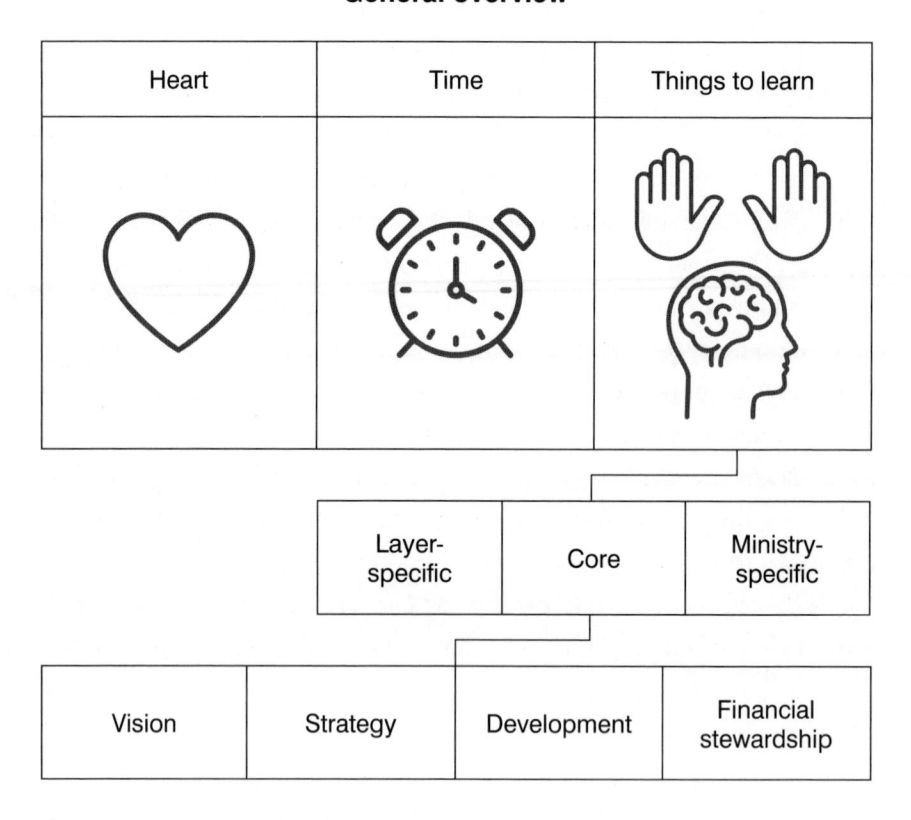

Heart	Time	Things to learn

	Layer-specific	Core	Ministry-specific

Vision	Strategy	Development	Financial stewardship

96 | WISDOM IN LEADERSHIP DEVELOPMENT

7
Pipeline 101

Over the past few chapters we've looked at the big picture of the leadership development framework and wrapped our minds around the three specific cultures needed for leaders to grow. Over the next five chapters we'll tackle two more tough topics: clearing up what leadership pipeline thinking is and how it works, and implementation, the trickiest hurdle of all.

The leadership pipeline is a simple concept to grasp but, since it's also a way of thinking that energizes and fuels itself, it will take effort before it becomes your unconscious default. To help this happen, we're going to survey the pipeline mindset from multiple angles to unpack the deeper logic of what it's doing and how it works. You'll get the concept itself but also the underlying 'why' that drives it.

Back in chapter 4, we introduced the pipeline architecture idea by saying it was a way of viewing different roles and layers of leadership so that there's clarity around what each role and layer is supposed to be doing and what differentiates it from other layers. It's where leadership progression, role definition and skill development all intersect.

A basic three-layer leadership pipeline looks like this:

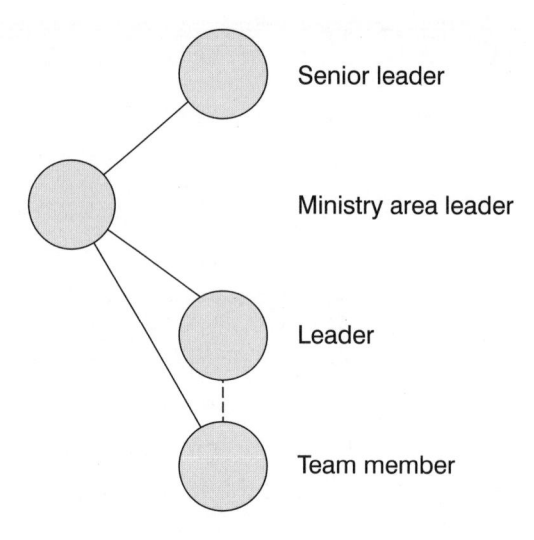

- Senior leader
- Ministry area leader
- Leader
- Team member

From overhearing the conversations between Luke and Phil and also Matt and Andrew we've already learned much about how and why the pipeline enables real leadership development.

Some people can get wary at this point because pipeline architecture can, at first sight, seem corporate and rigid—even distasteful. "That type of commercial philosophy won't darken my church." Fair enough. There's no virtue in doing things just because some businesses do them. We don't want the church to become like a business; we want it to actually do a good job.

But if you're sceptical of pipeline architecture because it means introducing leadership layers, the truth is you probably *already* have layers of leadership in your church. If your church has a senior minister, an assistant minister and a congregation, then you already have three leadership layers. And if there's a team somewhere being led by someone other than the two paid ministers, then you already have four leadership layers. Pipeline architecture isn't about adding layers to your currently layer-less church. Pipeline architecture is about helping you utilize those pre-existing layers more effectively and intentionally.

The key insight

The key insight at the heart of the leadership pipeline philosophy is that in any given ministry situation that involves a team—and so, therefore, some layers of leadership—the ministry-specific skills are *not* the main thing that you're doing.

Imagine a youth ministry made up of a team of volunteers and a youth pastor who is responsible for the whole youth ministry. Every one of them needs some specific youth ministry skills—let's say running games and leading a discussion group, along with some input on issues like self-harm, suicidal thoughts, disclosures of abuse and so on. These are all vital, and incompetence can at best lead to a weak youth ministry and at worse be catastrophic. They're important, and this is where we can be tempted to spend a lot of time and thought.

But pipeline thinking helps us to see that, though very important, these topics aren't the main thing that those leaders are doing or need to learn. Volunteer leaders need to learn how to *be on a team*, and that youth pastor needs to learn *how to lead a team*.

Most things are the same

From that critical insight flows one more: that the majority of ministry done in a certain role will be *the same* across different ministry areas. If the main thing that youth leaders need to learn is *how to function in a team*, and what youth team leaders need to learn is *how to lead a team*, then leading a team in youth ministry and leading a team in the women's ministry will be roughly 70% the same. Leading a team is leading a team.[12]

It often doesn't feel 70% the same when you first join a ministry—say when you become a youth leader for the first time. This is because learning youth ministry-specific skills feels existentially more pressing and urgent. And in one sense they are: you're on games next week! You'd better figure it out! But most ministry-specific skills are quite limited in

---

12 The authors and researchers of the book *The Leadership Code* concluded that 60 to 70% of all leadership is applicable to any domain or context. See Dave Ulrich, Norm Smallwood and Kate Sweetman, *The Leadership Code*, Harvard Business School Publishing, Boston, 2008, p. 9.

both number and complexity, whereas the skills needed to function helpfully in a team, or as a team leader, are more intricate and subtle. This becomes even more apparent in the layers above the leader layer, since by the time you reach that point you will have mastered the vast majority of those ministry-specific skills.

No, not every team can be treated and led exactly the same way. It's not all cut-and-paste. Every team is unique because every person is unique, and a team is a collection of people. What worked in one may not work in another. There are also a wide variety of differences that impact how a team functions: cultural, generational, intergenerational, life-stage, emotional maturity, relational skills, experience... just to name a few. However, the basic skills and abilities needed are the same, even taking into account the various factors. They'll need to be *applied* differently and creatively, but they'll remain fundamentally the same. This is what makes leadership an art as well as a science, and why it's always challenging and fun.

Only three things

Each layer of the leadership pipeline is made up of just three parts: the heart needs to be focused on; how time needs to be used; and things to be learned. As a leader moves from one layer of the pipeline to another, each of these three parts will change.

Heart

Heart	Time	Things to learn

As we saw in the previous chapter, the focus of the heart is the hardest change for new leaders. It's also the easiest element to misunderstand.

There are two common misconceptions. Firstly, we're *not* proposing a change in *values*. If we value the word of God, having Jesus at the centre and candour at the leader layer, then we'll be holding to those values just as firmly at the team leader layer. Secondly, when I say 'heart' I don't also mean 'love'. Love and care are central and critical in every layer of Christian leadership because love is central to both being a Christian and being a leader.

By heart I mean what a leader needs to focus on and how they feel about that focus. It's the focus of their *personal ministry contribution*. Someone at the leader layer needs to focus on their own individual contribution—they are focused on serving others in the specific things that they, themselves, do. However, someone who is leading a team needs to focus their contribution on getting things done by working *through* the people on their team. Moving that focus from contributing individually to contributing through others is what has changed. Another way to say this is that the *type of ministry* that needs to get done has changed.

Heart is also about how the leader *feels* about that focus. They need to move past a begrudging acceptance of this new reality to fully embrace the new state of play and feel satisfaction when they make a contribution *through their team* instead of personally. And this change in feeling is essential.

Time

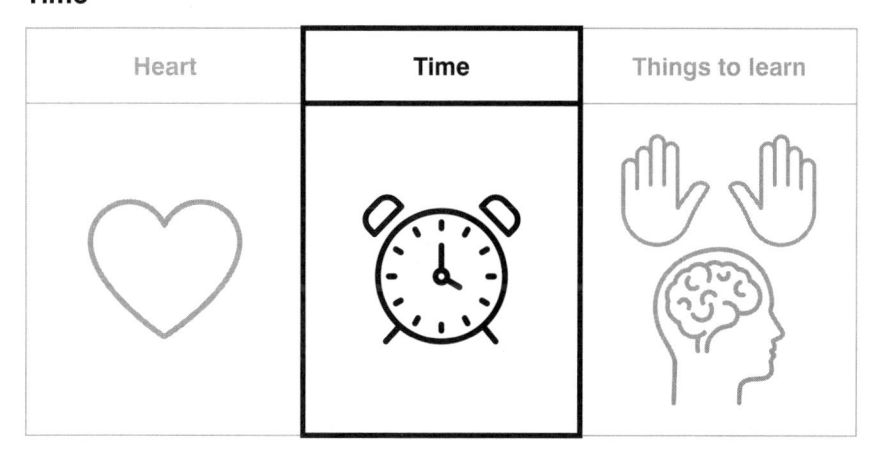

Heart	Time	Things to learn
♡	⏰	🧠

'Time' is partly about whether a leader spends their time getting things done themselves or building the members of their team, and it's also partly about the kind of time horizon the leader is primarily working with. Are they thinking weekly, quarterly or longer? Obviously, everyone needs to think about what is happening *this week* and the things they need to do and places they need to be. But the higher up the pipeline a leader moves, the more long-term they will need to think, partially due to the increased need for deeper strategic thinking.

We'll go through in detail what all this looks like for each layer in section two. For now, we're busy understanding the different pieces that make up each layer of the pipeline.

Things to learn

This piece of the pipeline layer triumvirate contains the most information and new skills to contend with, but it's also the easiest to grapple with. It breaks down into three smaller categories: ministry-specific skills, layer-specific skills and core skills.

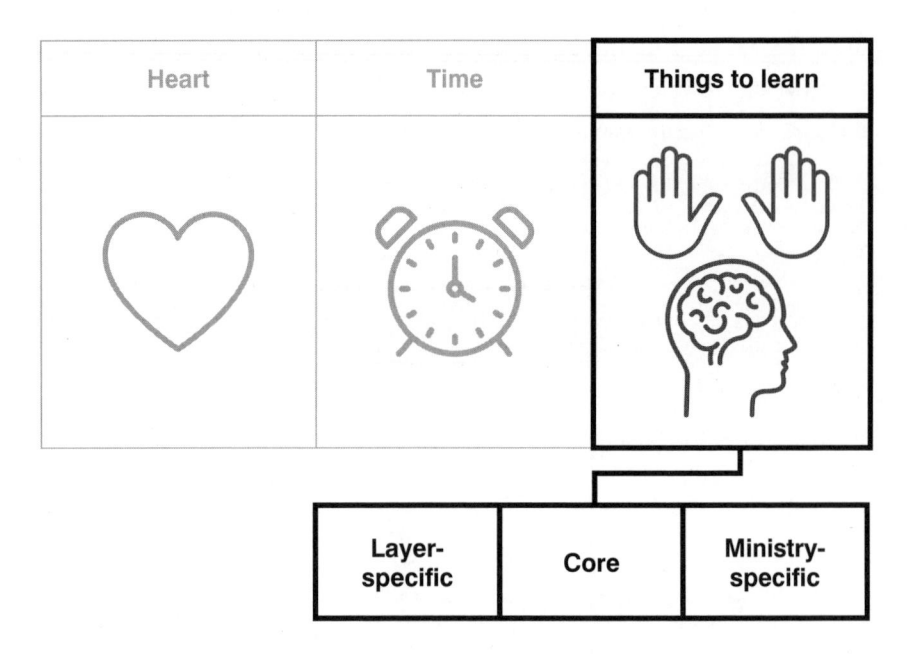

Heart	Time	Things to learn
♡	⏰	🙌🧠

Layer-specific	Core	Ministry-specific

We've already discussed ministry-specific skills. Layer-specific skills are the skills and concepts common to that layer of any ministry. In other words, the things that every member of a team needs to learn regardless of which specific ministry they are involved in.

For a frontline leader, these will be things like arriving on time, aiming for quality, and being flexible and encouraging. These aren't just youth ministry things or children's ministry things. For a team leader, it will be things like delegation, ministry monitoring, coaching and feedback, communication and so on. Again, we'll discuss more in section two.[13]

Lastly, of these three facets it's often the core skills that are hardest to get a handle on. Within core skills are vision, strategy, development and financial stewardship.

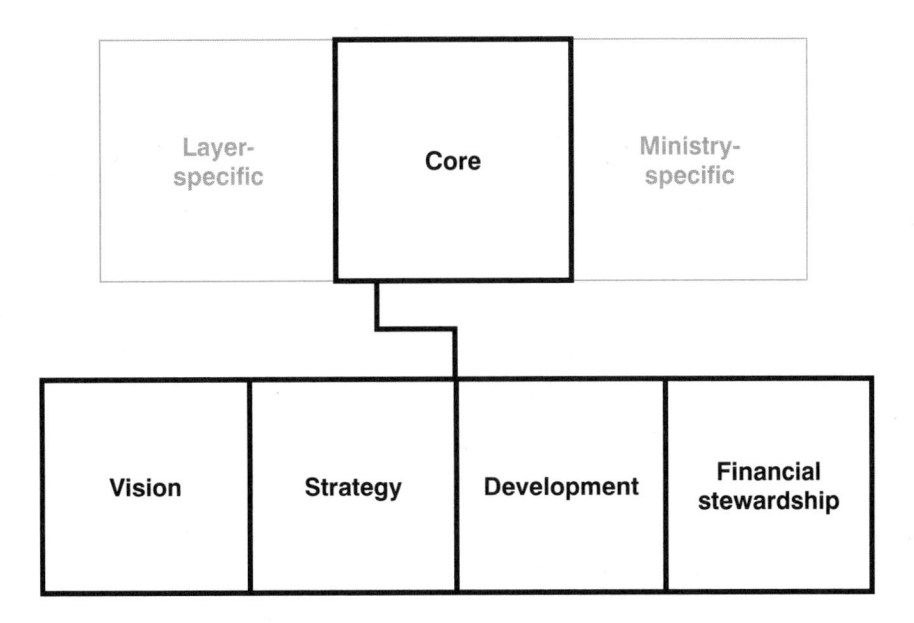

	Core	
Layer-specific		Ministry-specific

Vision	Strategy	Development	Financial stewardship

These skills are core because they *evolve* as a leader moves through the pipeline. Ministry-specific skills don't change. Running games is running games. Layer-specific skills don't change either, though you do learn further facets as you move through the pipeline. More are added at higher layers, but the key skills are built upon rather than morphed. For example, recruitment happens at every layer where a leader is empowered to recruit. A person could potentially learn all those recruitment skills at the

---

13 And if you're after a collection of training materials for developing leaders at any layer of the pipeline, make sure you head to revcraighamilton.com.

leader layer if they wanted to. They wouldn't need to, and it probably wouldn't dramatically help them improve their recruiting with their limited scope of authority, but they could.

But vision, strategy, development and financial stewardship aren't skills so much as they are attitudes and expectations. They are about the relationship a leader has to these four realities. And that relationship needs to morph and evolve as they change layers of the pipeline. For example, the leader layer's relationship with the vision of the ministry is that they need to know that it exists and be on board with it. But when they become a team leader, that relationship to vision needs to change. They now need to be able to *articulate* it because it's their responsibility to *transmit* that vision to the leaders on their team and so ensure that *they* know it and are on board. This is a change in *connection* to vision.

The pipeline is about clarity and multiplication

I hope you've grasped that each layer of leadership *within* a ministry, even while all layers are involved in, say, ministering to women, is actually doing distinct work. It has its own behaviours, priorities, time horizons to focus on and internal measures of personal success. Team leaders aren't just more organized or more responsible leaders; they are doing different, though complementary, ministry.

The leadership pipeline is where leader development, leader progression and role clarity all overlap. It's a philosophy and a framework for intentionally developing people in leadership so that we multiply leaders and so multiply the ministry that can be done. Pipeline architecture will help you love the people in your teams better by giving them clarity on what they need to do and how to thrive. You'll need to buy fewer leaders and thus be less inhibited by budget issues. You'll get more done, leverage more of the genius that already exists inside your people, and be consistently and intentionally raising up leaders at every layer of your church. That is, you'll be equipping the saints for the work of ministry.

Pipeline planning meeting 2

This will be the second time your team gets together to contribute their insights and build on the insights of others. The specific agenda of this meeting is to tackle the fourth and seventh clarity questions: What's our flavour? What's our top priority right now?

What's our flavour?

Your church's flavour is a mixture of some key values in your church as well as some relatively distinctive features that separate your church from the others around it. This isn't a marketing exercise where you work out your 'brand': this is self-understanding.

This question can be quite hard to come at cold, and you'll return to your flavour in another pipeline planning meeting later. Don't get hung up on getting it exact—whatever that means. This is a first pass, a rough outline, a quick sketch. Parts will be perfectly accurate. Some will be way off. It's preliminary.

Here's an exercise to do together to help.

    a) Choose three words or phrases *only* from the following list that you think best describe your church. Don't focus on what you think your church *should* be. Focus on what *actually is*.

- believes in the Bible
- focuses on Jesus
- filled with grace
- lives holy lives
- dependent on the Holy Spirit
- loves urgently
- sings passionately
- preaches powerfully
- devoted to prayer

    b) Again, choose only the three words that best capture your church.

- generous
- hospitable

- passionate
- fun
- welcoming
- excelling
- transparent
- high conflict (in a good way)
- united
- people take responsibility
- empowering
- inviting
- intentional
- proactive
- candid
- trusting
- encouraging
- creative
- innovative
- collaborative
- future-focused
- risk-taking
- formal
- casual
- nimble
- relaxed
- organized

c) Can you think of a word that describes your church that wasn't in either of those lists? Add it to your six.

You now each have seven words that you think describe your church. Write them down and take turns sharing them. Explain your choices, but don't make a big sermon about it. Display them somehow, such as on a whiteboard or via a projector. Don't write them in columns. Don't attach people's names to them. Just write them up in a big cloud of words. If someone says a word that's already been brought up, write it up again. You might have the same word appear lots of times.

Discuss anything you notice. Are there words that appear again and again? Are any of the words surprising? Let everyone share their perceptions.

One quick tip: just because a word appears a lot doesn't necessarily mean it's right or that the Lord is leading you towards that word or anything. It might be spot-on, but equally it might not be. Maybe we've *all* got it wrong. Maybe we're just copying each other because we thought that word felt like the 'right' answer. This is just a preliminary stab at it.

Keep a record of this word cloud so that you can come back to it in the future and move on to the next question.

What's our top priority right now?

It's time to figure out what you're going to focus on for the next season in your church life. Spend half the remaining meeting time gathering broad ideas and then the other half narrowing in and closing off options.

For this first attempt, go for a 90-day time horizon. It's easier to think of priorities for the next three months than for the next year. Plus, if you end up choosing something that isn't great, at least you're only stuck with it for three months.

Have everyone, by themselves, write down three potential priorities, one for each of the three priority pools (quantity, operation processes and discipleship perception).[14] Then go around the group and have people explain their thoughts. Collect and display their answers. Discuss what you see. Are there any patterns or commonalities? Are there any surprises? Did anyone suggest investing in areas of strength or is every option about fixing a weakness?

Whittle the list down to a manageable amount. You might ask people which item on the board jumps out to them, or you might ask them to pick their top four (with the caveat that they can only choose, maximum, two of their own ideas).

The endgame is to come away with a maximum of three priorities for the next quarter. (If you can't get there, the senior leader should take what you have and turn the options into a short list within the next week.)

---

14 See chapter 3 to refresh yourself on these categories.

Now we need to transform them into something actionable. The simplest way to do this is to think about a two-step process.

Step one is to translate the priority into a 'from A to B by C' formula. *From* six small groups *to* seven small groups *by* 31 July, for example. *From* our current ad hoc welcoming vibe *to* an articulated integration pathway *by* 1 October.

Step two is to break that formula down into the actionable steps that need to be taken. It's tempting to go big and list lots of things that you *could* do. In reality, you won't do *that much* because the regular churn of ministry will continue. Try and find the minimum that needs to be done to achieve the objective (or at least push the ball down the field a bit).

Someone will need to be assigned the responsibility for this practical priority translation task: either the senior leader or someone else on the team. The point is that *someone* owns it and they commit to getting it done as soon as they practically can.

Once you've locked in your first priority (or priorities), book in the end date to check how you went and to figure out the next priority. Hopefully it's starting to feel like you're getting things done and building some momentum.

8
The key impediments to starting a pipeline

Leadership development framework

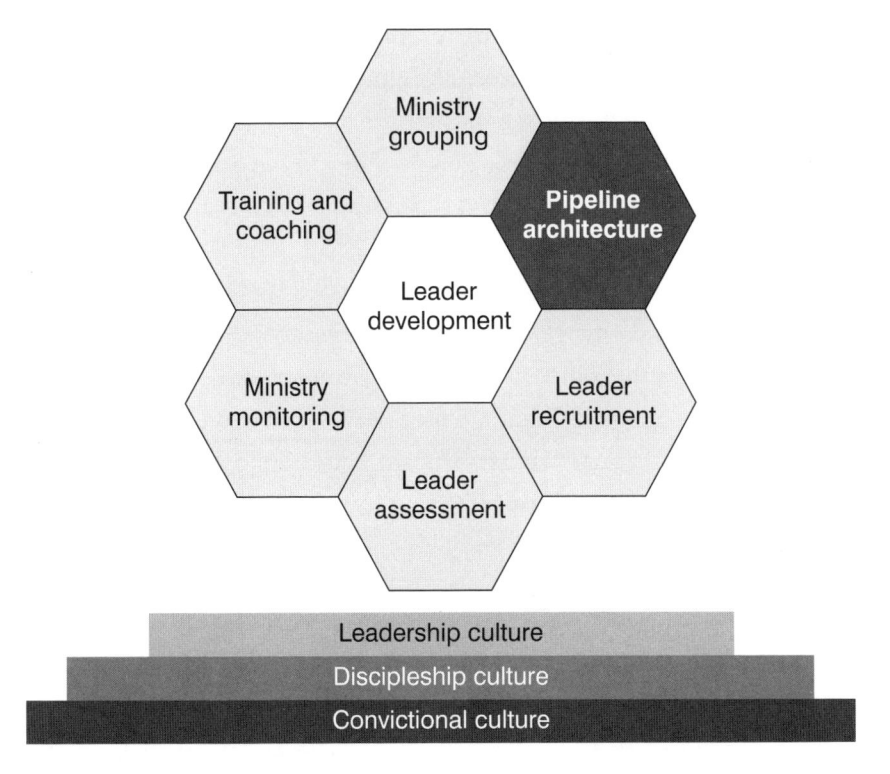

(Diagram: hexagonal framework showing Ministry grouping, Training and coaching, Pipeline architecture, Leader development, Ministry monitoring, Leader recruitment, Leader assessment — resting on layered foundation of Leadership culture, Discipleship culture, Convictional culture.)

The shadow impulse

It had been a tiring season at St Luke's: the calendar had been particularly full, and there had been several pastoral crises in the lives of church members. As the senior minister, Luke had been involved in varying degrees of intensity, but still, he admitted—he was weary. As he stood up from his desk and stretched his shoulders, his phone rang. It was his friend Chris who led a church on the other side of the city.

After chatting briefly about life and family, Chris got to the point of why he had called: "I've been implementing this leadership pipeline that we've been talking about. Well, I say 'implementing', but we haven't got far. I've talked it through with my staff, we think we understand the basic idea, and we're in agreement as to what we'll call each layer, but—"

"That sounds like you've done a lot!" Luke interrupted. "Getting to that point is no easy task."

"Well, true. But now we're a bit stuck. The staff have been struggling to get it running in their ministry areas, and honestly I've found it hard to implement in the ministries I'm responsible for too. The staff are all highly skilled in their ministries, and, under God, they've been seeing great results. The pipeline seems hard to install into something that's already working well. Though, when it comes to the Sunday welcoming teams, the team leaders there just aren't stepping up."

"Tell me more about that", Luke probed.

"Well, I'm the welcoming ministry area leader. We have three services, and a team with their own team leader for each service. I've been helping the team leaders shift to focusing on getting ministry done through others and all those things. And I think they've been working on that, but when I run the team meetings with each team before each service, the team leaders don't grab the responsibility like I want them to. Is there a step I've missed or a technique that might help?"

"I have good news and bad news", Luke said. "The good news: I think I know what the blockage is for your welcoming teams. It's very common. And I'm pretty confident it's the same blockage your staff are facing in their ministry areas."

"That is good!" Chris replied. "I can't wait to tell the team. What's the bad news? That the missed step is complicated to do?"

"The bad news is that it's not a technique or a step or anything like that. The blockage is you. And your staff. What's hindering your pipeline is pride."

"What... pride? You know how much Vanessa and I have sacrificed over our time in ministry!"

"I know you and your family have given up a lot for that church", said Luke kindly. "I thank God for your ministry regularly. I'm not saying you or your staff are terrible people who should be disqualified from ministry. I'm saying you're normal, pride is subtle, and ministry issues are often leadership issues. Not always, but my first instinct is still to see if the leader is doing or not doing something that is causing or contributing to the problem."

"That's fair", sighed Chris.

"And those problems are often tied to what those leaders believe. None of us behave perfectly in line with what we believe; we're all inconsistent and irrational to various degrees. It's part of being sinful. Leadership is often the crucible where our sin is exposed to us in ever deeper layers. Just when we think we've got to the bottom of some sin, something will happen to peel back another layer and we'll see that there's still far more to go."

"Yeah, that's true", Chris agreed. "The more you grow as a Christian, the more aware you are of the depth of your own sin. The more mature you are as a disciple, the more sinful you often feel."

"Exactly. And in my experience, pride can be the loudest and most obvious sin and yet also the most elusive and crafty. Sometimes it's hard to spot. It camouflages itself as something good. It frequently takes hold as the shadow impulse, and I think it's white-anting your pipeline in its beginning, fragile state."

"The shadow impulse?"

"People in ministry—paid or unpaid—have an impulse within them that wants to see people loved and cared for, helped, converted, grown and trained to follow Jesus through being taught and ministered to. But somewhere along the way the shadow impulse creeps in and grows until it replaces the healthy impulse. The shadow impulse is that we want to see people loved and cared for, helped, converted, grown, and trained to follow Jesus through being taught and ministered to *by me*.

"I'm passionate about people. I'm working really hard. I'm doing good things. But if you scratch a bit deeper, you'll find that I'm also passionate about being the one to do them and, often unknowingly, I'm passionate that I do them and that *you don't*. It's hard to notice the change, in ourselves or others, but the impact is huge. The shadow impulse stops the pipeline functioning properly because it keeps ministry confined to one person."

Chris cleared his throat. "And what made you think this was an issue for my team and me?"

"In one sense, the shadow impulse is an issue for everyone, since it's really just an outworking of pride."

"Okay", said Chris. "So the question we should be asking isn't: is it in me? Because the answer is: it is. It's in everyone."

"Right", said Luke. "A more important question is: are you aware that the seed is in your heart, and are you watering it? If you're watering it then it will grow, and as it grows it will choke your heart. That's what pride does."

"I think I'm getting it," Chris said slowly, "but was there anything specific that made you think this shadow impulse is causing our implementation problems?"

"Two things, actually. You said that your staff are highly competent in their fields of ministry. This is great, but it does mean that they're more susceptible to an overgrown shadow impulse. When I'm very skilled and the ministry is going well, then there's a high chance that pride will be twisting my passion for ministry being done into a passion for ministry being done *by me*. That obviously makes it hard to genuinely hand ministry over to others."

"The shadow impulse dissolves the pipeline because it's fundamentally opposed to leadership development", mused Chris. "We're on board intellectually, but deep in our hearts we're self-sabotaging. We've loved doing our ministries so much that we've accidentally tied together who we *are* with what we *do*. If the ministry is successful, I am successful. I can't hand that over to someone else."

"Excellent point", Luke said. "When our identity is tied up in our ministry, then we're in dangerous territory."

"Which means", Chris continued, "giving away ministry to others means I'm diminishing my own sense of worth. Of course I'll want to keep as much as possible!"[15]

---

15 See Hamilton, 'Don't let what God wants you to do get in the way of who God wants you to be', pp. 71-76.

"Exactly", Luke said. "You and your team are being hindered by a particularly sneaky configuration of pride."

"But if the ministry impulse and the shadow impulse are both present in our hearts, is there any way to check which one is dominant?"

"Well, that's a tough question. I don't have the definitive answer, but the kind of questions that have been helpful to me and the team here are:

1. Are you just as happy when people praise someone else for their sermon as you are when they praise you?
2. Are you just as thrilled hearing about someone becoming a Christian through what someone else did as you are when it's someone you ministered to?
3. Do you tell stories of other people's ministry successes and achievements as much as you tell your own?
4. When you have some big ministry success and people give the credit accidentally to someone else, do you correct them? Why?"

"Thanks so much for your time, Luke. This has been really helpful. Just one thing before I let you get back to what you were doing. What tipped you off that the shadow impulse was an issue for me? Now that I've had a chance to think about it, you're right. But what gave it away?"

"Oh yes, this was the second hint. You didn't let your team leaders run the meetings of their own teams. In that key moment, you took a responsibility back from them and did it yourself. And seeing as you did it because you oversaw the whole ministry, that signalled to me that something was going on with your view of what 'real' ministry was."

"Well, you nailed it. And I'm thankful that you pointed it out. Now."

"You're welcome!" said Luke. "Hey, before I go, if you want to talk to someone else who's begun implementing the leadership pipeline, give my friend Phil a call. He's the senior minister over at St Philip's. He's only just started, but he's overcome some hurdles already that might be helpful to hear about."

"Thanks, Luke! I will."

Not just for big churches

Matt had just finished his talk outlining the foundations of the leadership pipeline philosophy at the children's ministry conference. As he stepped down from the platform, a woman approached.

"Hi Matt", she said when near. "I'm Jess. Thanks so much for your presentation. It was fascinating, and I'm sure it was helpful for lots of churches. Do you mind if I ask you a quick question?"

"Hey Jess", Matt said. "Fire away!"

"I can see how the leadership pipeline would be helpful for a big church with lots of people and lots of layers of leadership. Is it just a big church thing? I mean, I just can't see this amount of structure fitting the culture of my church. We're 70 people on a Sunday on a good week."

"Oh, not at all", Matt replied. "Intentionally raising up leaders is for every size of church. In fact, some of the churches that are best at building leaders are churches with less than 100 people. Besides, if you had people leading teams in kids' ministry, wouldn't that free you up to do things you never quite have the time or brain space for?"

"I guess. So the pipeline's just a tool to help churches intentionally develop leaders?"

"Pretty much. Although maybe more importantly, it's also a mindset of different layers of leadership doing different types of ministry. I can imagine some people being put off by what looks at first sight like an 'over-structured' move away from ministry-in-relationship. But there'd be no more structure in a leadership pipeline than there'd be at your church right now—it's just that maybe no-one has drawn out what the structure now is. But it's there, probably with certain people being looked to for leadership and approval while others kick up a stink and effectively veto any decisions they don't like."

"It's like you've been to my church!" Jess laughed.

"Which means the issue with the pipeline isn't that it's structural as opposed to organic. Instead it's more like a rival structure seeking to replace a currently hidden structure with one that everyone can know and navigate. This will threaten some people. You'd need to be careful in how you go about implementing it. But the pipeline is all about getting ministry done with others and through others. It's all about relationships. Size doesn't stop relationships."

It's not just having multiple layers

Andrew and Tom had met at the same pizza place at the same time every year for the last four years. They'd become close friends at Bible college and, even as ministry took them to different sides of the city and consumed their time and attention, they still made it a priority to catch up. Andrew always looked forward to it. He eventually turned this year's conversation to the leadership pipeline, sharing how helpful it had been in his youth ministry. But he was surprised that it didn't seem to resonate much with Tom.

"Have you already heard of the leadership pipeline?" Andrew asked.

"Well, not exactly called that," replied Tom, "but basically. We've had leadership layers in our ministry since before I arrived at the church. But it's a good thing to do, though. I totally agree."

"Oh, how does it work at your church?"

Tom shrugged. "Pretty much every team has a team leader. We usually look around our church for people who have the skills and experience to lead a team, and then we deploy them into that role. It's been working really well. I'm not sure there's much more to it."

"Yeah, sounds similar", admitted Andrew. "But... what do you mean that you *deploy* them? Don't you have to train them?"

"They tend to come pre-trained from leading at their work or at a previous church. They already know what to do. We just release them to use those skills."

This didn't sound very pipeline to Andrew, but since Tom had been doing it for longer... "But what exactly do your team leaders do as they lead?"

"What all team leaders do, I suppose", blinked Tom. "They're usually one of the most organized people on the team. They're responsible for things like rostering and making sure people do what they're meant to, and they model what it looks like to be a good leader. They're often really experienced at, say, kids' ministry, so they'll lead and coordinate that team."

Andrew saw the difference now. "That's how it used to work at St Luke's as well. The problem we ran into is that highly trained people stopped arriving at our church. They used to come in waves as people moved into the area—though one time when the church up the hill imploded we got a tsunami. But the waves got smaller and further apart, and we started running out of leaders."

"Actually... we've noticed that recently too."

"Really? We realized we hadn't consistently been raising up and building our own leaders. We'd been benefiting from the work done by other churches or other ministries. Not that it was wrong to use the leaders who had arrived from other churches!"

"Every gift from above should be received with thanksgiving", Tom grinned.

"Exactly", Andrew laughed. "But we realized we need to raise up our own leaders, not just to fill roles but also for the sake of their own discipleship. Having leadership layers and deploying leaders isn't the same thing as a leadership pipeline. It might look the same on the surface, but the philosophy of the leadership pipeline is actually fundamentally different. It's about carefully clarifying what kind of ministry is being done at each layer, intentionally helping people make the difficult transitions from one layer to another, and raising up leaders throughout the pipeline."

"Oh", said Tom, much more engaged. "Tell me more."

So Andrew did.

9
The ten pipeline commandments

Leadership development framework

A hexagonal diagram with "Leader development" at the center, surrounded by: Ministry grouping, Pipeline architecture (highlighted), Leader recruitment, Leader assessment, Ministry monitoring, and Training and coaching. Below the diagram are three stacked layers: Leadership culture, Discipleship culture, and Convictional culture.

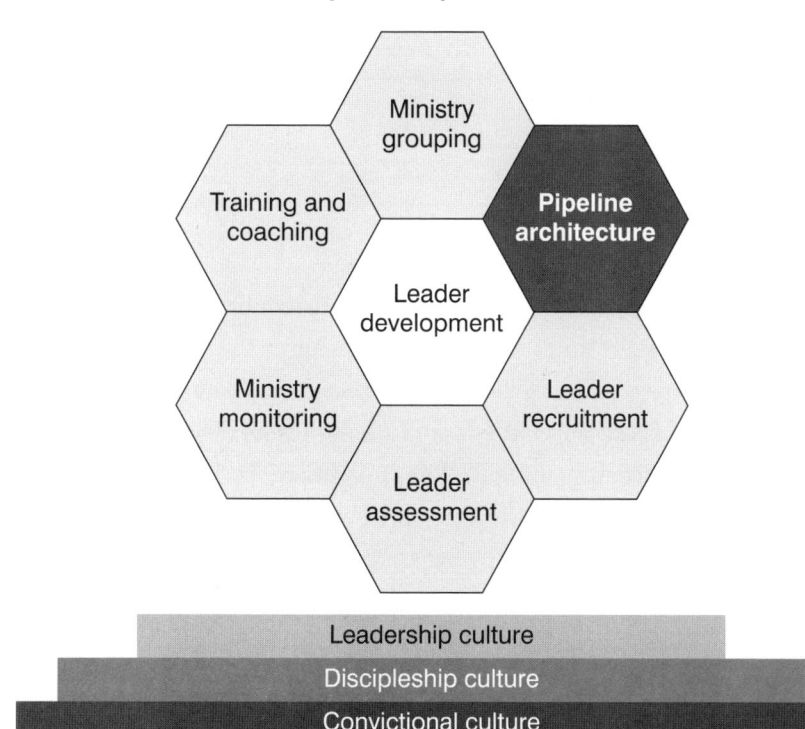

Once you've grouped your ministries, either across the whole church or within the ministry area you're responsible for, you'll then move on to the second element in the leadership development framework—pipeline architecture—and consider what kind of ministry should be occurring at each layer, crystallizing and clarifying those roles and responsibilities.

Like any tool, we need to understand the leadership pipeline to use it properly. A smartphone is an incredibly effective tool—but if you use it to hammer in nails its success will be temporary and limited. If you don't understand what the leadership pipeline is designed to do or how it's working, then you are almost guaranteed to clog the pipeline and unintentionally dismantle it without even realizing. It's not that the pipeline is particularly brittle, but it can't function when used poorly.

To help us wrap our minds around this pipeline mentality and move beyond a superficial understanding of the diagram, there are ten commandments that act as the central core of pipeline architecture thinking. Stay within arm's reach of these commandments and you'll have a good chance of successfully implementing the leadership pipeline in your church or ministry.

Commandment one

> Going from one layer to the next takes intentionality and specific training.

This is the most basic leadership pipeline commandment, but it's not as obvious as you might think. Learning leadership is the same as learning anything: you need to learn it. People are not born leaders. Sure, some people's personalities mean they lean towards leadership; some have an inbuilt talent for learning quickly and an aptitude for leadership; others grew up with more opportunities to learn leadership, informally or formally. All of this is true, but whether natural talent is present or not, leadership is still a collection of skills, constructs and concepts that can be, and need to be, learned.

I know lots of people who had above-average natural talent in some area yet never achieved what their talent indicated they were capable of. You probably know people like that too. Talent alone isn't enough to explain extraordinary achievement. As Angela Duckworth says in her book, *Grit*:

> Talent is how quickly your skills improve when you invest effort. Achievement is what happens when you take your acquired skills and use them.[16]

---

16 Angela Duckworth, *Grit*, Penguin Random House, London, 2016, p. 42.

Duckworth summarizes these thoughts into two simple equations:

> Talent × Effort = Skill
> Skill × Effort = Achievement

Duckworth acknowledges that this summary is simplistic and doesn't include several other factors that influence achievement, such as luck—or what we might credit as God's providence. The critical insight here is that *effort counts twice*.

People who are moving from one layer to another will need to be taught what needs to be done and how to thrive at that layer. They'll then need to deliberately put in the effort to learn those skills and behaviours. Most people who move from one leadership layer to another don't just intuitively pick it up, and "most people" includes you and me. The choice is between years of trial and error and slow incremental improvement to learn what's needed—or explicitly training in it. Clarity and intentionality mean that people learn more quickly, get less frustrated and stick at it longer.

And yet, as we saw back in chapter 6 with Dan the youth leader, intentional and specific training isn't necessarily a slam dunk. Even when training is happening, there's no guarantee that it will be intentional and specific about the right things.

Which means the obvious questions are: what do we need to be intentional about and what specific behaviours should we be training people to be doing? To commandment number two!

Commandment two

> The goal isn't to 'level up'.

The layers of leadership aren't levels: they're layers. As soon as you call them 'levels', a switch gets flipped in people's brains that makes them think their goal is to *rise through* the levels and score points and complete the game. Nope. We're not playing Donkey Kong.

We have a tendency to take the best and brightest from one layer and move them to the next because we often equate 'promotion' with recognition and honour. But promoting people to a higher layer of leadership is not a gift of thanks for services rendered. Just buy them chocolate and write them a nice card instead.

The goal of the pipeline isn't to ascend as high as you can. The goal is to find the place where you can best serve so that the body is built and the kingdom grown. Maybe that means a role higher up the pipeline, but perhaps it means staying on the frontlines.

We need to remind ourselves and those we lead that prestige isn't found at the top. Greatness is servanthood, and you can be great at any layer. Equally, you can fail to serve at any layer. The layers are just doing different ministry, not ranking people.

Commandment three

> Being good at a ministry doesn't mean you should advance up the pipeline.

It's often assumed that the main criterion for promoting someone to, say, a team leader role is that they are good at the ministry they are doing at the layer below. But high-level competence in the ministry-specific skills of one layer doesn't mean you should move up to the next. It doesn't make sense to take your most talented leader of kids and have them primarily deal with leaders. You want your best kids' leader actually leading kids.

Commandment four

> Being awesome at one layer tells you nothing about whether you'll be awesome at the next.

Again, this is so obvious, but we keep on falling for it. Someone is an awesome small group leader. People love being in their group and under their leadership growing in discipleship. And so what do we do with this person? We promote them to oversee all the other small group leaders (the trap we fall into when we ignore commandment two).

Not only do we need good small group leaders leading actual small groups, but leading small group leaders is an almost completely different skill set to leading a weekly small group. Being good at one doesn't mean you'll be good at the other. Now, *maybe* this person will also make a great small group team leader, but if they do it'll be because they're an exceptional and high-functioning human and not because *being a good small group leader prepared them for this*. It's equally likely—and in my experience, more likely—that they'll crash and burn as a team leader.

You'd be better off leaving them leading small groups—especially if that's what they're passionate about—and instead finding someone who might actually be good at team leading. If you wanted to capitalize on the gifts and experience of that great small group leader, there are lots of other options. Create a 'small group consultant' role and have them troubleshoot other leaders' issues. Have them talk through in leader training meetings some aspect of what they do. Add potential trainee leaders to their group so that they can watch and learn. They can do all these things while still leading a small group.

You need to break the habit of promoting your best and brightest. Of course, you still might ask them to lead at a higher layer, but you won't ask them *because* they're the best at their current layer. That doesn't help them, the people they lead or the kingdom.

Commandment five

> The behaviours that cause success at one layer will sometimes compromise it at the next.

There are dozens of skills, sub-skills and conceptual frameworks fundamental to good leadership at each specific layer. Some of those will help you at other layers of leadership, and others will actually *hinder* you. Some leadership skills and abilities are only useful at that layer, and so have a detrimental impact when employed at different leadership layers. The ways of doing things at one layer may need to be jettisoned entirely when you move to another layer. Sometimes the same underlying skills and mindsets *are* required at the next layer, but they need to be radically recalibrated to be useful.

We've seen one example of this in one of Andrew's leaders, Dan. Dan was highly competent and committed to quality and excellence as a frontline leader, but this passion needed to be redirected away from his own individual contributions once he became a team leader.

Another example is the frontline leader whose whole life is run week-to-week. This works fine for them; they thrive under pressure and need a crunching deadline to help motivate them. But when this person moves to a team leader role or a ministry area leader role, they have other people relying on them and needing clarity from them so *they* can then go and do their own work. Requiring the high pressure of the weekly horizon becomes dysfunctional. Besides, not everyone works well under pressure; some people need time to sit with something or for their plan of action to emerge through an iterative process. Other people have limited availabilities, and so if you don't get organized until today you may squeeze them out of being able to contribute simply because they were only free yesterday. A weekly timeframe rarely works when you have other people who can't do their ministry until you have *set them up* to do it.

A leader was leading a team they were intimately familiar with while also being highly skilled in that team's frontline ministry. This former team leader now oversees the entire ministry area—including teams and ministries they aren't knowledgeable about or competent in. They can no longer lead out of personal, hands-on experience, and can't coach from a place of insider knowledge. This personal experience was one of the main tools they relied on as the team leader; if they keep relying on it, they'll either struggle to lead at this new layer or they will favour the specific team that they came from.

If the goal is to find where a person can best serve, and if being great at one layer can actually *get in the way* of being great at the next, then how do you determine who should be asked to move up?

We'll discuss this important question in chapter 21, but for now the answer is: people should be moved up a layer because you think they have the capacity for that layer's ministry. You have some reason to believe they'll be able to do the work of the next layer.

"Should I ask Steph to start this new kind of ministry, with the different work and behaviours of that layer?"

"Well, do you think she'll be able to do it?"

"No."

"Then why are you even considering it?"

It's that simple.

To be able to answer this fundamental question, you need to know:

- what ministry at the next layer involves
- whether the person can already do those things, or you have some confidence that they'll be able to learn.

When I first started recruiting team leaders pre-2010, I didn't know the answers to either of those questions. The chances of my team leaders succeeding in their roles were like flipping a coin, and I was effectively gambling the success of the ministry. I probably would have had a better success rate if I just blindfolded myself and played pin the team leader on the donkey. In chapters 16-19, I'll outline which abilities and behaviours are required at each layer so you'll have the first key piece of knowledge needed to make a wise decision instead of a wild guess.

Commandment six

Don't skip layers.

No matter how tempting it may seem or how competent a person may appear, do not have them skip a leadership layer. It will cause harm later. When people skip layers, it creates gaps in their ability. Leadership development has a process, and that process needs to be honoured.

You want a leader to transition first to a team leader role before becoming the ministry area leader. This is a proper progression through each layer of the pipeline:

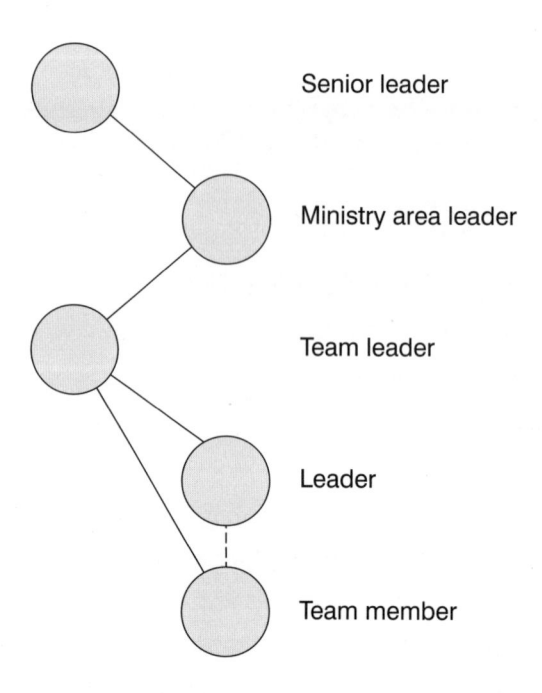

- Senior leader
- Ministry area leader
- Team leader
- Leader
- Team member

There are scenarios where you can be tempted to have a leader skip the team leader layer and jump straight to being responsible for the entire ministry area. For example, a person is a great youth leader so we send them to a Bible college for further theological training. Then they come out of Bible college and become a youth minister in charge of a whole youth ministry. But this almost always causes significant problems—and when it doesn't, it still causes serious problems.

Firstly, time allocation is harder to change than you'd first think. Shifting from primarily thinking in terms of a weekly horizon to thinking in 90-day blocks is a monumental change—so imagine trying to go from thinking weekly to thinking with a three-year horizon! And not just as a one-off, but consistently as your default frame of reference. That's a tough hill to climb without practice.

It's also the *kind* of thinking that attaches itself to those timeframes. Weekly thinking is likely to be tactical thinking whereas yearly thinking is more strategic. It's not just which view you use in your calendar, the weekly view or the monthly view—*how are you thinking* about what's in your calendar? People give up on making this transition if it's too far out of their reach.

Secondly, when you skip a layer you either skip all the things to learn at that layer, or you need to learn two layers' worth of things but you need to learn them both at the same time with no time to practise along the way. Why is this a problem, especially if some skills are tied just to one layer rather than flowing on to the next? Because the learning curves are graded. While some skills need to be left behind, many are built on, expanded and refined across that transition. You start learning something at one level and you master it at the next.

Responsibility and expectations are also graded—and the safety nets get smaller. Take recruitment: as a team leader, you begin thinking about team leader recruitment because you learn to bring someone from your team on the journey with you. But when you're the leader of a whole ministry area, you are wholly and solely responsible for recruitment, and so you'd better be competent at it. If you get the selection wrong, or you don't know how to manage that leader-to-team leader transition, you'll wake up after a year or so and find yourself in a mess.

Don't have people skip the building blocks needed for more advanced lessons to make sense and stabilize within their mental model of how life and leadership work. Don't take from them the opportunity to practise and refine skills with the safety net of someone else being ultimately responsible.

Sometimes circumstances conspire against you and literally the *only option you have* is to have someone skip a layer. If that's the case, do what you need to do. But you need to know that this is a terrible option. Don't fool yourself into thinking "It's not ideal but it'll probably be okay". It most likely won't be. You'll need to work twice as hard to backfill all the things that the person skipped. They'll have to be mentally prepared for their time to be even more gruelling than it would typically be and to fail and make mistakes more often than they usually might. You'll need to set up a rigorous and frequent coaching rhythm. But do consider whether you just haven't looked hard enough or long enough or creatively enough for another option. Are you *sure* there's no other way?

The exception to this commandment is if the person has done a good job leading at a higher layer before but is now leading at a lower layer for reasons other than competence or character. This could be because of work circumstances changing, health issues, other family issues or the like. In this case you may wish to skip them up a layer, but you'll need to be aware that the person will still take longer to adjust and you'll have to make a concerted effort to remind and refresh them on the skipped-layer skills.

Commandment seven

> The goal is not to be optimally proficient in every skill at every layer.

The leadership pipeline training modules break the leader, team leader, unit leader and area leader layers down into around 30 modules each. This is 120 modules! And even this isn't coming close to everything that a leader could learn and gain mastery in. This can seem overwhelming, especially if you tend to think in a short timeframe. If you need to reach proficiency in all that content by lunchtime tomorrow, then you might as well not even start. But people often overestimate what they can achieve in one year and grossly underestimate what can be done in three.

But you don't need to become an expert practitioner in every single facet of every single layer's competencies anyway. Each of us will be strong in some areas and weaker in others, and that's normal.[17] Being a good leader doesn't mean being the best at everything. It doesn't even mean being *good* at everything.[18] You just need to be minimally competent so that you don't cause problems—far easier to achieve than it is to be in the top percentile.

The goal is not to max out every skill at every layer. You need a working knowledge of all those skills, to be able to do all these things, but you don't need to be the best at everything. You just need to be *not inept*. Think damage control more than development. Mature your strengths while ensuring you are minimally proficient at the rest so those weaker areas don't hurt and hinder those around you.

---

17 Hamilton, 'Play to your strengths', pp. 99-104.
18 Hamilton, 'You're just the leader', pp. 175-177.

Commandment eight

> The further along the pipeline you are, the more things change.

At each layer of the leadership pipeline, the structure remains the same: abilities, time and focus. Things to learn, new ways to operate, and new priorities and feelings. Yet as you change layers in the pipeline, the *content* within this structure changes too. And the further you move through the pipeline, the more widespread and disruptive those changes will be.

For starters, your role description will become less precise. When you're at the first layer of leadership, as a member of a team, your role should be reasonably well-defined (being written down on paper isn't the determinative factor for being well-defined). At the leader layer, there will be a collection of reasonably contained tasks that are relatively quickly described and understood. If you're a Bible reader, your role is to read the Bible from the front during the Sunday service. That role, while not easy, is well-contained and defined. A leader in the youth group might: care for and build relationships with the high schoolers; take part in the program; assist with set up and pack up; and help with discipline and keeping people safe. This role is a bit broader than the Bible reading role but it's still well-defined and easy to grasp.

When you lead the entire youth ministry area, you are responsible for *overseeing* it: formulating a strategy to reach and grow high schoolers as followers of Jesus; setting culture; perhaps ministering to parents of teenagers and helping them to disciple their own kids. These are much less contained responsibilities. The senior minister will have input, but to a large extent you yourself will determine exactly what the strategy is and so what programs you'll have, start or stop. If you can't come to terms with this, you'll only ever be a reactive leader: always responding to issues and crises but never setting the agenda and determining what needs to be done.

Your role becomes less defined because it's increasingly complex. You begin to be responsible for more intangible things, like culture. You have a more extensive range of things that you oversee, which will often include items that are at odds with one another. For example, at the ministry area layer you are responsible for that ministry thriving, but you are also responsible for the overall health of the church. Sometimes what's best for the youth ministry isn't what's best for the wider church, and so the youth minister needs to be careful that he or she doesn't create, in his or her enthusiasm, a youth ministry ghetto, siloed away from the rest of the church.

Even within the youth ministry, sometimes what is best for the junior highs clashes with what is best for the senior highs. Often there isn't enough money to do every good thing and so you need to make trade-offs and hard decisions where not everybody 'wins'. This complexity is not the sole domain of the higher layers, but as you move through the pipeline it becomes the constant rhythm of life.

And you will be involved in more meetings. This results from the increasing complexity of your role and its place in the broader organization, but also from the fundamental truth of leadership: it's about loving people. Ministry is done alongside and through others, so you need to talk to them, meet with them. If you think that meetings are where good ideas go to die and where you go to not do 'real work', then as you move further along the pipeline you will struggle and be frustrated. It's part of your job to make sure the meetings aren't a waste of everyone's time.[19]

The further along the pipeline, the more structurally isolated you will be. You will have fewer and fewer peers working at the same leadership layer as you. This isn't a bad thing or a good thing—it's just *a* thing that you need to be aware of and manage, both it and your own expectations. You will need to take responsibility for building and maintaining peer relationships. The senior leader will need to look outside the church to find other peers and, depending on the size of the church, so too may the ministry area leaders.

One other aspect that changes as you experience more structural isolation is having fewer and fewer people seeing less and less of what you do, which means less opportunity for positive reinforcement and coaching in those things you're responsible for. My last boss saw almost nothing of what I did apart from preach and run staff meetings. He knew about it because I and others reported to him how things went, but he couldn't praise me or provide feedback on the vast majority of what I did.

---

19 See Hamilton, 'Meetings are where real work is done', pp. 387-394.

And that wasn't his fault, or because he did anything wrong; it was merely the result of where we were in the leadership pipeline.

Commandment nine

> The pipeline can get clogged at any layer.

The constant temptation and danger is for people to slip back into leading at the layer below their current role. This is rarely a conscious desire, but it's real nonetheless.

We heard about this in the conversation between Andrew and Matt in chapter 6. People will lead as though they are at the lower layer because they want to feel competent again, and they know they are competent at the things they used to be doing.

They can also go back down the pipeline due to fear—usually of failure or (closely related) making a fool of themselves. They may regress down the pipeline because they miss the amount of praise they received previously. Perhaps they move themselves down because they see the people they're leading not doing a good enough job and so they do it themselves.

Whatever the reason, they've now blocked the pipeline at that point. And as when any pipe gets blocked, nothing can flow through and what was moving gets sent back down. A leader dropping behaviourally down a layer creates a cascading effect, pushing the people at each layer down to the layer below. As you can imagine, the higher up the pipeline the blockage occurs, the more catastrophic it is for the entire pipeline.

Commandment ten

> Life is often not as neat as a pipeline.

The pipeline gives the impression that life and ministry can be ordered and organized, everything labelled and in its right place. For those who have been working in chaos, it manifests as an oasis. But this is a mirage. While the pipeline is definitely the way forward for you, it's no magic fountain.

In real life, the pipeline is messy because people are messy. Things won't turn out perfectly or the way 'the book' says they should. As you implement the pipeline, you need to remember it's normal to have to compromise, to be okay with 'close enough' and to make decisions that aren't ideal.

You'll have people (and most likely, you) ministering at different layers in different ministries at the same time—and sometimes different layers within the same ministry. Someone may be a team *member* in the ministry outreach to the homeless and a team *leader* on Sundays in the kids' ministry. Another person may be the small groups ministry area leader while also leading a small group under a team leader.

Also, in the vast majority of churches and ministries, team leaders won't be doing *exclusively* team-leader-only ministry. The kids' church team leader will often also be directly leading the kids—running games, giving talks, etc. This requires clarity in the mind of that leader to know when they are functioning in which role and the ability to communicate this to the rest of the team. It might sound silly, but it is very useful for the leader to explicitly say which hat they are wearing each time before they speak.

In the end, the key is to know when you're doing things un-ideally and what the consequences and costs will be, and to act to minimize those downsides.

In the IT world, some problems are tagged as PEBCAKs: Problem Exists Between Chair And Keyboard. When it comes to pipeline architecture, 99.9% of the issues are PEBCAPs—Problem Exists Between Chair And Pipeline. User error occurs when the simpleness of the basic principle—'the diagram'—deceives you into thinking that you have a complete grasp of what's going on. If you revise these ten commandments every so often, you will drastically reduce the frequency and seriousness of your PEBCAPs.

10
Common experiences in the pipeline

Luke called the meeting to order. He had been hosting these small gatherings at St Luke's for years now, inviting leaders from the surrounding churches who were implementing the leadership development framework to bring their questions and roadblocks so that everyone could learn from each other. They were helpful for those churches—and kept Luke sharp himself.

"It's great to have you all here this morning", he started. "I hope you'll all be able to stay for lunch at the end before you get back to the ministry waiting for you at your churches. Not all of you will know Chris. He's a senior minister who has just begun implementing the framework and the pipeline. Chris, it's good to have you."

"Not everyone here is a senior minister," Luke continued, "and we're all at different points in rolling out and embedding the framework. But no-one in this room is perfect and we're all facing challenges, so make sure you share your insights.

"Alright. Pose a problem, and we'll discuss how we've tackled it in our church or ministry."

Chris's roadblock: pipeline rookies

"Thanks", said Chris. "As Luke said, I'm still new to all this. Here's where I'm up to. None of my people have ever experienced anything like the leadership pipeline. They've been in hierarchies before, and some of them come from industries that have different levels—no, *layers*—of leadership. But they tell me the pipeline is different. Their schools and businesses have layers, but they don't function well and they don't bring clarity. It's like they don't know what to do with them. In fact, one of my high-level business guys said he's going to take the pipeline back to his company to see if he can implement it there, too.

"But anyway, I guess I'm after advice on how to help people who have recently moved up a layer—because for me that's literally everyone. Almost all of us are doing things we've not done before in a structure that none of us deeply understand."

"It's really hard", empathized Phil, sitting back to listen.

Chris's roadblock: read and re-read

"One thing I found when I introduced it in the youth ministry at St Phil's", Andrew said, "was that it was often two steps forward, one step back—sometimes two steps forward, two steps back—since people weren't doing what they should've been at their layer, but the layer above didn't intervene because they themselves didn't realize anything was going wrong. And that happened all the way up, including me.

"So keep reading and re-reading the layer descriptions, and keep trying to compare and contrast what is happening with what those descriptions say is *meant* to be happening. Look for the discrepancies. Then try and decide whether it's an acceptable variation within your specific culture or whether it's actually a mistake. You *will* get that call wrong from time to time. But it's an iterative process; it'll slowly get better as you notice what isn't right and make improvements."

Chris's roadblock: meet regularly

"That's really good", agreed Luke. "You need to start somewhere. I'd also suggest having regular pipeline development meetings with small groups of leaders to discuss issues and probe to find the specific misunderstandings and blind spots."

"That's a good idea", said Chris. "Should those meetings be with leaders who are all at the same layer, or leaders from the same ministry area but at different layers?"

"Either or both", replied Luke. "The point is to find a way to observe how the pipeline is functioning, even though you can't see it all in action.

There are pros to both ways: leaders from different ministries but similar layers get to share issues and solutions, whereas meeting with multiple layers of leaders from a single ministry means that entire pipeline can learn what proper performance looks like and so can better hold each other accountable."

"That makes sense", said Chris.

"Also, remember it's perfectly normal for people at a new layer to have challenges with their skills, time allocations and heart focus. There will always be a gap between how a leader should behave and how they actually behave. They need to be *developed* with their direct leader to pinpoint those gaps and work to close them."

Chris's roadblock: compare and contrast

"And what that means", said Matt, "is that their direct leader needs to actively observe to diagnose what they're doing well and what they have to work on. Those competencies are listed in the layer 'things to learn' summaries, so it's just a matter of compare and contrast.

"What I found implementing this in the kids' ministry at St Luke's", Matt continued, "is that leaders don't need to know the pipeline intimately to be able to compare their people to the list of competencies for that layer and spot the differences. It's also worth saying to your leaders that they should do their own gap-analysis and proactively seek out resources and mentoring for their self-development. Not everyone will, of course, but those who do are the ones you should keep an extra eye on since they might be good candidates for more leadership responsibilities."

"Yes," said Luke, "helping leaders begin to take responsibility for their own development is a good and healthy thing. So Chris, is that a good start for you?"

"Oh, absolutely. That's enough to keep me going for a long time."

Phil's roadblock: high-calibre beginners

"Great!" said Luke. "Okay, what's another roadblock someone is facing?"

"What do we do with people who have lots of leadership experience already?" asked Phil. "Or even someone who has loads of potential? We have a volunteer who leads at a very high level in his work, so we skipped him over the leader layer and moved him straight to the team leader layer. It seems to be going fine so far. We're thinking of doing the same thing with another lady. Is this a bad idea?"

"Yes", said Luke and Matt simultaneously. They looked at each other and Luke motioned with his hand that Matt should speak.

Phil's roadblock: faithfulness

"Don't get me wrong", Matt began. "I've skipped people over layers a couple of times when there was no other option. But if there *is* another option, you should take it every time."

"That's right", said Luke. "If you must, then you must. We've had to at St Luke's in a few ministry areas, but we hate doing it. Matt, tell them about what happened with Gayle."

"Great example", said Matt. "Gayle is a phenomenal leader high up in the corporate world, so we had her skip layers. She already possessed lots of pipeline skills—not all, but lots—and knew how to get things done from her job. But she didn't know how to get things done *at our church*. She didn't understand how the ministry functioned or what was important to us. She was good at making sure things got done, but that success was only ever temporary because she didn't know how to disciple her leaders and care for them as Christian brothers and sisters. On top of that, she didn't know how to lead volunteers, which is so different from leading staff."

"But if you knew those blind spots going in and had a plan to deal with them, could it have worked?" asked Chris.

"Well, yes, we went into it naively..." Matt paused, thinking about Chris's question. Eventually he said, "No, I still don't think it would have worked out well. She quit after six months. She was also volunteering in another organization and she realized she didn't have time to do both, so she chose to serve there. The difficulties would have been a part of that decision, but not the main part. What I learned is that the 'faithfulness buys responsibility' principle still applies even if you're a high-flying executive. We should have allowed her to move through the pipeline and display devotion to the ministry."

Phil's roadblock: count the cost

"Each case is slightly different," Luke said, taking his turn, "so you'll need to use wisdom to determine whether the cost of having someone skip a layer is more or less than the cost of not doing it. You'll only be able to make that call in the moment, and you won't ever know for sure that it's right. But, as a general rule, skipping layers is *very* costly."

"What does that cost look like?" asked Phil.

"There're usually three predictable results, and they flow out of each other. When a person skips a layer they are often, as Matt said, good at getting results in the short term. This means that underlying issues get masked because of their innate leadership ability—and it's the heart-focus shift that suffers most. This means there's little to no groundwork for sustainable results over time.

"What flows from *that* is that they functionally lead at a lower layer", Luke continued. "Because they haven't made that tough heart transition, every person down the pipeline will also lead below where they should. This is a high cost to pay. Now, the ministry might be going fine, but this will be through sheer force of will, not because everyone is working well as a team. And they'll get exhausted eventually.

"Which means, lastly, that their leaders aren't being developed properly either. Everything will incline them away from developing and coaching their team—whether it's the misaligned heart focus, their own meteoric 'rise' through the pipeline or their lack of skills in this area. One of the most important responsibilities of the leaders at higher layers is to develop the leaders below as much as they possibly can. A healthy pipeline—and so a healthy ministry and a healthy church—will have capable leaders at every layer. Skipping high-potential leaders up the layers puts all that in serious jeopardy."

Andrew's roadblock: finding people for the next layer

"Following on from that, then," said Andrew, "what should we be watching for when looking for people to move to the next layer?"

Luke thought for a moment. "First, wait until they are competent at everything required for their current layer before making any decisions about the next. They don't need to be an out-of-the-stratosphere-level expert, but they can't be incompetent either. Once they're able to do all they should at a basic level, invite them to begin learning some of what the layer above requires. You'll see how they go with those responsibilities while also giving them a taste of what that next layer is like."

"So you don't just move them straight into the role?" asked Chris.

"Not if you can help it", Luke said. "As with everything in the leadership development framework, there's what's ideal and then there's your specific circumstances. But you should always be aiming to bring people along slowly and incrementally."

Andrew's roadblock: temporary teams

"One of the things we've been doing at St Philip's", added Phil, "is invite leaders we suspect might be a good fit for higher-layer ministry to join one-off or short-term task forces focused on solving a particular problem or planning an event. This allows them to rub shoulders with higher-layer leaders and be exposed to higher-level discussions and decisions. Plus we get to observe them in that environment without everything resting on their shoulders."

"And what are you looking for in those prospective next-layer leaders?" asked Luke.

"Just basic things", Phil said. "Do they turn up? On time? Do they contribute ideas? Are they only critical of other people's ideas or do they suggest alternatives or solutions? And if there's work to be done before the next meeting, I try to ensure that some is assigned to them so I can see whether they are reliable or not and the quality of whatever they bring back."

Andrew's roadblock: moving within a layer

"When I have the forethought," said Matt, "one of the things I do is move high performers to more challenging roles within the same layer. One of the advantages of our kids' ministry is that there are several different teams in the same pipeline layer because we have multiple age groups at multiple services, plus mid-week ministries. I can move people to more difficult teams or assignments to give them a broader experience and to watch how they tackle it."

"Thanks Phil and Matt", Luke said. "Those are very helpful suggestions for how to take the opportunities that the pipeline provides to creatively develop leaders. In the end, eventually you have to pull the trigger and do it. Moving them up *will* result in multiple performance gaps, even if you've been training them for some time. So that's normal, and then you go back to those things discussed earlier about helping someone who has moved into a new pipeline layer.

Matt's roadblock: performance problems

"We have time for one more problem before I share the new thing I've been using the pipeline for—and then lunch! Who's next?"

"Well," started Matt, "my problem is less of *a* problem and more like *problems*. I currently have a few leaders, in various pipeline layers, with performance issues. They're just not leading where I think they should be."

"Do you mean that they are at the wrong layer?" clarified Luke.

"No, I think they are leading at the right layer, or at least *capable* of it. It's more that they aren't growing. I guess my question is: what do I do if people aren't getting better?"

"That's an excellent issue to raise, and I'm sure we're all dealing with it", Luke said. Everyone at the table vigorously agreed.

Matt's roadblock: look up

"When there are performance problems," started Luke, "I start with whoever is leading the person who isn't getting better. You need to check if it's a leadership issue. And even if their issue isn't completely explained by their supervising leader, you'll still want to know if they're exacerbating it. Is their leader being less than helpful?"

"And what kind of things do you look for?" Phil asked.

"There's an almost limitless number of ways that a leader can do a bad job", Luke sighed. "But some poor leadership patterns are more likely than others.

"First, check for micro-managing. Is the leader getting involved in decisions they shouldn't be? Are they dictating too much of not just *what* needs to get done but also *how* it gets done? Is there evidence of a lack of trust? Are they giving people responsibility without giving them the appropriate authority?

"Second, is that supervising leader working at the wrong layer? Have they failed to make the heart transition and so been competing with their team and pushing them down the pipeline?

"Third, have they been valuing the wrong things? For example, do they only value attendance and so only talk about *how many* people were there and ignore the quality of the ministry or the quality of the disciples being made? Or do they only value one part of the ministry and ignore anything else that isn't their pet project?

"Fourth, are they just bad at personnel selection? Do they select the wrong people to be their key leaders? Do they only ever ask their friends or those who demand it? Or the loud or the charismatic? Do they overlook character in favour of skills? If so, then their direct key leaders aren't that good because their selection was based on other criteria.

"Fifth, maybe the supervising leader is vague with role definition. How clearly have they communicated the role to their leaders? How obvious have they been about the ministry-specific and layer-specific skills they are looking for? Often what looks like resistance is just a lack of clarity.

"Sixth, are they a poor communicator? At the higher layers of leadership, communication becomes one of the main things you do. You communicate your care for your people through a huge number of things that everyone needs to understand and agree with to be able to succeed together. And communication isn't just verbal. How's their written communication? Their non-verbal communication?

"Seventh, are they giving their leaders adequate resources? If you don't provide the bricklayer with enough bricks, it doesn't matter how good they are—it'll be drafty in the winter. Do their leaders have what they need? Our ministries don't need to be elaborately and expensively resourced, but there are essentials to get the job done.

"Eighth, are they too lazy or scared to coach their team? You get what you allow. Is this leader being clear on what they expect and holding their leaders to that standard? Are they telling their leaders what they're doing well and where they need to improve? Sometimes leaders don't get better because no-one's told them they aren't or helped them improve. Pointing weaknesses out, gently and lovingly, is one of the central responsibilities of their leader. It's worth finding out whether this is happening in a healthy manner.

"Basically, poor performance in a team—or a team member—should send you straight to the leader of that team to check whether the problem starts upstream."

Luke's final thoughts

Luke looked at his watch and said, "It's almost time for lunch. Let me quickly share with you how I've been using the pipeline recently, and then we can close in prayer and go eat.

"Perhaps you've already been doing this, but it's a new idea for me: I've been using the pipeline as a self-evaluation tool. When my weaknesses get foisted upon my consciousness with great clarity and no small amount of agony, it's obvious where I need to grow. But when things are just coasting along and there's not much feedback from external sources, I find it hard to self-diagnose where I am weak. That's when the pipeline list of competencies has been helpful. Am I unconsciously competent, consciously competent or consciously incompetent? I try and be honest with myself on what areas have the most room for improvement and then I find ways to learn and improve."

"Sounds like a good idea", Phil agreed. "Do you look at your layer, the senior leader layer, and work through those?"

"Actually I start two layers below—for our church that's the unit leader layer—and compare myself to those competencies first, then the area layer above that, and *then* my own. This helps me find the skills I might have accidentally missed on the way so that I can backfill them, and the skills I used to be competent at but that have atrophied due to lack of use or misuse."

"What about skills or insights that aren't in the layer summaries?" asked Chris. "How do you keep learning things that aren't included in the pipeline?"

"I make sure I keep getting to conferences and reading books. One of the most important things you can do as a leader is to keep learning. Just like I want to keep growing in my biblical and theological understanding, so I want to keep growing in my leadership understanding. If people are going to be coming to me to drink, I want to make sure I'm a flowing stream and not a stagnant pond."

With that, Luke thanked everyone for coming and for their thoughts and input. After sharing that he had thoroughly enjoyed himself and been sharpened by their time together, he declared it lunchtime. "Is there someone who could please pray for us to close?"

11
Before you install

By now you probably have lots of thoughts about leadership development swirling around your brain: things you like; things you want to know more about; things you're confident will never work at your church; things you already know you need to change or introduce. To round off this first section, here are some overarching considerations to think through before you get started. Doing so will put you in the best position to successfully implement the leadership development framework in your ministry.

Change management and the Red Queen

Anything you do from here is a change initiative, especially if you plan on implementing the pipeline architecture. This means you'll need to be familiar with the Red Queen syndrome from *Wisdom in Leadership*.[20] You'll need to create urgency, build a coalition of allies and create a vision for change by deciding between options, finding the feeling and crafting the elevator pitch. That will get you through the first three steps of that nine-step process. I recommend that you read or re-read that chapter before you get started here.

Implementing the leadership development framework is already very difficult, but putting yourself behind the eight-ball by neglecting the process of change management will almost guarantee that this plan is sunk before you even get out of the harbour. Make sure you are familiar with the Red Queen and put a plan in place to outrun her.

---

20 Hamilton, 'Red Queen syndrome', pp. 447-472.

Start and iterate

It's critical to think iteratively. Things don't have to be perfect before you can start, nor should you install every part on day one. It would be *impossible* to implement the entire framework at once. You've got to get culture under control *while* also thinking about how ministries are grouped and how recruiting happens, *while* setting up systems and expectations for monitoring ministry and assessment, revamping training and getting coaching up to speed *and* putting in place the entire leadership pipeline across all ministries. Maybe there's some freak who could all that simultaneously, but you are not that freak. Don't even try.

But don't wait until you have every step mapped out either. If you have a rough idea where you want to end up and a few key milestones set along the way, start the journey. You'll make course corrections and solve problems once you're on the way. Most of the issues you'll face you won't even know exist until you bump into them anyway. As General George Patton once said, "A good plan violently executed now is better than a perfect plan next week."[21]

The rule of thirds

Any new initiative will have three basic responses: some love it and are on board instantly; some hate it and think it will ruin everything; some aren't sure or don't care. It's the rule of thirds.

Hate it	Not sure	Love it

Most people's instinct is to spend time and energy persuading the haters to become lovers. It makes sense—but it's the wrong thing to do. It shows

---

21 General George S Patton, Jr., 'Quotes', *General Patton*, accessed 18 November 2020. www.generalpatton.com/quotes/

people that complaining gets your attention, which means over time you'll be creating complainers. It signals to the unconvinced middle that maybe the haters are right since you're spending so much energy there. It discourages the lovers and early adopters that you're spending so much time with the haters and neglecting putting energy into the actual good idea that they agree with. In summary, you'll encourage the unsures to become haters and complainers while some of those already onboard will drop out too. Whoopsie.

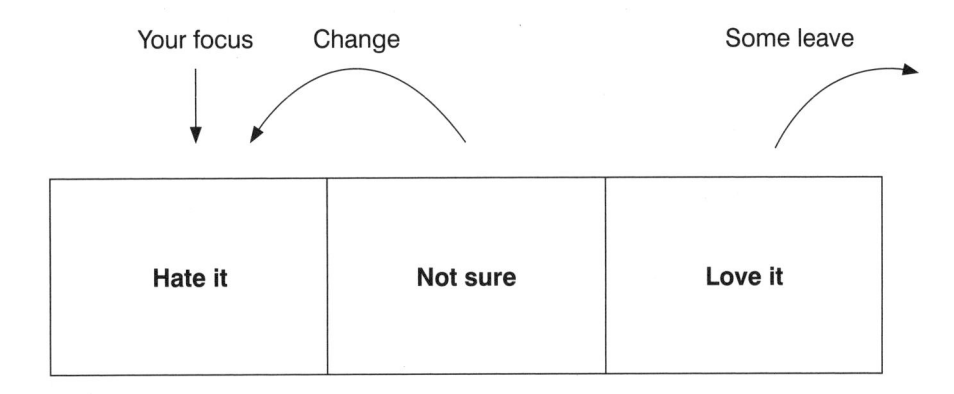

Your focus	Change		Some leave
Hate it	**Not sure**		**Love it**

Instead, spend time with the early adopters to make the idea work as beautifully as you can. Then when it takes flight the uncertain people will be compelled to join the team, and you may even convince some of the haters.

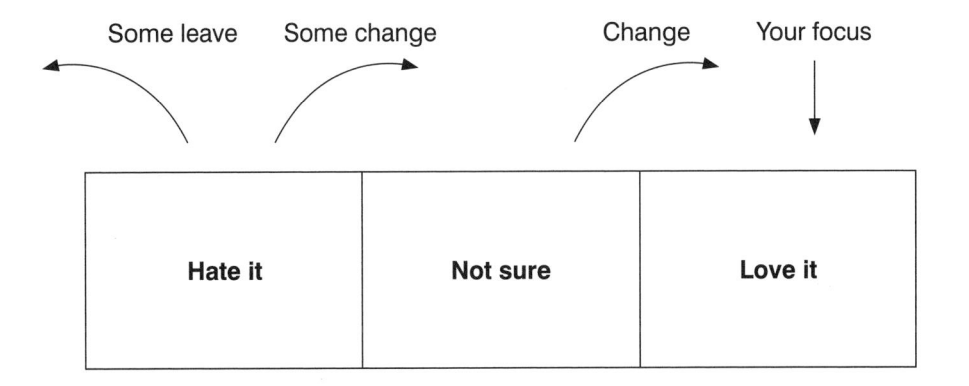

Some leave	Some change	Change	Your focus
Hate it	**Not sure**		**Love it**

11 // BEFORE YOU INSTALL

Five-year forecast

You'll need to get your expectations right. Establishing the framework in your church, including the pipeline, isn't a year-long project. Think three to five years. The pipeline is the most difficult to implement. For most people, although it will make intuitive sense almost as soon as they hear it, it's a significant change in mindset. It takes at least 12-18 months for it to become the new normal, if not longer.

Five years may sound like a long time to you, and in one sense it is, but come on—we're talking about a culture change and a leadership revolution! But this doesn't mean you won't see any fruit for five years. Far from it.

Here's roughly how those five years might break down (you might move more quickly through some steps and take longer on others).

Year one: planning and building a coalition

The temptation will be to skip through this quickly so that you can 'get on with it', but resist. You can't rush the foundation. In this phase you'll be creating urgency, building a coalition of allies, clarifying your culture, grouping your ministries and designing your pipeline architecture. It might feel as though you aren't doing anything, but that isn't true: you're waiting.[22] The more disciplined you can be now, the better and easier everything else will be.

Year two: implement in one ministry area

Choose the most straightforward ministry with the most enthusiastic leaders and implement it there—then learn everything you can so that it's smoother and easier next time. This is when you'll train your leaders in the pipeline philosophy as well as tackle the final four elements of the leadership development framework.

Year three: roll out to all ministries

Bring all the other ministries in, explain the framework and talk it through to help them understand it, then begin rolling it out across the church.

---

22 See Hamilton, 'Waiting is doing something', pp. 477-482.

Year four: begin cross-training

Gather everyone leading at the same layer, from every ministry across the church, and train them all at once. For example, get all the team leaders talking to each other about their challenges and learning from each other as you together try and create your church's 'best practice'. Do this perhaps once or twice a year.

Year five: keep improving

Things will still feel new and fragile. Most leaders will need reminding to think in a pipeline mindset and make conscious decisions. You'll need to keep improving pipelines by unearthing blockages and helping people get unstuck, as well as embed everything down into the systems and culture of your church so that it starts to become 'the way we do things around here'.

This'll take time

Finally, let me again emphasize that this will all take time. Implementation is hard, consistent work. This is not a quick fix for your leadership woes where you just add water and bake for 40 minutes at a moderate heat. It will take discipline, patience, humility and lots of effort. But the hard work is worth it for the results: more ministry, less weariness, stronger discipleship, lives changed and glory to Jesus. In the end, that's what it's about.

Pipeline planning meeting 3

This meeting will be spent tackling the remaining two clarity questions, most of it as individuals working on their own ministry area. Yes, this all *could* be done by people in their own time, but if your team is anything close to normal then it will be far more likely to happen if there's a time externally set aside with the positive peer pressure of everyone doing it too (i.e. a meeting).

Who's doing what?

The goal is to create the first drafts of the fundamental operations for the ministry areas.

Get everyone working on their individual ministry areas by breaking the ministry up under four broad headings that encapsulate the entire ministry. If any of the headings seem unrealistically broad, break it down again into two smaller areas. You can do this up to four times. The maximum workable number of fundamental operations is eight, but the fewer you can realistically have the better.[23]

Everyone creates at least two different breakups of their ministry area, coming at it from different angles or starting points. Experiment, then either pick the best set of fundamental operations or combine several to create the best.

You could have each person share their ministry's fundamental operations, with the team saying what they appreciate and perhaps any areas that may have been overlooked. (You almost always overlook something on your first pass at fundamental operations.)

What authority do we have?

Out of everything we'll do in these pipeline planning meetings, clarifying this question will, in most cases, produce the single biggest leap forward in productivity and creativity. When people have clarity and genuine authority, they suddenly get smarter.

The goal is to empower the people you oversee by producing first drafts of what will become their decision-clarity quadrants.[24]

First, have every person write a list of all the types of decisions that are or could be made in their area of responsibility. These might be decisions they themselves have made, decisions their overseen leaders made on their behalf or decisions they wish they could make. They then allocate each decision to one of the four decision-clarity quadrants, putting them where they think they should go. If any further decisions come to mind, of course, add them in.

---

23 See this question in chapter 3 for more details on fundamental operations.
24 See this question in chapter 3 for more details on decision-clarity quadrants.

That's as far as you'll go regarding authority in this meeting. From here, everyone will send a copy of their draft to their team leaders and propose a possible date and time in the next fortnight to meet and discuss these decisions.

Before that meeting, each of their team leaders will make any adjustments or additions to the draft decision-clarity quadrants and bring both versions to the meeting. The leader and team leaders will together clarify this snapshot of the decision authority—and then get on with the ministry God has given them.

Section two

12
Culture and leadership development

Leadership development framework

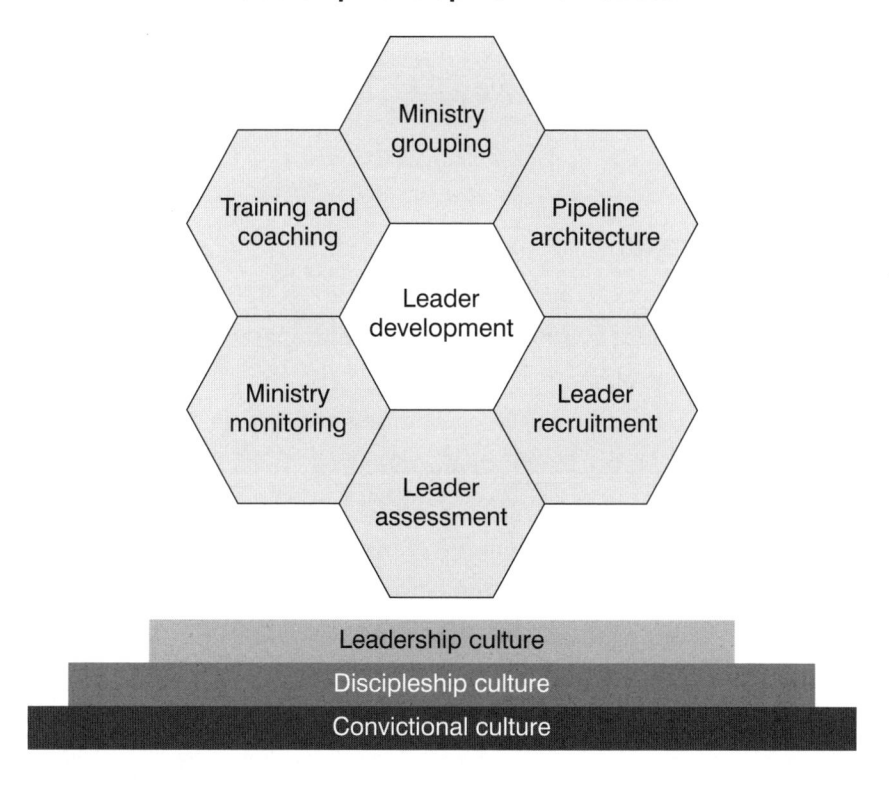

- Ministry grouping
- Training and coaching
- Pipeline architecture
- Leader development
- Ministry monitoring
- Leader recruitment
- Leader assessment

Leadership culture
Discipleship culture
Convictional culture

Culture is in more than just yoghurt: it's a feature of every group, organization, country and church. As we talked about in chapter 5, if you want high-functioning ministry leaders at your church, the culture-soil needs to have essential nutrients. Without a healthy culture it will be next to impossible to grow a vibrant leadership development system. This chapter we're going to dig into how culture impacts leadership development and what steps you can take to change the culture of your church.

Culture is the set of assumptions, attitudes, values, beliefs and behaviours that govern and guide what an organization does and how and why they do it. It's often implicit and subliminal, the silent language of your church—which is what makes it so hard for insiders and long-timers to recognize it.

In 2008, HSBC was positioning itself as "the world's local bank" and produced a series of ads highlighting the differences that local culture and values can make. One poster had a picture of three grasshoppers. Under the first one was written: "USA: pest". Under the second it said: "China: pet". And under the third it read: "Northern Thailand: appetizer".[25] Culture impacts even how we think and feel about insects. It shapes and impacts everything. Understanding the culture you're in will help you be more effective in it.

Healthy or toxic

Culture as a concept can be difficult to really grasp since it's so vague and amorphous. Would it be nice to have some examples of possible church cultures? Happy to oblige.

Your church culture may be welcoming and evangelistic, casual or formal. It could be organized or disorganized. It might be relaxed or highly strung. It may be caring. Your culture could be one of excellence or more "close enough is good enough". Your church may have a culture of holding the word of God very highly and authoritatively, and alongside that have a culture of grace and encouragement—but you could equally have alongside that fear and critique.

You may have a collaborative, enabling leadership culture, or you may have an autocratic, command-and-control leadership culture. Your leadership culture might really be more of a helper culture, or a "the staff are paid to do it" culture. Perhaps your culture honours and respects leaders, or maybe they're criticized and distrusted. Your leadership culture might be one of guilt or constant politicking.

---

25 HSBC, 'Never underestimate the importance of local knowledge', accessed 25 November 2020. www.adeevee.com/2002/03/hsbc-banking-shoes-crickets-football-print/

Ask the new people at your church. They'll know. Some parts of your culture feel very foreign to them and they bump into it the most often, which will probably make them the best at articulating what it is or feels like.

Even just from this quick list of cultural possibilities, you can see how much culture impacts both *what* gets done and *how* it gets done. Culture can be healthy, productive and fruitful, or toxic, counter-productive and stifling.

What might a toxic culture look like?

- highly critical
- disorganized
- low morale
- low trust
- lack of clarity
- high confusion
- high levels of politics
- low productivity
- high leader turnover

Churches like this exist. Imagine for a moment being in one. How much would the church be getting done compared with what it *could* be? How effective do you think this church would be, even if full of faithful people? They're probably not raising up many leaders. Any leaders they do accidentally raise up likely aren't leading to the extent they could be—and leave once the culture becomes something they are conscious of and when their frustration outweighs the guilt of going. If you worked at this church, you probably wouldn't be that excited to turn up each day. You'd spend time politicking or managing hurts and frustrations rather than building disciples and growing the kingdom. You'd feel disempowered, disillusioned, discouraged and demotivated.

And a healthy culture?

- highly appreciative
- organized
- high morale
- high trust

- maximum clarity
- minimal confusion
- minimal politics
- high productivity
- low leader turnover

Wouldn't you prefer to be a part of *this* church and on *this* team? If everything else were equal, you'd get much more done and raise up more leaders who grow into what God has for them. This church would be raising problems to the surface, finding solutions, and then moving forward in implementing them so much more than the first church. The power of culture impacts everything you do and is always in play.

Maybe you're now thinking, "Sure, but I don't know much about how to impact, influence and change those things. I'll stick with my processes—church services, teaching, financial systems, strategy, small groups, ministry grouping and pastoral care—because that seems more straightforward." But remember what we discussed in chapter 5: all this culture stuff impacts everything in that processes list of things happening at your church (which are either smart or dumb) by either *multiplying* them or *undermining* them.

Culture cradles and shapes—and in one sense necessarily limits—everything done in your ministry.

Culture is a punishable offense

Another way to come at this question of what culture is and how it plays out is to notice that, since a key ingredient of culture is values, culture is an expression of what you're willing to be *punished for*. It's the things that, if people don't like it or other groups don't reward you for it, you'll still do anyway.

Perhaps you have a culture of being a safe place for anyone at all who wants to come and hear the word of God. Then one Sunday someone whose sins are outside the acceptable, domesticated sins that your church is comfortable with turns up. Their sins are of the taboo variety. People in your church complain that they don't want *that kind of person* in *their* service. Either you tell that new person that they have to leave, or people from your church will leave instead. What will you do?

If one of your deeply held values as a church is being an open and welcoming place for sinners to hear the word of God, then your culture isn't threatened by the 'sinner' but actually by the *complainers*. And so, to uphold your values and express your culture, you are willing to be punished by having some people leave.

Patrick Lencioni, a leadership author and consultant, tells a great story about what it looks like to be punished for the values and culture of your organization. In the US, there's an airline with a deep commitment to a culture of humour. They won't hire anyone who doesn't have a sense of humour, and this culture is embedded so deeply that they make jokes during the pre-flight safety announcements. After one of these funny safety announcements:

> A frequent flyer wrote to the company's CEO complaining that a flight attendant was making jokes during the pre-flight safety check. She was upset that the employee was trying to be funny while he was talking about something as serious and important as safety.
>
> Now, most CEOs would respond to that complaint by thanking the customer for her time and her loyalty to the airline and assuring her that safety was, indeed, important to the organization. They would then promise to look into the matter to make sure that the flight attendant adjusts his behaviour to avoid offending any other passengers who could be uncomfortable with the jokes. That would be reasonable enough, I suppose, unless your core values have to do with humour.
>
> Well, the CEO of this company took a different approach. Rather than apologizing to the customer and asking the flight attendant to moderate his behaviour, he wrote her a short note with three words on it: "We'll miss you."[26]

---

26 Patrick Lencioni, *The Advantage*, Jossey-Bass, San Francisco, 2012, pp. 94-95.

Now, before we all begin gleefully replying to all criticisms with "We'll miss you", it's important to note that the takeaway isn't to respond to any and all complaints in a swift, monosyllabic manner. The point is that the complaint was attacking one of their core values, a profoundly integral part of their culture. This is why there was no leeway, surrender or apology. It was who they were and it wasn't negotiable. The punishment of a lost customer was preferable to undermining their culture.

Quantifying culture

By now you must be asking yourself, "What's my church's culture?" As you hunt for the answer, you'll be sorting what you find into four categories of values.

The first category is *core* values. These are the traits and characteristics that you hold in highest esteem. These might be things like the lordship of Jesus, the Bible as the central authority, honesty, being Spirit-led and so on. These are the foundation of who you are and how you operate. They're often the things that a church *must* be; they're permission-to-play values.

The second category of identifiable values is *aspirational* values. These are what you hope and pray that one day your church will be like—but that day is not today. They are still worth pinpointing—they belong in the same bucket as your vision or mission in that they're part of the preferred future that you are working towards—but they need to be visibly designated as such. With work, they will move from ambition to reality and become core values.

The third category is *accidental* values. These are cultural norms that exist in your church or ministry, but they aren't there on purpose and you don't particularly want them. Maybe your culture is tense but you'd love to be relaxed; slow but you'd prefer nimble; timid when you'd love to be bold. Good work: you've diagnosed toxic elements of your culture. These are areas that you'll want to work on to transition your culture to a healthier place.

Lastly, there are cultural values that uniquely set your church or ministry apart: *differentiating* values. These aren't things that a church *must* be: they're things that a church *could* be. Maybe you're fun, casual and innovative. Now, when I say that these are values that make your church unique, I don't mean absolutely, qualitatively unique, where there's no other church like this in the whole world. These traits or values are *relatively* unique to your church.

If you want to include some permission-to-play values here in your differentiator values, you need to make sure that you embody them in a unique measure. If you include 'welcoming', you must go above and beyond with your welcoming so that your church stands out from the pack in this area. This is the same for all those fundamental values, like hospitable and generous. Otherwise, people will interpret all this values and culture stuff as empty rhetoric and you'll be planting the seeds of cynicism and apathy—which will begin the process of adding *those* traits to your list of accidental values.

The categories we've just talked about function as a framework to help organize and group the thoughts and impressions that you and your team come up with while brainstorming what your culture is. You'll ask questions like: Is this *really* who we are or is this who we would like to become? Is this who we are and we're embarrassed by that and want to be different?

But you might be wondering, "Where does flavour fit?" We talked about flavour back in chapter 3, and it's a mixture of the most important and distinctive pieces from both your core and differentiator values. It's those core beliefs and values that define and drive you—what you're willing to die for—and then also the less-important-but-still-distinctive characteristic features that differentiate you from other similar groups. Flavour describes the personality of your church or ministry—an articulation of what makes your church *your church*—and it's best to limit this description to fewer than ten words or ideas so that it's more easily understood.

Two traps

It's worth keeping your eyes peeled for these two related but opposite mistakes that people make while uncovering their culture.

First, people sometimes limit themselves to only their *core* values and so describe their cultural values so basically and broadly that the description is useless. "Trusting in Jesus; kind; speaking the truth": these are so generic that, sure, they cover everything, but they don't have any real power to describe *this* church. These kinds of core values are the compulsory, permission-to-play values. Bible-believing, Jesus-centred, honest, kind, prayerful... all of these are describing what it means to be a church, any church, rather than *this specific* church. They're the first category of values you need to uncover in your culture, but they're not the whole shebang.

Of course, if you didn't have these values functioning at some level in your church, there'd be a problem. If trusting in Jesus isn't a core value of your church then are you really even a church? It's just that when it comes to describing *your* church as opposed to the one down the road, they are too generic.[27] When unveiled on your church's new stationery, the crowd will go mild and eventually grow apathetic.

The second, opposite, error people make is expressing only what they *wish* their culture was like instead of what it's *actually* like. Using only the aspirational values is just as useless as the first mistake.

I spoke with one leader who had just completed a significant examination of his church culture's core values, and on the list was 'evangelistic passion'. I was excited to hear this because evangelistic passion was something we wanted and were working on at our church. I asked him to tell me more about how this played out at his church and what this passion for the outsider looked like. He said, "Oh no, our people aren't evangelistic at all, but that's where I want us to get to."

It's a mistake to think about cultural core values in this way because writing the words down or putting them up on a cross-stitch in the foyer doesn't inspire anyone to actually live up to them. It just makes people cynical. They see "casual and relaxed" embroidered on the official church quilt—and then look at the staff and key leaders stressed out of their brains and triple-checking the agenda for the meeting in six-weeks' time to address whether service leaders are allowed to say "Good morning everyone" or whether they must stick with "Greetings in the Lord". It's evident to the discerning mind that "casual and relaxed" is disconnected from actual reality—and the 'official core values' are 100% irrelevant and therefore completely ignorable.

---

[27] Having said this, I could imagine a context where a church believing the Bible wasn't as common as it is in my context and where, therefore, 'Bible-believing' could be an actual differentiator. Then it would be important to include it in your cultural descriptors.

How do I change the culture?

My answer: with much pain and difficulty. Culture change is no easy thing. It takes a long time and an almost obsessive discipline. It may be one of the most challenging leadership endeavours there is. Sorry to be the bearer of bad news.

If your culture isn't what you think it should be, what do you need to do to go about changing it? A common way that people try is to write down what they think the culture needs to be and then send that out in an email, mention it in a meeting, maybe preach a sermon on it—and then that's that. Nothing changes.

The good news is that changing a culture is the same species as any other change initiative—it's just an incredibly sophisticated specimen. Just do all the same things you'd do with any change initiative.[28]

Changing culture will, most likely, take you years. It won't be easy-peasy lemon squeezy; it'll be difficult-difficult lemon-difficult. The next few pages outline the overarching steps needed to alter a culture, but they aren't the only things you need to consider. There are other factors that you need to take into account, like how long it takes for the majority of your church to turn over. Depending on the dynamics, changing the culture may take five to ten years, perhaps even longer. Think long-term.

The first step

Before you change anything, you need to know as exactly as possible what the current culture is.[29] As we've discussed, this will be difficult to discern if you've been in the culture for a while, but it's even harder if you are the long-term senior leader of the church or ministry. If you've been there for, ballpark, more than five years, the current culture is a reflection of you—both strengths and weaknesses—and a reflection of what you have allowed. It can be hard for you as the senior leader to face up to those things.

So you'll need to be absolutely real. Real with yourself and real with the people you lead. There's no point overlooking the faults and downsides of

---

28 This whole process is outlined in chapter 73 of *Wisdom in Leadership*, 'Red Queen Syndrome'. There's a lot there to help you get your mind around what it takes to complete a change initiative successfully.

29 See Hamilton, 'Where is here?', pp. 349-354.

your culture, even if it's a painful process. To some degree this will be about unearthing your personal flaws and your leadership inadequacies. You must confront the brutal facts. This will take humility, discipline and self-control.

This will also mean that you'll need to give your team permission to speak these facts without fear of consequences. This is much harder than it sounds, especially if part of your culture has been to make people too afraid of you to raise issues. It's extra-hard to extract the truth from a team that has been trained to minimize or supress bad news. When a leader refuses to listen, eventually they end up surrounded by people who don't say anything worth listening to. In this case, you may need to go outside your direct team to find people who will tell you the truth.

People stumble at this first hurdle of articulating reality not because they aren't smart enough, but because they sabotage the effort (often unintentionally). They ignore negative feedback, minimize the perspectives that contradict their own mental model of what the culture is, or are blocked by their own pride from hearing the truth. But if a leader refuses to see the problems, then the problems aren't the problem.[30]

Towards the aspirational

Let's assume you've dug down deep and mustered all the humble leadership you could and were able to articulate the current culture of your church or ministry with pinpoint accuracy, warts and all. You had an honest conversation with yourself about how many of those warts came from your own heart. You've identified your core, aspirational, accidental and differentiating values. Now what? Next, you need to be able to articulate the kind of culture that you want—your *aspirational culture*.

Here the real work begins, and it begins with you. Again, this will take effort: a lot of effort, though the basic formula for culture change can be articulated in a deceptively simple way:

---

[30] If you suspect that any of this could be relevant to you, then read or re-read chapter 77 of *Wisdom in Leadership*, 'Bad news is good news', before you try and articulate what's defective in your culture.

Culture change = Clarity + Modelling + Consistency +
Normalizing + Communication + Time

We've already discussed clarity, but the next step is *not* to draft an email to everyone. You first need to *be* the culture you want to see. You'll need to *model* it. As I said in *Wisdom in Leadership*:

> Whatever the culture you want to create, it always starts with you, the leader. If it's not who you are, or who you want to be, it will never be the culture."[31]

And once you've begun acting differently, you need to make sure you *keep* acting differently. It can't just be a short-term change; it needs to be *consistent*.

All throughout this process you'll be chatting with people about the culture you're labouring to create. But what you *won't* be doing is any broad communication. No getting up during announcements and waxing poetic about "our new culture". Too early. At this stage, your communication will be low-key and ad hoc.

As others begin to pick up the new culture and behave in line with it—becoming allies alongside you—you'll need to point it out, celebrate it and help people see and feel that this new culture is the *new normal*. Change may be small to begin with, so you'll need to be concentrating to spot it. This celebration will be especially important if the new culture is also producing better 'results'; highlight them and the behaviour that helped produce them. Show that this new way of behaving isn't just something that *you* are doing, but instead that *we* are doing. This all takes intentionality, so keep it on your radar.

Once you've *become* the new culture and that behaviour has started to form new norms, values and assumptions in others around you, *now* it's time to teach and speak publicly about it. The new culture needs to be explicitly *communicated*. Write that email, call that meeting, draft that newsletter—whatever medium you think is best.

All the while the old culture will be fighting back, but this battle will probably be fiercest once the new has been explicitly communicated and

---

31 See Hamilton, p. 366.

the line in the sand has been drawn. Persevere. It's highly unlikely that this pushback will be deliberate; it's usually old habits dying hard. But even if it is conscious, you still need to graciously keep up the pressure and refuse to go back to the old ways.

The final ingredient of culture change is time. You'll need to be active and attentive, encouraging the new culture and discouraging the old, for a long while to come. The new culture will grow and spread so long as you continue to behave in line with it and so long as you celebrate it when you see it, as well as pointing out when the old culture rears its head. The new culture will need both promotion and protection, and so will require your attention.

To change a culture, prepare and plan for a long journey.

13
Navigating the culture

When a highly competent person moves to a new church—either as a staff member or a congregant—often their competence doesn't travel with them. They were very effective at the last church, but their effectiveness takes a long time to approach those same heights. Things just don't seem to work out. We'll talk about this more in chapter 22 on hiring staff, but for now we'll focus on one of the contributing factors to this lagging competence: navigating the new culture.

No matter how successful you were at your previous church, the culture of your current one needs to be reckoned with. Past achievements don't allow you to transcend the influence of the current culture. It's simply not how it works. How well you assess, understand and navigate the new culture will either amplify your effectiveness or derail it altogether. Don't ignore this reality.

New kids on the block

Imagine a church hired two new staff members at the same time: David and Tina. The onboarding process was the same for both. Michael, another staff member, met with each of them and talked through their role descriptions, clarified their responsibilities, provided the historical background to their ministries, discussed people around the church they needed to be aware of, gave them key objectives for their first year, pointed out the low-hanging fruit and some easy and visible wins, and outlined the church culture and the idiosyncratic way things worked there.

Tina and David each responded very differently to these meetings. Tina was interested in learning how the church operated and its 'unwritten rules', what her key objectives were, and how she could get some easy and early wins to build trust and display competence.

David's response to the suggested easy wins—what they would be for him and why they were so necessary—was to protest: "I'm not here to impress anyone". Michael tried to explain that it wasn't about being impressive but about building momentum on multiple fronts. David made it clear that he had been successful at his previous church and he was planning on getting straight on with the job.

Tina and David's first few months were about them getting to know people, setting up their houses and offices, finding their groove. David had far more experience than Tina and was insightful when it came to things like putting together Sunday services and thinking through the dynamics at play in each congregation.

Then, like clockwork, after six months both new hires were hit by the shockwave of culture clash as they started trying to actually do something. The things they assumed would happen or exist didn't. They dropped balls they didn't know they were juggling.

Both leaders wanted to get straight on to getting things done, but only one of them thought it was important to learn how to get things done *at this church*. By the end of their second year, Tina had got an astronomical amount done and was able to make substantial changes to her ministry area. Things looked and felt very different. David, on the other hand, had accomplished very little. His ministry area looked, for all intents and purposes, exactly the same as when he had arrived.

David grew increasingly frustrated and disillusioned. Worst of all, he blamed everyone but himself. He could never reconcile how Tina had been able to get so much done while he had been unable to make progress.

Two individuals, working at the same church, on the same team, for the same boss, at the same time, with vastly different outcomes in their ministry and ability to get things done. The key factors weren't experience, love for people, preaching skill or pure leadership expertise. Culture and character made all the difference.

Navigating the culture

Every time you join a new church or organization, you enter a new culture. Sometimes joining a new ministry within the same church can still involve joining a unique culture. So what should you be looking for as you enter? How can you diagnose some of the principal features of the culture so that you can avoid culture shock, get up to speed faster, feel like you belong more quickly and start to contribute more effectively?

Here are six of the critical factors that will help you to navigate the culture. While they do overlap somewhat, it is helpful to distinguish them.

Relationships

The first thing to notice is how relationships are formed and built, particularly in the teams that you'll be a part of. Do people have one another over at each other's houses? Do they go out for coffee or to the movies? Do they hang out before or after meetings? Are emails and messages places to joke and banter, or strictly for work only?

Especially when it comes to a staff team, are people friends or co-workers? Do they hang out together when it's not an official work event, or are their friends in different circles? The latter doesn't mean that they don't like each other or that the team isn't loving and cohesive. It just means that the relational expectations aren't that you'll all be best friends sharing family holidays and ice cream cones.

Collaboration

The second thing to keep an eye on is how collaborative the team is. Do people work together or do you go off to do your own job and check in every now and then? Do people bring problems to a meeting for advice or help? Are decision-making lines clear and never violated or are decisions made by the team?

How do people talk about the ministry: 'I' or 'we'? A friend of mine worked at a church once that was a reasonably collaborative team, and when it came to communicating ministry from the front they always used 'we'. They decided as a staff team to make a particular Sunday in November a baptism Sunday and assigned the organization to a new-ish staff member.

When he announced the upcoming baptism Sunday, he consistently used 'I' as he spoke and never once 'we'. He said that 'he' thought that baptisms were really important and wanted to put more emphasis on them. Whether or not this is what he meant, it *sounded* to the rest of the staff like he was contrasting himself with them. Every staff member except for one noticed and discussed it over the next few weeks, as did a significant number of church members. In itself, it wasn't a big deal, but it had violated the culture and people could tell.

Communication

How does the team communicate with each other? Do they send emails, or is everything done face-to-face? If they are big email senders, what exactly gets sent in those emails? Do they *discuss* via email? Do they *decide* via email? Do you need to initiate and foster relationships face-to-face before people will get on board with your plan, or can you just flick an email to another team member and that person will rocket a reply back agreeing to do what you ask regardless of how relationally close you are? Are they big social media users or not?

When it comes to meetings—staff or ministry team meetings—are they formal with agendas and points of order, or are they free-wheeling with items raised as they go? Are they rigidly directed or loosely organized; prepared or spontaneous?

In those meetings, do proposals and problems need to be written and sent in advance before the issue can be presented, or can they be shared and discussed without notice? Are anecdotes from Mrs Jones at morning tea about how "lots of people aren't happy" enough to sway decisions or is more data needed? Are issues debated or rubber-stamped?

When communicating, do people respond well to strong recommendations and staunchly held viewpoints, or do they respond better to a softer interaction of possibilities and perhapses? If both are used, what order is the most effective? Do people put forward hard, opinion-as-fact positions and then retreat from them, or begin with loose, lightly-held thoughts that then become firmer throughout the discussion?

If the church or ministry has multiple pipeline layers, how do people communicate with higher layers? Can you bring issues straight to your boss's boss? Does this need to be pre-approved? Do you need to flag it with your team leader before you meet up with *their* leader, or can you just talk to anyone about anything?

Authority

You need to know who has authority. It might not be obvious. In some churches, the highest authority is clearly the senior leader, but in others it's no-one on the paid staff. It may be one of the lay elders or wardens, or someone who doesn't hold any official office but who has been influential and respected for many years. The most powerful person in the parish might be the receptionist or administrator, or the wife of an elder or the senior leader.

You also need to know how is authority given. Ask, "What is the basis for authority?" Is it positional or based on competence? Does authority come from quality preaching or from exhibiting care in relationships? How much of a role does tenure play?

If authority is mainly derived from a person's position, and so is given, then when you have a position you can just get on with doing things and making changes. But this is rarely how authority *really* works. You'll need to determine how it's built in *this* church: who is respected, whose opinions matter the most, who is loved and esteemed, and what they did to engender that authority.

Decision-making

How do decisions get made? Or probably more importantly: *where* do decisions get made? Churches and ministries have their official decision-making processes—staff meetings, parish councils, congregational meetings and the like—but these may or may not be where the *actual* decisions are made.

If decisions do get made in meetings, is it all decisions or only some? If it's only some, what kind of decisions are made in meetings and which ones are made through another process? Do meeting-made decisions always get implemented as decided, or do tweaks (or large-scale changes) happen through another, informal decision-making mechanism? Are decisions made in a ministry area meeting only provisional until they have been vetted by the senior leader?

A friend of mine worked at a church where decisions that the staff made during a staff meeting were never final. The decision was then discussed with the senior minister's wife and sometimes completely changed. Decisions had to be taken into 'the house' and then re-emerge before you could rely on them. And the house always won.

When things are decided in meetings, are they decided in the same meeting where the issue is first raised, or does it take multiple conversations? Is it necessary to find other churches who have made the same decision to show a precedent, or is there comfort in being innovative? Is there a pattern as to which decisions get changed later and which are implemented unscathed? Does it make a difference if it's written down compared to verbally agreed upon?

Does the team lean towards action, in which case decisions are made quickly and analysis is low, or is the team slow to make a decision, requiring a high degree of analysis—perhaps over-analysis—and consensus?

How change happens

How does change occur in this culture, and how welcoming is it of *outsiders* bringing change? In most churches and organizations, the answer would be "not very". This overlaps with authority and decision-making. Even when people *say* that they want you to come in and make changes, they often won't fully mean that. Misreading the culture at this point can be at best frustrating and at worst catastrophic. The most significant factor is not *what they said* or *what you were told*, but rather how people *actually behave*.

Is it possible in this culture for change to happen from just one person imposing their will without any other support? This is so unlikely that it's best to assume not. You'll need to work out the unwritten rules for how change happens in this specific culture, how power works, and how many and what kind of allies you'll need.[32]

Which relational connections do you need to accumulate? Whose

---

32 See Hamilton, pp. 453-459, for an overview of how power and allies work in a church context.

approval do you need? Is there someone whose *disapproval* you need to avoid? What factors do people care about and which don't worry them? How sensitive is the leadership to criticism towards newly minted changes? Do they immediately undo the changes, or do they try and help the critic understand the rationale? Under what circumstances do they do one and not the other? Can you be highly assertive and fast-paced in your pursuit of change, or do you need to engage in dialogue, build a coalition and only then propose a change? Is the leadership *more* receptive to change during a crisis or *less*?

It is highly unlikely that anyone will directly answer these questions for you; you'll need to observe and figure it out.

Follow me and watch for the changes

These six areas aren't the only ways that the new culture you enter may be different from the one you left; they're just the *first* six for you to notice! There will be multiple other cultural distinctives where you will just be slightly out of step, and these misalignments will cause you grief. The difficulty is that these other cultural frictions could be almost anything, which makes them hard to predict, plan and write advice for. This reality means that the best way forward is to learn how to, if not diagnose with precision, at least highlight areas of potential disjunction that will require further attention and concentration.

Be especially sensitive to how people are behaving that is *different* from your personal norm yet is *similar* to each other. That is, you want to look out for behaviour that is distinct from yours but is common to the group. This behaviour, over time, will settle into patterns that you can begin to recognize. You'll then start to predict and anticipate how people will react in the next situation and learn some behaviours that you may need to adopt to navigate this culture.

Two enabling qualities

We've talked about paying attention to the current culture—assessing, understanding and navigating it—but your ability to navigate a culture successfully will be determined by two personal qualities. Before you look to and assess the culture, you'll need to examine and evaluate yourself for *humility* and *self-awareness*.

It's not intelligence that hinders people from navigating culture successfully; it's pride. It's the foolish notion that my manner and preferences of how to get things done are unassailably right and any other method, purely by not being mine, is inferior or even wrong. And even if my way really is better, pride leads me to think that everyone else should—and will—simply fall in line because I expect them to. But life doesn't work that way, and most of the time we need to learn how to succeed in a culture before we can begin changing it.

Humility also requires self-awareness to be able to differentiate what I do from what *should* and *must* be done. It's also needed so that I'm able to realize what I assume and value compared to others around me. This contrasting of cultures is not easy and requires wisdom and discernment.

When I first started at a church I was working at, I struggled in both of these areas. I was arrogant and believed unquestioningly in the power and insight of my opinions. I was sure I knew "how to get things done" and that there should be no distinction between that and "how to get things done *here at this church*". I found it hard to work out why things weren't working interpersonally with the other staff like I assumed they should. My ideas and plans kept getting blocked, and there was constant and escalating friction. I was regularly frustrated.

It dawned on me one afternoon in my office that I could keep on whining about the weather—which would only result in rain-soaked clothes and the shivers—or I could start accepting how things were and start using an umbrella. So I directed my energy towards solving the puzzle of why I wasn't able to make things work and what the invisible rules were that governed how this church operated. In other words, I started thinking about navigating the culture. It was then that everything changed.

David and Tina weren't much different in their love for people or preaching prowess. But Tina was humble and self-aware. She was conscious of the new culture she was entering and willing to take on board the wisdom of others on how to navigate it successfully. As is often the case in matters of leadership, when it comes to successfully navigating the culture, character is king.

Pipeline planning meeting 4

Now that you've wrestled those key clarity questions to the ground, or are on the way to doing so, it's time to tighten up your church's leadership development. The place to start is with culture. You had a preliminary go at articulating your culture when you worked on your church's flavour; now you're going to try and capture all its uniqueness. This will take discipline and humility since not all the news will be good.

The objective for this meeting is to create one list of core values and another list of accidental and differentiating values that describe your specific church or ministry.

Getting set

For this meeting you may need a wider group than you've had before. This depends on who has been a part of things up until now, what size your church is and how leadership and decision-making functions there. In order to articulate culture, you need to hear from whoever will be able to help you. This might include laypeople who have been at the church forever or perhaps some switched-on newcomers. You might stick with the pipeline planning group you've got and then meet up with another group as well. Decide what you think is best.

Describing culture is challenging because it's the 'vibe'. There's a reasonably high level of abstraction at play. People always know more than they are able to articulate—which means sometimes the best they can do is to scratch around the edge of something without being able to put their finger on it, unable to explain *why* this is how they think it is. Be prepared for that and don't punish people for being vague.

Some people may also need time to build up the courage to say something negative about the culture of the church they love, or they may wait to see how you handle it when someone *else* says something negative before they share their insight. Be very careful and deliberate to thank everyone for their input and resist the impulse to defend yourself or challenge someone's opinion. In fact, when you feel this impulse, it's a good reminder that you should be even more open and gracious than you might typically be and invite people to expand on the negative insight from their point of view. The goal of this exercise is not to make yourself feel good. The goal is to get to the truth of your current culture no matter how disappointing that truth might be.

This process may require multiple meetings because it can take people a while to get into the mind frame of diagnosing culture. Plus, most people have their best and more insightful ideas on the way home from a meeting!

Meeting plan

Make sure everyone understands what you mean by 'culture'. It's a nebulous concept at the best of times.

You want to harvest people's insights, and there are lots of ways to get people to start sharing their thoughts. Because there may be a lot of bad news being given, it might be helpful to use a method that allows a level of anonymity and a way for people to separate themselves from their opinions. It can also be hard for some people to move their minds past core values like 'Jesus-focused' or 'Bible-believing'. This method navigates around both these issues.

1. Hand out five small pieces of paper to each person.
2. Have everyone write five different words or phrases they think describe the values at the core of your church's culture, one per paper. They need to write clearly so someone else will be able to read them. (This allows people to give those central, more obvious and perhaps generic core values their due and get them out of their systems.)
3. Put all the pieces of paper into a big messy pile.
4. Each person reaches in and takes five pieces of paper at random (it's okay if they end up with some of their own).
5. Everyone takes turns reading out the five papers they chose. The words should be recorded where everyone can see them.
6. Invite everyone to make observations about these words. Are there ideas that come up again and again? Are there ideas that were only mentioned once? Are there different words that actually point in the same direction?

Now move on to describing the accidental and differentiating cultures of your church. These might be good or bad, noble or embarrassing. Follow the same process as before: five pieces of paper, your clearest handwriting, pick random pieces of paper and read their words or phrases, discussion.

It is often harder for people to articulate the vibe. Here is a list that people can draw from if they get stuck:

- lethargic
- paid people do the ministry
- backwards-looking
- fearful
- generous
- hospitable
- passionate
- dispassionate
- fun
- serious
- sombre
- welcoming
- insular
- excelling
- last-minute
- critical
- political
- transparent
- high conflict (in a good way)
- high conflict (in a bad way)
- gossipy
- selfish
- us versus them
- united
- people take responsibility
- empowered
- inviting
- intentional
- proactive
- passive
- controlling
- suspicious
- poor communication
- candid
- trusting
- encouraging
- creative
- innovative
- collaborative
- future-focused
- risk-taking
- formal
- casual
- slow
- nimble
- timid
- tense
- relaxed
- organized
- disorganized

Now that everyone's words are written up, depending on how disappointing those words are you may all feel quite drained. It may be best to stop at this point. Make sure everyone has a copy of all the words and phrases. If possible, put them up where everyone can see them regularly. After two or three weeks of the words bubbling on the backburners of their minds, gather the team again and continue the conversation. What new thoughts or connections have people had? Out of all the words that were chosen, which five would people choose now? Should any new ones be added?

At this point, bring back the flavour you drafted a while back. Compare and contrast. Do your earlier thoughts resonate with where you are now or are they miles apart? Has any new insight cropped up? Do changes or additions need to be made?

You may also want to begin articulating any aspirational cultures you'd like to cultivate. Again, this can be hard to think of from scratch, so you might need to sneak up on the idea. One way to do this is to name some people from your church who embody what you wish everyone was like. Write up five to ten names and then try to tease out what it is about these people that got them up on the board. What are the similarities between them? Once you've compiled that list of aspirational cultural principles, delete the names and focus on those values. This will get you started towards working out what kind of culture you would like to have at your church.

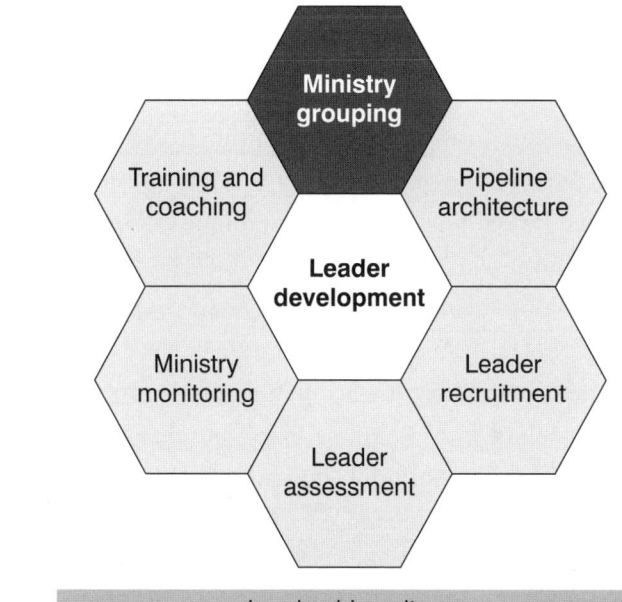

14
Ministry grouping

Leadership development framework

[Diagram: Hexagonal framework with "Leader development" at center, surrounded by "Ministry grouping" (top, highlighted), "Training and coaching", "Pipeline architecture", "Ministry monitoring", "Leader recruitment", and "Leader assessment". Below sit three tiered layers: "Leadership culture", "Discipleship culture", "Convictional culture".]

The first piece of the leadership development framework is ministry grouping. This is where you conceptualize and visualize the shape and structure of the ministry, basically creating an organizational chart. You're clarifying which ministry relates to what and who is responsible for whom.

This step in the process of developing leaders is often under-appreciated and overlooked... because it sounds potentially useless and definitely boring. I'm constantly trying to avoid tasks described by those adjectives, so if ministry grouping really was one of them then I'd be the first to petition that it walks the plank. But while it might *seem* useless, it's definitely not (I will concede that it may be a little bit boring). Ministry grouping is like cutting your toenails. It's not exciting, but if you don't do it then sooner or later your shoes won't fit. Ministry grouping is a prime source of clarity, one of the most valuable assets that a leader trades in.

Ministry grouping exists because you are a finite human with finite resources. You don't have the ability or the time to do everything. So, fellow mortal, here are six reasons it's worth learning the skill of ministry grouping.

One: allows growth

There may have been a time when you ran your church or ministry area all by yourself. You thought everything up, set everything up, cleaned everything up and locked the door. And you might still be having a great time doing this! But if you keep doing it all, you'll have to choose: make sure the ministry stays small and don't tell any new people about Jesus, or allow new people in to hear about Jesus but over time do a worse and worse job as it becomes too big. *Or* bring more people onto the team and share the responsibility with others so that more and more people can hear about Jesus. Those are your only options.

As soon as you invite just one more person to join you in the ministry (whether staff or volunteer), you have created an organization and so you now have a chart. It looks like this:

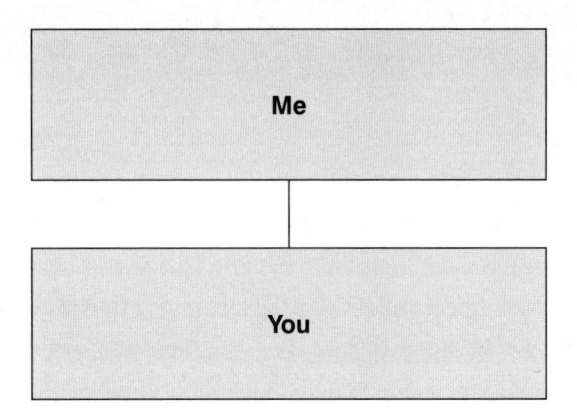

```
┌─────────────────────┐
│                     │
│        Me           │
│                     │
└──────────┬──────────┘
           │
┌──────────┴──────────┐
│                     │
│        You          │
│                     │
└─────────────────────┘
```

I'm not saying it's a complicated chart. But there it is: that's what the organization looks like. Whether you like it or not, you now have two layers of leadership.

Ministries get more complicated as they grow—and the more complication you have to deal with, the more you'll need others to help shoulder the load. This means breaking up the work into smaller pieces and giving it to others to accomplish. Through thoughtful distribution, over time you'll get more done (and done faster) than when you were alone.

Two: provides clarity

The second purpose of ministry grouping is to bring clarity so people can minister to their full potential. They need to be able to answer: Who am I responsible to? Who is my boss? Who do I report to? Who do I ask for help?

These questions all ask, "Who's in charge?" If people aren't sure, they won't know who to ask when they get stuck and they won't know who to listen to when multiple people are telling them what they should be doing. This lack of clarity will mean they start playing it safe by only doing what they know every one of those people who *might* be in charge, or who *speak* like they are, would approve of. It will also mean—to avoid 'doing the wrong thing'—that they surrender their initiative and only do what someone explicitly tells them to. People will behave and perform at a far lower level than they could have if they'd known who was in charge.

A clear ministry grouping also shows people where they fit in the big picture. They see how their individual piece contributes to the whole ministry's outcomes and are more motivated to slot it in.

Three: achieves care

Ministry grouping is necessary for achieving a span of care. Good, clear authority provides care. People need to know who to go to when they need help. They need to know who cares about them, not just in terms of the ministry work being done, but as individuals, disciples.

Most of us know that we should care for the people on our teams and make sure they *feel* cared for, even if we're not sure how to do it. But some of us have too many people under us to be able to adequately care for any of them like they need and should expect. If your chart looks like this...

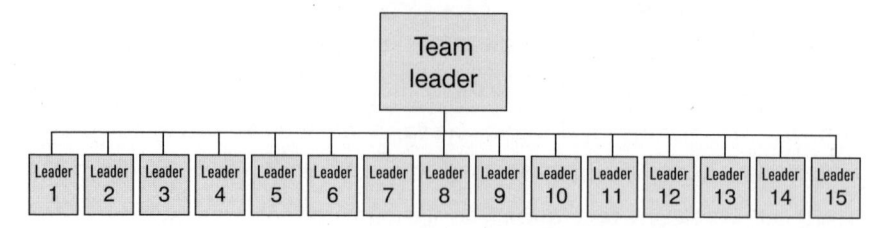

```
                            Team
                           leader
   ┌──┬──┬──┬──┬──┬──┬──┬──┼──┬──┬──┬──┬──┬──┐
 L1 L2 L3 L4 L5 L6 L7 L8 L9 L10 L11 L12 L13 L14 L15
```

...then it is highly unlikely that you're able to care for all of those people properly. If this diagram describes you *and* you are also involved in preaching, funerals and other pastoral care, not to mention administration and correspondence, then having this number of people directly reporting to you is a mistake. Rare is the person with an effective span of care for 15 people in a ministry context—especially if they're volunteers—and odds are you are not that person. These 15 people won't have the access to you as their team leader that they require. Their biggest problem is going to be *you*—getting answers from you, getting time with you, having you remember what's going on in their ministry and in their world. Ministry grouping helps us group these 15 leaders into smaller teams with much more realistic spans of care:

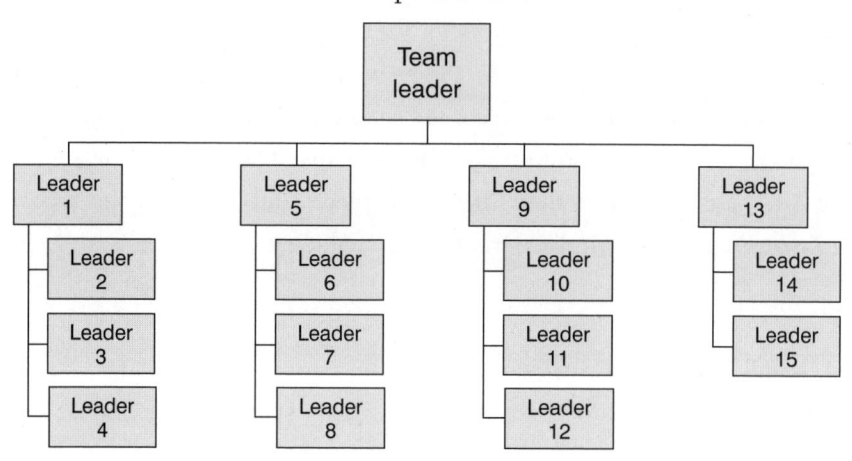

```
                         Team
                        leader
      ┌──────────┬──────────┬──────────┐
   Leader     Leader     Leader     Leader
     1          5          9          13
     │          │          │          │
   Leader     Leader     Leader     Leader
     2          6          10         14
     │          │          │          │
   Leader     Leader     Leader     Leader
     3          7          11         15
     │          │          │
   Leader     Leader     Leader
     4          8          12
```

The team leader now has four people reporting to them that they care for, with everyone else reporting to one of *those* leaders. That original team leader is now leading a team made up of *team leaders*, with other leaders organized beneath each of them.

Four: makes the invisible visible

As we covered in chapter 4, ministry grouping shows you the shape of the organization—whether the whole church or an individual ministry area. This shape reveals how people are clustered within ministries, along with who is responsible for what and whom. Often the process of seeing the organization visibly symbolized helps you to spot something that has been in front of you the whole time but that you weren't able to perceive.

You might remember this picture:

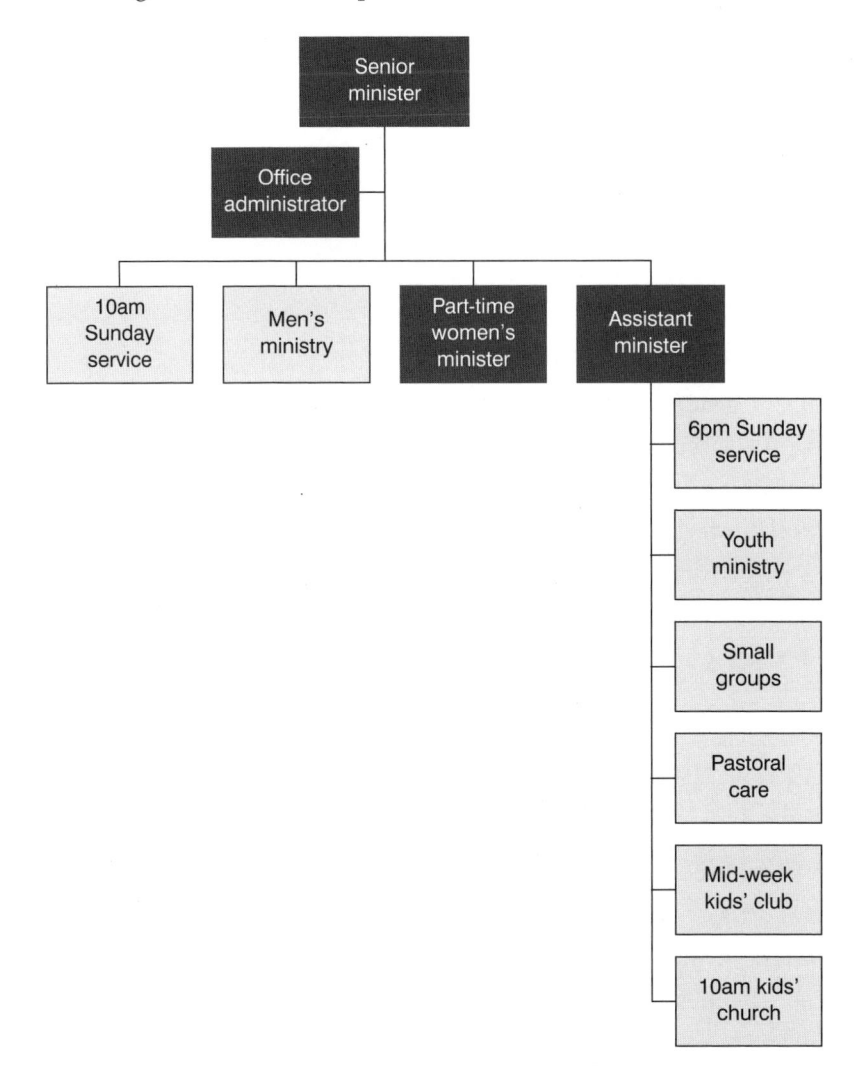

```
                    Senior
                    minister
                      |
           Office ----+
           administrator
                      |
        +------+------+------+------+
        |      |      |             |
      10am   Men's  Part-time    Assistant
      Sunday ministry women's    minister
      service         minister      |
                                    +-- 6pm Sunday service
                                    +-- Youth ministry
                                    +-- Small groups
                                    +-- Pastoral care
                                    +-- Mid-week kids' club
                                    +-- 10am kids' church
```

This senior minister probably didn't organize things like this for the assistant minister because he hates him—although technically that's a possibility. This probably happened because the senior minister wasn't concentrating; he has no idea of the pressure this assistant is under. Meanwhile, the assistant minister might feel over-burdened but not have the insight or the language to articulate why. The senior minister likely only sees how badly all these ministries are functioning and interprets that with a story about how incompetent the assistant minister is.

Imagine the flood of clarity that will wash over both when this diagram is put on the table. Suddenly the assistant is shown that their poor performance isn't a competence issue but a structural issue. If anything, it is the senior minister causing problems for everyone else.

Ministry grouping makes that which is usually invisible visible, raising the intelligence and insight of everyone involved.

Five: gives you a blueprint

Ministry grouping is essential because a diagram of the organization becomes a blueprint for the new roles that will need to be created. Changing and rethinking things on the page creates a plan for the future to work towards.

Imagine that this organizational chart is yours:

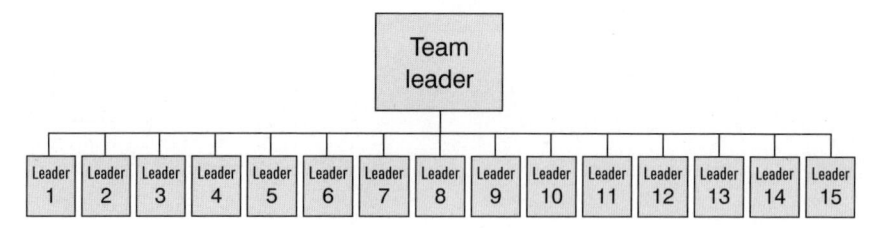

```
                           Team
                          leader
  ┌────┬────┬────┬────┬────┬────┬────┼────┬────┬────┬────┬────┬────┬────┐
Leader Leader Leader Leader Leader Leader Leader Leader Leader Leader Leader Leader Leader Leader Leader
  1    2    3    4    5    6    7    8    9    10   11   12   13   14   15
```

You've realized that you can't effectively lead this number of people, but you aren't sure who, out of these leaders, could step up to lead a team, or how long it would take to develop a handful of people to take on those responsibilities. Six months? A year?

If you're going to be leading these 15 people anyway for the time being, what if you charted how you want to reorganize things *before* you can? Something like this:

```
                        ┌──────┐
                        │  Me  │
                        └──────┘
      ┌─────────┬──────────┴──────────┬─────────┐
   ┌──────┐  ┌──────┐            ┌──────┐   ┌──────┐
   │  Me  │  │  Me  │            │  Me  │   │  Me  │
   └──────┘  └──────┘            └──────┘   └──────┘
```

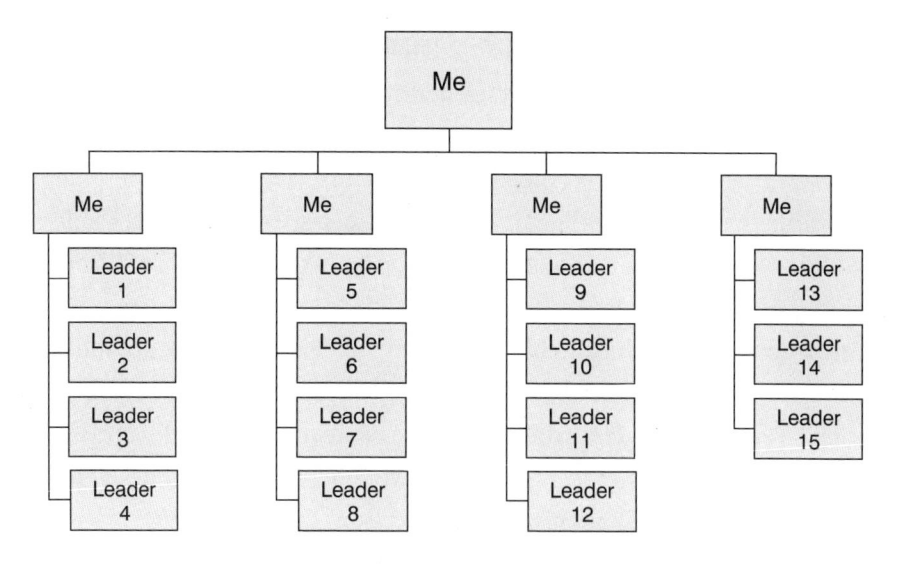

(Org chart: "Me" at top with four "Me" sub-nodes, each leading Leaders 1–4, 5–8, 9–12, and 13–15 respectively.)

You create four teams where *you* are the team leader of each. You create the team leader roles and you begin modelling how you'd like these teams run. Your people start to get an idea of what this is meant to look like and how it's supposed to work. Now you can start training people to take over existing roles, rather than having them learn a role they've never seen before.

So over time you fill those team leader roles until your organization looks like this:

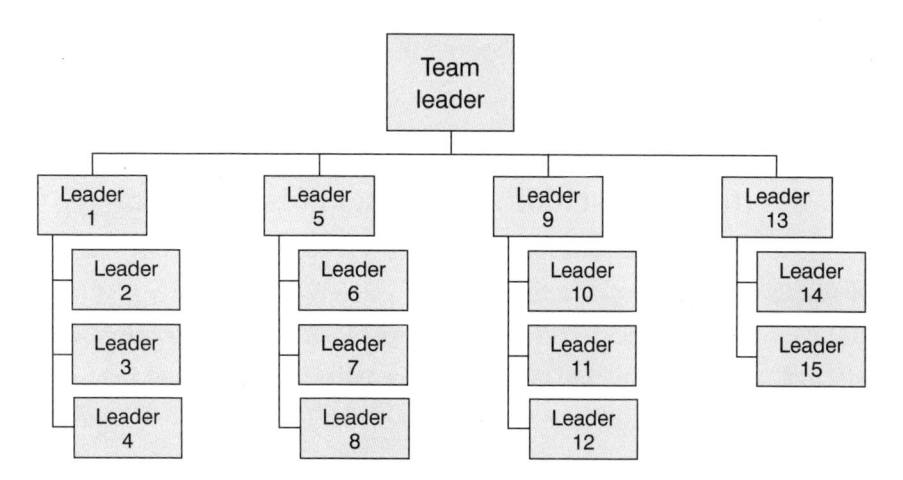

(Org chart: "Team leader" at top, with Leader 1, Leader 5, Leader 9, and Leader 13 reporting to it; each of those leads Leaders 2–4, 6–8, 10–12, and 14–15 respectively.)

Ministry grouping gives you and your team something concrete, if still only symbolic, to mentally grab hold of and tangibly work to create.

14 // MINISTRY GROUPING | 181

Six: enables the leadership pipeline

Ministry grouping is definitely under-utilized, but at least people are aware that organizational charts are a thing. More unknown, and therefore even less utilized, is pipeline architecture. This tool is the potent missing puzzle piece when it comes to raising up high-level leaders within your church or ministry. But to design and build a robust leadership pipeline, you need to have first grouped your ministry areas. We'll break down the pipeline architecture layers in chapters 16-19, but the key thing now is that the leadership pipeline clarifies the specific work that each layer and its leaders do as opposed to what any other leadership layer is doing. It's both a mindset and a framework for intentionally developing leaders that is clear about what's required from them.

For pipeline architecture to be effective, it needs to be overlaid on top of your ministry grouping structure: your organizational chart. If you skip the ministry grouping step, you'll likely have a structure that is more complex than necessary that will collapse under its own weight. There'll be too many layers, too many roles and too many people with not enough ministry work to warrant the amount of complexity. People will leave to join other ministries and teams where they are more needed, and the pipeline will crumble.

You can't install a leadership pipeline without a ministry grouping structure to apply it to. It's a necessary foundation for everything else in the leadership development framework.

How is the pipeline different from ministry grouping?

In the next chapter we'll unpack how to go about ministry grouping, but before we do it's important to distinguish clearly how ministry grouping differs from pipeline architecture. At first glance the two seem very similar, and because the pipeline so heavily relies on the grouping structure it can be hard to tease them apart in the beginning.

So what is the difference between an organizational chart and a pipeline?

The organizational charts you'll create are attempts to represent visually the authority relationships in your church. Who reports to whom? Who is responsible for whom? Who is a peer of whom?

Here's the representative chart that we looked at earlier:

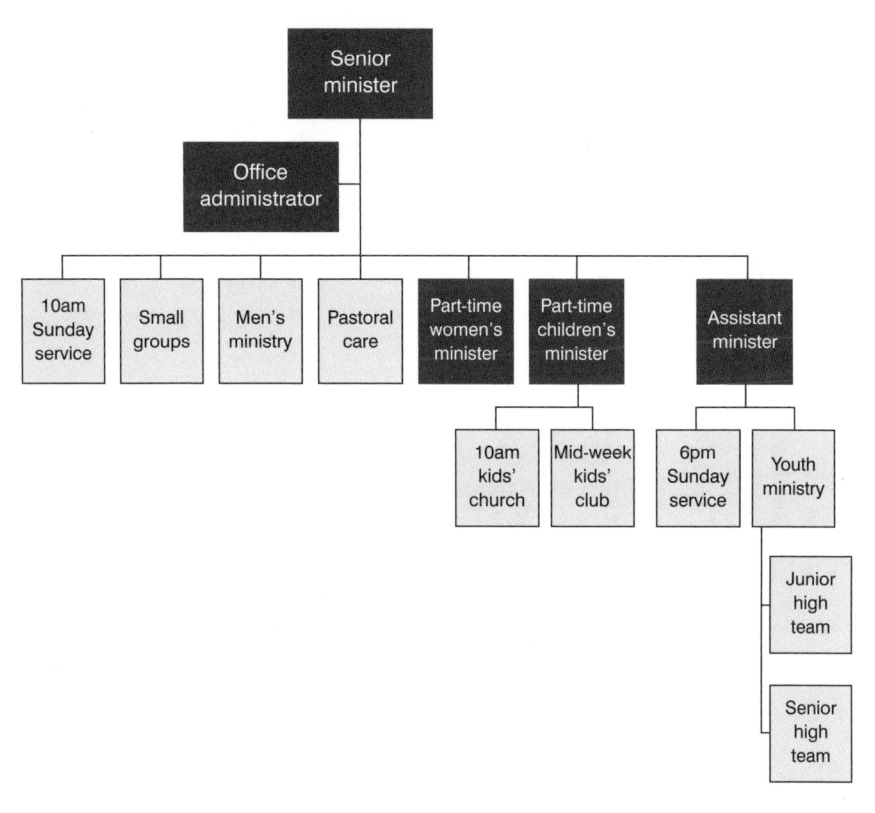

```
                        Senior
                        minister
                           │
        Office ────────────┤
     administrator         │
   ┌──────┬──────┬─────────┼─────────┬──────────┬──────────┐
  10am   Small  Men's   Pastoral  Part-time  Part-time   Assistant
 Sunday  groups ministry  care    women's    children's   minister
 service                          minister   minister
                                                 │           │
                                          ┌──────┴──────┐ ┌──┴──────┐
                                         10am    Mid-week 6pm      Youth
                                         kids'   kids'    Sunday   ministry
                                         church  club     service
                                                                    │
                                                              ┌─────┤
                                                             Junior
                                                              high
                                                              team
                                                              │
                                                             Senior
                                                              high
                                                              team
```

This diagram shows the official authority relationships in this church. I say "official authority" because while there is formal, structural authority and leadership in a church—which is captured in the organizational chart—there is also unofficial authority that exists off the grid. This authority is just as real, but it's harder to recognize and quantify, despite often being stronger and more influential than any official position or title. This kind of unofficial leadership influence can be built in many different ways, such as longevity, recognized competence, relational loyalty, investing love and care during crises, controlling the church's calendar and being the hub of the church's gossip grapevine. This authority plays a massive role in the dynamics of a congregation. So, as we think about ministry grouping and diagramming authority relationships, just remember it's only showing the official authority and positional influence.

So what can we say about this church from its ministry grouping?

1. The office administrator, women's minister, children's minister and assistant minister all report to the senior minister.
2. The senior minister directly leads the 10am Sunday service, small groups, men's ministry and pastoral care.
3. The office administrator is in a slightly different relationship to the senior minister than the various ministers are.
4. The women's minister, children's minister and assistant minister are peers on the same authority level.
5. The children's minister directly leads the 10am kids' church team and the kids' club team.
6. The assistant minister directly leads the 6pm Sunday service team and oversees the youth ministry (though he doesn't directly lead the junior and senior high teams since he has two team leaders doing that).
7. The women's minister is the only leader in the women's ministry at this point. There isn't yet a team of leaders.

With an organizational chart, you're thinking about who's above you and who's below you, with the *primary* consideration being whose team you are on. One way to think about it is to number the layers from the top down, like this:

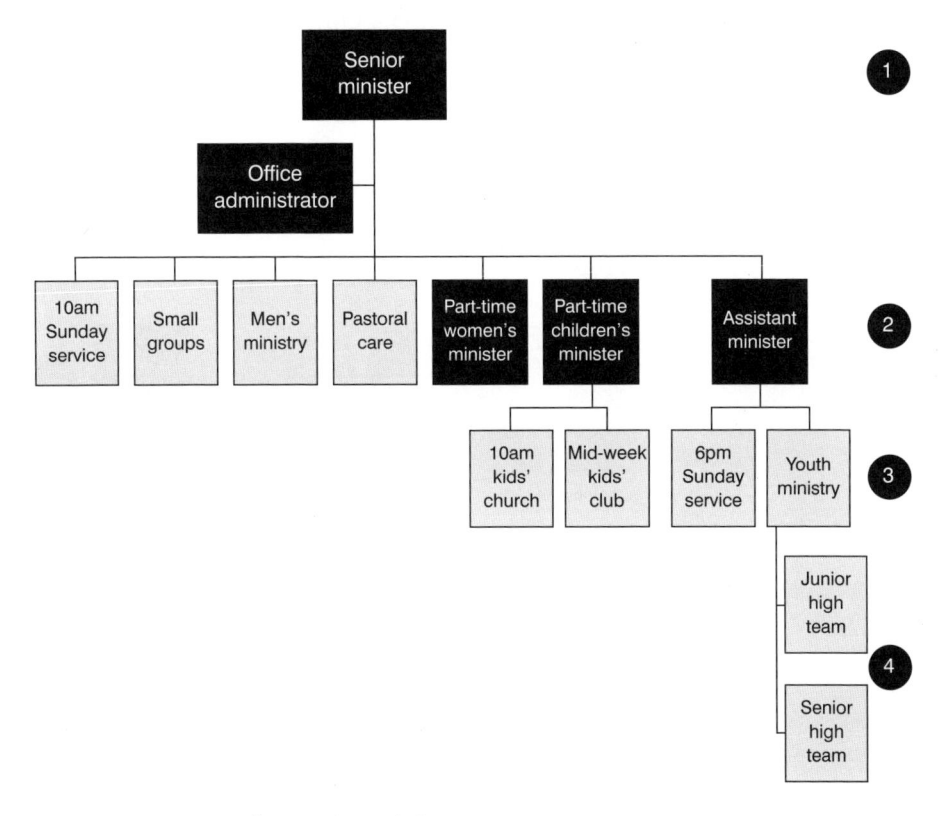

```
                    ┌──────────────┐
                    │   Senior     │                    ①
                    │   minister   │
                    └──────┬───────┘
          ┌────────────────┤
    ┌─────┴──────┐         │
    │   Office   │         │
    │administrator│        │
    └────────────┘         │
  ┌──────┬──────┬──────┬───┴──┬──────┬──────────┐
┌─┴──┐ ┌─┴──┐ ┌─┴──┐ ┌─┴──┐ ┌─┴──┐ ┌─┴──┐ ┌────┴────┐
│10am│ │Small│ │Men's│ │Past│ │P-T │ │P-T │ │Assistant│  ②
│Sun │ │grps │ │min  │ │care│ │wmn │ │chld│ │minister │
└────┘ └────┘ └────┘ └────┘ └─┬──┘ └─┬──┘ └────┬────┘
                           ┌──┴──┬──┴──┐  ┌────┴────┐
                         │10am │Mid-wk│ │6pm Sun│Youth│  ③
                         │kids │kids  │ │service│min  │
                         └─────┴──────┘ └───────┴──┬──┘
                                              ┌────┴────┐
                                              │Junior hi│
                                              │  team   │
                                              └────┬────┘      ④
                                              ┌────┴────┐
                                              │Senior hi│
                                              │  team   │
                                              └─────────┘
```

- *Layer one* is the senior minister.
- *Layer two* is the women's minister, children's minister and assistant minister (along with the office administrator, acknowledging that this person fills a specialist role at this layer).
- *Layer three* is the kids' church team, the kids' club team, the 6pm Sunday service team, and the junior and senior high team leaders.
- *Layer four* is the junior high team and the senior high team.

But when it comes to pipeline architecture, we're not thinking primarily about authority relationships or which team we are on. Instead, our attention is on the type of work being done at each layer. In that sense, we're focusing more on counting from the bottom up. To do this properly, we need to look at each branch of this organizational chart individually, rather than assuming that everyone in layer two is doing the same work simply because they're peers on the same layer on the same team.

Let's look at each ministry one at a time. We'll start with the assistant minister. Counting from the bottom up, that ministry looks like this:

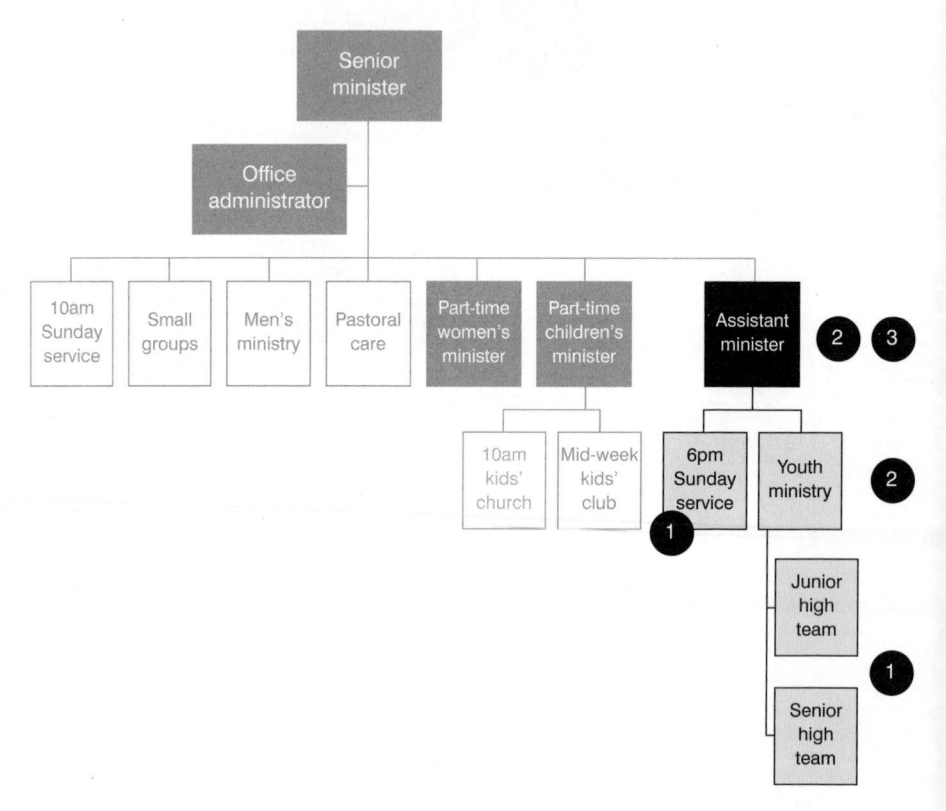

- *Layer one* is the junior and senior high teams. They are frontline leaders directly leading those high schoolers. Layer one is also the team who runs the 6pm Sunday service.
- *Layer two* is the team leaders who lead the junior and senior high teams, and also the assistant minister as he leads the 6pm Sunday service team.
- *Layer three* is the assistant minister as he leads the two youth ministry team leaders.

186 | WISDOM IN LEADERSHIP DEVELOPMENT

In terms of the leadership pipeline, the assistant minister is a part of *two different* pipelines: one with two layers and the other with three. In the youth ministry he leads a *team* of team leaders; at the 6pm Sunday service *he* is the team leader.

Now let's examine the children's ministry:

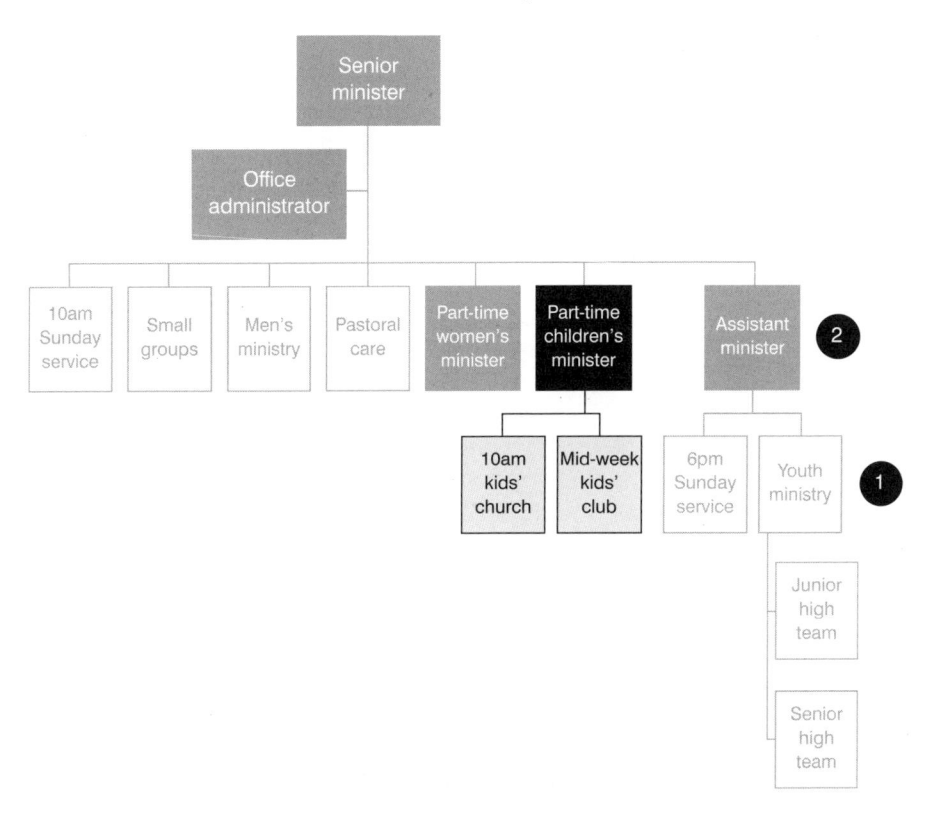

[Organizational chart showing Senior minister at top, with Office administrator beneath. Reporting to Senior minister: 10am Sunday service, Small groups, Men's ministry, Pastoral care, Part-time women's minister, Part-time children's minister, Assistant minister (labeled 2). Under Part-time children's minister: 10am kids' church, Mid-week kids' club. Under Assistant minister: 6pm Sunday service, Youth ministry (labeled 1). Under Youth ministry: Junior high team, Senior high team.]

This ministry area is much simpler.

- *Layer one* is the kids' church and kids' club leaders on the frontlines leading the kids.
- *Layer two* is the children's minister, who oversees the entire children's ministry area while also functioning as the team leader for both of the layer one teams. They are a ministry area leader who also is doing team leader work.

Lastly, the women's ministry:

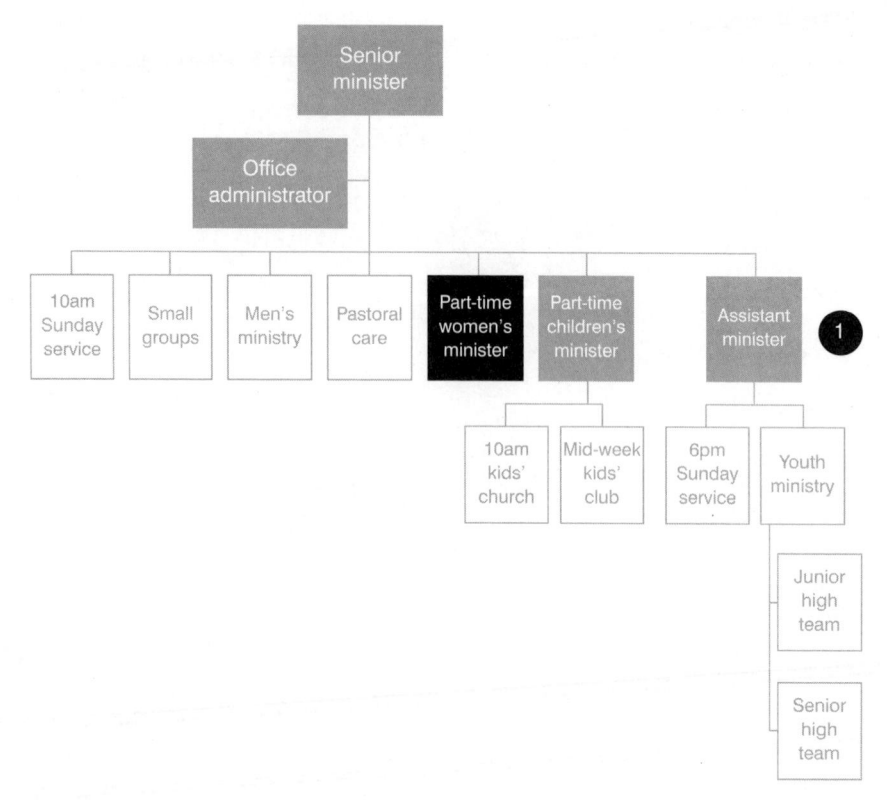

```
                        Senior
                       minister
                          |
                   Office
                administrator
    ┌──────┬──────┬──────┼──────┬──────┬──────┐
  10am   Small  Men's  Pastoral Part-time Part-time Assistant  ①
  Sunday groups ministry care   women's  children's minister
  service                       minister minister
                                   ┌──────┤      ┌──────┐
                                 10am  Mid-week 6pm    Youth
                                 kids'  kids'  Sunday ministry
                                church  club   service
                                                        │
                                                     Junior
                                                      high
                                                      team
                                                        │
                                                     Senior
                                                      high
                                                      team
```

This ministry area only has one layer and the part-time women's minister is the only leader. She leads the entire ministry area while also doing the frontline leader ministry.

The ministry and leadership exercised by each of these staff members are very different from each other. So, while the ministry grouping organizational chart helps us see that the three ministers are all on the same team (the senior minister's), the leadership pipeline shows us that, while each oversees an entire ministry area, they are doing distinct work with differing levels of complexity. The assistant minister needs to be exercising a much higher degree of leadership than the other two.

Ministry grouping visualizes the official authority relationships and who is on whose team. Pipeline architecture reveals the work being done by each layer and how the ministry is being distributed through the organizational chart.

15
How to group ministries

Leadership development framework

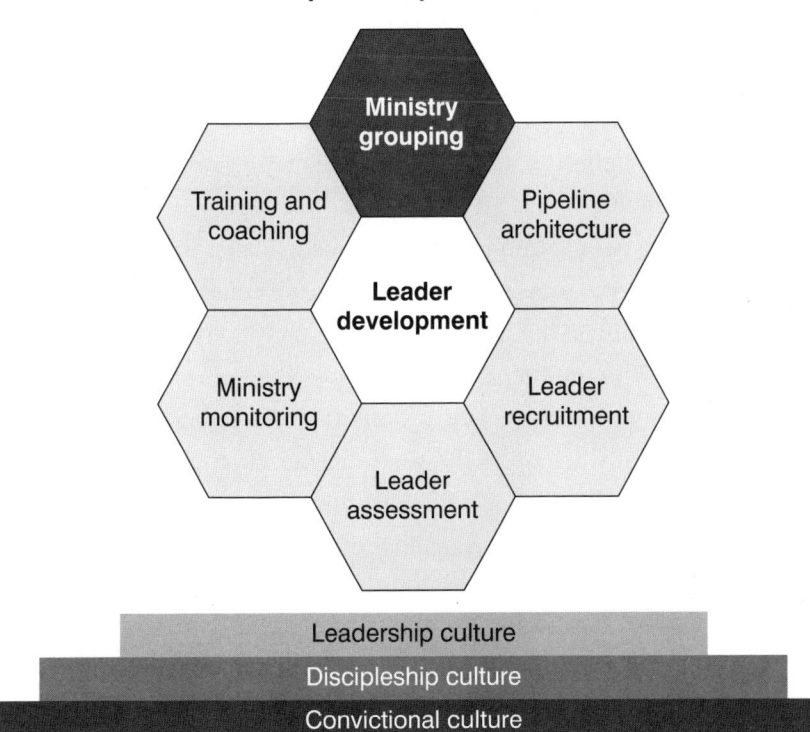

(Diagram: hexagons around central "Leader development" — Ministry grouping, Training and coaching, Pipeline architecture, Ministry monitoring, Leader recruitment, Leader assessment. Below: Leadership culture / Discipleship culture / Convictional culture.)

Ministry grouping is necessary and valuable, so it's a skill that needs to be learned. There isn't only one correct method, but there *are* two groups of principles to come to grips with. In this chapter we'll talk through the main ministry grouping lenses that you need to be familiar with that will get you 80% of the way towards a valuable ministry grouping.

Most important

The first and most crucial step is to clarify why your church or ministry exists and what it's aiming to do. What is the mission, the purpose? You group ministries to help you achieve this mission, so be clear on what it is. The second step is to clarify the basic plan of what you're going to do to get that done. This is your strategy: your plan for achieving what you want to achieve.

In other words, ministry grouping will be difficult to figure out if you skipped all those questions back in chapter 3. Don't make things harder for yourself; turn back there now.

Having clarified all that, *then* you can ask, "What basic grouping of ministry do we believe will best enable us to achieve the mission at this moment in time?"

There are two options at this point: visually representing *what actually exists* or reorganizing it to *what you think it should be*.

If you go with door number one, you need to keep asking, "Who oversees that? Who oversees them?" Think carefully through what happens in your church, starting at the frontlines, and ask, "Who runs it and who do they report to? Who are they responsible to and who would they ask for help?" Go as far up the chain as you want. If you're trying to diagram the whole church then work up to the senior leader; if it's a single ministry, stop at the person who leads the ministry area.

If, however, you're trying to *reorganize* the structure of the church then, first of all, you need to know all the ministries and events that happen so that you can make sure they're included in the structure. Write a list so you don't leave anything out.

Once you have a pretty good idea of everything that needs to be reorganized, whether it's an entire church or a whole ministry area, decide which of the following lenses will be best in helping you organize your ministries so that you achieve what you want to achieve.

Ministry grouping lenses

There are three broad lenses that you can use to guide your ministry grouping project: geographic, demographic and functional. These are the general categories you'll think in before you make more fine-grain modifications.

Geographic

Perhaps you are a church that has multiple physical locations and you want each one to have its own identity and autonomy. In this case, you might organize geographically as the primary lens, which means decentralization.

Let's say you are a church with a north campus and a south campus. If you organize with a hard-line geographic lens, then the north would organize its ministries independent of the south. North would have a kids' ministry and south would have a separate kids' ministry. They would plan, operate and make decisions separately because geography is the primary lens.

You can also include under this principle different times that ministries run: the 8am Sunday service, the 10:30am Sunday service, the 6pm Sunday service. While all three services meet at the same geographical location, the people are turning up at different times. It's temporal geography. In this case, you want each service to have the autonomy to run as a unique congregation with its own minister preaching its own sermon series while choosing its own songs and running its own welcoming and pastoral care systems.

The advantages of this lens are:

a) it gives those 'on the ground' maximum input in shaping ministry to reach those they are ministering to

b) it forces the local team to take responsibility

c) it enables more innovation, which can then be copied by the other locations if they wish

d) it's clear who is in charge at any one location.

The disadvantages are:

a) it's resource-heavy since there's a lot of duplication across sites

b) there's a higher probability of things being done sub-optimally somewhere

c) when people from one service visit another, it feels like they are visiting a completely different church.

Demographic

The second organizing lens is to group your ministries in terms of things like age, gender or ethnicity. Your main ministry groupings could be to do with life-stage: kids, youth, young adults, families, seniors. You could distinguish based on gender, such as men's and women's ministries. Some churches will include specific cultural ministries, like a Korean-speaking congregation or a Sudanese congregation.

The advantages of this lens are:

a) you can make the ministry appropriate to that slice of the population, such as music style or service format

b) communication can be done well if language barriers make it necessary to run separate ministries

c) gathering with similar people is a comfortable and natural human tendency

d) it's often easier to organize gatherings because schedules are more likely to align. Young part-time workers are more likely to attend night services because they are more likely to work shifts on Sundays, whereas young families are more likely to attend morning services because it fits with meal and sleep times for young children.

The disadvantages are:

a) people may never mix with those outside their unique life-stage and so are disconnected from those who would perhaps be helpfully challenging to relate to

b) people who don't fit into the majority categories have no official place to belong in the church's ministries

c) it implicitly trains people to expect that the church exists for them and their consumer needs and that they will be made as comfortable as possible rather than challenged.

Functional

The third lens is to organize ministries in terms of broad areas doing the same overall task or with the same overall objective. You might break things up into Sunday services, welcoming and integration, and growth groups. Another option could be events and gatherings, creative and communication, people and pastoral care, administration and technology. Some people refer to this as ministry portfolios. You could also think not in terms of tasks or objectives but instead of processes that cross various ministries, like evangelism, discipleship and training.

The idea is to organize together ministries that have common features or objectives. For example, rather than three different people planning three different Sunday services, you'd have one person planning all three.

The advantages of this lens are:

a) it minimizes duplication of thought and activity

b) it standardizes these processes across the church, with the benefits of sharing resources and people, increased expertise and faster learning and implementing of best practices.

The disadvantages are:

a) standardization becoming the dominant virtue discourages innovation due to the inherent disruption that accompanies new ideas

b) passing people from one ministry function or process to another can be done poorly if not attended to thoughtfully

c) with no-one directly responsible for, say, the 10am Sunday service—since people are instead responsible for various functions that operate *within* that service—problems can arise and fester before anyone notices and takes action

d) since there is no one person officially leading the 10am service, it can be hard for people to know who their minister is if they aren't taught the way things are organized.

Not everything is neat

These lenses can make the process of grouping ministries seem very neat and tidy, but in real life it's extremely rare to apply one lens monochromatically across your whole church and at every layer of ministry.

Geographic, demographic and functional aren't mutually exclusive categories, and sometimes you'll want to use all three simultaneously at various stages or layers of your restructuring. One layer might be organized demographically, but then within that, at the next layer down, it might be best to organize functionally. Often either the ministries or the people that you have to work with—or lack thereof—mean that you have to mix and merge the lenses into a hybrid application. (This is the positive way of saying that you create some kind of organizational Frankenstein's monster. But most churches are Frankenstein's, and there's nothing wrong with that. Some of my best friends are Frankenstein's.) The lenses aren't there to restrict you but instead to help you be conscious of what you're doing and the advantages and disadvantages that come with that choice.

As with many arenas of leadership, ministry grouping is both science and art. Yes, there are principles, categories and classifications, but then the mess of real life needs to be taken into account. So, even once you've done some thinking through of these three lenses and how they might best be applied to your particular church, there is still fine-tuning to be done.[33]

What about a matrix?

So far, we've been talking about organizational charting and ministry grouping in a traditional hierarchy. But matrices are all the rage; should we be considering one?

The purpose of ministry grouping is to organize ministry so that it can become what it needs to be to achieve its mission. So far we've been talking about using one primary grouping lens—geographic, demographic or functional—to design the upper layer of your chart. But typically churches use a hybrid of lenses to design that crucial layer that bears the primary load for executing the strategy, still keeping it as a single, primary layer. The difference in a matrix structure is that you carry the strategic load by

---

33 For examples of what this might look like in a real ministry, and to explore the priority dials that will help fine-tune your thinking, check out revcraighamilton.com.

using two or more of the grouping principles and arrange them into equally important dimensions. Which means you end up with two equally important, *equally primary* layers. It can be complicated to get your head around as an abstract thought, so let's see it in action.

Let's say a church is structured like this:

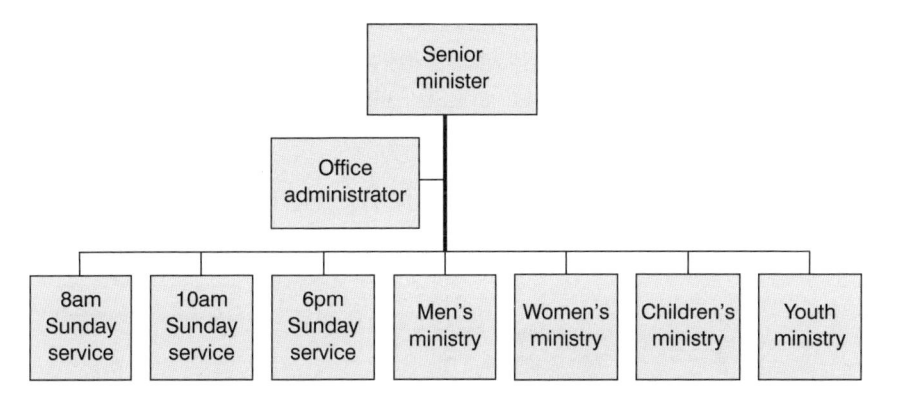

```
                    Senior
                   minister
                      |
          Office ─────┤
       administrator  |
    ┌──────┬──────┬───┴──┬──────┬──────┬──────┐
   8am    10am   6pm   Men's  Women's Children's Youth
  Sunday Sunday Sunday ministry ministry ministry ministry
  service service service
```

Everything done at this church is found somewhere under this first layer grouping. This ministry grouping bears the strategic load of seeing this church accomplish its purpose—presumably something to do with growing disciples of Jesus. You can see below that they've grouped things at this layer in a hybrid of both geography (that is, temporal geography regarding what is happening in the one building at different times across a Sunday) on the left side and demographics on the right.

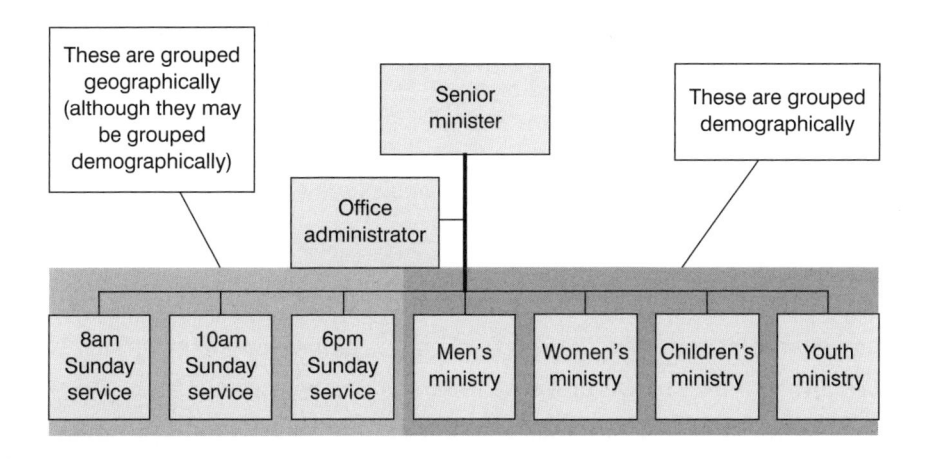

```
  These are grouped                              These are grouped
  geographically           Senior                 demographically
  (although they may      minister
  be grouped
  demographically)
                    Office
                 administrator
    ┌──────┬──────┬──────┬──────┬──────┬──────┐
   8am    10am   6pm   Men's  Women's Children's Youth
  Sunday Sunday Sunday ministry ministry ministry ministry
  service service service
```

15 // HOW TO GROUP MINISTRIES | 195

(It could be that the 8am service is a seniors' service, the 10am is for adults who don't consider themselves senior, and the 6pm service is the youth service, in which case the entire layer is designed around demographics. We can't tell that just from this chart.)

If the church decided that this ministry grouping wasn't able to bear the required strategic load, they might switch to a matrix structure. To do that they would need to elevate the other lens (in this case, functional) to equal importance with the two already being used. The structure would then look something like this:

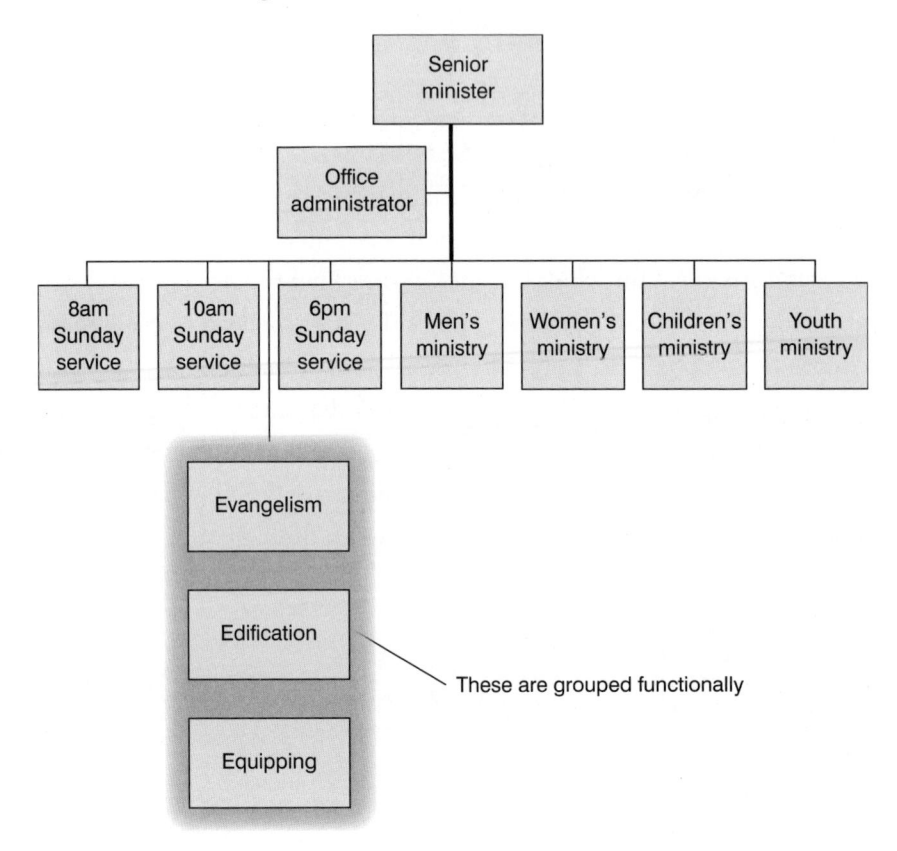

These are grouped functionally

The church has now added in three functions—evangelism, edification and equipping—as *equally important* organizational dimensions. This is the pivotal move. In the previous hierarchical configuration, these three functions would still have been happening in all these ministry areas. What has changed is that they are now equally important to the existing ministry areas in *structurally* shouldering the strategic burden. The people responsible for evangelism, edification and equipping are now direct reports of the senior minister, along with those already across the top of the organizational chart. They now oversee these three functional areas across all of the church and have the same level of responsibility as the existing ministry heads; the evangelism pastor has the same level of authority and responsibility as the 8am Sunday service pastor, for example.

The challenge at this point is that there is an immediate conflict of responsibility. Who is responsible for evangelism in the 8am Sunday service: the evangelism pastor or the 8am service pastor?

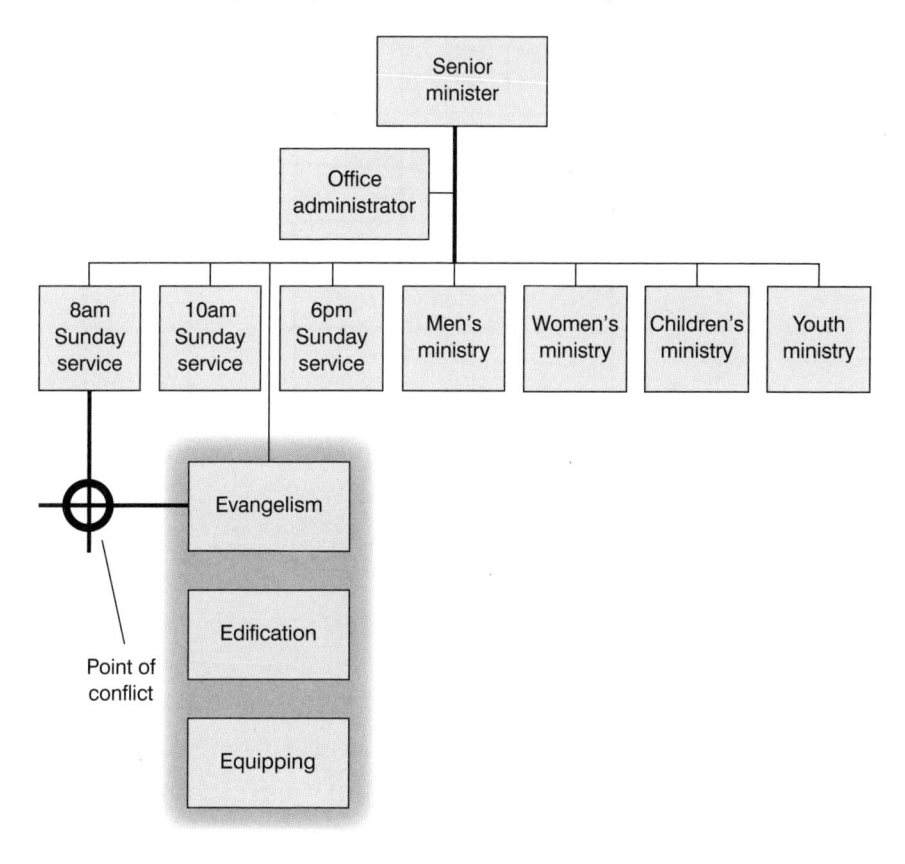

This same question now repeats itself at every intersection.

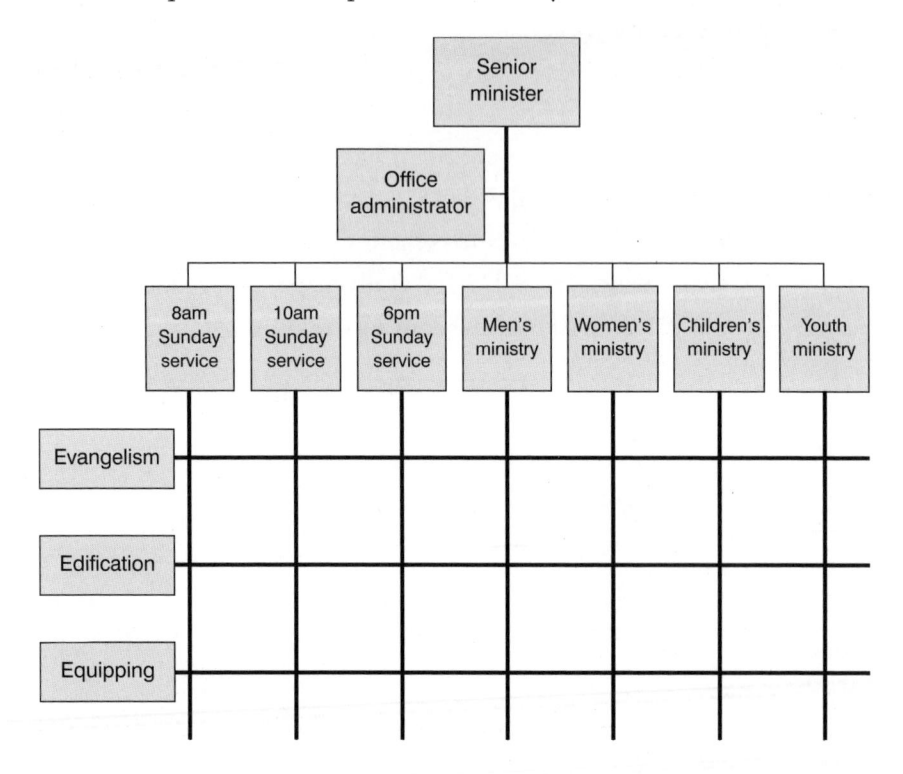

```
                           ┌─────────────┐
                           │   Senior    │
                           │  minister   │
                           └──────┬──────┘
              ┌─────────────┐    │
              │   Office    │    │
              │administrator├────┤
              └─────────────┘    │
    ┌──────┬──────┬──────┬──────┼──────┬──────┬──────┐
  ┌─┴──┐┌──┴─┐┌───┴┐┌────┴┐┌────┴┐┌────┴┐┌────┴┐
  │8am ││10am││6pm ││Men's││Women││Child││Youth│
  │Sun ││Sun ││Sun ││min. ││min. ││min. ││min. │
  └────┘└────┘└────┘└─────┘└─────┘└─────┘└─────┘
```

Evangelism							
Edification							
Equipping							

This high level of conflict is often seen as evidence that matrices are bad and don't work, but it's the opposite. Conflict is evidence that a matrix is working and that diverse views are being encountered and considered. Matrices are *supposed* to increase conflict. For those of us who are conflict-averse, this sounds like some kind of living nightmare, but suppression of conflict is a sign of a poorly functioning team since healthy, productive conflict is a sign of trust and mutual respect. So long as the culture is healthy and the leaders are competent, are emotionally stable and display vulnerability-trust, then a matrix full of conflict will be a positive thing.[34] (If your culture is unhealthy and your team is dysfunctional, adding a matrix into it could well be the straw that sends the camel to get a lawyer and pursue other opportunities.)

In this book I'm not going to focus on matrix organization for the simple reason that if you are reading it to learn and grasp the art of

---

34 See Hamilton, 'Two foundations of team-building', pp. 245-251.

ministry grouping—congratulations, good job—you're probably not ready to go head-to-head with the raging bull that is the matrix. However, here are a few brief points before we move on to the specifics of each pipeline layer.

If it isn't clear already, matrices are hard and complex because:

a) It means that people have multiple bosses they report to. If these two bosses aren't on precisely the same page then...

b) ...people will have two or more sets of (sometimes competing) objectives, instructions or expectations, which means...

c) ...conflict is an iron-clad guarantee. For example, the person responsible for the planning across all Sunday services might want to create economies of scale by duplicating the service plan and song choices across all services, which undermines the work of the service pastors in creating a sense of community and identity at each service.

Conflict isn't necessarily catastrophic, and there are numerous ways forward, but it does slow down decision-making. This lengthening of decision-making isn't necessarily a bad thing either, because by lingering on an issue both competing objectives are given the attention they should have.

d) Any matrix necessitates even more clarity because—as well as clarifying roles and responsibilities—you also need to clarify authority at every intersection. One way to do this is to say that either the functions or the demographics always have the final say. However, this kind of blanket decree is almost never a good idea and often doesn't work in or match reality. The decision needs to be more nuanced. A well-functioning matrix is one where the different axes are equal in power. But this doesn't mean that *all* decisions must be joint or consensus decisions. It may be that one dimension has authority over a specific set of decisions, the other dimension has authority for another set, and a third set of decisions are to be decided by agreement or by the layer above if agreement cannot be reached. But however you slice the decision authority, you can see the increased level of clarity required.

e) A matrix requires (and to some degree fosters) collaboration more than traditional hierarchies do. In a conventional hierarchy it can be easy to create ministries that accidentally become little fiefdoms, especially if the integration occurs high up and it isn't on the senior leader's radar to break down ministry area silos. In a matrix, because ministry areas will be structurally bumping into others at regular intervals, it's much harder for ministry ghettoes to evolve.

f) Lastly, since in a matrix there are more often decisions that impact your ministry that you don't have the final authority to make, you need to rely on influence much more than authority in your leadership—which means you need to be a highly capable leader. In any church there exists both executive power and persuasive power, so even when you have authority you still need influence (especially when it comes to leading volunteers), but in a traditional hierarchy executive power is at least an available tool. In a matrix, for certain decisions, you simply can *never* rely on executive power because that power resides in someone else's hands. If the decision is vitally important then you'll need to be a highly proficient influencer to ensure the right outcome—and most of us aren't naturally highly proficient influencers.[35] Command and control leaders will find a matrix too hard for them to lead within and not worth the effort.

The point is not that matrices are for good leaders and traditional hierarchies are for mediocre leaders. That's not true, and you can't judge a leader based on what type of structure he or she is leading. There are good reasons not to use matrices, and many amazing leaders lead traditional hierarchies while there are atrocious leaders heading up a matrix. It's your call which is best for your church, taking into account the complexity of what you're trying to accomplish and the baseline competence of the leaders. But this book will focus on, and assume you're leading within, a traditional hierarchy. If you are leading within a matrix, you're hopefully wise enough to make the appropriate translations into your context.

---

[35] See the detour on the dynamics of executive and persuasive power in Hamilton, 'Red Queen syndrome: a nine-step process for implementing change', pp. 454-456.

Ministry grouping is the foundation for all the other aspects of the leadership development framework. It's the skeleton that all the other pieces flesh out. This is the first step to making sure your leadership development is smart.

Pipeline planning meeting 5

The goal of this meeting is to clarify the ministry grouping for the whole church and to personalize and agree on the pipeline architecture you'll install there. This will be easier if you are an average-sized church and more difficult if your church is larger and thus more complex. But putting in effort here is necessary so you can work out what pipelines you have active or need to create. Remember, while ministry grouping is not pipeline architecture, the pipeline relies on grouping.

Ministry grouping

This meeting isn't about changing and reorganizing the church's groupings. The objective is to describe *what is*.

Draw the top layer of grouping for the whole church so that everyone can see it. In other words, you'll draw up the senior leader's team of direct reports and name any specific ministry areas the senior leader is directly responsible for. Check that nothing has been left out. Everything should live somewhere under this first layer.

The next step is for everyone to work by themselves to fill out what the ministry grouping looks like for their ministry areas. Each area should be drawn down until reaching the frontline leaders. Put each grouping up so that everyone can see the structure of the whole church.

This process of making the groupings visible might highlight some situations where a single person has 37 direct reports and needs to create some smaller groupings and raise up some team leaders. That realization is invaluable and a project for that leader to work on in the following months.[36]

---

[36] Don't forget to check out revcraighamilton.com for some practical examples of how that might be done.

You now have clarity on what the grouping structure is, or will need to be, for your whole church. This means you can move on to personalizing the pipeline for your church.

Personalizing the pipeline

The pipeline in this book is the standard model. Tweak it if you feel you need to. Don't like what the layers are called? Change them. Don't like what each layer does? Move things around. Don't like calling it a pipeline? Call it something else. Think there should be more layers? Add them. Think small group leaders should be in the team leader layer? Put them there. Think it should be flipped so that instead of going *up* the pipeline you go *down* to reinforce that the senior leader is the servant of the whole church? Do what you think is best and make it work for you.

To personalize the pipeline, make sure everyone is familiar with what each pipeline layer does in broad terms. "Team leaders lead a team and area leaders lead a whole ministry area." Things like that. Then get agreement with whoever is necessary (staff, area leaders, elders) on which pipeline layers are active across your church. This will help you determine whether you need the unit leader layer.

Now comes potentially the hardest part of today's meeting: agreeing on what to call each layer. You absolutely must call each layer the same thing across every ministry in your church. You want the maximum amount of clarity and simplicity you can get—and 14 different names for the same role ain't that.

Work out what you already call these layers across your church. Are team leaders always called team leaders or are they called leaders, coaches, managers, deacons or something else? Does every ministry call them something different? Are ministry areas called 'areas' or 'departments'? Every ministry will think their label is the best and most transparent, but that's just because it's the one they thought of or the one they've been using for the last 20 years. Some people and ministries are going to need to change.

Note: once you've decided what the layer will be called, those who need to change don't have to change that day! Maybe it's just that on their role descriptions (which we'll work on in a couple of meetings) they'll need to add the new label in brackets. For example, instead of 'kids' ministry coach' it says 'kids' ministry coach (team leader)'. Then next year it becomes 'kids' ministry team leader (coach)'. The year after that, it's finally 'kids' ministry team leader'. Remember, don't think one year, think five ahead.

Last, explicitly define the pipelines in each ministry, since not every one will have the same number of layers. The active pipeline architecture needs to be decided. Don't over-structure a ministry if you don't need to. Some ministries will realize that they need more layers and so will have one person fulfilling multiple layer roles while they work on developing their leaders and bringing them up the pipeline. This is normal, messy church life.

This final step of defining each ministry area's pipeline could be made homework rather than completed during this meeting. If so, start the next pipeline planning meeting with show-and-tell where all the area leaders present their pipelines and who exactly is at each layer so that everyone gets on the same page.

16
Full outline of the pipeline: leader

Leadership development framework

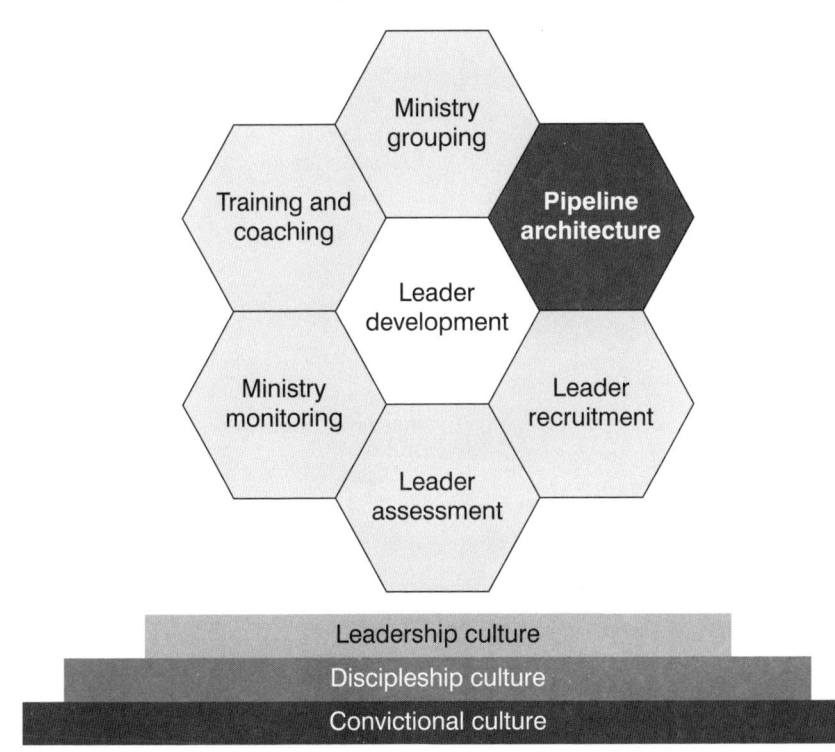

- Ministry grouping
- Training and coaching
- Pipeline architecture
- Leader development
- Ministry monitoring
- Leader recruitment
- Leader assessment

Leadership culture
Discipleship culture
Convictional culture

In section one we got our heads around the basic idea of the leadership pipeline philosophy: building layers of leadership that each do different ministries while still being united in seeking to make disciples. Now it's time to break down the four main leadership pipeline layers—leaders, team leaders, area leaders and senior leadership—and get a handle on what should be happening at each and the consequences if we get it wrong.[37]

Definition

This first layer of the pipeline is the leader/team member layer.

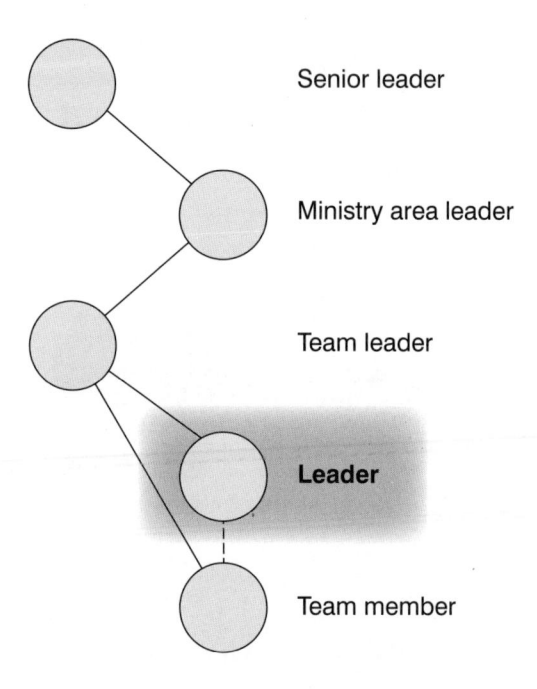

Senior leader

Ministry area leader

Team leader

Leader

Team member

In the pipeline framework, a leader is someone who serves by directly leading group members or performing a ministry task, and who has another leader directly responsible for their oversight. They're a member of a team.

This *part of a team* thing is one of the defining facets of this layer. Someone's solo ministry—going out under their own steam to knock on doors and talk about Jesus, offering to mow people's lawns in Jesus' name, leading the members of their family—is great, but it's not part of a leadership pipeline because there's no pipeline. This doesn't make it less

---

37 Large churches or complicated ministries may need to consider a fifth layer, the unit leader layer. I've included a breakdown of that layer in the appendix.

valuable—there's nothing wrong with being the Lone Ranger—but it's not what we're talking about here.

A leader is at the frontlines of the ministry they are involved in. If it's kids' ministry, then they directly lead the kids. If it's the greeting ministry on a Sunday morning, they're standing at the door saying hello and handing out the weekly news sheet. Whoever the recipients of the ministry are, the leader is directly interacting with them. The youth leader leads the youth. The small group leader leads the people in their small group.

Some churches will call everyone in this layer a leader. Other churches will want to distinguish between those whose ministry is life-on-life—like a kids' leader or a youth leader—and those whose ministry is focused on performing tasks—like the person at the sound desk or the Bible reader. Both types of ministry are crucial but obviously different, and so are the expectations for those roles, even though they are both on the same layer.

Whether you call this layer the leader layer or the leader/team member layer is about preference and culture rather than right or wrong. The point is that this is the frontline layer of whatever ministry we're talking about, whether kids', youth, small groups, sound, visuals, pastoral care, welcoming, men's, women's or feeding the poor.

Key distinction

These people have gone from doing ministry by themselves to doing ministry in a team. Every Christian can minister to others wherever and however they like; they're responsible to the Lord. But when a person joins a team and becomes a leader in the pipeline, they're now also responsible to the other members of their team and to their team leader. The critical thing for them now to learn is how to function well in a team.

As we've talked about in section one, every layer of leadership can be broken down into:

1. heart focus
2. time considerations
3. things to learn.

Heart focus

This is the most significant and difficult area, as well as being a tricky category to pin down. It's about what you focus on and how you go about your ministry. It's the focus of your *personal ministry contribution*. But it's also about your heart, about how you feel about what you're doing. It's about *liking* this layer of ministry. Generally this will be the pipeline layer that we like—doing these tasks or ministering to these people. And there's nothing wrong with liking what you're doing! It just becomes more of a challenge in the following layers of leadership (or a real problem, as we saw in chapter 6 with Andrew's youth leadership team).

As we mentioned back in chapter 7, some might refer to this as the 'values' needed at each layer, but this is unhelpful. When people think of values, they think of things like honesty, integrity and perseverance. Then, when you say that as leaders change layers they need to change their values, it sounds like we move away from honesty as we rise up the layers. But what is meant by 'values' here is 'the type of work being valued'. This will make more sense as we work through the layers, but at the leader layer the work that needs to be valued is individual contributor work. Stick to using 'heart focus' for this area and stop the misconception before it starts.

The heart focus of the leader layer manifests in three main concerns:

1. getting results through personal proficiency
2. high-quality work
3. accepting and embodying the ministry's values.

If "getting results" conjures up images of ruthless boardrooms and ranting about the bottom line, please know that I just mean the inevitable process whereby you do something and then something happens *as a result*, good or bad, intended or unintended. We live in a world of cause and effect, and the causes we're thinking about at the leader layer that lead to specific effects are causes performed by individuals.

A leader is focused on getting results through personal proficiency; they get better at the things they're doing. Once you see it in action it feels obvious. The youth leader runs a game. They aren't very good at running games, so the result is a not very good game. They would like to get better at running games so that better games are run. The small group leader is very good at running their small group. People feel a sense of belonging, share their thoughts and ideas freely, are guided to a correct understanding of the passage, are cared for and prayed for and are helped to grow in love and obedience to Jesus. The leader is highly personally proficient, and that results in a great small group. None of this undermines God's sovereignty, since he works in, through, above and in spite of all things.[38]

Linked to this is that the leader needs to be focused on doing high-quality work. You might think, "What's the alternative? Focusing on sloppy work?" But people might not be focused at all on the quality of their work, or unaware that they could be getting better. The leader should be focused on doing the best they can do and seeking to improve so that they can do even better next time.

Lastly, a leader at this layer will need to focus on accepting and embodying the church or ministry's values. As we've said, every church's culture will be slightly different from the next, even if they share many or all of the same core values. Some churches will be contemporary in style, while others will be planning for next year like it's 1983. Whatever the culture is, the leader needs to accept its values. They may not approve of them all, but they need to accept them and embody as many as they can.

If the church has very few values that you can embody with a good conscience, maybe it isn't the right church for you. But generally, the church you're at expresses *enough* common values that you can belong and want to serve there. In which case, embody the values that are biblical and that you think should be perpetuated. The others you may want to respectfully challenge and even seek to change. (This kind of change is tough and you should proceed with caution.)

One way to summarize the heart focus for the leader layer is that they are serving alongside others as an individual contributor in a team of individual contributors.

---

[38] For more on this see Hamilton, 'God uses means' and 'Focus on doing your job', pp. 55-64.

Time considerations

Time and the use of it is an essential variable for every layer because everything done is done *in time*. But time isn't used or conceived of the same way at every layer.

At the leader layer, time is primarily thought of in weekly increments. The kind of questions a leader will ask are, "What's happening this week? Am I on anything? What about next week?" They'll need to think about arriving on time, reliably, and whether to leave on time or not.[39] They will have tasks or responsibilities that have due dates.

Ultimately, they need to learn to manage themselves and use their time and energy to fulfil all the responsibilities in their life, including their responsibilities to the ministry team.[40]

Things to learn: core

You'll remember that the things to learn at each layer are broken up into three groups: ministry-specific, layer-specific and core. Ministry-specific things are the skills, frameworks and processes needed that are specific to each ministry area. For example, early childhood development and behaviour management for kids' ministry; vocal training for music ministry. Due to the colossal range of what *could* be involved, we won't be delving into the ministry-specific things to learn at all. We'll focus on the layer-specific and the core.

The core group is broken down into vision, strategy, development and stewardship. These areas continue into all layers but evolve as we transition into new ones. Let's break each of these down for the leader layer.

Vision

What I mean by vision is the answer to why your church exists and, under God, what it's seeking to achieve. You can call this vision or mission or priority, but the point is that you have clarity on the preferred future you're working towards as a church.[41]

---

39 See Hamilton, 'Arriving on time isn't what you think it is', pp. 115-117.
40 See Hamilton, 'Time management won't help you', pp. 111-114.
41 See Hamilton, 'The point is clarity, not labels', pp. 337-344.

At the leader layer, you should be aware that you have a vision, know roughly what it is and support it. This isn't as simple as it sounds. Awareness of the vision is one of the hardest parts of having one, which is why repetition is critically important.[42]

It doesn't help anyone if members of your team aren't on board with what your church is doing and are heading in a different direction. If your church is seeking to "make new and deeper disciples of the people in our city", but people are joining ministry teams to save the rainforest, over time they'll be trying to revolutionize the ministry to impact the Amazon and getting frustrated with your stubbornness, and you'll get annoyed at them for continually trying to derail the main mission. At this layer, you want them aware of the vision and supportive of it.

Strategy

Strategy is the general plan for how you are going to achieve your vision. We talked about this in chapter 3. In the church world, if the vision is to evangelize the city, then the strategy might be enabling and empowering people to invite their friends to church and also be confident to lead people to Christ individually. The tactics would be when and what we'll train people with to be able to make that happen. Alternatively, the strategy to evangelize the city might be to hire a stadium and run an evangelistic rally. That will require very different tactics.

At the leader layer, you want your people to know the overall strategy and serve effectively in it. They should understand how what they do connects to the bigger picture. That way they'll be able to offer you intelligent feedback as to whether what they're involved in is actually doing what it's supposed to be doing.

Again, this sounds simple and straightforward, but it's surprising how often a person at the frontlines of a ministry doesn't know how what they do connects to the broader goals. When people don't see this link they will often lose enthusiasm, because if they think what they do doesn't matter, or if it seems random and thoughtless, they'll move on to something else that they can see matters.

---

42 See Hamilton, 'Your people should be able to do a good impression of you', pp. 421-428.

Development

The third core area is development: people development. At this layer of the pipeline, we're helping people develop the skill of *being developed*. This doesn't come naturally for a lot of people. They need to:

1. learn to be open to receiving feedback
2. expect to improve
3. participate in training
4. have the humility that enables the first three to happen.

You want a culture of development from the ground up in your church so that everyone is continually growing as disciples and as leaders. Set the tone from day one that being a part of this church, and in particular being a part of this ministry, means being willing to grow. This means helping people to develop the ability to receive coaching.

Stewardship

Stewardship is being able to use what has been entrusted to you wisely.

Leaders should display capability in their own financial stewardship. Whether or not the cliché is true—the wallet is the last part of a person to be converted—financial stewardship is often at least sluggish. You want to help people to grow in this area of discipleship, particularly in light of the seriousness that Jesus gives to this issue: you cannot serve both God and money (Matt 6:24). You want the leaders in your church, as people whom others will be following and imitating, to excel in the grace of giving (2 Cor 8:7), because it's a significant heart issue and it signals a serious commitment to the growth of the kingdom and the ministry of their specific church.

Leaders should also show faithfulness to an allocated budget. This might not apply to some ministries at your church, but others will have weekly or term budgets where people are allocated a certain amount, perhaps to buy prizes for a kids' ministry game or to buy supplies for an activity on the youth camp. Leaders need to learn to stay within the budgeted parameters because it shows faithfulness and responsibility but also because the ministry only has limited resources. We can't all overspend by $50 every week. This faithful stewardship is also crucial if a person ever moves to another layer in the pipeline where they may have more significant amounts of money to oversee and spend. Showing faithfulness with little shows that they can be entrusted with more (Luke 16:10).[43]

If your ministry doesn't have regular allocated budgets but you have a person you want to develop to become a team leader, get them to help you plan a one-off event and provide them with a budgeted amount for an area of responsibility. This way you give them experience and you get to see them show faithfulness in this area. If they blow the budget, then it's good it happened now with a (presumably) smaller amount and you gain a chance to coach them and give them another try.

Things to learn: layer-specific

These are the skills, frameworks and mindsets that leaders need to learn at this initial stage of their leadership. They are on the frontlines, presumably leading others, so most of the 'other person' leadership skills they'll need will be in the ministry-specific arena. Having said that, the two most important things leaders need to learn at this first layer are actually self-leadership (if you struggle to lead yourself, you'll definitely struggle to lead others) and how to be a helpful member of a team.[44]

I'll include a breakdown of layer-specific skills at the end of each of these layer-focused chapters. These are my recommendations of things to learn, not something sacred handed down for thousands of years, so add or subtract things to reflect what is needed in your specific context. That said, they're still good lists, so don't feel as though you must change them. I won't unpack each skill in great detail (otherwise this book would be *way* too long), but where possible I've pointed to the corresponding chapter in *Wisdom in Leadership*.

---

43 See Hamilton, 'Faithfulness buys responsibility', pp. 187-189.
44 For more on the importance of self-leadership see Hamilton, 'Lead yourself', pp. 85-90.

Layer summary

If this is your first time encountering a pipeline philosophy, the detail might feel overwhelming. To help you and the people you will be training in pipeline thinking, each layer has a one-sentence summary that captures the heart of what's going on. You can summarize the leader layer, perhaps crassly, as:

> I succeed when I succeed.

This layer is about being a faithful and effective *individual contributor*. The key distinction is that they have gone from *doing ministry alone*—like talking to workmates about Jesus—to *doing ministry with others*.

What happens if they don't learn these things?

Time allocations, heart focus and things to learn aren't there just to make leaders' lives complicated. When leaders don't learn them, there are observable consequences that play out as they move through the pipeline.

The first consequence if a leader doesn't learn a foundational thing—leading themselves, relating to other people well, reliability, any of them—is that they'll instead learn bad habits. These will be harder to break the longer they go on, and if they move through the pipeline they will replicate these bad habits with the people they lead. Then you have an epidemic on your hands, and it'll be too late to find patient zero. It's now become a culture change problem—which will take a long time and a lot of energy to correct. Prevention is better than the cure.

Secondly, if leaders make their way through the pipeline with these gaps in their leadership, they will clog it. Imagine a leader who lacks humility, doesn't contribute positive energy to the team, doesn't encourage people, nurtures mindsets that are unhealthy and hates taking initiative. Then they become a team leader with the primary responsibility of developing the people they lead into strong and healthy leaders. Fat chance! This leader doesn't have the internal resources to do that well because they haven't learned or personally become what is needed themselves.

The things that hold back team leaders are often issues overlooked from the leader layer. If an underdeveloped leader keeps rising through the pipeline, they'll clog it because they'll be unable to build leaders beneath them. And a clogged pipeline causes issues well into the future.

For example, vulnerability is a difficult trait to foster, and it requires a particular environment to grow and flourish. It needs to be modelled by the team leader to develop in the members. If the entire team is full of people who ooze vulnerability, this *can* overpower the influence of the team leader, but this is extremely rare. If the environment set by the team leader is hostile to vulnerability, this will most often discourage those who are willing to be vulnerable from acting that way around the team. The influence of the team leader is key.

A healthy pipeline should look something like this:

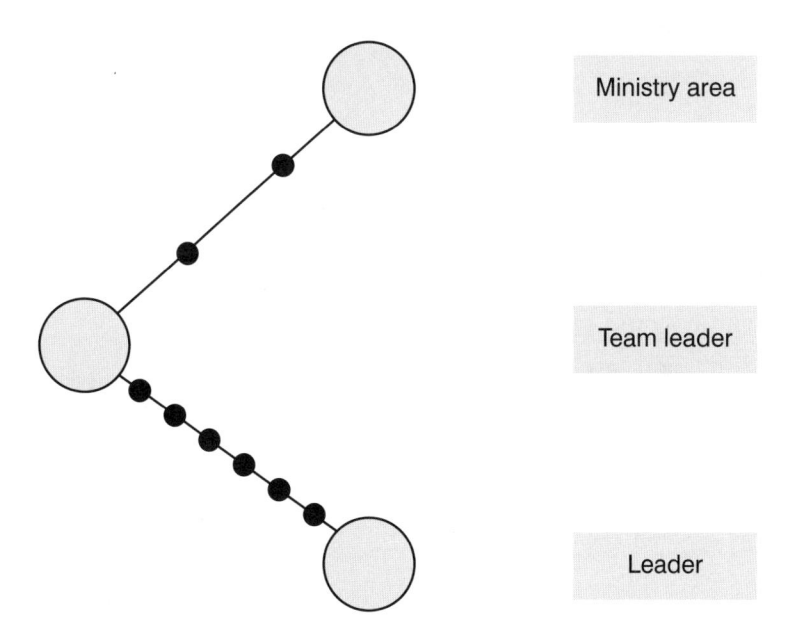

	Ministry area
	Team leader
	Leader

Here we have a ministry area with two team leaders and a whole bunch of leaders in those two teams. In the leader layer it's reasonable to have leaders at all different stages of development; some leaders are new and so are barely proficient whereas others are highly competent and are now learning what it takes to be a team leader. Some could probably start leading a team tomorrow if needed. The two team leaders in this pipeline have been doing a good job raising up the leaders underneath them.

Here's a clogged pipeline:

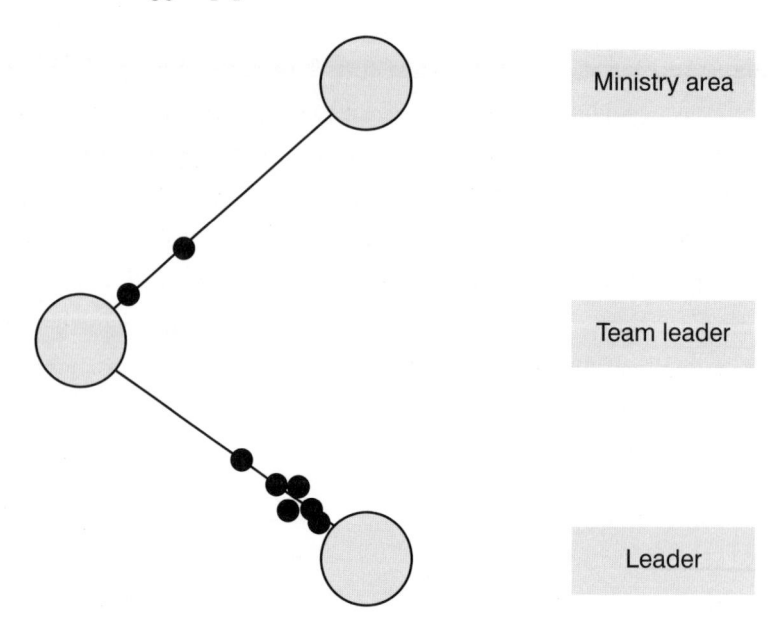

Ministry area

Team leader

Leader

A pipeline can look like this for lots of reasons, but in this case those two team leaders didn't learn what they needed to at the leader layer but have still gone on to lead teams. The leaders on their teams are not being developed as leaders. Not everyone is at the same place in their development, and there's even an outlier who is pulling away from the pack, but no-one is even close to being ready to lead a team if needed. Not tomorrow or any time soon.

It's unlikely that a pipeline would ever get entirely clogged, since there's usually at least one exceptional person who can grow and develop in spite of the input they receive from the leadership above them—but this is cold comfort. We want to build a church and culture where people can exercise their gifts and grow; we want to build a mighty river of leaders, including people who never thought they had it in them. But a deficient leader who rises up the pipeline will turn that river into a trickle, and they will cripple bruised reeds who *could* be leaders but who need care and investment to realize that potential.

Clogging the pipeline isn't just an inefficient waste of resources: it's cruel and unloving. Leadership is always about love, and bad leadership is always unloving.

The third consequence of a leader not growing in these areas is that if the leader doesn't specifically deal with pride and learn to accept coaching—stumbles in the development core skill—then they will become increasingly blind. If they haven't learned to receive feedback, they haven't developed humility and vulnerability either. This will be crippling for them and the ministries they lead.

Humility is one of the most essential characteristics a leader needs.[45] Firstly, it's rational and obvious that I'm only good at a breathtaking minority of things. The vast majority of things in the world that I *could* be good at, I probably don't even know exist. Secondly, we're following the crucified king who came to serve rather than be served. It's incongruous to follow him and not want to become like him. Thirdly, humility means that our leadership is about others, not us. It's about the cause of the kingdom, the glory of the name of Jesus. Fourthly, humble people are ready to learn. They can handle being wrong because they know it means they can discover what's right.[46]

The higher you go in the pipeline, the harder it is to receive critique: it's more difficult for the people you lead to give feedback up the chain than it is for feedback to come down; there are fewer people above you to give it; you are less supervised; and the more expertise you gain, the more you can start to believe your own press and think you have nothing to improve. So if you become the boss who can't receive feedback, the people you lead will learn not to tell you bad news and there will be an ever-increasing number of things that you don't know that everyone else does. Without leader-layer humility, you will grow increasingly blind. This blindness leads to the fourth consequence, which is that the leader will become increasingly dangerous.

In *How the Mighty Fall*, Jim Collins traced the decline of big and powerful companies and the common features that led to their collapse.[47] He observed that an organization can actually be more than halfway through the process of decline while everything still appears to be going

---

45 See Hamilton, 'Humble and hungry', pp. 253-259.
46 See Hamilton, 'Bad news is good news', pp. 487-492.
47 Jim Collins, *How the Mighty Fall*, Random House Business Books, London, 2009. This book is a must-read.

well. That should keep you awake at night. Conversions can be up, giving can be up, the number of volunteers can be up, everything can be going up—while under the bonnet you're about to give out. His second observation is that hubris kicks off decline and then its results—pride, arrogance, a lack of humility—speed the process.

How the Mighty Fall isn't a Christian book; it's a secular business leadership book, and it has still noticed how critical humility is to a healthy organization.

If leaders with this deficiency rise through the pipeline and a lack of humility spreads, you're seeding time bombs throughout your ministries. When those people eventually implode or explode, innocents will be caught in the blast and there'll be a lot of slow rebuilding to be done.

Who should become a team leader?

How then do you know whom to invite into a team leader role? Answer: you never know for sure. People are too complicated, and life moves too quickly. But just because you can't know 100% doesn't mean you are left entirely in the dark. You can have degrees of certainty.

Since this is such a common challenge, I've written a whole chapter about it: chapter 21. But for now, here's a quick set of questions that will help you consider a person's suitability for team leadership:

1. Are people following them in other spheres of life? Are they already influencing the people around them?
2. Do they make things happen in their lives, or do they wait for things to happen?
3. Are they energized or overwhelmed by responsibility?
4. Are they enthused by a challenge? Do they respond well to a difficult person?

If you'd answer 'yes' three or four times, you've probably got someone who would be a good potential candidate for being a team leader.

One-page summary

Leader/team member (individual contributor)

Serves by directly leading group members or directly performing ministry tasks.

Summary: I succeed when I succeed.

Key distinction: shift from doing ministry alone to doing ministry with others.

Things to learn: layer-specific	Things to learn: core	Things to learn: ministry-specific
• ongoing character development and repentance • convictions • working in a team • relationship building	*Vision:* aware of and support *Strategy:* know and serve effectively in *Development:* able to receive coaching *Stewardship:* faithfully utilizing personal resources, staying within allocated budget	• technical proficiency • using ministry tools, processes and procedures • reporting

Time considerations	Heart focus
• arrival and departure • meeting personal due dates for projects (usually short-term) • managing self to use time well	• getting results through personal proficiency • high-quality work • accepting and embodying the group's values

Leader: layer-specific things to learn

Leading yourself
- Lead yourself[48]
- Play to your strengths[49]

Character
- Five C's[50]
- Character is king[51]
- Humble and hungry[52]

Handling the Bible
- Basic exegesis
- Biblical theology overview: big point/parts
- Biblical theology overview: plot/structure

Tools to be an everyday evangelist
- What does it mean to be an everyday evangelist?
- What is the gospel?[53]
- Sharing your testimony
- The place and power of prayer[54]
- Learning an easy way to share the gospel

Building a team
- Recruitment[55]

Loving a team
- Reliability and punctuality
- Planning and flexibility
- Quality

---

48 Hamilton, 'Lead yourself', pp. 85-90.
49 Hamilton, 'Play to your strengths' pp. 99-104.
50 Hamilton, 'The five C's', pp. 261-267.
51 Hamilton, 'Character is king', pp. 47-50.
52 Hamilton, 'Humble and hungry', pp. 253-259.
53 Hamilton, 'The gospel is God's power', pp. 35-41.
54 Hamilton, 'Prayer is mandatory', pp. 43-46.
55 See chapter 20 in this book.

- Encouragement
- Being a positive presence in the team
- Serving your leader
- Introduction to emotional intelligence
- Relating to all ages
- Relating to the opposite gender
- Relating to leadership: followership

Developing a team member

Developing a healthy mind

- Vulnerability[56]
- Mindset and hopetimism[57]

Using a healthy mind

- Creativity and new ideas[58]
- Forward-thinking and initiative
- Basic decision-making
- Understanding church size dynamics

---

56 Hamilton, 'Two foundations of team building', pp. 245-251.
57 Hamilton, 'Hopetimism', pp. 159-168.
58 Hamilton, 'Creativity is a lost art', pp. 365-374.

17
Full outline of the pipeline: team leader

Leadership development framework

- Ministry grouping
- Training and coaching
- Pipeline architecture
- Leader development
- Ministry monitoring
- Leader recruitment
- Leader assessment

Leadership culture
Discipleship culture
Convictional culture

The team leader role is challenging to transition into. The vast majority of leaders in your church will be in the first layer of the pipeline—leaders and team members—with few being team leaders and fewer again being ministry area leaders. This means that the majority of transitions will be from leader to team leader, and this is the transition that is the hardest for the heart focus, as we saw in the conversation between Andrew and Matt.

Definition

The team leader is the second layer in the pipeline and, as the name suggests, serves by leading a team of leaders. You might have a team of leaders who love and serve the three-to-five-year-olds during your Sunday service with one leader leading that team. The team leader leads a team of leaders who then directly lead the kids.

Some ministries in your church will not have or need a team leader layer. If you imagine an accordion, in this situation the team leader layer would fold up into the layer above, and the ministry area leader—whose role we'll outline in the next chapter—would take on the responsibilities of a team leader. Perhaps a youth ministry has 10-15 high schoolers and a team of four leaders. If this team were to have a team leader layer as well as a youth minister at the ministry area layer, it would probably be over-structured. But if a youth ministry had a junior high group and a senior high group that met on different days, rather than the youth minister leading both they may instead choose to concertina out a team leader layer.

Most team leaders will be like a player–coach, responsible for the whole team and overseeing the plans and strategies while also being on the field running after the ball. This is harder and more complicated than doing a 'pure' team leader role. The player–coach will need to find ways to use their 'player' moments to coach those around them. The kids' church team leader shouldn't *merely* run games or give talks; they should run games and give talks in a way that brings a less-experienced leader with them to observe, help and then do.[59] Perhaps they bring people in to work on understanding the Bible passage together and finding the teaching point. Maybe they say to everyone, "Listen carefully to the talk today and watch for things I'm doing to connect with the kids and apply the passage; afterwards we'll talk about what you noticed and what I could improve". Leading at multiple layers at the same time can be challenging, and the potential for confusion is high, but often you won't have any other options.

---

59 For more on this, see chapter 25 on training and coaching.

What about small groups?

The team leader layer can get confusing when it comes to small groups in a church. Is the small group leader a team leader or a frontline leader? A small group looks a lot like a team. It's particularly muddy if you envision small group leaders as disciple-makers more than discussion facilitators, who develop each person in their group to speak the word of God to the others in the group as well as head out into the world as a disciple who ministers to the people around them. This sounds like team leader work. And yet the small group leader is on the frontline of small groups. So how should you organize and conceptualize them?

It's your church and you're allowed to do what you want. If you want them to be team leaders, go for it. But my advice, from my experience of helping churches implement a leadership pipeline: it's best to have your small group leaders at the leader layer. Yes, they'll need *some* of the layer-specific skills of a team leader, such as coaching and running a meeting, but it's still best to put them with the other frontline leaders.

For a start, conceptualizing small group leaders as team leaders will lead to an imbalance. If you have 100 people in ten small groups, then the small groups ministry has 100 leaders and ten team leaders. If you were to call a meeting of all the leaders in your church, you would have the youth leaders, kids' leaders, other ministry leaders—and then literally everyone who just sporadically attends a small group.

As well as this pragmatic reason, conceiving small group leaders as team leaders is a category confusion. Leaders serve by directly leading the members of—or recipients of—a ministry. In almost every ministry the 'recipients' will also be ministering to each other—the kids in the Sunday kids' program minister to each other—but in small groups this is more explicit. Small groups don't strictly consist of 'the leader' and 'those ministered to' but rather a group of disciples seeking to disciple one another with a leader who fosters, encourages, exemplifies, guides and is responsible for the whole process. In that sense, the members of the small group are the recipients of *that specific* fostering rather than a team serving those outside the team.

Key distinction

The distinction between the ministry of a team leader and that of a leader is the shift from 'doing the ministry' to 'getting ministry done *through others*'. The team leader needs to understand that moving away from the frontlines isn't a move away from caring and loving people, nor is it a step away from *actual* ministry (whatever that means). It's a move to a multiplication of ministry, to facilitating and enabling ministry; it's a move from directly caring for *these select ones* to making sure *all these ones* are cared for. It's not *less* ministry but a *different mode* of ministry. Both the leader and team leader have the same objective: that the people are ministered to. *Through others* is the momentous change that happens.

Heart focus

As we saw in chapter 6, this *through others* shift is the most difficult and painful shift in the entire pipeline because it needs to take place in the heart.

Every layer transition in the pipeline requires an internal revolution for success. The transition to team leader is internally violent because, for almost everyone, it involves the death of the leader you were previously in order to be the leader you need to be. The infection of pride runs deep within us, and even when we shine a light and deal with what we find, the rest retreats further into the darkness. Moving into a team leader role exposes the infection, and so the often-unknowingly prideful leader needs to be put to death so that a healthier leader can emerge.

This might sound a bit dramatic, but we saw some of the ways pride shows itself in chapter 6. When a leader becomes a team leader they are no longer primarily an individual contributor. They used to be a highly proficient frontline leader, but they've suddenly lost their high competence. They're doing tasks they're not good at since they're still learning them. And because it's a role with higher visibility, more people can see that incompetence and struggle. This is tricky territory. There's a powerful temptation to drop back down and do the ministry of the leader layer again in order to feel as though you're doing a good job. Sometimes this is conscious, but often it happens without a deliberate decision.

It also provokes hidden pride because doing ministry through others means that my work manifests in theirs. My effort has now gone into making someone else able to do a good job, so when it's time for people to praise someone they'll give it to the one who actually performed the task—which was not me. The team leader's best work is hidden. My leadership fruit will start to grow on other people's trees.

The team leader must be passionate about the success of their team members because them doing a good job ministering to people is the objective. All our various roles tie back into making disciples, but team leaders focus on making disciples of the people in their ministries *by* developing and discipling the leaders in their team. They need to experience team success as personal success.

Lastly, team leaders need to hold themselves accountable and be held accountable by others for the success of their leaders. As well as processing team success as personal success, they need to feel team failure as their personal responsibility. It's the team leader's job to develop their team, help their leaders do a good job and put them in positions where they can succeed. You share accountability for the actions of your team.

Time considerations

The team leader needs to move from thinking only weekly—"What am *I* doing this week?"—to also thinking quarterly—"What are *we* doing this term and *who* is going to do *what* each week?" This is essentially a transition to increased strategic thinking. It's not just "Who is doing what each week this quarter?" but "What are we planning to achieve this quarter?", "What will we work on and improve this quarter?" and "What are we building towards this quarter?" The team leader keeps their eye on the weekly while prioritizing the quarterly.

For some, it might mean going from being a last-minute person to a forward-planner. If at school you handed in assignments with seconds to spare after starting them the day they were due, it will be hard to instead work progressively over a prolonged timeline and hand things in early. Staying the same isn't an option though; other people are counting on you.

The other way that doing ministry through others impacts the time considerations of the team leader is around whom your time belongs to. At the leader layer, time is about preparing for what you have to do: writing the Bible study, cooking the food, moving the chairs. When other people on the team ask you questions, they are essentially interrupting you. You might not mind, but they are still stopping you from getting on with what you need to do. If you've ever worked in an office, you'll know how this feels. One or two people coming over to "just ask a quick question" is no big deal, but if they keep piling up they begin to feel like what they are: disruptions that prevent you from getting your work done.

When you're a team leader, this changes. Your time is *for the team*; you need to make it available to them. The interruptions by the members from your team are no longer distractions from your work: they *are the work*. They're moments of coaching and development. Yes, you still have individual work that only you can do, but those 'interruptions' are now part of what "only you can do".

Time is not only to be used reactively for the team but also proactively, spending it listening, asking questions, coaching. We'll talk further about this in chapters 24 and 25, but here it's enough to flag that the team leader's time is available to the people on your team, both at their request and at yours.

Things to learn: core

At the leader layer the core items were knowing and agreeing with the vision and strategy, being coachable and faithfully managing personal and allocated resources. These now change and grow due to the increased levels of responsibility and authority the team leader possesses, along with the way their modelling is multiplied through the leader layer.

Vision

The team leader needs to be able to clearly articulate the vision, not just be aware of it. This means being able to say it in the words that your church has chosen, whether that's "We will impact the nations for Christ by transforming people through the gospel to passionately treasure Christ above all else" or "Seeing all our community bow the knee to Jesus and loving others for him". They must articulate it word-for-word because they'll be passing it on to the people in their team. Yes, their team will hear it from higher layers and read it on whatever documents are handed around, but their team leaders will be the ones who will most likely explain it and clarify any questions.

This means team leaders also need to be able to *implement* it. They'll know how the ministry they're involved in and their specific team connect to the overall vision. This allows them to shoulder the responsibility for their own motivation and also communicate and re-communicate the connection to their team, because people need to know why they do the things they do. If the connection between what they're doing and the mission gets fuzzy, so too their motivation will wane. A key component of motivation is *knowing* that what you do matters. When we think that what we do doesn't matter or make a difference, we wonder why we bother. Team leaders need to keep connecting their team's work to the bigger vision for them.

Strategy

The team leader unites the team around the strategy so they can execute it. The team leader needs to be able to explain it, believe in it and show their team that it makes sense.

In the ideal world, everyone joins the team because they want to do what this ministry is doing. In the real world, people join for all kinds of reasons and ministering *this way* is sometimes not one of them. For example, the strategy of your pastoral care ministry might be to partner with small group leaders to care for the people in their small group (unless the issue is too big, in which case the matter goes to either staff or an outside professional). The focus is on people being cared for and walked alongside by their existing small group leader. Is this the only way to organize care in a church? No. Is it even the best way? Who knows, but it's how *this church* is going to do it. It's not hard to imagine a person joining that pastoral care team and not being on board with that strategy because *they* want to care for every single person. Maybe they are a deeply compassionate person, or perhaps they have some unresolved issues and need to be needed. If they execute *their own* strategy, they will cause massive problems not just for those on the pastoral care team, but also for the small group leaders and the people who need pastoral care.

It's also possible that leaders have genuinely good ideas that don't fit within the strategy. In these cases, the team leader needs to know the strategy well enough to diagnose and evaluate these ideas against it. They can't just reject them; they need to explain *why*.

Development

The team leader needs to be able to receive coaching, just like the leader does. It would be wise to stress this to those new to the layer, since people sometimes assume that coaching isn't required now that they are the team leader. Everyone needs to have the humility to take advice and feedback.

But as well as continuing to receive coaching, a team leader must also give it. Perhaps it was modelled well to them; perhaps not. Even if it was modelled well, that doesn't mean they understand what made it that way.

Learning how to give coaching can be difficult; it's where the time considerations and the heart focus shifts overlap and find expression. If the two main shifts—of investing in their team members and not seeing them as interruptions, and viewing their ministry primarily as getting things done *through* others—are made correctly, they'll be expressed concretely in coaching and development.

Stewardship

The team leader needs to continue to manage the resources they are allocated, although those resources now include humans. That's quite a corporate way of speaking about people, but it highlights that being asked to do a task or come to an extra event means a time and energy cost for that leader. This becomes significant at the ministry area layer, so the framework for it needs to start here.

Depending on the church, a team leader may be allocated a budgeted amount of money. Managing finances faithfully and responsibly is more of the same from the leader layer, though perhaps now the amounts are more substantial. If you have followed the principle of 'faithfulness buying responsibility', this should be a straightforward evolution.

The other innovation at this layer is that the team leader is now responsible for explaining to their team what the use of the money needs to achieve and the budget restrictions in terms of amounts and anything off-limits. They also need to deal with any—probably inevitable—accidental over-spending. When a leader goes over budget, what will happen? Is there a policy, or is it a case-by-case response? Does the leader who overspent need to cover the extra or does the ministry absorb the cost and spend less elsewhere? Is this a decision the team leader can make or do they need their oversight leader? This will be a new set of questions for most team leaders, and the consequences of their answers are both financial and pastoral.

Things to learn: layer-specific

The layer-specific things for the team leader to learn are skills and frameworks that enable them to care for and love the people on their team. When a team is led poorly, it negatively impacts not just that team but the effectiveness of what they are seeking to achieve. If what we seek to achieve is of eternal significance, we must do everything we can to have high-functioning teams.

The layer-specific things to learn are organized into the same categories as the previous layer, however this time the focus is on leading the team and leading *through* the team rather than being a helpful individual contributor *on* a team.

These aren't things that you can only learn *once* you reach this layer; you can learn them anytime you'd like. But it's at this layer that you'll mainly need them, so this is the *latest* that you should be learning them.

Layer summary

This layer is all about the transition from being an individual contributor to leading and serving through others:

>I succeed when you succeed.

The key distinction of the team leader layer is shifting from directly doing the ministry—leading the small group, feeding the poor—to getting that same ministry done through others. That ministry—as well as the scope of your influence—is now multiplied through the efforts of the people in your team.

What happens if they don't learn these things?

We've already seen in chapters 1 and 6, through Andrew and his team leader Dan, some of the effects of a team leader not making the transitions needed, but let's spell them out here.

Firstly, a team leader who isn't leading will stunt the growth of his or her team. They won't develop the leaders underneath them and will instead see this as a distraction from the role rather than its essential component.

Secondly, this dysfunctional team leader will compete with their team members, acting as an individual contributor performing the same ministry as their team—but doing it better. This clogs the pipeline, and the discouraged team members will stop behaving like team members. If this isn't corrected and the dysfunctional team leader continues progressing up the pipeline, this will wreak havoc on the entire ministry area.

Thirdly, the team leader will become a bottleneck and a restrictor of ministry. The job of the team leader is to multiply and amplify their teams, but this requires clarity and trust to achieve. If they don't work hard here, the new team leader will restrict and control their teams and so slow the ministry down.

Which leads lastly to the whole ministry area being affected. At the team leader layer—and above—any of these substantial pipeline misalignment errors will hinder the entire ministry area from executing its strategy.

For example, let's imagine a youth ministry. The way this ministry ecosystem works is that students graduate in from kids' ministry—some Christian and others not. The youth ministry disciples them in various ways, depending on where they are in their faith or their lack of it. Once these students finish high school, some of them will never be seen again, while the majority of those who hang around will either lead in kids' or youth ministry and the process will iterate once more.

Now imagine that the team leader of the senior high youth group doesn't actually lead at the team leader layer but functions as an individual contributor, pushing all the other leaders down the pipeline to function as leaders in title only. Without the leaders involved, contributing and discipling those students, people keep coming because they are committed, but their growth as disciples stagnates. The group externally looks healthy since numbers don't drastically drop, but for those with eyes to see it's limping along.

As a couple of year groups finish high school, an usually high percentage drop off from Jesus and church, with the majority of the remaining students heading to lead in children's ministry. Just two come to lead in youth ministry. The church has an influx of three male leaders from the unfortunate implosion of a nearby church, so there are enough for the junior high boys; the female leaders for the junior high girls are something of a skeleton crew.

These female leaders do a heroic job trying to love and disciple the female students, but they can't look after them all by themselves. The number of female students dwindles to the number these leaders can manage. By the time this second generation gets to the end of high school, there is a small but committed core group of keen Christian female students. Some of them come back and lead in the youth ministry. There are, once again, not enough leaders for the junior high girls...

This is obviously a simplified story, but you can see how one team leader not making the mental and heart revolutions required creates a problem for female leaders and disciples for generations of high school ministry.

How to help new team leaders make the transition

Clear onboarding

When a leader moves to be a team leader, you must communicate with them clearly, early and regularly about the transitions they need to make in terms of things to learn, time and heart focus. Merely being aware will help the new team leader navigate the transitions: they'll at least know what they need to grow in and what categories they're making mistakes in. Their heart focus need to change, or they cannot remain at this layer or move on to higher one. I would generally give a person two years to become proficient, assuming that after one year you can point to evidence, even if slim, that development in all three arenas is taking place.

Ministry monitoring

We'll break this concept down later in the book, but for now it's important to flag that you cannot 'set and forget' a new team leader. They need someone to walk with them and constantly remind them what's important and how things have changed. The layer above—the ministry area or unit leader—is responsible for clarifying the team leader's role and making the parameters of their authority explicit. They'll need role clarity, observation and regular checks on the progress towards critical objectives.

This supervising leader must be carefully observing the new team leader to see where they are struggling. This will not be a question of *whether* they are struggling; they *will* be. They'll need to be around enough, talking to them enough, to figure out where exactly it is, because noticing changes in heart focus and leadership values is tough. It's a good idea to meet with a new team leader more frequently to begin with so that you can help them begin to make these shifts.

One of the most helpful things you can do from the layer above is to ask questions about—and reward—what you want to see from them. For example, yes, ask the team leader whether they've put together the term's roster, but also ask if they've booked in to meet with each member of their team this term. Instead of holding them accountable for whether or not every newcomer at the event was welcomed, hold them accountable for whether or not *their team* met every newcomer. "Did Mr Jones get welcomed? Why not?" implicitly puts the focus on merely whether it happened, and the easiest way for your team leader to ensure that is for them to do it themselves—the danger they are already leaning towards. Instead ask, "Who on your team met Mr Jones?" or "Why didn't your team meet Mr Jones?" This pushes the focus to the team leader's primary responsibility for seeing ministry happen through their team.

This is where ministry monitoring begins to cross over into…

Coaching

As well as the ongoing clarity of ministry monitoring, the new team leader will also need coaching (we'll talk about this later too). The new team leader will have to learn the new skills and will require feedback to help them grow and improve. The direct responsibility for the coaching and development of team leaders rests on the layer above. As the team leader gets more comfortable with their new skills and the rhythm of their role, they'll gain intrinsic motivation (and be less afraid) to use and value them more.

What if someone cannot make the transition?

As I've been saying all along, there's no guarantee that someone will transition to the next layer and thrive there. However, just because there's no ironclad way to determine whether someone will be successful doesn't mean that sometimes there aren't good reasons for it.

There will be some people who simply find they cannot, or don't actually want to, make the transition and the heart focus revolution that goes along with it. They love frontline ministry. They've tried the team leader layer and they don't like it.

Great! There is nothing that says a person needs to progress up and through the pipeline. Higher is not better. The pipeline is an attempt to help people find where they can best serve and grow as the disciples God has made them to be. Not everyone is wired to lead at higher layers and not everyone needs to. Most people will serve at that first layer. Do everything you can to discourage the assumption that the pipeline is about getting to the top, so if people say they don't want to or don't like it then that's good: now you know and knowing is better than not knowing.

But this means you might need to create an 'expert resource pipeline'. This is a pipeline that isn't about leading people but is instead about intentionally growing in and becoming an expert in frontline or technical skills. These experts can teach those specific skills. For example, you may have a graphic design ministry because you have some keen self-taught designers or maybe one or two professionals in your congregation. They might not be interested in leading a team of graphic designers, but they may be keen to teach others the skills that they have. You'll encourage them to become more highly skilled and help create opportunities and environments where they can teach and train others. The expert resource pipeline honours elite individual contributors without forcing them to climb into roles that aren't best for them or aren't as useful to the ministry.

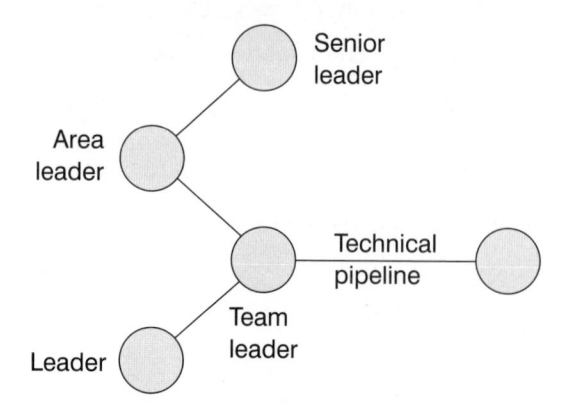

It's worth making this pipeline as official as the leadership pipeline so that everyone knows it's an actual thing with your endorsement. It also means you will minimize the effect of 'the Peter principle' in your church and ministry.

The Peter Principle, a satirical book, puts its finger on a pattern often seen in organizations: a person who is competent at their job will keep being promoted until they reach a position where they lack the skills needed and where they'll stay for the rest of their career. The principle states: "in a hierarchy every employee tends to rise to his level of incompetence".[60] The expert resource pipeline mitigates the Peter principle in your church by having an alternate track that people can take.

---

60 Laurence J Peter and Raymond Hull, *The Peter Principle*, Pan Books, London, 1970, p. 22.

One-page summary

Team leader
(from individual contributor to leading through other leaders)

Serves by leading a team of leaders.
Summary: I succeed when you succeed.
Key distinction: shift from doing the ministry to getting ministry done through others.

Things to learn: layer-specific	Things to learn: core	Things to learn: ministry-specific
• ministry distribution/delegation • performance monitoring and coaching • performance measurement • rewards and motivation • communication and climate setting • monitoring resources	*Vision:* clearly articulates and implements vision *Strategy:* leads team to unite around and execute strategy *Development:* able to give and receive coaching *Stewardship:* faithfully gets best results with allocated resources and helps team to understand resource parameters	• technical proficiency • using ministry tools, processes, procedures and reporting

Time considerations	Heart focus
• term planning • setting priorities for team • making time available for team members (at your request and theirs)	• getting results through others • success of team members • team success as personal success • accountability for the success of leaders

Team leader: layer-specific things to learn

Leading yourself
- Beginning to think strategically[61]
- Dealing with pain and criticism[62]
- Running a productive meeting[63]
- Improving understanding of emotional intelligence
- Decision-making as a team[64]

Building a team
- Recruitment for growth
- Recruitment from within[65]

Running a team
- Situational leadership and leadership styles[66]
- Life cycle of a team[67]
- Leading volunteers[68]
- Planning and assigning ministry in the team life cycle (situation-dependent)
- Distributing the ministry workload
- Accepting weaknesses[69]
- Motivating and inspiring a team[70]
- Quality communication[71]
- Giving direction with freedom[72]

---

61 Hamilton, 'The point is clarity, not labels', pp. 337-344.
62 Hamilton, 'If you're planning on not being hurt then you're planning on not being a leader', pp. 133-141.
63 Hamilton, 'Meetings are where real work is done', pp. 387-394; and 'People deserve to know the truth', pp. 281-293.
64 Hamilton, 'Decide how decisions are made', pp. 435-442.
65 See chapters 20-22 in this book.
66 Hamilton, 'Change your default style', pp. 105-110.
67 Hamilton, 'Understand the life cycle of a team', pp. 277-280.
68 Hamilton, 'Free volunteers aren't cheap', pp. 325-329.
69 Hamilton, 'Everyone already knows', pp. 219-220.
70 Hamilton, 'Communicate from the inside out', pp. 205-208.
71 Hamilton, 'Team communication is exponential', pp. 239-243.
72 Hamilton, 'You're just the leader', pp. 175-177; and 'Get out of the way of good people', pp. 317-320.

- Giving credit and taking blame[73]
- Conflict resolution
- Celebrating[74]

Developing a team
- Finding the awesome in people[75]
- Emotional climate change[76]
- Coaching: how often should you meet
- Coaching: fundamentals[77]
- Ministry monitoring[78]
- Feed-forward: people hate feedback[79]
- What to do when people let you down
- How to run an end-of-year evaluation meeting[80]

---

[73] Hamilton, 'Give credit and take blame', pp. 321-324; and 'Praise publicly', pp. 183-186.
[74] Hamilton, 'Celebrate', pp. 493-495.
[75] Hamilton, 'Find the awesome', pp. 295-301; and 'Fail forwards', pp. 209-217.
[76] Hamilton, 'Learn relaxed concern', pp. 395-398.
[77] See chapter 25 in this book; Hamilton, 'Shut up and listen', pp. 229-234; 'Ideas are born ugly', pp. 197-203; and 'Anything worth doing is worth doing badly' pp. 179-181.
[78] See chapter 24 in this book; and Hamilton, 'Treat them like children' pp. 303-306.
[79] Hamilton, 'People deserve to know the truth', pp. 281-293.
[80] See chapter 23 in this book.

18
Full outline of the pipeline: ministry area leader

Leadership development framework

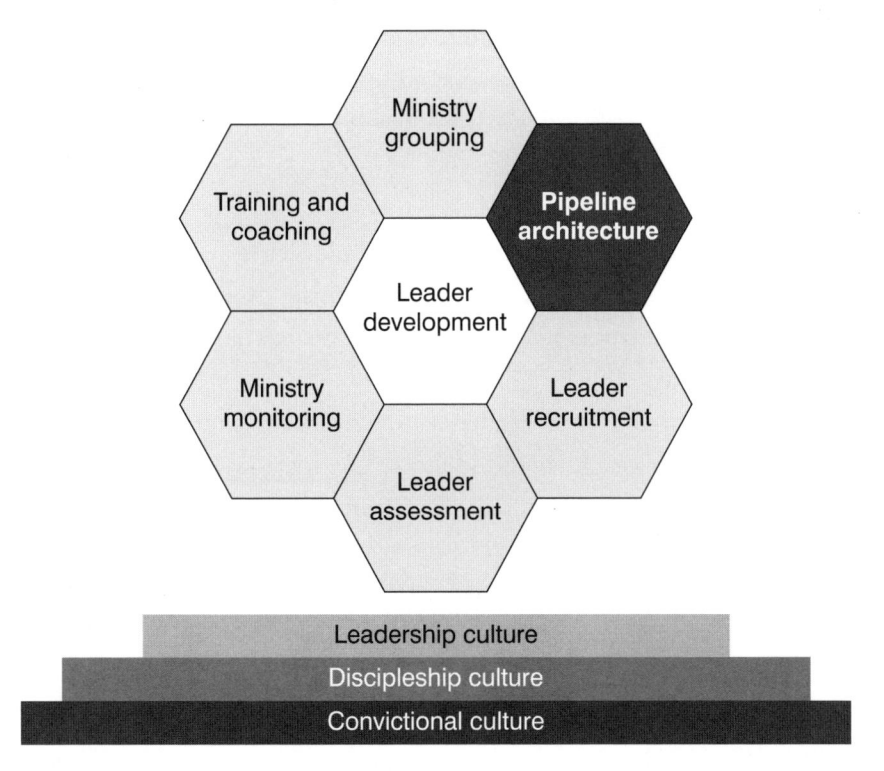

- Ministry grouping
- Training and coaching
- Pipeline architecture
- Leader development
- Ministry monitoring
- Leader recruitment
- Leader assessment

Leadership culture
Discipleship culture
Convictional culture

The move to the ministry area leader layer is another challenging transition, even tougher for some than the team leader transition. Often it is a move into full-time paid ministry. This isn't universal; some will lead an entire ministry area as an unpaid volunteer, while others will experience full-time ministry as a team leader (for example, those who join the staff as a trainee or intern) or a unit leader (in a large church).[81]

The ministry area layer also often brings with it the most leadership culture shock. There is a vast difference between running a team within a ministry area and being responsible for it entirely. It may contain multiple distinct ministries and everything that goes along with that: systems for recruiting and training, budgeting and financial responsibilities, high-level strategic planning, administration required... not to mention the jump in ambiguity and complexity. It's one thing to lead the team who lead the five-to-ten-year-olds on a Sunday morning; it's quite another to lead multiple teams across multiple services on a Sunday *and* the various teams who lead the midweek kids' groups or ministry in the local schools, *plus* organize multiple holiday camps and events throughout the year, *and* ensure that all are adequately resourced financially and with personnel.

Definition

As the name suggests, the ministry area leader leads an entire ministry area, like kids' or youth, men's or women's, small groups, integration, or perhaps the entire 10am service. Or it might be that they lead a 'purpose' area like maturity.

Often the ministry area leader will be overseeing multiple ministry units. The pastor responsible for the entire 10am Sunday service will oversee the welcoming team, the music team, the sound and behind-the-scenes team, those who lead from the platform, the morning tea team, the welcoming team and those who pastorally care for the congregation. But defining a ministry area as a collection of separate ministry units isn't always accurate; small groups aren't usually able to be decomposed into smaller units the way that a youth ministry can be.

Whether you think of a ministry area as a demographic, a function, a purpose or a collection of ministry units, the point is that it's a broad area of ministry that can be intelligently distinguished as a relatively isolated, though necessarily interdependent, sphere. While the area leader may find themselves still primarily leading teams, the difference is that they

---

81 See the appendix for an outline of the unit leader layer.

are leading more than one, and their responsibilities have greatly expanded.

Key distinction

The area leader must shift from focusing on 'doing it better' to asking, "Should we do this?" This is a move from a primary focus on efficiency to a primary focus on effectiveness, from getting better at the things we're doing—and helping others to also improve—to thinking about what to achieve and whether this is the best way to do so.

This layer is going all-in on strategic thinking. Before we wanted leaders to begin to think more strategically and long-term, but now the strategic questions are centre stage: What do we want to see happen for these people? Is what we're currently doing getting them there? Is there a better way?

People are *allowed* to ask these questions before this layer—in fact, it's better if they do—but now they *need* to. (Thinking like this earlier than this layer will be one of the possible signals that you may be looking at someone to bring to the area leader layer.)

Heart focus

As we've said all along, heart transitions are painful, and the area layer is no different. This time the shift isn't a revolution tied up with our personal pride, but is instead a relational transition that plays into our feelings of loyalty and disloyalty: an unconscious bias towards the unit of origin.

Before you were a part of the Friday youth group, and though you were involved in the wider youth ministry area and cared about its other units, you weren't invested in them. They weren't *your* ministry. But now you're the leader of the entire youth ministry area, you mustn't play favourites with that ministry unit—even though it's the one you came up the pipeline through and it's instinctually where your loyalties will lie. It's where you gained your leadership experience, learned painful lessons, had thrilling ministry successes, forged strong relational bonds. Of course you're attached!

And that needs to change. Now you need to value all units appropriately. It may be right to *value* one over another—not all units are created equal—but not due to favouritism. Favouritism can show itself through the over-allocation of financial resources, the deployment of people when they would be more useful elsewhere, or by extra personal time and attention. It's not lost on the other units, and if there's a quicker way to destroy their morale and motivation, it'd be a photo finish. Your ministry unit of origin needs to be assessed as fairly as possible alongside all the others, even though it can cause anguish since it feels disloyal to the ministry and leaders you love.

While this reprioritization is going on, the new area leader also needs to re-evaluate which team is their primary team. Where do their chief loyalties lie? It surprises most that their primary team is not the one they lead but the team they are part of. For most at this layer, this will mean the wider church staff team. And you don't turn up to team meetings with your youth ministry hat on, arguing and lobbying for your constituency. When you sit at that meeting, you need to wear your whole-church hat. This means learning to see your ministry area in its wider context, making big-picture decisions that are best for the whole church—which perhaps might mean privileging another ministry area at the expense of yours.

Wait a minute. We just talked about how the ministry area as a whole needs to be prioritized rather than an individual unit, since the *area* is where loyalty needs to lie. And yet, when it comes to the team the ministry area leader is a part of as opposed to the team they lead, they *cannot* prioritize their area? This can feel contradictory, but both actions are the result of a single principle: *not showing favouritism*. In the team I lead I am not to show favouritism by preferencing my unit of origin at the expense of the whole ministry area. In the team I am a member of I am not to show favouritism by preferencing my ministry area at the expense of the whole-church ministry. This can feel as though I'm being disloyal everywhere I turn, but if I see the underlying rationale I can work through those feelings and retrain myself to experience things the way they really are.

Time considerations

The ministry area leader's time is all about expansion. Usually, they will be spending more time doing ministry now than they did at any layer below. They also need to substantially expand the horizon of *when* they are thinking. At the team leader layer, time was generally spent thinking in three-month increments; now annual planning is the norm.

The ministry area leader thinks about budgeting, projects, campaigns and events—the calendar. They are responsible for *what* the ministry does across a year as well as *when* they do it. This is a shift even deeper into strategic thinking. They ask, "What are we doing this year? Is that the best way to achieve what we're trying to achieve?"

The ministry area leader also needs to begin thinking three to five years into the future. Where do we want to be in five years? What will be happening in our church? Obviously this won't be in the same level of detail as the weekly roster, but overall direction should be determined. It's about projecting forward what seems to be happening—or alternatively, what to change to set a new course—and considering what will need to occur to continue.

The ministry area leader must think both long-term and short-term. If they focus on the short-term and neglect the long-term, they'll be so busy watching their feet that they won't notice the pole until they smack into it. But if they value the long-term without considering the short-term, then they're planning a fantastic holiday with a fabulous itinerary that everyone is too malnourished to travel to. The area leader needs to manage the tension between the urgent and important.

The ministry area leader will be tempted to use their time to fix problems, since by now they are very good at it. It seems intuitive: they are the ones responsible, plus they have the experience. If they are a staff member the temptation will be even stronger: "Isn't this what they pay me for?"

This knee-jerk instinct needs to be resisted and replaced with careful thought. The reason they have experience solving problems is due to *their* leader wisely allowing them the opportunity to do so. (Maybe it was because their leader was lazy and absent, but let's give them the benefit of the doubt!) When a problem erupts in one of the area leader's teams, they need to resist the instinct to jump in and fix it and instead they need to spend more time with that team leader. They need to ask questions and help *the team leader* to think it out. They need to coach the team leader through solving the problem since it's actually the team leader's *direct* responsibility.

Sometimes the problem will be too big, complex or consequential for the team leader to solve. *Sometimes.* After resisting the instinct to solve every problem, the ministry area leader needs to discern which problems they *need* to solve. But even then a clever ministry area leader will bring that team leader with them on the journey. It's coaching. Ultimately, the ministry area leader spends less time solving tactical problems—taking problems away from the team leaders and therefore disempowering them—and more time building a strong team.

Lastly, the ministry area leader needs to lead through all kinds of meetings: one-to-one meetings, meetings with all the team leaders, whole team meetings, meetings that they're in but don't run, meetings, meetings and more meetings. The typical response to this reality is complaining. But leading through people means talking to them about what's happening, and talking is a meeting. These meetings might have a spectrum of formality, from *very* to *not at all*, but they're still meetings. And if the ministry area leader doesn't like meetings or finds them boring, well, now they run most of them, so it's up to them to make them better. But they're unavoidable: that's the job.[82]

Things to learn: core

Up until this point, all of the core things to learn have been about implementing and executing. This now shifts towards creating. The ministry area leader needs some autonomy to determine what is best for the ministry area while still submitting to the vision and priorities of the whole church. If you haven't already, you begin to live in the tension of autonomy and submission. This is related to the favouritism we've discussed; that same dynamic is at play when it comes to vision and strategy.

---

82 For more on what to do in meetings, see Hamilton, 'Meetings are where real work is done', pp. 387-394.

Vision

The ministry area leader needs to deeply understand the church-wide vision and be able to translate it for the specific ministry area. How does this ministry area connect to the broader vision? If the church is about making disciples and impacting the nations, then how does kids' ministry fit into this? The ministry to the poor? You are responsible for articulating the ministry-specific vision in light of where the whole church is heading.

Strategy

This is where the ministry area needs some autonomy. The ministry area leader is responsible for designing the strategy to achieve what they are seeking to achieve because it necessarily varies from area to area. This is very different to being a team leader, uniting the team around the decided strategy and executing it. As a ministry area leader, the responsibility for the strategy itself rests on your shoulders.

This newfound autonomy shouldn't be taken too far, however. Whatever strategic choices are made must still fit within the overall church strategy and integrate with other ministry areas, particularly those it rubs against. For example, if the women's ministry's strategy is for every woman to be in a female-only small group, they should have a conversation with the small groups area leader to talk about its impact on the mixed-gender small groups across the church.

Development

At this layer, personal leadership development becomes mostly self-directed because the amount of supervision is drastically lower than at the previous layer. This can be jarring, especially if your supervisor when you were a team leader did a good job and made development conversations part of the regular rhythm of your relationship. That simply cannot happen as much at the ministry area leader layer: you will be doing things your direct supervisor won't be around to watch. They also may not have the expertise to know what you need to learn to excel in your specific ministry area.

Your leader will still be helping you improve, but those conversations will start to become geared towards helping you find the paths for development rather than being the primary method of development itself. You will need to seek out books, podcasts, training courses, conferences, expert practitioners and mentors. "No-one's training and developing me" is no longer an excuse you can use. The responsibility is mostly yours.

Stewardship

The ministry area leader is responsible for shepherding the church's resources. Whether it's income from an entry fee for a weekly activity or a line item in the church budget, the ministry area leader creates a ministry-specific budget and makes decisions about where and on what that income should be spent. This will be new territory. Team leaders had to manage the money assigned to them, but most of the time it was to be spent on specific items or activities. The ministry area leader decides what those items or activities should be. They need to think through questions like: What does wise stewardship of these resources look like? How much should be spent on advertising? How much should be spent on tangible consumables? How much should be spent on training and development of leaders? Is it appropriate to spend any of this money on celebrating?

Things to learn: layer-specific

While maintaining a relational orientation to ministry—ministry is fundamentally about people and Jesus—the ministry area leader also needs to pay attention to the ministry itself. This is the distinction between working *in* the ministry and working *on* the ministry. They need to think about structures, systems and processes, as well as the people who will exist within them, *for the sake* of those people. It's loving to pay attention to these non-people factors because when you neglect systems it's people who get hurt.[83]

From a pure skill set perspective, the ministry area layer is probably the hardest transition since it comes with the most extensive volume and variety of new things to learn.

---

83 See Hamilton, 'Why systems matter', pp. 375-381.

Layer summary

The one sentence summary of the ministry area leader layer is:

> I succeed when we succeed differently.

The challenge of this layer is leading multiple ministry units doing different ministries. If I'm the kids' minister, that ministry may have a variety of age ranges across the Sunday ministry and mid-week ministry, plus a schools ministry, an administration and resources team, and maybe even a media and photography team. These units are all quite different from each other, and the area leader needs to understand what success looks like for each one and lead them all to succeed accordingly.

Why this matters

There are four main consequences if ministry area leaders don't transition properly. Each of these consequences can manifest on its own, but often they wrap around each other as a package deal.

First, as with every layer, if a ministry area leader doesn't turn the corner in the pipeline, they will begin to clog it. One way they may do this is by holding team leaders accountable for the wrong things. If team leaders are asked questions about and rewarded for frontline leader ministry, then the ministry area leader is training that team leader to clog the pipeline. Team leaders must be held accountable for team leader work: getting ministry done *through* their teams.

Another way ministry area leaders clog the pipeline is by not instilling the right heart focus in the layers they lead because they don't understand the pipeline mindset. For example, they insist on choosing the best individual contributors or the longest-serving to move to the team leader layer rather than selecting those who are true potential team leaders.[84]

The second main consequence of a ministry area leader failing to transition is that team leaders will be disempowered. Not only will there

---

[84] Choosing team leaders is one of the most critical responsibilities of the ministry area leader, and useful selection criteria can be a particularly challenging hurdle, so there is an entire chapter on it in this book: chapter 21.

be the standard pipeline problem of competing with the layer below you, but those down at the leader layer will be accidentally trained to bypass their team leaders and bring all of their issues to the ministry area leader. Over time this teaches everyone that the team leaders don't have any authority or function and the pipeline will begin to collapse.

The third consequence ties into this erosion of the team leader layer: the ministry area leader will start to drown in details. If they are trying to handle the things they are responsible for *while also* solving problems that team leaders should handle *while also* trying to do the rest of the team leader's ministry, they will quickly be overwhelmed. They will drop balls and cut corners, all the while brewing a cocktail of frustrations with leaders and team leaders who "aren't doing their jobs properly". This anger will eventually burst out, directed at everyone but themselves, and the unjust accusations will accelerate the ministry area's tailspin, while the ministry area leader still doesn't realize their woes are self-inflicted.

The final consequence is that the whole church will be wounded. This may sound like catastrophizing, but a poor ministry area leader will impact more than just that one ministry. Ministry areas don't exist in separate spaces, even if they appear quite siloed. They feed and bleed into each other. Kids' and youth ministries are closely linked, and if a church has a significant young adult population then that will also factor in. A weak welcoming and integration ministry will have noticeable effects on the rate of growth of the entire church. And if small groups are struggling, that will flow on into the maturity of people across the church and impact evangelism and welcoming.

In the end, a ministry full of struggling and disempowered leaders will create a toxic culture that will seep across a church. Dysfunction never stays sealed away. At the ministry area layer, errors hurt the whole church's ability to execute its plans, and a clog in the pipeline can create a leadership vacuum that can last for years before it can be rehabilitated and cleared.[85]

---

[85] If you are or you know a struggling ministry area leader, I've got a list of warning signs and ways to help at revcraighamilton.com.

One-page summary

Ministry area leader
(from leading leaders to overseeing several ministry units)

Serves by leading an entire ministry area (i.e. children's, youth).
Summary: I succeed when we succeed differently.
Key distinction: moving from 'doing it better' to "Should we do it?"

Things to learn: layer-specific	Things to learn: core	Things to learn: ministry-specific
• designing roles • designing strategy • setting priorities • dealing with complexity • coping with high visibility, especially from below	*Vision:* translates church-wide vision for ministry area *Strategy:* designs ministry strategy for area that fits within church-wide strategy and integrates with other areas *Development:* self-directs development *Stewardship:* effective in managing resources	• technical proficiency • using ministry tools, processes, procedures and reporting

Time considerations	Heart focus
• three-to-five-year planning • equally valuing short-term and long-term • spending less time solving tactical problems • spending more time building a strong team • leading via meetings	• valuing all units appropriately • viewing own ministry area in the context of the wider church and making big-picture decisions

Ministry area leader: layer-specific things to learn
Leading yourself
- Maintaining a posture of learning and listening
- Functioning in ambiguity
- Working without supervision or guidance
- Comfortable being a public figure
- Self-regulating from basic work week to 24/7 on call
- Understanding common cognitive biases
- Advanced emotional intelligence
- Balancing energy and efficiency[86]

Building a ministry area
- Ministry grouping[87]
- Selecting team leaders[88]
- Grasping paradigms and translating them into a specific church context
- Purpose and programs[89]
- Competent recruiting[90]

Running a ministry area
- Creating clarity[91]
- Making your teams wise
- Setting overall direction for teaching
- Curriculum development
- Strategic thinking[92]
- Systems thinking[93]
- Prioritizing

---

86 Hamilton, 'Energy is more efficient than efficiency', pp. 191-195.
87 See chapters 14 and 15 in this book.
88 See chapter 21 in this book.
89 Hamilton, 'What are you trying to achieve?', pp. 345-348; 'Think in steps', pp. 355-358; and 'Hold hands with your programs', pp. 359-363.
90 See chapters 20, 21 and 22 in this book.
91 See chapter 24 in this book.
92 Hamilton, 'The point is clarity, not labels', pp. 337-344.
93 Hamilton, 'Why systems matter', pp. 375-381.

- Leading effective meetings[94]
- Fundraising
- Resource planning
- Leading in unfamiliarity
- Complexity
- Understanding the ecosystem[95]
- Change management
- Dealing with emergencies
- Negotiating
- Having hard conversations

Developing a ministry area
- Transition accountability
- Building external relationships
- Skipping layer meetings

---

[94] Hamilton, 'Meetings are where real work is done', pp. 387-394; 'Ignore the org-chart', pp. 429-434; and 'Hellos and goodbyes matter', pp. 443-445.
[95] Hamilton, 'Where is here', pp. 349-354.

19
Full outline of the pipeline: senior leader

Leadership development framework

- Ministry grouping
- Training and coaching
- Pipeline architecture
- Leader development
- Ministry monitoring
- Leader recruitment
- Leader assessment

Leadership culture
Discipleship culture
Convictional culture

There is probably no church position that has been more debated or has experienced more change in the past 50 years than that of the senior leader. In the West, on a rising tide of prosperity, expectations of excellence in all spheres of life have risen and churches have become more attentive to the quality of their ministries. As cultural Christianity has waned, the biblical literacy of unchurched people has dropped and assumptions about life have become diverse. This has led to churches being more sensitive to the differences among people and hence ministry and outreach has become vastly more complex and requires a larger pastoral staff. This increased complexity has led to a transformation in the responsibilities of senior leadership.

It's no longer enough to be a competent Bible teacher with a desire to care for the flock through pastoral home and hospital visits. Senior leaders are now *leaders*, a role that was not always so prominently necessary. There is also an increase in the administrative, secretarial and compliance demands on the senior leader from within the church itself as well from external structures, both denominational and governmental (most of which is good and right).

Parallel to all of this has been the debate over what factors produce a healthy, numerically increasing, faithful, unified, energetic and loving church that grows disciples who make disciples. Many have championed the importance of a healthy small groups ministry; others have stressed ministries to children and youth. Factors proposed include having adequate and attractive physical space; the role of laity in planning and decision-making; excellent biblical preaching; and an outstanding welcoming and integration ministry. Should we minimize denominational affiliation, either in terms of liturgy or branding, or create a thicker liturgical life with a renewed sense of the transcendent? And there are arguments for the importance of a highly competent and specialized pastoral staff, while others promote the agility of the generalist.

Laid out like this, the sheer scope argues quite strongly against one single factor that explains or catalyses a healthy church. However, within this mosaic, I would argue that the senior minister is a factor near the top of the list.

I would also hasten to add that the role of the senior leader in a small church is vastly different to what's required in a large church. The typical small church teaches the senior leader to *react* to circumstances and to primarily lead by *enabling* the initiative of others, whereas the large church wants a senior leader who will *respond* and *initiate*. The small church senior leader is a jack-of-all-trades, whereas the large church needs a minister who can specialize in a few areas, delegate other responsibilities to dedicated staff and then spend a large portion of time leading those staff. Smaller churches place a premium on relationships and having a direct connection to a senior leader who conducts one-to-one ministry. The large church typically needs a senior minister who is an excellent preacher, who can inspire and mobilize the church to a vision, who works primarily *through* their staff, and who understands the value of relating to people in groups rather than primarily one-to-one.

An increased understanding of these profound differences has led to many church nominators, pulpit search committees and denominational boards and officials to question and overtly reject the traditional wisdom of becoming a senior minister of a large church by first serving in two or three smaller parishes. These people have seen that serving as the sole pastoral staff member is not good preparation for becoming a senior leader of a large church, since the assumptions and instincts honed and calibrated for the small church are harmful in the new context.

The purpose behind all this background is to demonstrate that the senior leader layer will shape the church the most directly while also having the most variety in the specifics of what that role entails across churches and denominations. In some churches, the senior leader will be an individual supported and assisted by other ministers or committees. In others, the senior leadership will be a *group* of leaders—a board or a plurality of elders. There may be any number of other configurations.

The senior leader layer, as the name suggests, is whoever makes up the highest stratum of leadership where the final authority lies—humanly speaking—at the local church level. This may be a straightforward decision, with the answer already made for you by your denominational structures, or it might take more thought and discussion to work out.

Whatever the church's size, the senior leader layer will require proficient leadership over a range of skills. Errors at this layer—whether in the choice of senior leadership *itself*, the personnel choices made by the senior leadership, or mistakes made by the senior leadership in other arenas—are often more severe than at other layers simply because of the number of those affected. The range and quality of leadership required at this layer makes it demanding even for the most gifted.

One final preliminary comment is that it has been increasingly common for churches to follow the military model of the unit commander with an executive officer. This means they structure themselves with a senior pastor who typically focuses on preaching and vision and an executive pastor who takes the lion's share of the other traditional responsibilities of the senior leader layer (including hiring and oversight of the rest of the staff). In this structure the senior leader layer is probably best conceived of as shared across a two-person team with the senior pastor being the 'senior-est'.

Definition

The senior leader layer can be one of the hardest to define, due partly as explained by the variety of church polity, but also because of the range of possible pipelines that can exist across churches and the varying complexity of the ministries offered. Pipeline layers concertina and collapse into each other when they're not needed. The vast majority of churches will not need the unit leader layer. Some may not have the ministry area leader layer, with the senior leader instead overseeing all ministry areas. Some churches may not even have the team leader layer (though in most cases I would advise its creation as soon as possible).

The pipelines that a senior leader may be overseeing could look like any of these:

Same layer

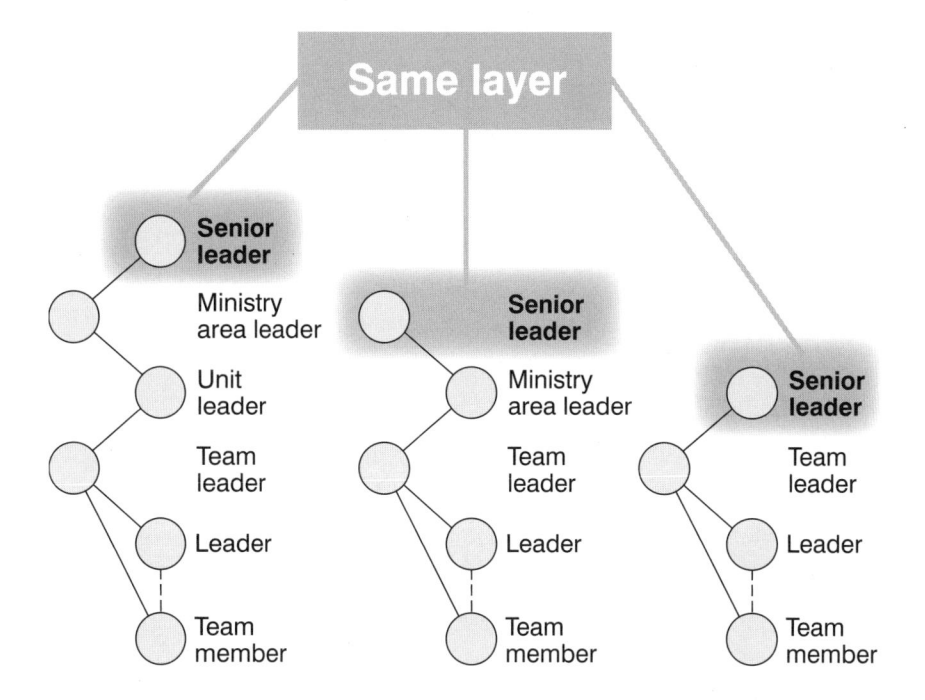

```
Senior leader — Ministry area leader — Unit leader — Team leader — Leader — Team member
Senior leader — Ministry area leader — Team leader — Leader — Team member
Senior leader — Team leader — Leader — Team member
```

No matter how much all the layers concertina into each other, the two outer layers always remain: the leader and senior leader layers. As you expand or contract these middle layers, the leader layer remains basically the same, while the senior leader layer changes dramatically. Some elements in the role remain constant, but others change significantly as they absorb the ministry area or unit leader responsibilities and mindsets. A further factor that makes the senior leader layer challenging to quantify is the different expectations of diocesan and regulatory bodies.

As with every layer of the pipeline, you will need to modify and translate the requirements so that they make sense within your particular context and constraints.

Key distinction

The buck stops here. There may be a bishop or some other diocesan official somewhere else, but this is the highest local level of authority. This layer is responsible for the growth and discipleship of the entire local church or para-church ministry.

Linked with this, and worth making explicit, is that this layer is not merely responsible for those already in the church and disciples of Jesus. The leadership at this layer, like all the others, is shaped by the cross, which means it will also be concerned for those outside its walls and the sheep who aren't currently within the fold.

This external focus is closely linked to the internal responsibility to disciple the whole church, because as the church follows Jesus and becomes more like him, they will become more and more concerned with the lost, the harassed and the helpless. Like Jesus, they will expend effort and energy to see others saved. Therefore, the senior leader layer is also responsible for asking, "How can our church bless a wider circle?" Others in the church hopefully already have a heart for the nations, but it is the senior leader layer's responsibility to help the *entire church* to catch that global vision.

Heart focus

The heart focus here is made up of three separate shifts. Two of them are finalizing shifts where the majority of the transition work should have been done earlier, while the third is unique to this layer.

The first heart shift is to value the success of others as personal success. This battle should have taken place way back at the team leader layer, but unfortunately it can be a difficult war to win. Sometimes what looks like victory is just a truce or the opposition going underground to strike again later. Often that later is now.

The second shift is to value multiple ministry areas and think in terms of a portfolio of strategies. This means asking questions like: How do all the ministry areas of this church work together to achieve our purpose? How can all the strategies dovetail and reinforce each other to maximize our effectiveness? How do we rein in any disparate forces?

Moving from one ministry area to all ministry areas has parallels with the shift that occurs for ministry area leaders as they move from one unit to multiple units. For the senior leader, this transition is ramped up because the ministries will significantly broaden in variety and number, and thus complexity. The temptation is unsurprisingly to stick to the known, but the senior leader needs to come to grips with the ministries' individual strategies, understand how they interact with each other at the macro level and ensure that this variety works together as a whole.

The new third shift is that the senior leader has the final responsibility for their congregation. This means additional psychological pressure as they come to terms with this reality: the cavalry is not coming.

Time considerations

Comparing the time considerations of the ministry area leader and the senior leader, you find that the vast majority are identical. These all must continue:

- three-to-five-year planning
- equally valuing the short-term and long-term
- spending less time solving tactical problems
- spending more time building a strong team
- leading through team meetings.

At this layer, the senior leader must spend a *significant* amount of time with the ministry area leaders building a strong team.

In an orchestra, the conductor doesn't make a sound, but everyone looks to them for leadership. As the famed conductor of the Boston Philharmonic Orchestra Benjamin Zander put it, the conductor "depends for his power on the ability to make other people powerful".[96] That's the job of the senior leader: making the ministry area leaders powerful. The senior leader must spend time with them, invest in them, build and develop them, problem-solve with them, find the awesome within them and engage and multiply it for the good of the world and the glory of God. Time spent here is multiplied across the church.

At this layer, more than any other, the leader must be comfortable achieving through others. The ministry is too broad to be done by one person. Even in a very small church, ministry will be done by others in the congregation —it just may not be *formal* ministry. Ministry will be being done and led

---

96 Benjamin Zander, 'The transformative power of classical music', TED, 27 June 2008, accessed 8 December 2020. www.youtube.com/watch?v=r9LCwl5iErE

by others, and so the senior leader must invest in *them* as a priority.

The other unique shift in time allocation is spending more time on concerns and people external to the church. The senior leader layer will invest time into relationships with neighbouring churches and their leaders to be a support to them in the mutual work of the gospel and in order to learn from and be sharpened by different paradigms and practices. They may even begin spending increasing time investing in the broader church structures to which they belong, whether diocesan bodies or fellowships and networks. They may serve on boards or committees; they may lecture at local theological colleges; they may speak at various conferences or other churches' gatherings. As the face of the church, the senior leader will spend time with local school, business and government leaders—not to build fame or influence but for the good of the wider community and for the spread of the gospel in that place.

This transition can be a difficult path to navigate as there is no formula for how to assign time to external versus internal work. Some may end up spending too much time on external concerns. This could all be useful for the gospel while still being detrimental to their specific church. In other circumstances this will all be wasted time, adverse to the gospel and only about the senior leader ego-stroking. Others spend too little time on external concerns and so find themselves stuck in a rut with an anaemic and myopic vision and no community influence.

The time spent on external concerns is from one point of view a sacrifice by the whole church as their leader invests in people who are not them. But it is also in the best interests of the local church in that it pays dividends in unexpected ways. When the senior leader spends time with other leaders in other contexts solving other problems, growth and development will take place. There is no-one within the church responsible for developing and coaching the senior leader, and a church is blessed by having a growing leader.

Things to learn: core

The senior leader is responsible for their core things to learn, but this doesn't mean that they must be devised by them alone. They may be but they don't *have* to be (though it's best if they are involved in the process). Whether the senior leader decides these unilaterally or as part of a wider team, they must own them and champion them with all they've got.

Vision

The senior leader layer is responsible for creating, guarding and modelling the vision of the church *in line with the Bible* rather than any personal desires. The vision for the church cannot be to increase both the appreciation for and playing of the bagpipes in the surrounding suburbs, even if a noble dream. The vision must be an outworking of God's revealed priorities, contextualized and formulated for this specific church at this specific point in time.

As well as creating it (and by *creating* I mean applying the vision and mission given to the people of God in the Scriptures), the senior leader must guard that vision. People will continually join the church who will have their own strong ideas as to what its vision should be. You must prevent your church from being distracted towards other worthy but less central bagpipe-related pursuits.

Lastly, as previously discussed, the senior leader will need to embody and model the vision, values and culture of the church in their lives and decisions.

Strategy

At this layer, as well as coordinating multiple ministry strategies to work together as a coherent whole, strategy will also involve thinking about *priorities* for the church. In light of the vision, what are the key strategic priorities at this exact moment? What is most essential for us *right now*?

In the same way that others will have alternative ideas for the vision, some in the church will also have opinions about priorities. Usually their priorities will either be the ministries that they are involved in leading or those that most impact them. You may be convinced that the top priority is to plant a church in the suburb over to the east and they will think it best to plant in the suburb to the west. You'll be working towards rebuilding the kids' ministry and they will feel the priority is expanding the ministry to the poor. Both options may be important and needed.

It is the senior leader's responsibility to see the whole and, after gathering wisdom from trusted sources, to make the decision. This strategic prioritization will have far-reaching effects, from the calendar to budgeting to what is preached on and spoken about from the front, and it may even impact personnel movements between ministries and staffing levels.

Development

As we mentioned earlier, at the senior leader layer development is entirely self-directed. There's no-one local to report to or who is responsible for coaching and developing you. You need to take the initiative and the steps required to continue to grow as a leader.

Stewardship

This layer is the chief fundraiser for the entire church. Ministry costs money, and the senior leader is responsible for finding the funds required to see the vision become a reality. This means instruction on money and generosity in the normal rhythms of the church's preaching and teaching, managing the church's money in a transparent and trustworthy manner, and leading any extra giving programs such as capital campaigns.

This layer is also responsible for faithfully stewarding the allocation and prioritization of resources, both financial and human. In some church structures, budgeting may not be the sole decision of a single senior leader, but even then it is still the responsibility of the senior leader layer. This layer must decide on the best allocation of funds based on the strategic priorities. If the priority is the new church plant then it makes no sense to put all the money into buying new carpet and a jumping castle for the current site.

Things to learn: layer-specific

From one perspective, the senior leader layer is simply a continuation and intensification of the ministry area layer. Your thinking needs to continue to be relational and structural, holistic and atomistic. You're thinking about the content of what you teach while also considering the systems your listeners must operate within. You focus on your patch while also looking beyond.

Integrating ministry units becomes integrating ministry areas. In this sense, the senior leader transition is a change in degree rather than kind.

However, due to the increased scope, complexity and responsibility of the senior leader layer, this shift can also feel completely new, and it can be easy to get intimidated and lost in the transition. And, for most people, there is no-one helping and guiding you through it like there should be at other layers. Fortunately, while the pipeline doesn't give you a 'guide by your side', it does provide a 'roadmap for the role'.

The senior leader layer has the fewest layer-specific things to learn out of all the layers, but it does rely upon the proficiency built up previously. Any cheating or fudging as you made your way through the pipeline will come back to bite you. And if you skipped any of the four core layers on your way to the senior layer, you have things to learn to backfill, and a treacherously steep learning curve.

Layer summary

The one-sentence summary of the senior leader layer is:

> I succeed when our ministries succeed together.

The challenge of the previous layer was that it involved leading multiple units doing different ministries. The general shape of that challenge continues into the senior leader layer, except now the differences are even more pronounced since it's not within one area but within one wider church. The objective is integration and alignment to enable the whole church to be effective for the kingdom.

The challenge is also increased because, depending on the church, there may be too many ministry areas for the senior leader to understand them deeply or know how they achieve success. Instead, the senior leader will need to depend on the expertise of the ministry area leaders, the systems for reporting what is happening in those ministry areas, and their own wisdom to assess the strategic plans of the ministry area leaders.

Why does this matter?

As we've seen, this layer has a lot of parallels with the ministry area layer in terms of its skills and competencies and in how it generally functions. But when it comes to the heart focus shift, it parallels the team leader layer in working *through* others and getting out of the way *of* others.

And like the team leader layer, this is also an extraordinarily dangerous layer. If the senior leader usurps the ministry area leader's authority, this will ripple down that entire pipeline, pushing each layer into the layer below. And ripples in one ministry area pipeline can cause problems in its neighbours. For example, a person involved in two ministries can bring bad habits from the affected pipeline into another one. If the leaders in that pipeline don't notice the newly aberrant behaviour, then the infection will spread throughout that pipeline as well—and the chain reaction will continue. If the senior leader layer does its job poorly, most people in the church will suffer the consequences.

Also like team leaders, senior leaders might have to give up doing the ministry they enjoyed and replace that with ministry that is new, unfamiliar, risky and hard. The temptations that plague the team leader layer—going back to the familiar, the comfortable, the successful, the highly praised—are again active.

Lastly, this layer may involve tearing down a ministry that the senior leader themselves built previously but that no longer fits the direction of the church or has run its course. The sheer power of nostalgia can make it extremely difficult to make, from the outside perspective, the easy and obvious decision. This indecisiveness, like all indecisiveness, can lead to a lack of confidence from others. It can also hinder the church since resources—financial and human—continue being used by a dying ministry instead of being better deployed elsewhere.[97]

It is worth saying that this conundrum is only an issue when you have a senior leader who has come from within. The hired-from-outside senior leader can close ministries with no personal attachment or concern. This brings its own challenges, especially if the newly-appointed senior leader doesn't understand the cultural and nostalgic loyalty and significance of

---

97 For an in-depth look at the signs of a struggling senior leader, visit revcraighamilton.com.

these ministries or doesn't understand the more subtle contributions a ministry might make. In either case, decisions must be made thoughtfully and carefully, but they *must be made*.

One-page summary

Senior leader
(from leading a ministry area to overseeing all ministry areas)

Serves by leading the entire church.
Summary: I succeed when our ministries succeed together.
Key distinction: the buck stops here; how can our church bless a wider circle?

Things to learn: layer-specific	Things to learn: core	Things to learn: ministry-specific
• Building a strong team • Leading the 'culture' side of church life • Leading from a distance • Shouldering final responsibility	*Vision:* takes responsibility for creating, guarding and modelling the vision and values of the church in line with the Bible *Strategy:* thinks strategically about, and sets priorities for, the church as a whole *Development:* wholly self-directed development *Stewardship:* faithfully allocates and prioritizes resources; funds the vision	• technical proficiency • using ministry tools, processes, procedures and reporting

Time considerations	Heart focus
• spends significant time with ministry area leaders • spends increased time with external people and wider concerns	• accepts final responsibility • values the success of others rather than hands-on success • shifts from an individual strategy to a portfolio of strategies

Senior leader: layer-specific things to learn

Leading yourself
- Loyalty to the wider church over a single ministry
- Helping set the culture and pace for the whole church
- Succession planning[98]

Building a church of ministry areas
- Leading from the pulpit
- Seizing opportunities
- Building a strong team

Running a church of ministry areas
- Thinking large and small
- Making unpleasant decisions
- Seeing what could be
- Being the chief fundraiser
- Using authority without vetoing
- Understanding how each ministry functions
- Communicating with multiple constituencies
- The courage of vision
- First-principles ministry in a changing environment
- Guarding the culture
- Resource allocation
- Creating a thriving team environment
- Dealing with the media and responding to national/global issues
- Anticipatory leadership
- Initiating and managing change
- Deeper systems thinking[99]

---

[98] This depends on the polity and systems of your wider church structure. However, you should seek to do what you can within the bounds you have to operate within to ensure the continued strength of the church after you have gone.

[99] See Hamilton, 'Why systems matter', pp. 375-381.

Developing a church of ministry areas
- Being a coach/consultant for ministry area leaders
- Creating a developmental church

Pipeline planning meeting 6

The goal for this meeting is to decide on one or (at most) two ministry areas where you will explicitly install the pipeline architecture and prepare a timeline for doing so. This will be the first of three components you'll need to line up; you'll set up the others in the next two pipeline planning meetings.

If you set people homework after the previous meeting, start this one with their presentations about which pipelines are active and who has which roles in their areas.

By this point you should agree on which pipelines are active in your church, whether you need the unit leader layer and what you will call each layer. Also, you will have just read the detailed breakdown of what ministry needs to be happening at each pipeline layer. You're now ready to plan the installation of some pipelines!

When deciding on which ministry you're going to start with, pick the one where you have the best chance of the pipeline being installed with ease and enthusiasm. You want it to be a big, fat, unmitigated success that builds momentum and positive associations around all things pipeline. This will make it easier for you to convince the gatekeepers, the naysayers and the unsure middle to get on board when it rolls out in their ministry because they'll have seen it triumph.

Those two factors, ease of installation and enthusiasm, may not be present in full measure in any one ministry at your church. Pick the best option out of the unideal ones. Lean towards enthusiasm over ease, since installing the pipeline will only ever be *relatively* easy. Going with enthusiasm means that, even though you'll need to keep people motivated to persevere, you'll be starting from a better position.

There's no one sure-fire way to install the pipeline. As you implement it in one ministry, you will learn how implementation goes at your church rather than just in this book. Different churches will have different hurdles and varying ways they are already ahead of the curve that can be leveraged to shrink the size of the change.

Having chosen your ministry areas, the next objective of this meeting is to put together a plan for how you'll roll this pipeline thinking out into this ministry area. You can't just declare: "This is now happening. Do it!" This is essentially a change management exercise and you need to help people come with you, so gather all the brains you can and squeeze as much genius out of them as possible.[100]

Any change is, on some level, the implicit answer to a problem. How will you help people see and feel the problems that pipeline architecture will solve? How will you help explain the philosophy to them? Which chapters from this book will you read with them—6 and 7 maybe? Who are the small group of allies that you'll gather first? How will you gather them? What steps will you take? If you've chosen two ministries, will you combine forces and run co-meetings with both areas or will you work independently with your teams and only talk together informally?

The ministry area leader will need to be the one implementing this plan, so resist the urge to plan every last detail for them. The role of this whole pipeline planning team is to help cover all the angles and provide as much advice and perspective as they can. Identify potential allies and possible roadblocks and plot out some milestones.

By the end of this meeting you should have a draft plan and timeline for how you'll roll the pipeline out into the ministry area. Don't forget this roll-out will start in a few months—we've still got two more pipeline planning meetings to help get you ready.

---

[100] You might want to re-read Hamilton, 'Red Queen syndrome', pp. 447-472, to re-familiarize yourself with the basic pieces of successful change.

Layer summary

	Explanation	Summary	Key distinction	Layer-specific skills
Senior leader	Serves by leading the entire church.	I succeed when our ministries succeed together.	The buck stops here; how can our church bless a wider circle?	• self-directed ongoing growth as a disciple and helping your team grow • selection of key positions • willing to address ministry monitoring problems quickly with key staff • using the power of veto judiciously
Ministry area leader	Serves by leading an entire ministry area.	I succeed when we succeed differently.	Moving from 'doing it better' to "Should we do it?"	• ongoing growth as a disciple and helping your team grow • leading self • leading the ministry in teaching and structure • leading the ministry as a ministry area • leading the ministry as a team of individuals • designing roles • designing strategy • selecting team leaders • developing team leaders • dealing with complexity • coping with high visibility, especially from below • leading effective meetings • being less dumb • advanced wisdom on dealing with people
Team leader	Serves by leading a team of leaders.	I succeed when you succeed.	Shift from doing the ministry to getting ministry done through others.	• ongoing growth as a disciple and helping your team grow • team dynamics • running a team • developing a team • entrance to higher-level leadership • recruitment
Leader/ team member	Serves by directly leading group members.	I succeed when I succeed.	Shift from doing ministry alone to doing ministry with others.	• ongoing character development • handling the Bible • tools to be an everyday evangelis • loving your team • developing a healthy mind • using a healthy mind

Time considerations	Focus and feelings
• spends significant time with ministry area leaders • spends increased time with external people and wider concerns	• focusing significant energy on only two or three key, long-cycle objectives • from immediate gratification to sustained progress • taking advice from parish council/elders • educating parish council/elders so they provide informed advice • asking questions and listening to a broad spectrum rather than a single trusted advisor
• annual planning—budgets, projects, campaigns • three-to-five-year planning • setting priorities for ministry area • spend less time solving tactical problems • leading by team meetings • financial management	• main job is to grow team leaders • integrating the ministry of the teams directly reporting • equally valuing the short-term and long-term • able to view own ministry area in the context of the wider church and able to make big-picture decisions (even at the expense of own area)
• term planning • making time available for team members • setting priorities for team	• getting results through others • success of team members • accountability for the success of leaders • team success as personal success • visible integrity
• arrival and departure • meeting personal due dates for projects (usually short-term) • managing own time	• getting results through personal proficiency • high-quality work

20
Leader recruitment

Leadership development framework

- Ministry grouping
- Training and coaching
- Pipeline architecture
- **Leader development**
- Ministry monitoring
- **Leader recruitment**
- Leader assessment

Leadership culture
Discipleship culture
Convictional culture

The first two pieces of the leadership development framework—ministry grouping and pipeline architecture—are usually the most foreign out of the six. Now we turn our attention to the remaining pieces, which are probably already active in your church to some degree. These chapters will sharpen what you're already doing.

The third piece of the leadership development framework is recruitment. Having considered the culture that cradles and supports the entire framework, designed the ministry grouping that will help you achieve what you seek, and begun thinking like a pipeline architect, now you're ready to bring real people into these abstract structures you've created.

We'll first discuss recruiting volunteers from within your church, and then in the two chapters following we'll talk about selecting team leaders and hiring staff for the pipeline.

When it comes to recruiting, often the first thing we think of is that moment when we ask someone to join a ministry. But before we get to the words you use and the methods you employ (important but not as important as you might think), we need to step back and get our heads around the theological foundation of recruitment and its three main drivers.

Increase the pond

You make recruitment easier by increasing the pool of people who are, at some level, willing to be recruited. This happens as the Bible is taught and the Spirit applies that teaching to people's hearts and lives.

There are lots of different ways this teaching and application can happen so that people develop a passion to serve. It should be a part of your weekly preaching and teaching. It should be embedded in your small groups and one-to-one ministries. You should look for ways to set a culture of serving, such as highlighting and celebrating those who serve throughout the year or talking about that expectation with those who newly join your church. Don't just think sermons. Leverage as many opportunities as you can to regularly demonstrate the importance of the lordship of Jesus over every aspect of life and the significance, excitement and privilege of the mission he has left for us to do.

As you teach from the Bible the lordship of Jesus and his call to people to carry their cross and follow him, this hopefully sees people become disciples—which means more people who might swim in your pond. It also equally hopefully sees people grow as disciples who understand the mission Jesus has left for them and the foundational nature of sacrificial servanthood. Not everyone who is a follower of Jesus is necessarily ready to be recruited. We all know people who are genuinely converted but perfectly happy to turn up on a Sunday, listen to a sermon, say hi to a few people and then leave, not to be seen again until next week. They are disciples of Jesus, but they aren't in the pond you can recruit from. The way to get them into that pond is to disciple them.

Know what you're thinking

You need to know what the Bible says about serving and discipleship, not just (or even mainly) so you can speak it to others, but most importantly so you can speak it to yourself.

Do you believe that the goal of discipleship is to be conformed to the image of Jesus? Do you believe that serving is Christlike, an essential part of discipleship? Do you believe that becoming like Jesus is the best thing a person can become, the path to real joy? Do you believe that serving others is a mix of joy and hardship and joy *in* hardship? Do you believe that ministry is motivated by love for God and love for neighbour and so is a natural consequence and expression of that love? Do you believe that every person called to Christ is also called to ministry? Do you believe that ministry is an act of worship? Do you believe that ministry done for Jesus glorifies him? Do you believe that the pastor's job is to equip and release people for ministry? Do you believe that within God's family we belong to each other, need each other and have obligations to each other? Do you believe that God has given us gifts and abilities so that we can serve others? Do you believe ministry is about partnering with God, an enormous privilege?

If you do, you won't be apologetic about asking someone to give up his or her precious time to serve in ministry. If you're tempted to feel as though you *shouldn't* be asking anyone to serve, it's either because your ministry actually is a waste of time—in which case, stop doing it—or it's because you don't believe some of these things right down to the core of who you are.

Believing these things doesn't mean it's always right to ask *this specific* person to join *this specific* ministry. Maybe this isn't the ministry for their skills or perhaps they are already very involved in serving. But that's different to feeling guilty about asking someone to sacrifice their time to serve in the first place. Your recruitment should never be, "Sorry, would you please come and help me?"

Ministry is all about growing as a disciple, expressing that discipleship, glorifying God, serving others and doing something significant. Make sure you have that rock solid and crystal clear in your own heart and mind before you begin recruiting others.

Character and prayer

Before we go any further, let's unearth two foundational assumptions. Before we get to the 'how' of recruiting, while we're still on the 'who'— character can never be emphasized enough. It's very rare that people's leadership crashes into a ditch because they lacked skills; far more often it's a lack of character that demolishes a ministry. In the pastoral epistles, the apostle Paul underlines this importance in his list of qualities that need to be looked for in those who wish to be leaders (1 Tim 3:1-13; Titus 1:5-9). When you're thinking through who to recruit, make sure you ask, "Is their character becoming increasingly Christlike?"

The recruiter must also be prayerful as they consider who they might enlist. If recruiting is all about asking then the first person who should be asked is God. You should pray to the Lord of the harvest to raise up workers for the harvest field (Matt 9:38). If you lack leaders, he's the first port of call; you do not have because you do not ask. Prayer will be a component when you have potential people, too. You'll want to pray for wisdom and insight, courage and clarity.

One of the striking features of Paul's letters to Timothy and Titus where he explicitly discusses recruiting overseers, elders and deacons (leaders of various kinds) is that he *doesn't* tell Timothy or Titus to pray about it. I don't want to make too much of this. I don't think this omission means Paul would think it was wrong to pray or that he doesn't expect and assume that Timothy and Titus will pray. I think this is a feature because, having thought and prayed carefully, a decision still needs to be made: by you.

Key drivers

Once you've set that theological foundation for recruitment (a major driver itself), it's time to turn to the three often-overlooked recruitment drivers.

The first driver is relational loyalty. You build genuine relationships with people. You are there for them in the highs and lows of life—you baptize their child, help them move house, turn up to their kid's birthday party, counsel them through messy heartaches—you do life together. This creates trust and relational loyalty. This isn't to say that you do these things to gain 'recruiting power', but it's just a fact of life that relational loyalty—sometimes called relational capital—is one of the factors in recruiting.

The second driver is displayed competence. People need to see that you vaguely know what you're talking about and that when you set about to do something you give it a real go. You don't need to be the best; you just need to show that you are basically competent in a few areas. However, everyone will have their subjective view of what competence looks like. For some, no matter what you do, you'll never be competent enough. For others, so long as you turn up and are at least half of the time facing the right way, they're happy. Most will be somewhere in the middle, and they're just looking to see if you've done some things that turned out okay. They're looking for runs on the board. They want to know that they can trust you, that you'll do what you say you'll do, that they won't be wasting their time or leaving them high and dry.

The third driver is vision. This is an intimidating area for leaders who feel as though their vision must be something that wows people with mesmerizing rhetoric. They're imagining a carefully crafted pitch of emotional words and pithy sound bites, all tied together with a memorable anecdote about a young boy on the streets of Guam. But they don't know anyone from Guam, so a compelling vision is out of their reach. There's nothing wrong with using those elements—if you can, you should—and over time you'll get more confident and natural as you share your ministry's vision. But none of these steps is necessary, or even what I mean by 'vision'. Those elements are tools, tips and tricks that help you *communicate* vision, not vision *itself*.

Vision is a normal and very ordinary part of life. You are casting vision all the time without even realizing it.[101] Vision is just answering three key questions clearly enough that people understand: Why are we doing this? Why is this important? What do we want to see happen as a result? You need to know and be able to tell people what the point is, why they should bother, and why this would be a potentially good use of time. Finish this sentence: "This idea will help us make disciples and honour Jesus because..." If you do that: boom. You've communicated a vision.

To grossly oversimplify things, in an average-sized church the effectiveness of these drivers goes in the order we've just looked at them: relational loyalty is the most potent, then displayed competence, and lastly vision. Each church will have unique cultural and historical factors that will shape how recruiting works there, but that's the general rule of thumb.

Since vision is the least effective of the drivers, 'casting vision' might not seem as urgent as some books make it out to be, leading some churches to ignore it altogether. This is the correct diagnosis but the wrong remedy. It's true that vision, as a *single lever*, doesn't have the same weight in driving recruitment and forward movement in the average church, but that just means the wise leader will understand the role it plays *along with* the other drivers. Vision is a necessary ingredient playing a support role alongside relational loyalty and displayed competence, multiplying *their* effectiveness. On its own, vision doesn't move many people to action, but without it the other drivers are far less effective.

This order of effectiveness, in the average church, also explains why it can be challenging to recruit people early after arrival: relational loyalty and displayed competence haven't had time to gain momentum. After around eighteen months, recruitment gets easier as these two drivers begin to gain traction.

Assuming that you are teaching and discipling people from the Scriptures about the nature of the Christian life and the place of service, these drivers will influence whether or not people join a ministry. But once people are involved, these drivers will also enable people to remain serving in that ministry—apart from their own theological convictions, of

---

101 See Hamilton, 'Your people should be able to do a good impression of you', pp. 421-428.

course. People will serve as an expression of their love for God and neighbour as they follow the suffering servant—sometimes in spite of you and your leadership. But there are lots of ways for those impulses to be expressed, and not all of them involve serving in *this* particular ministry or even primarily within a local church. These three factors keep people from being frustrated and taking their convictions to serve elsewhere.

In the larger-than-average church, the order of effectiveness basically reverses: vision is the most impactful driver, then displayed competence and lastly relational loyalty. In a group above 175 or so, people know they don't know everyone and that there are too many people for the pastoral team to 'do life' with all of them. There are more options available, and thus preference is a more significant factor, as well as ministry effectiveness. People want to do something that will make a difference in achieving the vision and positively impacting people's lives.

I was told about a larger-than-average church where a ministry area was finding it particularly hard to recruit leaders. The ministry area leader had formerly worked with a single congregation, and unfortunately wasn't alerted that the three recruitment drivers are inverted in larger churches. He relied on relational loyalty and displayed competence—but after two years had recruited no-one. It took too long to spread deep relational work over such a large number of people, and having minimal leaders in his teams over that time meant the ministry wasn't effective and did not display his competence well. When he moved on from his role, someone else took over that ministry area and began recruiting based on vision. After one (rather mediocre) announcement at all the Sunday services, this new ministry area leader had recruited for and filled all teams at all services and had begun building the ministry structures and developing the team.

Knowing the key factors of recruiting is critical to success, as well as understanding how they generally play out in the size of church you're in—and then figuring out how they work in your specific church. The techniques and systems are essential and helpful—we'll talk about them now—but they don't just 'work'. Life and leadership are complicated, and recruitment techniques need to be employed while carefully considering each environment.

Specific advice on the ask

Having been theologically grounded, let's get to the nuts-and-bolts advice on the specifics of recruitment. Here are seven concrete things you can do this Sunday to kickstart your recruitment.

1. Ask

You'd be surprised how many people overlook asking, and perhaps how often *you* overlook it. If you want to recruit people, you need to ask people—lots of them. Yes, you can come up with lots of reasons why this person will say no or why they can't do it. They're almost certainly excellent, persuasive excuses. But you need to ask that person anyway because if you don't, you'll never recruit them. You dishonour them when you don't ask them. You strip them of the opportunity and responsibility of making their own decision.

If you know it's going to be tough for them to say yes, or if there are good reasons why they will say no, don't hide those issues. It's not like they're secrets. Bring those complications up early in your chat. It shows that you have thought about it and you understand what you're asking of them. Here are some phrases to get you started:

> "I know this is a big ask…"
> "I know this is a longshot…"
> "I know you have a lot going on right now…"
> "I have a crazy idea for you…"
> "I have an idea that would totally ruin your life and your plans…"

Whatever you say, make sure you *actually ask* people to be involved.

2. Be careful with needs

You need people because your ministry has holes that need people to fill them. This is one way to look at your recruitment decisions, and there's some truth to it, but it's also not the most helpful or accurate perspective, nor does it communicate what you deep-down think about the opportunity to serve in ministry.

That's not to say that you should *never* say the word 'need', it's just that you should be careful that it doesn't become the dominant paradigm that people hear and view serving through. If people think that ministry is about filling needs, then they'll think it's about helping *you* out. They'll think it's transactional and temporary. They won't think it's any of those things you just said you believed about ministry. If people feel that disconnect, they'll start to think that these 'holes' are not actual ministry. In other words, you'll teach people one thing with your words from the Bible but train them in another through your recruiting talk in announcements and conversations.

3. Ask from the inside out

Instead of asking from need, you should ask by talking about the why first. I discussed this in *Wisdom in Leadership*: communicating the why before the what, the how or the next step.[102]

Here's the difference:

> Option 1: "We need two people to help out in our three-to-five-year-old room during our Sunday service this week, otherwise it won't happen."

> Option 2: "During 'Kids on Sunday' our preschoolers learn God's word each and every weekend. Come and join our team and help our three-to-five-year-olds understand God's love for them."

One uses guilt and fear as motivators, the other vision and purpose. Both have a good chance of 'working', but only one will help you recruit the right people for the right reasons. Option 1 might get you bodies in the room, but there's a good chance they'll be begrudging, dispassionate and uncommitted. Someone is more likely to join enthusiastically and with commitment if they are recruited to a cause where they understand why it matters.

---

102 See Hamilton, 'Communicate from the inside out', pp. 205-208.

4. You're not a sinking ship

Flowing on from the last point, be careful of painting your ministry as a sinking ship—most likely it's not. But even if it is, don't lead with that. That's like asking someone out on a date by saying, "I'm ugly and I have no friends or job prospects, but I do have excruciating body odour. Oh, and a fun personality." Lead with that last point!

Generally, people don't want to get on a sinking ship. They don't start following a sports team who are at the bottom of the table. Okay, there are *some* people who will love the idea, because they want a challenge or to serve in an 'extraordinary' kind of way, but most people will quickly, and perhaps subconsciously, mentally move on before you've even finished talking.

5. Take the pressure off

Very few people like making a decision on the spot. When I'm pressured to decide *right now*, I feel like there must be a trap... but I haven't had a chance to work out the scam... I'd better say no just in case. Without time to think through the implications, people will lean towards rejection in case your proposal clashes with something that they can't remember this minute. It's safer to say no.

Give people time to think: "Here's my idea, but I don't want you to say yes right now. Take some time to think about it, talk to people and pray. I'll check with you next week to see what you think." This takes the pressure off, allows them to really consider it—and prevents you from coming across as desperate and needy.

To do this, you need to be organized. If you actually, desperately, need people by next week then you don't have time to take the pressure off like this. Recruiting properly means thinking more than a week ahead. But if you're further along the pipeline than a frontline leader, you should be thinking more than a week ahead anyway.

6. Get ready for a basketful of rejection

The people you ask will turn you down most of the time. This is normal. The sooner you come to grips with this, the better. It might take you ten asks to get one yes. Sometimes the yes will come straight up, other times you need to wait. If you're not prepared for this, it can wear you down.

You need to go into it with your eyes open so that it doesn't surprise you. You'll hear the word no more than the word yes. Accept it as a fact and move on.

7. You're never finished

Recruiting is an ongoing process. You'll never be done. There will be pauses and reprieves, but it'll never stop. People will be constantly moving on, or the ministry will grow—or both. Either way, recruitment.

It is, however, wise to not be *constantly* enlisting. People need a break from you surveying them as potential recruits, and you yourself need a break. You need to invest in the people you already have and figure out a way to make it work with *this* number and *these* people. But don't let yourself get tricked into thinking this is the new status quo. It's not goodbye forever; it's just see you soon.

Multiply recruiting

Two of the major recruitment challenges are the time it takes to do it (no instantaneous mind-reading available on this planet) and the network of relationships needed (do you know the people you should be asking?). You can solve both problems by pushing recruiting into every layer of your pipeline instead of keeping it at yours. This multiplies the recruiters you have and so the amount of recruiting that can be done.

Your current leaders will likely be your best recruiters: they know what's involved in the ministry and they're more likely to be passionate about it. They also may know someone you don't, or something you don't—they may have been in a conversation where a person has said they'd love to be involved!

Empowering your leaders to recruit is as easy as telling them. You simply say to them that, if they know anyone who might be keen or who they think would be a good fit for the team, they should feel free to have a conversation with them.

At this point, you may be thinking to yourself, "What if they recruit the wrong person? If I'm the person responsible for this ministry area, don't

I need to have input on who joins the team?" Yes, you should definitely have input on who joins the team. But it's not *either* you recruit everyone and have input *or* you multiply recruitment throughout the pipeline with no control over who joins.

First explain to your team what kind of person would be a 'good fit'. What that means is, in one sense, up to you, though I would suggest a solid place to start your thinking would be the five C's: character, convictions, competencies, chemistry and capacity.[103] Let your leaders know what the prerequisites for leadership are as they think through whom they might recruit to the ministry.

Here's what a talk giving your leaders some parameters for a kids' ministry might look like:

> As you know from your own experience, joining the kids' ministry team helps people grow both as people and as disciples of Jesus. If there are people you think should consider joining the team, you are totally competent and authorized to talk with them and invite them to consider it. They can come to 101 in January and scope it out for themselves! Here is the checklist:
>
> **1.** Are they already a part of a ministry? If so, leave them alone. We don't poach people from other ministries. The stronger other ministries are, the stronger kids' ministry will be. People might be planning to move on from other ministries, but that's different from us explicitly seeking to recruit people away.
>
> **2.** Are they a Christian?
>
> **3.** Check their character qualities. All of us have issues, so they aren't necessarily a disqualification, but are there glaring character holes?
>
> **4.** Check their modelling. If kids were to imitate their way of life, would it be a generally good thing? They can't be perfect, but are they growing and repenting?

---

103 For more on this, see Hamilton, 'The five C's', pp. 261-267.

5. Check their commitment to church life. Have they committed to meeting together with God's people on Sundays and in a small group?
6. Is being a leader an unhealthy need in their life? Do they love to boss people around? Do they love to be admired and looked up to?

The only automatic no is the second criterion: are they Christian? The rest are more like yellow flags: proceed with caution. So if there are people you think would benefit from being involved in kids' ministry, feel free to chat with them!

This ministry has given its leaders the framework they need to begin to think and then talk to the people they know at church who might be interested in the kids' ministry. They're armed with the information they need to do a discerning job with their newly deputized recruiting authority.

You'll notice this list has no requirement for kids' ministry skills; they will be taught. Your ministry may legitimately need a specific skill set before people can join. Notice too the high focus on character—they will be observed and mimicked by the children. Lastly, you'll see that three of the criteria are being a Christian, being committed to Sunday services, and being in a small group. Your ministry may or may not require all those prerequisites, but they are worth serious consideration.

The other item that may have stood out was the reference to 101. Clarifying what a good candidate for recruitment looks like is a great first step, but it won't mean that everyone recruited by your team is the kind of person you yourself would have recruited. Sometimes this will be a good thing and they'll recruit a person you would have overlooked or had never met before, but sometimes they will recruit a person who clearly doesn't fit the requirements of your ministry area. This is where 101 comes in, a step that helps you to filter those who are, at worst, dangerous and, at best, not ready yet.

101

When your leaders recruit people, you haven't given them the authority to recruit people directly on to the team. They recruit to a preliminary stage that I call a 101 meeting, which is like an expression of interest. Make it clear to your team what authority they have.

At 101, the ministry area leader meets with people and explains to them the vision of the ministry, how it works and what the requirements and expectations are for leaders who join the ministry, and then gives people a chance to ask questions.

At the end of this meeting, give people a week to think and pray about it. Tell them you'll get back to them to discuss whether this ministry is for them or whether another ministry might suit them better. This gives them time to think—remember, take the pressure off!—and it gives you the chance to talk with their small group leader or anyone else relevant if you don't personally know them and their discipleship to double-check their Sunday commitment and general suitability.[104]

The 101 process is critical if you want to decentralize recruitment and spread it throughout the pipeline: it allows you get many people out there recruiting without sacrificing the high standards you have for leadership. It also allows you to share the authority for recruiting without surrendering that final decision of who joins the team. You're training leaders for higher layers while choosing leaders.

Since it's so important, it's vital that the process is simple and communicated. It needs to be the automatic, default rhythm of your ministry area. It also needs to be a process you honour.

A friend of mine was at a church where a ministry area was in the middle of a severe leadership shortage. They implemented the 101 system. The ministry area leader gave his team the authority to recruit to a 101 meeting, outlined the type of person that would be good and set them loose. One leader recruited a friend of his who was keen to be a part of the ministry and happy to come to 101. The ministry area leader also did some recruiting, and signed some people up to temporarily fill the gaps for one week—then cancelled the 101 meeting, saying that the friend

---

[104] You can download an example set of 101 documents at revcraighamilton.com.

wouldn't be needed since others had filled the gap for that week.

That week! Absolute madness.

As you can imagine, no-one else on the team ever recruited anyone, and the leader who had recruited their friend left that ministry at the end of the year because they were so frustrated by the short-sightedness on display.

When you dishonour the recruitment process, you dishonour the people who have put in effort within the process. You don't need to say yes to everyone who's been recruited to be honouring, but you need to play by the rules you set up.

Onboarding

Getting people to agree to join the team isn't the end of the recruiting process. You also need to help them *onto* the team, which means onboarding.[105] Joining a new ministry or team can be both daunting and difficult. There are people to get to know—both those you serve and those you serve alongside—unfamiliar processes and ministry-specific skills to learn, and maybe some layer-specific skills too. It can be overwhelming.

Onboarding is about helping people get up to speed as quickly as possible on how the team does its ministry, what precisely the new leader's individual role is, and how that role fits into what the rest of the team does. You'll focus on three goals for them: becoming real friends with the people in their team, having role clarity, and fast gaining effectiveness in their role. In other words, you want to move them from being an outsider to being an insider. Left to happen organically, this can take about a year. Onboarding is about making this timeframe as short as possible: what if you could shave it down to ten or even six months?

Think carefully about what you can do to help people. Remember, being *on* a team isn't necessarily the same as being *part of* a team. I suggest you work both angles at once: help the team leaders to be active in onboarding the new team members, and also help the new team members

---

[105] The technical term for this is 'organizational socialization'. You may have also heard it called integration, orientation or induction.

to themselves be proactive and intentional. If things are happening both top-down and bottom-up, there's a far stronger likelihood that the onboarding will actually happen well.

On the ministry area side, do the following:

1. Have a clarity conversation

Have the team leader discuss the role and its responsibilities with the new leader. You should have already talked about it at 101, but once is never enough. A good rule of thumb is to presume that people haven't memorized everything you say. Go over it again and make sure they know what is expected from them and what they are meant to be doing.

2. Buddy them up

Assign a member of the team to look out for them for the first six months who can translate on the ground what the team leader said in case the new leader didn't understand. This way the new leader can ask questions that they may not feel comfortable asking of the team leader or the ministry area leader, and they will have at least one peer they are confident will help and support them.

3. Create environments where they can build friendships

This should be happening anyway in your team, but think carefully about how to create moments that facilitate relationships forming. This could be time spent in pairs or triplets sharing about life and praying for each other during a team meeting. It could be going out for a burger as a team after you have finished your ministry together for the week. Perhaps have the team over at your home for a meal.

4. Encourage open dialogue

You'll want to explicitly encourage and repeatedly reinforce that the new leader can come to you (and the team leader below you, if there is one) and discuss anything without fear of getting into trouble—and when they do, don't punish them for it! If things don't make sense to the new leader—if they are struggling, if interpersonal issues are happening, if they need help in any way—they need to know that you see it as your job to see them succeed. You'll need to emphasize that their questions aren't interruptions or distractions from you getting your work done because those questions and interruptions *are* your job. (Remember the heart shift from the team leader layer?)

In most people's experiences, both from their work and from other church contexts, this will not be how team leaders normally function, so you'll need to remind them and reassure them that you mean it.

5. Check in with them

The supervising leader should check in with them about their onboarding once a month for the first six months (though if you are onboarding a staff member, do this more frequently: once a day for the first week, once a week for the first month or two, then once a month for the remaining months). Ask them if anything is confusing, who they have met and spoken with so far, if they need any resources or if they have any questions.

On the other hand…

Now that we've covered five top-down onboarding steps, let's look at five things the new recruit can do to get themselves settled on the team and proficient as quickly as possible. Most of these are the flip side of the previous; they focus on helping the new recruit build real relationships with the people in their team as they gain clarity about their role and become effective in it.

1. Ask lots of questions

The new team member needs to be told that they are allowed to ask questions. Lots of them. Often a team leader or ministry area leader will try to think of all the things that need to be explained, but because they have likely been a part of the ministry for a long time, they won't be able to remember or notice all the unique things that happen. They need the newcomer to point out what needs explaining.

The new team member needs to ensure they ask their questions with humility and sincerity, rather than in an accusatory way meant only to highlight their disapproval. New team members who overlook this vital distinction may find their fellow team members rebuffing these ones; not all questions are equal.

2. Schedule regular one-to-ones with your team leader

The team leader should be scheduling one-to-ones with the leaders in their teams, but a great many things that *should* happen in the world *don't*. New team members need to pursue these meetings with their team leader. If the team leader organizes the one-to-ones as they should, then the new leader has lost nothing; if the team leader doesn't, then they've gained since they now have a chance to meet and learn from the team leader.

3. Get to know your team

The new team member shouldn't just passively wait for the current team members to befriend them; they should proactively seek to get to know their fellow teammates. If the team is seeking to get to know the new member *and* the new member is seeking to get to know the team, this will only improve the relationships and how quickly they grow strong.

4. Don't wait for feedback

This again is something that team leaders *should* do but may not, especially if they are insecure or uncertain. Having the new member of the team seek out feedback proactively helps both sides get better at their roles. It also means the team member will begin learning the skill of leading up.

5. Accept the challenge and be prepared to fail

This reinforces the expectation for everyone new at any layer: you will not be good at it to begin with. That's part of what it means to be new at something. It isn't a sign of deficiency but that learning is taking place. The only way to learn something is to not know it, struggle, make mistakes, get feedback, try again and keep improving.[106]

What helps the team member navigate this painful, early segment of

---

[106] See Hamilton, 'Fail forwards', pp. 209-217; and 'Treat them like children', pp. 303-306.

the journey is keying their expectations to reality. Everyone around them who's great now started out not that good, just like the new member, and those experienced people are there to support them, not to ridicule them. With those truths in place, they can tackle the challenge of the new head-on.

Pipeline planning meeting 7

From this point on, our pipeline planning meetings won't follow the order of the leadership development framework. The phases of the framework are organized logically, but this isn't usually the best way to implement it. For example, recruitment is placed after the conceptual work of ministry grouping and designing the pipeline architecture, however in real life your ministry probably already exists and has people serving in it. It's better to develop those who are on the team before focusing on bringing new leaders in.

Over these past months, you've hammered out some serious clarity on the anvil of these pipeline planning meetings. Now you'll take all that work and make it digestible by others through the second component you'll need to roll out the pipeline philosophy: clear and simple role descriptions for every ministry.

Your role descriptions should state what the role is, what layer of the pipeline it's in, the essential pieces of what it needs to do and how much time should be spent doing it. Some of your ministries may already have role descriptions that you can use as a base to work from. Flick forward to chapter 24 to see an example of what they could look like; there are more at revcraighamilton.com. They may seem sparse and straightforward, but crafting that simplicity takes more time than you might think, especially if you've never tried to do it before.

It's vital that you use very similar layout and formatting for every description across your church. It doesn't matter too much what that looks like, so long as it's clear and consistent. If you have many existing variations of role descriptions, take the time to debate which to use as the standard across every ministry.

Once you've decided as a team on the structure of your role descriptions, it's time for individual work in crafting, as simply as possible, each role and layer in a ministry area.

If ministry areas have significant overlap, collaborate and use each other's best phrasing to describe the parts of the roles that are similar. In the same way, when you get to the team leader layer these descriptions will be very similar, so you may want to collaborate as a whole team on a baseline description that can then be tweaked to suit each specific ministry.

By the end of this meeting you want to have as many role descriptions drafted for as many ministry units and pipeline layers as possible. These are *drafts*. After the meeting, put them in front of other key leaders from the ministry areas for feedback and input.

You now have two of the three components needed to begin installing the pipeline: a short-term timeline for installation into a specific ministry, and role clarity.

This hasn't been wasted time for those who must wait to install the pipeline into their ministry area. They now have a stack of role descriptions which they can begin using immediately. Role clarity is valuable for your leaders in and of itself, pipeline or not!

21
Leader recruitment: selecting team leaders

Leadership development framework

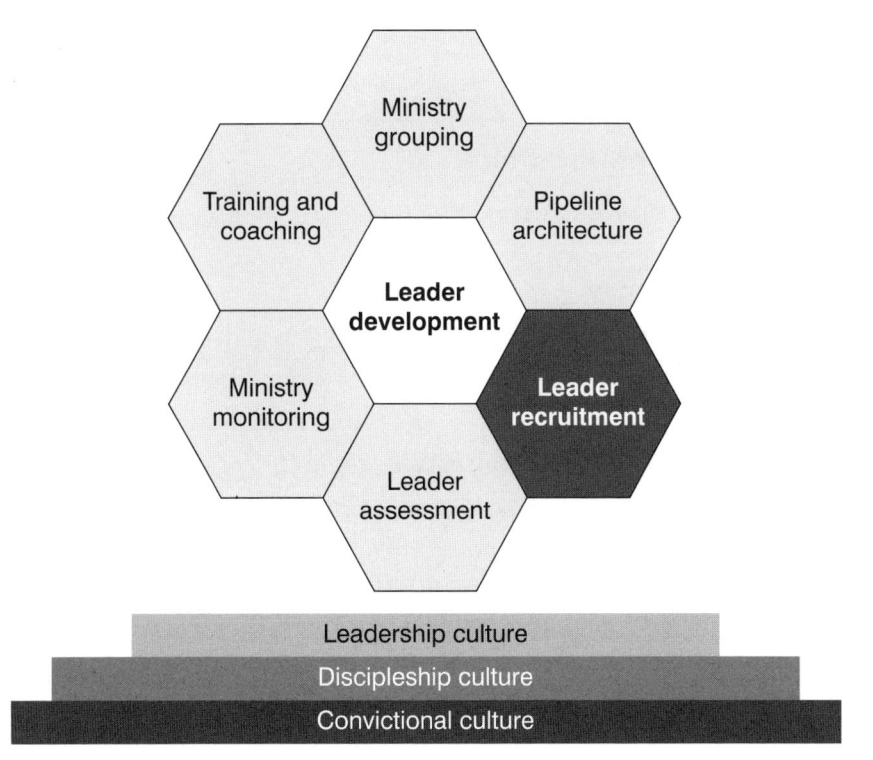

- Ministry grouping
- Training and coaching
- Pipeline architecture
- Leader development
- Ministry monitoring
- Leader recruitment
- Leader assessment

Leadership culture
Discipleship culture
Convictional culture

Selecting team leaders is one of the most important tasks for the senior, ministry area or unit leader who oversees that layer. A wrong choice here will result in decreased effectiveness for the whole ministry area and may result in catastrophic problems in the leader layer or even in nearby pipelines.

It's a challenging task too since you can't *know* with complete certainty whether a leader will thrive at this layer. Remember pipeline commandment four (being awesome at one layer tells you nothing about whether you'll be awesome at the next) and commandment five (the behaviours that cause success at one layer will sometimes compromise it at the next). It would be nice if God whispered in your ear and told you, "Tracy is everything you need in a team leader, thus sayeth the LORD". But he doesn't—at least, he's never done so for me. Instead, you need to use your wisdom in discerning who is the 'right' person.

No-one who has appointed team leaders for any length of time has a 100% success rate, but there are some general principles that will help you improve your win/loss ratio when it comes to personnel selection.

Six primary requirements

Let's start with six primary requirements.

Humble and hungry

They are humble and hungry. Character is king and will always be so. Long live the king. But presuming there's no glaring character issues, the two specific qualities to gauge in a person are humility and hunger.

By hunger I mean a deep, unshakable commitment to the cause. They have a desperation to see people loved and served and saved that motivates them to find a way around any roadblocks. They're hungry for the mission.

Amongst all the essential 'permission to play' character requirements for Christian leadership, humility and hunger are the top must-haves for someone you're considering moving up the pipeline.[107] This combination produces a servant-hearted attitude where the leader has the drive to accomplish the mission for the sake of others rather than self. These are critical because leadership has a way of stoking the embers of pride, a particularly nasty inhibitor at the team leader layer.

---

107 To dive more deeply into these two characteristics—and in particular the power that comes when they are combined—see Hamilton, 'Humble and hungry', pp. 253-259.

As you recruit and assess all your prospective and current leaders, you'll be thinking about them through the lens of the five C's—character, convictions, competencies, chemistry and capacity. You'll probably have a slightly lower bar for some of these C's when it comes to joining your teams as a team member or leader, but when someone is moving up to a team leader position you need to put that bar back up for character, convictions and chemistry (they'll need the capacity to do the role and a certain level of competence too, but we'll talk about that below).

Good relationally

They have healthy social interactions. Leadership is about relating to people. Without getting too technical, you're looking for someone who has basic common sense around others. This includes emotional intelligence—knowing and recognizing your own emotions, handling those emotions so that they are relevant to the current situation, being able to gather up your emotions and push on towards a goal in spite of self-doubt or lack of motivation, and being able to recognize the emotions of others—as well as the ability to relate well with different genders and ages. It also includes being able to listen and understand what people are saying (as well as what they're *not* saying). Specifically check what their anger levels are like and how they react when people let them down or when they're told no.

Effective

They are effective and do a good job with the responsibilities they have already been given. If you're considering asking someone into the team leader layer who is incompetent and ineffective, you should probably take a good look at yourself.

You might be thinking, "But didn't Craig just say that pipeline commandment four was 'being awesome at one layer tells you nothing about whether you'll be awesome at the next'? How does that fit with making sure the person is effective?"[108]

Commandment four helps us be clear that being awesome at the

---

108 Great question and great memory.

leader layer doesn't *guarantee* being awesome at this next one. Effectiveness can't be used as the sole criterion—but it should certainly be weighed up. You want them to have been at least generally effective and to have met the baseline expectations of competencies. You want to see that they can learn and improve, receive feedback and get better. Another reason is that you want the team leader to have the respect of their peers, which we'll discuss below.

Internally motivated

They show internal motivation. You don't want someone who needs to be reminded and cajoled and tacitly threatened in order for them to do what they said. You don't want someone who only does things when you explicitly tell them to. You don't want someone who's only there because all their friends are. You don't want someone who's always threatening to leave and who loves being begged to stay. You don't want someone who is always trying to find a reason to be upset, offended or demotivated. You're looking for someone who is internally motivated: they want to do this ministry because *they want to do it*. You want someone who takes the initiative and puts in the effort because it's the right thing to do.

Interested in responsibility

They show interest in increased responsibility. Being a team leader means more responsibility. Does this person even want that? Have they ever taken on more responsibility at the leader layer, or are they content with the basics? There's nothing wrong with only wanting to do the minimum; people have other things going on in their lives. But to be a team leader, they'll need to have shown a willingness and interest in taking on more. Wanting to be the *team leader* isn't the same thing. If they don't want more responsibility, they only want the kudos that comes with a title.

Respected

They have the respect of their peers. If they don't, that's a sign that there's something going on in their life that you perhaps haven't noticed yet. This isn't about popularity—who is liked the most or has the most best friends. To lead a team, you need to be worthy of respect.

You have Mort, the most incompetent person on the team. He talks as if he's the best and knows everything but he always makes a mess that everyone else then has to clean up. If you promote him to a team leader position, you're almost guaranteed to breed both bitterness and cynicism when it comes to the team leader role. Not only will he crash and burn, but the gravitational force of his incompetence will negatively impact how people view the other team leaders and even perhaps the very *idea* of team leaders.

Three subtle requirements

Those are the six primary requirements you need to be looking out for when selecting team leaders, but there are another three requirements to consider. These are more subtle, though no less important.

Keen to learn

They display an interest in learning leadership. They want to get better. Perhaps they read leadership books or listen to leadership podcasts. They soak up training and are interested in taking it further or discussing it more. They ask why you do things a certain way or how you solved that issue or why you structure meetings the way you do. They want to learn and be taught.

Don't assume that because they don't express their interest in learning the same way you do—reading books, perhaps—that therefore it isn't there. What you're looking for is the interest itself, not the method. Not all leaders are readers (a rhyme doesn't make it true). But all leaders will be learners (alliteration: more trustworthy).

Interested in the success of others

They show a genuine interest in the success of others. As well as being a key component of emotional intelligence (and just being a thoughtful human), this is also a crucial quality for team leaders. We discussed this when we looked at the pipeline architecture element: missing this quality undermines the team leader layer. If someone already possesses it, they're starting miles ahead.

On board

They are passionate about their church and this ministry. People don't have to love their particular church or ministry to begin serving. It's preferable, obviously, but not required. However, when people start to *lead other leaders* it becomes more important to get that culture fit right. You don't want a team leader who doesn't like your church and isn't particularly thrilled about being involved in a ministry the way that it currently is. That attitude will be contagious, and with the added authority of team leadership it will spread with great potency.

If you have team leaders who aren't on board with what your church is doing or what this ministry exists to do, the strategic plan, the flavour of how you get things done or any of those fundamental clarity questions, then you're creating problems that you'll need to expend serious energy in the future to fix.[109] You'll accidentally create little enclaves of boss-haters and, once you have this ghetto of grumblers, it will be tough to quarantine them and reverse their effect on the wider team.[110]

At the team leader layer and above, people must be positive about your church, where you're going and how you're planning on getting there. This isn't because you want a court of yes-men, but because you want people who will champion the ministry and love it enough to be a genuine and thoughtful critic.[111]

Three subtle positive patterns

Along with these nine requirements are another three patterns to be aware of in a prospective leader's life. These aren't prerequisites, just preferred behaviours; extra insights to look out for.

Leads already

They are followed in other areas of life. This can be hard to know about and even harder to gauge, especially if you don't see or hear much about

---

[109] For more on these questions for clarifying your ministry, see chapter 3.
[110] For more on boss-haters, see Hamilton, pp. 273-274.
[111] For more on what it means to be a genuine critic, see Hamilton, 'Public fans and private critics', pp. 235-238.

the rest of their life. Do your best to figure it out. Here are three broad categories that you might use:

1. Are they the *ringleader* of their peers? Does everyone naturally follow them? Are they the one who organizes and corrals the group?
2. Are they the *linchpin* of their friends? They might not be the official 'leader'—the alpha-dog—but if they don't go to the event or gathering, do things seem to fall apart? If they do go does everyone else seem to be there too, but if they don't go only a few turn up? That's a linchpin.
3. Are they a *gatekeeper*? Do people look to them for approval? Are their opinions influential in the group?

These are all varied and subtle forms of leadership that happen organically without positional authority.

Integrates knowledge

They can integrate new knowledge. Not only are they interested in the information, they also take it and integrate it into what they already know and do. They learn something at a conference and they put it into practice in their ministry or life. They learn something from a book or from the church down the road and they adapt it for their context.

Suggests solutions

They are willing to put forward ideas in a peer setting. If they have thoughts about what could or should be done, they are comfortable sharing those in a meeting—growing comfortable leading other leaders. Find ways to get potential team leaders into a room where you can see them solving problems and sharing ideas. This will help you to know whether they're beginning to develop in strategic thinking and questioning. You'll also see whether they are growing in confidence in their own ideas and are willing to take the initiative.

This one isn't foolproof. Some people have confidence in their ideas when they probably shouldn't, whereas others are shy and unsure. Discernment is required to work out what's actually going on, since this can be a sign of latent leadership *or* toxic immaturity.

Recruit slowly and stay in touch

There are two final issues that you need to think carefully about when it comes to selecting team leaders: speed and proximity.

The temptation will be to bring people up into a team leader role quickly and therefore early. You'll either be without a team leader layer but wanting one as soon as you can, or you'll already have this layer but a team leader has moved on to a different role or church before you were ready and you need to fill the vacant slot as soon as possible. But, if at all possible, recruit slowly to the team leader layer. It's a perplexing layer to move into, and it can cause a lot of damage if the person ends up leading poorly.

As much as you're able, be constantly drip-feeding team leader training to the leader layer and seeing who responds and is interested to learn more, then find avenues to foster their interest in learning the skills, time and focus of the layer above them. This might be through informal conversations, sharing books, invites to conferences or more formal tasks. This way, any new recruits will have already been learning pieces of the team leader role and the jump won't be so big and potentially overwhelming. Flattening out the learning curve like this means that the ramp up to the team leader layer will be elongated; just by doing this you'll therefore be recruiting more slowly.

The other side to this drip-feeding coin is that you'll need to get to know those who are at the leader layer. Presumably, if you are looking to select team leaders, you are either a unit leader, ministry area leader or senior leader—two layers above the leader layer.

- Senior leader
- Ministry area leader
- Unit leader
- Team leader
- Leader
- Team member

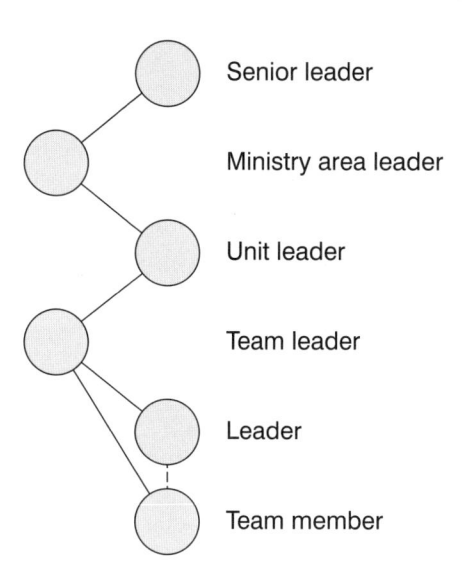

This means that you may not be meeting with the leader layer at all, or at least not very often. But when the time comes to select a new team leader, they are your pool of potentials.

Your current team leaders should not have the authority to select their own replacement. Of course, you'll listen to their thoughts and opinions—you'd be a fool not to—but the final decision should be yours. You need to know who these leaders are, what they're like and what they're about so that you can think through the primary and secondary considerations for team leader selection.

This is what's known as staying in touch with the skip layer. You can do this informally, formally or both, depending on the size of your church and the specific ministry. Informally means you are in genuine relationships with them: you see them at church, you chat with them about life over morning tea, you may even hang out with them or have them over to your house for meals.

But you might also want to meet with them infrequently but regularly in formally organized skip layer meetings. At these meetings you talk about their personal and their spiritual lives as well as the ministry, how they're going in it and what they think about it. These meetings are valuable as a chance for you to play your part in caring for them and to pray with them. They will also help you to gauge their suitability for being a team leader in the future and whether information is making its way down to the leader layer or up from that layer to you. Sometimes, but not all the time, information doesn't make it through the team leader layer. Sometimes this can be intentional duplicity, but most of the time it's accidental and the result of incompetence rather than conspiracy. Either way, skip layer meetings will help you to work out whether this information blockage is occurring and, if so, why.

Discerning the right people to invite to the team leader layer is difficult and puzzlingly mysterious. Sometimes those you think are a sure bet end up striking out whereas those who are more of a lineball end up as home runs. However, while recruiting for this layer will never be an exact science, you can increase the frequency of getting that pick right by being alert to these 12 aspects in the life of the prospective team leader.

22
Leader recruitment: hiring staff

Leadership development framework

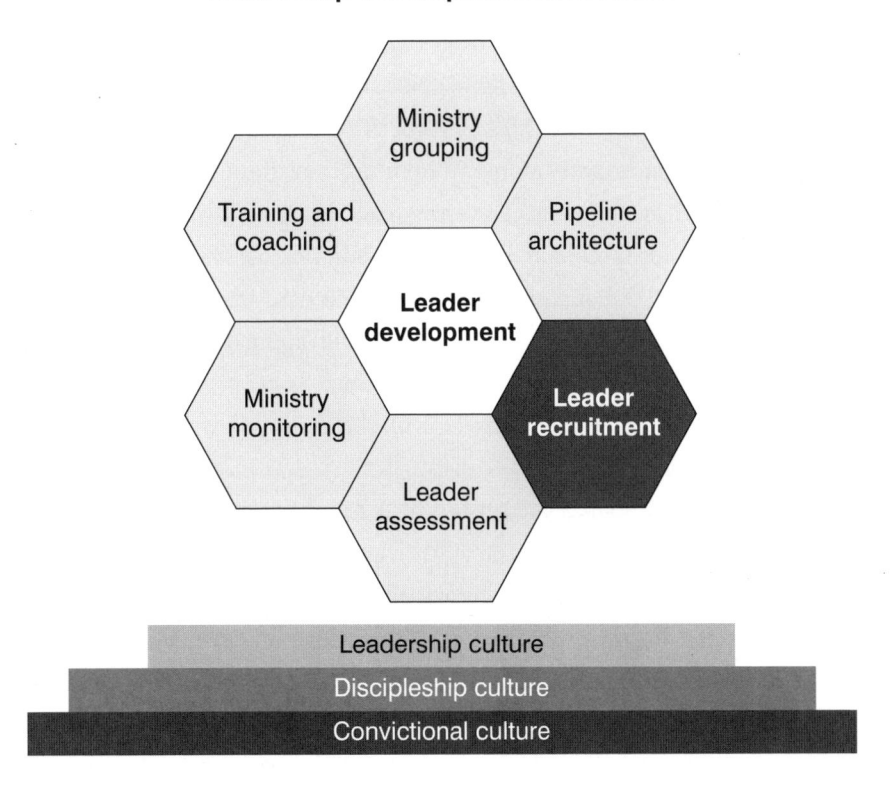

- Ministry grouping
- Training and coaching
- Pipeline architecture
- Leader development
- Ministry monitoring
- **Leader recruitment**
- Leader assessment

Leadership culture
Discipleship culture
Convictional culture

Not many of us will ever hire anyone, and those of us who will won't do it often, so this chapter's skills will be used infrequently. However, because it's a rare but hard task, it's worth being equipped so that if you suddenly need to you have somewhere to start.

This chapter isn't based on my own experiences of hiring people;

together we are gleaning the insights of those who have studied hiring as a practice over the last hundred years or so.

Hire around the five C's

Your best recruiting and hiring tool is the five C's that we covered earlier: character, convictions, competencies, chemistry and capacity. When it comes to certain volunteer positions in your church, you have some flexibility in how well you expect people to meet the five C's. Perhaps people don't need to be highly competent: you'll train them. Maybe they don't always need to have a high capacity. There may be a sliding scale of conviction necessary, such as a high bar for a small group leader and a lower one for providing morning tea biscuits.

But when it comes to hiring a staff member, skip one of the C's at your peril. What are their convictions? Where do they align with and diverge from your own? Is that divergence acceptable or not? What is their character like? How competent are they at the central aspects of the role—and how do you know? What about their leadership competency? Will they be able to lead at the appropriate pipeline layer and, again, how do you know? What is their capacity like? Will they be able to keep to the pace your church runs at? And do they mix well with the chemistry of your team; are they a good cultural fit?

This last question is frequently unasked when hiring decisions are made. If a new hire doesn't fit the culture and isn't humble and self-aware enough to navigate the transition or is uninterested in changing to suit, you will have constant problems until they move on. By then, both they and you will be frustrated and disillusioned. If your new hire is great in every other C but chemistry, you'll get a person focused on getting things done but who won't be able to get them done at your church.[112]

Your new hire will hit the culture wall after about six months. We talked about this shockwave back in chapter 13 when we talked about Tina and David. When new hires start actually trying to do something, reality asserts itself. Things that were automatic and obvious at the last church

---

112 For more on entering and navigating a new culture, see chapter 13.

aren't that way here. People don't respond the way they did at the previous place. The new hire will usually struggle and persevere for the next 12-18 months before they either conform or look for another church to move to.

Over and again, of all hires to senior positions, research shows that half fail and leave within 18 months.[113] And when it comes to churches, almost all hires will be to senior positions. Now, no research has been done into church staff retention rates as far as I know,[114] but anecdotally the rate isn't vastly different. Making chemistry a factor in the hiring process can prevent someone (and their family) from having to endure a frustrating and painful employment experience. Also, the astonishing costs of a poor hire are estimated to be up to ten times the yearly salary of the position.[115] These costs include ministry that should have been done that wasn't, high-performing people having to devote their time to preventing or fixing the problems of the low performers, and staff turnover issues such as the role being unfilled while the position is advertised and the time taken to interview potentials. Hiring for cultural fit will save a church time, money and ministry.

There is, of course, a tipping point when it comes to cultural fit. Similarity can create overconfidence; when we all agree, we never question our assumptions. This creates complacency and a failure to process information and circumstances as carefully as we should. So what's the right level of cultural fit? The answer is complex, but one of the main factors is the size of the staff team. When the staff team is under ten people, cohesion is vitally important.

---

[113] Some examples: Ron Ashkenas, 'Hire senior executives that last', *Harvard Business Review*, 3 August 2010, accessed 15 December 2020, hbr.org/2010/08/how-to-hire-senior-executives.html; Dan Schawbel, 'Hire for attitude', *Forbes*, 23 January 2012, accessed 15 December 2020, forbes.com/sites/danschawbel/2012/01/23/89-of-new-hires-fail-because-of-their-attitude/#114d869b137a; Jean Martin, 'For senior leaders, fit matters more than skill', *Harvard Business Review*, 17 January 2014, accessed 15 December 2020, hbr.org/2014/01/for-senior-leaders-fit-matters-more-than-skill.
[114] You can tell me otherwise at revcraighamilton.com.
[115] Bradford Smart, *Topgrading*, Penguin Group, New York, 2012, pp. 73-76.

A common trap

If a decision has to be made between hiring an outsider or someone from within, don't compare the written strengths of the outsider with the experienced weakness of the insider. It will feel like wisdom, like you're simply comparing one with the other, but you're not. You're comparing apples and oranges.

Firstly, the strengths you're taking into account are just what someone *tells* you they are good at. Maybe some referees vouch for them, but again that isn't the most reliable data. Is what they think of as high performance the same as your definition? Was that performance mostly the result of the individual or the result of many factors? (Hint: the result of many factors, as we'll see below.) On the other hand, you know the strengths of the person from within. You've ministered alongside them—you've seen them, what they do and how they do it. Their strengths are experienced strengths.

Secondly, you haven't experienced the outsider's weaknesses—yet. You don't know what they are. Maybe they told you some in the interview, but you can't *know* whether there is a whole extra menagerie of woes they didn't mention that will be foisted upon you the moment you take them on. They may have said they "work too hard" but they probably didn't mention their gross incompetence in some of the fundamental aspects of the job. Funny that. But again, you know the internal candidate's weaknesses, their extent and significance. There are no surprises there.

Thirdly, the weaknesses of the internal candidate will loom large in your thinking. That's human nature; they are visceral experiences. Your mind will lean towards making them seem more significant than they are, turning an orange into a grapefruit.

When you compare internal and external candidates like this the outsider will naturally look like the winning pick—but is this always a good idea?

The reality of the experienced outsider

Hiring from the outside is the common practice for many ministries—perhaps a Bible college graduate or a practitioner from another church.

There are many reasons for this: the requirements of diocesan bodies; the desire to get someone with experience and 'runs on the board'; the common thought that outsiders bring new ideas and perspectives. The virtue of hiring an experienced outsider is a well-loved rule of thumb. But is experience a valuable differentiating factor in hiring, and is hiring outsiders actually a good idea? Let's look at each.

Back in 1998, researchers Frank Schmidt and John Hunter analysed 85 years of data to see how well selection assessments predict job performance.[116] They looked at 19 different selection techniques and found that the best predictor of successful job performance was a work sample test (giving a person an example of the type of work required and assessing how well they complete it). Sample work tests had an R^2 of 0.29, which basically means they can predict 29% of an employee's performance.[117]

For church jobs, sample work tests are hard to come up with because the work is so varied and generally relates to people rather than discrete tasks. Even a sample sermon is only somewhat helpful since, though extremely important, the majority of what a minister will do is not the sermon—even if it takes 20 hours to prepare.

The second-best predictor of success is a tie between general cognitive ability and a structured interview, both an R^2 of 0.26. General cognitive ability is so predictive because it's not only raw intelligence but also the ability to learn. A structured interview is a consistent set of questions asked of each candidate, with the same criteria used to assess the quality of each candidate's response. The idea is that all variation comes from the difference in candidates' responses and not the judgements of the assessor. (Asking different questions of each candidate has an R^2 of 0.14.) Assessment of conscientiousness has an R^2 of 0.1, while a reference check has 0.07.

116 Frank Schmidt and John Hunter, 'The validity and utility of selection methods in personnel psychology', *Psychology Bulletin*, 1998, vol. 124, no. 2, pp. 262-274.
117 Technically, R^2 is a measure of how much one or more variables predicts an outcome. The R^2 value is on a scale of 0 to 1, and the closer you are to 1, the closer you are to that variable confidently predicting the outcome. Because of how complex real life is, a single variable almost never gets close to 1. R^2 values are worked out based on the likelihood of events occurring together: their correlation. Correlation is not causation, and neither is R^2. However, correlation is a decent starting point for figuring out what works and what doesn't. There's no way hiring performance causes job performance, but it can predict it.

Years of work experience has an R^2 of 0.03—just 3%. That's right: nearly 100 years of research shows that work experience does not predict job performance. The higher in complexity the job is—and church ministry is highly complex—the lower still the correlation between experience and job performance.[118] There is some evidence that people with more than five years of experience will produce a slightly higher job performance than those with less, but this is only a subtle, fleeting difference. There's absolutely no point in requiring more than five years' experience; it tells you nothing about the person's ability to do the job.

So hiring for experience is a general waste of time. Sad news for someone seeking an employee. What about hiring an outsider? Well, hiring someone from outside the organization is a good idea... sometimes.

In 2000, Rakesh Khurana and Nitin Nohria studied CEO turnover at Fortune 200 companies between 1980 and 1996.[119] They found that if a company was performing reasonably well, not wonderfully but not terribly, then bringing in an outsider was linked to a fall in performance and things getting predictably worse for three years before starting to improve. (Of course, if that CEO leaves before the end of three years and things are still performing adequately but not *as* adequately, bringing in another outsider then means things get worse again for another three years.)

Bringing in an outside CEO bolstered performance only when the company was in serious trouble—such as financial difficulties, senior management embezzlement, or if the outgoing CEO was fired for poor performance. In these cases, bringing in an outsider was linked to performance increases; the company clearly needed new skills or values and a message sent that there was a new sheriff in town and the old villains were gone.

Your church needs to assess itself carefully to know which side of the outsider value proposition it's likely to fall on if it has both external and internal candidates. But if experienced outsiders are, generally speaking, not a guaranteed winner, does that mean that we're back to insiders being the answer?

---

118 Michael McDaniel, Frank Schmidt and John Hunter, 'Job experiences correlates of job performance', *Journal of Applied Psychology*, 1988, vol. 73, no. 2, pp. 327-330.
119 Rakesh Khurana and Nitin Nohria, 'The performance consequences of CEO turnover', *SSRN.com*, 15 March 2000, accessed 15 December 2020. ssrn.com/abstract=219129

Filtered versus unfiltered

Winston Churchill was never supposed to be the prime minister of Great Britain. Although he entered politics young and rose through the ranks quickly, by the end of 1936 his political career seemed basically over. People had decided that he didn't have what it took for the highest offices; he was brilliant, but he was also a paranoid loose cannon. Very few respected his discernment as he'd made enormous mistakes in his various roles. He'd switched parties twice, in a way that certainly seemed from the outside as though he'd sacrificed his principles on the altar of personal ambition. He was dogmatic and pugnacious, seeing enemies and threats to Great Britain everywhere—some real, many imagined.

But he was the only politician who saw Hitler as a threat. This was partly because Hitler *was* a threat and partly because Churchill saw a stiff breeze as a threat. Neville Chamberlain, the prime minister at the time, was the quintessential British leader and he thought Hitler was "a man who could be relied upon when he had given his word".[120] Churchill knew that Hitler wasn't to be trusted and needed to be confronted and removed at all costs; Churchill thought that about pretty much everyone.

His forcefulness, zealotry, paranoia and brutishness nearly ruined Churchill's career, but it was those exact qualities that Britain needed heading into World War II. It took perhaps the greatest crisis that Britain had faced to overturn people's view of Churchill's suitability for the position, and even then it was a close call. Chamberlain only resigned when it became clear he had to, and pretty much everyone still preferred the other possibility, foreign secretary Viscount Halifax. But Halifax didn't want the position, and so Churchill was the only remaining option.[121]

The point of this history lesson is that success is not just about innate talents and work ethic. Effectiveness in one environment doesn't guarantee effectiveness in the next. As in the case of Churchill, context and culture play a huge role in ministry success.

Gautam Mukunda, author of *Indispensable*, makes a distinction

---

120 Gautam Mukunda, *Indispensable*, Harvard Business Review Press, Boston, 2012, p. 138.
121 For a nice summary of Churchill's career, see Mukunda, pp. 155-190. For a brief but comprehensive biography of Churchill, see Paul Johnson, *Churchill*, Penguin Books, New York, 2009.

between the filtered leader and the unfiltered leader. The filtered leader comes up through the system and is the kind of person the organization wants and rewards. Filtered leaders follow the rules, maintain the status quo and all think and act very similarly. Unfiltered leaders, in contrast, somehow bypass the filters of the organization and gain power before being thoroughly evaluated. Insiders are very often filtered leaders, which makes them safe choices.

Mukunda compared historians' rankings of US presidents and found that the most effective presidents were the unfiltered leaders. Abraham Lincoln is the quintessential example. He is considered by almost everyone as an extraordinary political leader, yet he was a dark horse candidate. But there's more. The sobering twist in the story is that the unfiltered presidents were also the *least* effective. It was either feast or famine. Unfiltered leaders are outsiders who get the job by a fluke. This means they will do things quite differently and often make a huge impact. Many times that impact cripples or destroys the organization, but sometimes it can be very positive. In the middle of the pack were the filtered leaders.[122]

Filtered leaders are usually the very definition of average because the extremes get sifted out. Unfiltered leaders are either much better or much worse. They're high-risk, high-reward types of leaders. So if insiders are often filtered, making them solid but unspectacular, and yet unfiltered outsiders are either the best option or very possibly the worst, maybe the answer is to find an outsider who has a track record as a star player.

The star

What makes someone a star performer? If I find a star who's looking for a job, will they then be a star at my church? The answer to the latter question is, unfortunately, probably not—because the answer to the former is that what makes someone a star has little to do with *them*. When high performers move from one place to another, they usually become mediocre performers.

The reason Churchill was so spectacularly successful was the context

---

[122] Mukunda, pp. 30-31.

he found himself in. As Mukunda says:

> The unfiltered leader who is an amazing success in one situation will be a catastrophic failure in the other, in almost all cases. It's way too easy to think, "I've always succeeded, I am a success, I am successful because I am a success, because it's about me, and therefore I will succeed in this new environment." Wrong. You were successful because you happened to be in an environment where your biases and predispositions and talents and abilities all happened to align neatly with those things that would produce success in that environment.[123]

Your effectiveness isn't just about you. It's about knowing yourself—your strengths, weaknesses and unique attributes—as well as the people around you and their impact, along with the unique culture you are in and how that magnifies, intensifies and resonates with your own values and behaviours. All this created your effectiveness. The same goes for your applicants.[124]

Harvard Business School professor Boris Groysberg studied star stock analysts to see what happened as they moved from one investment bank to another. This is an industry where people change who they work for but continue to turn up to literally the same place (Wall Street) to do the same work. Groysberg discovered that when these financial wizards moved from one bank to another, they stopped being financial wizards and their plummet in performance continued for at least five years after moving to a new firm.[125]

Groysberg noticed the same thing as Mukunda. Again, as with Churchill, context is critical. Naturals, geniuses and wunderkinds aren't amazingly effective because of who they are. They produce results due to

[123] Eric Barker, 'Gautam Mukunda of Harvard explains the secret to being a better leader', *Barking Up The Wrong Tree,* accessed 15 December 2020. bakadesuyo.com/2013/03/interview-harvard-business-school-professor-gautam-mukunda-teaches-secrets-leader/
[124] When researchers studied the performance of 2086 mutual fund managers between 1992 and 1998, they found that 30% of a fund's performance could be attributed to the individual manager and 70% to factors related to the institution: Klass Baks, *On the performance of mutual fund managers* [dissertation], University of Pennsylvania, 2002.
[125] Boris Groysberg, *Chasing Stars,* Princeton University Press, Princeton, 2010, p. 63.

a whole package of factors that must be taken into account because the collection of factors will be so complex and unique that you can be confident they won't be replicated for the star who joins your church. The best you can expect is a rough approximation.[126]

Effectiveness signals likely failure

Since culture has such an impact on effectiveness, those who were most effective in their previous culture will have the hardest time understanding, adapting and being accepted by a new one. They'll have a difficult time being effective at all, let alone being as effective as they were previously.

This happens for several reasons. The person who most embodies a culture and has deeply internalized it will naturally find it painful and time-consuming to relearn and change to a new one. A person who was relatively aloof from their previous culture, and so not ultra-effective in it, will be able to adapt more readily.

Being a star reinforces routines and habits that are specific to a church or organization. These routines can often become calcified into scripts, shorthands and rules of thumb that then *hinder* performance at the next church. These cognitive and behavioural rigidities can make even communicating difficult within that new environment and culture.[127] Imagine wearing thermals and a thick coat during an English winter, being transported to the Australian outback, then not understanding why you're suddenly sweating. What helped you in one environment can hold you back in another.

---

126 Groysberg noted that there were circumstances that didn't coincide with plunging performance: moving to a firm with better systems and facilities or superior personnel to work with, the star's team moving with them, more entrepreneurial work. Another fascinating finding was that women's performance was more portable than men's. Groysberg concluded this was largely to do with the increased due diligence that female stock analysts did on companies they were potentially moving to.

127 Dennis Gioia and Peter Poole, 'Scripts in organizational behavior', *Academy of Management Review,* 1984, vol. 9, no. 3, pp. 449-459; Paul Allison and J Scott Long, 'Departmental effects on scientific productivity', *American Sociological Review,* 1990, vol. 55, no. 4, pp. 469-478; Gina Dokko, Steffanie Wilk and Nancy Rothbard, 'Unpacking prior experience: how career history affects job performance', *Organization Science,* 2009, vol. 20, no. 1, pp. 51-68.

The conclusion to all this is that hiring is hard. There is ample opportunity for cognitive biases to trip you up. The rules of thumb are wrong as often as they're right. Choosing well-trained insiders, experienced outsiders or star players is no guarantee that you'll have someone who will do a good job. In fact, the likelihood is that they will underperform.

Overcoming these barriers will require, on your part as the *hirer*, intelligent hiring processes that minimize bias, consider cultural fit and seek to understand why a candidate has been successful previously. And from the *hiree*, you should be looking for humility and self-awareness along with everything else the role may require.

Pipeline planning meeting 8

The objectives for this meeting are to brainstorm and begin building a theology of serving/ministry/recruiting and to brainstorm potential leaders to develop.

From the last two meetings you have the structures and clarity in place to begin installing your pipeline. The final component in this foundational stage is figuring out who you can immediately invite to the next layer.

There may be some obvious candidates who are ready to be invited to a team, unit or perhaps even ministry area leader layer and begin training and coaching—or you might not have any of these people available. In that case, sit tight with people leading at multiple layers for a while. It might also be that you don't *need* anyone to step up into a new layer position.

Have everyone spend time individually thinking theologically about serving, looking at verses, passages and examples from the Bible that address ministry in the context of discipleship. Then share those thoughts as a team; write them up on a whiteboard or on big pieces of paper and have a conversation. Are there any overlapping ideas? Any that connect with each other? Does one idea flow from another? Is one the foundation for another? The goal is to draft what your church believes about these things and gain clarity about how your theological foundation informs—or should inform—how you speak and think and act when it comes to serving, ministry and recruitment.

Next build a list of potential leaders for development. While you want everyone in your church to grow, there will be some who will be more strategic for you to invest your time in. Consider individually the people in the areas you each have responsibility for who *might* have potential for development. Be generous. You're not thinking of people who could step into a role *tomorrow*. You're looking into the future with the eyes of faith and thinking, "If we intentionally invested in this person and if they wanted to grow, they could possibly get there".

Also make a list of people you've noticed in other ministry areas or who aren't involved in ministry at all but who you think have potential for leadership.

Now that you have these two lists, come back as a group and share them and discuss these people. Pray for each person mentioned.

Have each person choose three people that they will take a next step with. (Don't choose people who are in someone else's ministry; that'll just get messy.) Spend time thinking through exactly what the next step is. You might have a different idea for each person or you might do the same thing for everyone. You might offer to read the Bible with them over the next six months. You might offer to read a Christian book or a leadership book with them. Maybe have a conversation about being involved in ministry, or invite them to help you plan an event or attend a conference with you. There are lots of possible options! Figure out what you think is best for each person. Have everyone share their plans with the group.

You now have the three pieces you need to begin installing pipeline architecture into your chosen ministry. Within the first week after this meeting, the ministry area leaders responsible for your initial rollout should meet with the senior leader to finalize and double-check the plan so they can implement it.

23
Leader assessment

Leadership development framework

- Ministry grouping
- Training and coaching
- Pipeline architecture
- Leader development
- Ministry monitoring
- Leader recruitment
- **Leader assessment**

Leadership culture
Discipleship culture
Convictional culture

Whether they're at school, the doctor's or at work, most people hate assessments and the fact they're being assessed. It often feels like a way of saying "you aren't good enough". But bosses want to know whether their employees are doing well at what they're being paid for. Schools need to know whether their students have understood and can do what they're supposed to have learned so that every student can reach full proficiency.

The time we're most okay about being assessed is when we're sick but we don't know what's wrong with us. The more the sickness impacts our quality of life, the keener we are to endure whatever inconvenience and pain is necessary to find the cause. Last year I finally learned why my throat had hurt for two years straight. The assessment process was, let's say, uncomfortable, but I looked forward to it because I didn't want to stay in the pain I was in. I knew the assessment wasn't about my value as a person, but it would tell me where I was going wrong and what I needed to do.

Why it's important

Leader assessment is an essential piece of the leadership development framework because we need to know *who* needs help with *what* to get better. It's tough to improve when you don't know what needs improving. It's as simple as that. Plus we also need to know who might be a good option to lead at the next layer.

We want people to get better because it's good when people do a good job. It's no fun when you know you suck at something but you don't know how to improve. When people get better it's also good for the ministry; it means people are being helped, loved, taught, evangelized and discipled as well as we know how.

Nice and unloving

Not assessing leaders is both unloving and unrealistic. It's unloving because it means we don't care whether that person can do what we've asked them to do. We might have sent them off to struggle and fail until they can't handle it any more and they quit in frustration and despair.

Imagine you are at the beach with your friend and his children. The beach is a great place of fun and relaxation, but it's also quite dangerous. People die in the water. So there you all are, and your friend's children run off into the surf. You ask him, "Do your children know how to swim?" He replies, nonchalantly, "Oh, I have no idea". Your friend is not acting lovingly towards his children because he has not assessed their ability to not drown.

Not assessing leaders is also unloving to the people they will lead. Maybe Steve is keen to be involved and he's got that servant heart you're looking for, but if he cannot *do* the ministry then he's not actually serving—and *you* are not serving him or those you are ministering to by inflicting him on them.

I'm not saying that people need to be perfect at whatever the ministry is before they are allowed to be a part of it. If that were the case, I wouldn't be involved in anything. But when someone new starts, I already know they're not good—I've *assessed them*. Because I know this I can help them, train them, slowly release responsibility to them and build them up to be able to do the more difficult parts. We'll talk more about this in chapter 25 when we talk about training and coaching, but you won't be an effective trainer if you don't know what needs tackling.

Which brings us to the second point: not assessing people is unrealistic. You already assess people now. Maybe you do it consciously or unconsciously, formally or informally, but you do it. You have ideas already about whether people are competent, faithful, punctual, team players and a whole host of other factors.

So assessments are loving and avoiding them is unrealistic—why do we hate them so much again? Sometimes it's because they're too much like arbitrary school exams or glorified popularity contests, or we suspect they'll be a personal attack or a farcical waste of time. Or the problem is us: we're anti-assessment because we don't realize we're not doing well or we know but don't care about getting better.

We need our assessments to be more like the doctor's. We can help people be passionate about getting better by showing them that the assessment has nothing to do with their value as a person but it will help them see what's wrong and the steps they can take to improve. The questions we need to be asking are, "How should you assess leaders? How accurate and helpful are your assessments?" Though perhaps an even more basic question that needs to be asked is: is accurate assessment of other people even possible? And perhaps surprisingly and deflatingly, the answer is: no.

What the data says

Humans aren't good at rating other humans. And by "aren't good" I mean "completely cannot", especially when it comes to rating people on complex behaviours like, say, being a team player. Our assessments are inconsistent and depend a lot on what *I* think being a team player means, how valuable *I* believe that particular trait is, how much *I* consider *myself* a team player, or how tough a rater *I* am.[128] It's the same for other complex qualities like strategic thinking, potential or ministry acumen.

How considerably does this impact my ability to assess people? Considerably. In 2000, Michael Mount, Steven Scullen and Maynard Goff researched what performance ratings were actually measuring. How much of a rating was about the actual performance, how much was random error and how much was to do with the rater themselves?[129] They had 4392 managers rated on general role performance and also specific performance dimensions—like "fosters teamwork" or "analyses issues". Two bosses, two peers and two subordinates rated each manager (a classic process typically known as 360-degree feedback).

They found—I've probably already spoiled this for you—that the majority of a rating told you about the *rater* rather than the *ratee*. Of all the reasons that one manager was rated more highly than another, actual performance accounted for only 21% of the variance. The largest amount of variance in people's ratings was explained by the rater's individual idiosyncrasies: 62% of the rating! Which means that 62% of the assessment told us nothing—*literally nothing*—about the person being rated. The researchers called this the 'idiosyncratic rater effect'.

Amongst the different categories of rater, the bosses had the lowest idiosyncratic rater effects; their rose-coloured glasses or personal feelings impacted the rating by 51%. The highest levels were in the self-ratings:

---

128 Robert Wherry and CJ Bartlett, 'The control of bias in rating: a theory of rating', *Personnel Psychology*, 1982, vol. 35, no. 3, pp. 521-551; Michael K Mount et al, 'Trait, rater and level effects in 360-degree performance ratings', *Personnel Psychology*, 1998, vol. 51, no. 3, pp. 557-576; Brian Hoffman et al, 'Rater source effects are alive and well after all', *Personnel Psychology*, 2010, vol. 63, no. 1, pp. 119-151.

129 Michael Mount, Steven Scullen and Maynard Goff, 'Understanding the latent structure of job performance ratings', *Journal of Applied Psychology*, 2000, vol. 85, no. 6, pp. 956-970.

71%.[130] This is consistent with other findings about how terrible people are at rating themselves. People often overestimate their abilities compared to other people, like how most people think they are an above-average driver.[131] The researchers concluded, "For peer, subordinate, and self-ratings, the idiosyncratic component was larger than all of the other effects combined".[132]

None of us is as dumb as all of us

"But Craig, this is the genius of 360-degree feedback! Even if an individual is unreliable, many people won't be. None of us is as smart as all of us! When we compile all the ratings, we'll end up with a pretty good picture. One person might be biased, but if six people say you're 'not pastoral' then it's probably fair to say that you're not pastoral. Right?"

Wrong.

In 2004 James Surowiecki published his brilliant book *The Wisdom of Crowds*.[133] The book starts with the true story of British scientist Sir Francis Galton—the half-cousin of Charles Darwin[134]—who in 1906 went to a county fair and watched as hundreds of people individually guessed the weight of an ox to win a prize. The answer turned out to be 1198 pounds. After the contest was over, Galton asked to borrow the 800 tickets containing everyone's guesses and averaged them. This average? 1197. Aggregating the judgement of the many consistently ends up being astonishingly accurate.

The way this 'miracle' works is that knowledge is often scattered broadly about; one person has one piece, another has a few more scraps, a third has an even more important nugget and so on. When it came to the ox, one lady vaguely remembered the weight of 1905's ox; the butcher contributed his years of experience and expertise; a third person had bought meat in bulk once. Hundreds of people added their shaving of

---

130 Mount et al, p. 963.
131 Michael Roy and Michael Liersch, 'I am a better driver than you think: examining self-enhancement for driving ability', *Journal of Applied Social Psychology*, 2013, vol. 43, no. 8, pp. 1648-1659.
132 Mount et al, p. 966.
133 James Surowiecki, *The Wisdom of Crowds*, Little, Brown Book Group, London, 2004.
134 Fun fact!

knowledge to the pile. At the same time, of course, they contributed their biases, misinformation and mistakes, creating a pile of wrong as big as the pile of right. However, the pile of right increasingly pointed in the same direction while the pile of wrong was pointed every which way. As the correct guesses zeroed in, closer and closer to the correct answer, the wrong ones kept nullifying each other.

And so you're now thinking, "Yes, 360-degree feedback is like that". Except it's not. The title of Suroweicki's book—*The Wisdom of Crowds*—was itself a play on another, much earlier, book quaintly titled *Extraordinary Popular Delusions and the Madness of Crowds* and published way back in 1841. A crowd is wise when those in it are well-informed. In the case of the ox, everyone whose opinion was aggregated came from the surrounding farmlands and so they had an idea of the weight of oxen. But what if they'd never weighed an ox in their lives and didn't know anyone else who had either? What if they'd been asked to guess how friendly the ox was? Or its potential?

This is what happens when a group of people is asked to rate you. They don't see a lot of the things you do, don't interact with you enough to know well your abstract attributes, and they'd all have a different definition of each attribute anyway.

The other problem with a 360-degree rating is that it combines one person's uninformed rating of you with six other equally ignorant ratings. Errors average out when they are *random*, when they point in different directions. If you're taking someone's temperature with a faulty thermometer, the errors are systemic rather than random, and adding them together and finding the average doesn't miraculously correct them. When it comes to humans rating other humans, all our instruments are faulty.

Assessment will be happening, consciously or not, and in order to love our people, it needs to be—despite the fact that we're not good at rating complex performance skills. Is there a way forward?

When we are better

There is a way forward. In fact, there are many ways forward, so long as we think carefully about what we're assessing and rating along with doing what we can to minimize the idiosyncratic rater effect.

The first thing to realize is that assessing for traits such as potential, being a team player or strategic thinking is so difficult partly because they are actually categories made up of a myriad of smaller traits and factors. Being a team player isn't a *thing*; it's a mosaic of being punctual, having a positive attitude, being encouraging, telling the truth, admitting mistakes, listening to others, putting forward ideas, accepting feedback, being flexible, being willing to give extra help, forgiving others, asking for forgiveness, caring for the team... the list could go on and on.

If I rate you out of 5 on 'being a team player', what am I actually doing? To remind you from chapter 4, I'm trying to conjure up a list of all the behaviours that I think go into what a team player looks like, rate you on all those sub-factors, aggregate all those ratings into one meta-rating and so thus give you a, let's say, 4. But have I really gathered and rated 100ish separate dimensions fairly and accurately, and then weighted each appropriately in the cumulative total? Highly unlikely. I've probably thought up a handful that I at this moment in time consider the most important because they're the ones that people have not been doing and it's really annoying me right now. If you asked me tomorrow I might think differently. And what does a 4 in 'telling the truth' mean? Or a 3 in 'being flexible'?

Don't panic. While these meta-qualities are extremely hard to rate accurately, it's easier to rate more singular behaviours, especially if they are displayed competencies: "when running a game, regularly gives clear instructions". It's either yes, no or sometimes.

This is where the pipeline framework helps us. It breaks down performance at each layer into smaller pieces. "Being a good team leader" is broken down into its constituent pieces like ministry distribution and running a meeting. Each of these can be broken down further into smaller and smaller units that assist in a more accurate assessment. You can ask: did this team leader meet with each member of her team this quarter? If the answer is yes, you can say with some certainty that she has "coaching: how often should you meet" under control. You don't yet know if she's doing anything helpful while she's meeting with her team members, but that's a separate question. And if the answer is no, now you have something to have a conversation about. Maybe there was a good reason, maybe there wasn't, but you can coach with a bit more intelligence having assessed that particular facet of team development.

Another way to think about it is in terms of health. Health is an abstract term like teamwork—we don't try to measure health. Instead we measure various components we know make up that abstract notion: body mass index, resting heart rate, glucose levels, cholesterol, etc. Focusing on these components of health enables us to measure more reliably and act on the result more usefully. None of these measurements gives you the whole picture on its own, and some will be more central than others, but they'll be more helpful for creating a plan of action than giving you a blanket rating of '4 in health'. In the same way, pipeline architecture helps us break down these abstract concepts and deal with them more reliably.

Self-assessments

"Craig, the research showed that self-assessment was the rating *most* affected by the idiosyncratic rater effect and is the least accurate. Why should I bother using it?"

For a start, because it accurately tells you what the person thinks. Sure, maybe it tells you that they think that they're the best when you think they're not, but at least you now know. This will help you significantly in shaping your coaching conversations. If you both think they're below competent in an area then you can broach the topic fairly easily; if they think they are highly competent but you don't, you'll need a bit more tact. This is useful information to a compassionate and emotionally intelligent leader.

You can also use self-evaluations to have your people assess the ministry rather than themselves through questions like:

- Do you feel that what is expected of you has been adequately explained?
- Do you feel that you have been adequately equipped to fulfil these expectations?
- How clearly has the purpose and vision of this ministry been explained to you?

Presumably you attempted to do these things—here you are asking, "Did it work? Have I achieved what I set out to achieve?" If they answer no, this is bad news that is good news because now you get to try again. It also gives you an opportunity, at least once a year in case you forget otherwise, to ask your team where they think the ministry can do better. You could ask:

- No-one thinks this is a perfect ministry. Where do you think we can improve? What is this ministry missing? What could we do to improve? Be specific.
- In your opinion, what is the best part of this ministry?
- In your opinion what is the worst/most badly-executed part of this ministry?

As long as you can constructively accept the answers without getting hurt or angry, this will be a powerful tool for opening up a conversation with the members of your team. (If you get defensive or combative, then you have other issues that you need to deal with before you worry about the assessment element of the leadership development framework. You have some heart work to do and some maturity to gain as your top priority.)

Another reason to use self-evaluations is that they can be a brilliant training tool. When you give people a list of things to assess themselves on, it shows them what is valued and what you think they are supposed to be doing. This will work especially well if you show and explain their self-evaluation document in March but have them complete it in November. It's like giving people the answers to the exam.

Lastly, self-evaluations communicate that you have a culture of development and that you want to help people continually improve. They will also demonstrate a culture of honesty if people are allowed to say what they really think when they give their feedback through them.

When I first left school, I worked in retail at a large chain store. The manager told me that the store valued honesty and progress, so if we had ideas on what could be improved we should feel free to share them. Soon after I was asked what I thought, so I naively and non-combatively gave some feedback. And I received a written warning. I vowed then that if I ever led a team, this would never happen. I want my people to say what they think and disagree with an idea—even my idea and even in front of everybody—without being afraid of getting into trouble for it if they are respectful and have actual reasons.

And why wouldn't you value their opinions? People are smart and insightful; they see things that you don't. Besides, the moment that boss punished me for trying to make things better, I was taught to mentally check out from that job. I came in, I worked hard, but I didn't care. In the ministries I lead, I don't want people turning up without caring or trying to improve things. I want their hearts and brains too; all of us all together making this ministry better.

If development, honesty and valuing what the team thinks are not currently a part of your culture but you are committed to seeing them become so—moving from aspirational to actual—then a self-evaluation process can be one helpful element to begin to shift your culture.

The way I do all this in my ministries is that at the end of the first quarter we give everyone a self-evaluation that is actually a ministry evaluation. We flip the usual probation period and instead of us evaluating *them*, we ask them to evaluate *us*. We also give them the self-evaluation that we'll be asking them to do at the end of the year. Throughout the year we coach and train them to improve, and then in the last quarter we give them the same self-evaluation they looked at earlier—no surprises—but now they fill it in and talk it through with their team leaders.

Leveraging our assessing strengths

But as well as assessing individual competencies and performing self-assessments, we still need a *fair* way to assess other people (since it's going to happen anyway). Fortunately, there is a simple yet profound shift we can make in the way we approach assessment and in the types of questions we ask that ensures our assessments tell us more about the ratee than the rater.

Markus Buckingham and Ashley Goodall write, "To see performance at the individual level, then, we [need to] ask team leaders not about the *skill* of each team member but about their own *future actions* with respect to that person".[135] In other words, while people are consistently inconsistent when it comes to rating skills, they are *very* consistent when it comes to rating what they will do. They know their own feelings and intentions.

So, instead of asking team leaders what they *think* about the people on their team, we ask them what they will actually *do* with that individual. And rather than asking about whether they think that person has a certain quality, we ask how they would *act or react* if that person *did* have it.[136] Here are five sample questions you can use to get better and more accurate assessments of the people in your team. After you start to understand how these questions work, you can begin inventing your own to assess different facets:[137]

1. I always go to person A when I need extraordinary results. (This evaluates "produces high-quality work".)

Notice how this question doesn't ask you to rate the person on a five-point scale or to abstract and synthesize something in order to make a judgement. It simply asks what you do. If you need something done and done well, do you ask this person?

2. I choose to work with person A as much as I possibly can. (This statement connects to "being a team player".)

Again, notice how this question asks what you currently do. It's not asking you to rate a broad range of concrete behaviours and then aggregate them into a numerical summary of an abstract category. Here are three more options:

3. I would promote person A today if I could.
4. Does person A have a performance problem that I need to address right now?
5. If I had to do it again, would I re-hire/re-recruit person A for this position? Or perhaps to a different position?

---

135 Marcus Buckingham and Ashley Goodall, 'Reinventing performance management', *Harvard Business Review*, April 2015, accessed 13 February 2021. hbr.org/2015/04/reinventing-performance-management
136 Buckingham and Goodall, p. 156.
137 These questions are modifications of the questions in Buckingham and Goodall's article.

The fundamental point here is that you are asking your team leader to tell you about their own actions, either current or future, rather than the behaviours, qualities or characteristics of the person being rated.

Even knowing all these things, some people will still want a foolproof, objective and always accurate system. That system cannot exist because we are imperfect and complicated people dealing with other imperfect and complicated people. If you do nothing before you're certain it'll be 100% accurate, you'll still be making assessments unconsciously, and it's almost guaranteed that they'll be worse than any of these suggested evaluations.

The process will never be straightforward; you'll need discernment and wisdom. Assessment and evaluation are subjective and open to argument. But to develop the leaders in your team you need to know where they're at, what they can do and where they still need to learn so that you can train and coach them.

A leadership pipeline with strong leaders at every layer means inviting some to step higher. You'll have to make some judgement calls. But base them on how people actually react to a person. This kind of assessment is humbler, simpler and more reliable—and those three things alone are a noble and useful achievement.

Pipeline planning meeting 9

In this meeting you will revisit the first drafts of the fundamental operations that you created back in pipeline planning meeting 3 and, if you haven't already, line up your regular one-to-one meetings.

Have everyone go back to their fundamental operations and see if there are any new insights or additions they'd like to include. Then have each person work down the pipeline layers to clarify the fundamental operations for each. See how much of this you can get done before you either run out of time or people get restless and bored. You might then have each person share their finalized drafts with the wider team to help people share ideas.

It's time for people to conceptualize and organize their one-on-one meetings. Have each person create a list of people whom they already meet with or whom they need to start meeting with. They should then determine the frequency of those meetings. Weekly? Fortnightly? Monthly? Quarterly?

The final step, if appropriate, is to message or email each person with something like:

> Hey NAME, I've realized I could do a better job of caring for you as a ROLE in MINISTRY and so I think it would be good for us to meet up every FREQUENCY for an hour and half or so to chat about life and the ministry and whatever. Does DATE AND TIME suit for us to have our first go at it?

Tweak it so it sounds like you. Ensure you communicate the purpose of the meetings, how often you're thinking they'd happen and how long for each time. You also want to signal the content of the meeting and give them a concrete next step. Lastly, maybe this has never happened to them before and they might feel a bit awkward, so take the pressure off by hinting that it's nothing to be afraid of.

For senior leaders

In the next pipeline planning meeting we're going to zero in on self-evaluation assessments. It's extremely important that you first draft a three-month evaluation for the ministry area leaders who report to you to complete where they *evaluate the church's ministry* (for now skip any leaders in ministries where *you* are the ministry area leader). Give those leaders the evaluation and a couple of weeks to fill it in, then meet to hear more about their answers. This is a big leadership moment for you and it's easy to screw up. Don't be defensive and combative—especially if you disagree with them! Be curious. What are they seeing that you're not? You want to hear what they really think. Don't punish your people for telling you the truth.

It's important to do this before the next pipeline planning meeting because they're going to do the same process with their people. They will do a better job if they've experienced what it's like to be on the other side of the evaluation.

24
Ministry monitoring

Leadership development framework

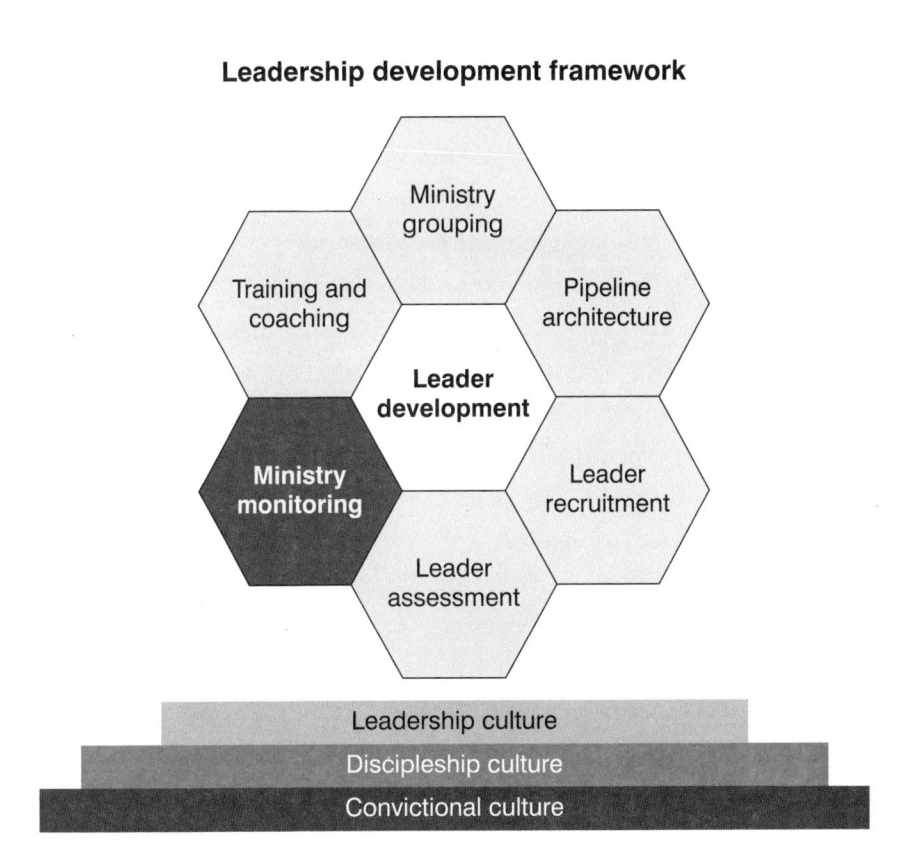

- Ministry grouping
- Training and coaching
- Pipeline architecture
- Leader development
- Ministry monitoring
- Leader recruitment
- Leader assessment

- Leadership culture
- Discipleship culture
- Convictional culture

The second law of thermodynamics states that all closed systems tend towards entropy. Things fall apart when left alone. Your kitchen will veer towards chaos and the floor of your car will get increasingly messy until you intervene and wash those pots and pans and throw out the McDonald's wrappers hiding under the driver's seat. Order doesn't happen by accident: you need to expend energy to create it and keep it.

Ministries are the same. They need to be monitored. Once you have set one up, recruited leaders and assessed where they are at, you can't walk away and let that ministry run itself. It will unravel into a frothy chaotic soup. It needs constant attention just to keep the basic operations ticking over. This is the *management* side of church leadership.

We may think, "Great; I've got someone leading that ministry. They'll chat to me if they have a problem or I'll chat to them if I hear about a problem. They'll just get on with doing a good job, and I'll focus on other things." This is a common but catastrophic mistake. Active ministry monitoring needs to happen at every layer of ministry. Senior leaders need to monitor the ministry of their ministry area leaders, ministry area leaders their team leaders, and team leaders their leaders.

This is *not* micromanaging. Micromanaging is when you withhold from the leader the freedom or authority to take ownership of the ministry, make decisions and fix their mistakes. Ministry monitoring is about caring for your leaders, helping them process what's happening in their ministries and reminding them of the things they said they'd do, while also providing an experienced and somewhat external perspective to point out what they may not have noticed or may *not be able* to notice because they're in the thick of things.

Ministry monitoring is made up of three pieces: providing clarity, reinforcing trust and giving time.

Clarity

In chapter 3 we talked a lot about clarity and the key questions you need to have answers for. The fifth question was "Who's doing what?" Every person in every team should know exactly what you want from them or they won't be able to know within themselves whether they've done a good job. You'll remember that we broke the ministry down into its fundamental operations (the handful of things that *must* happen for this ministry to be); we'll soon see how you use these fundamental operations and make them worth the effort when we talk about giving your leaders time by meeting with them. But before we get there, we still need to provide more clarity so that your leaders know what they are supposed to be doing.

This is where role descriptions come in. You need a clear role description for every position in every layer in every ministry in your church. These don't need to be elaborate or even formal—they just need to be clear. That's the objective.[138]

There are lots of good ways to create them, but I think the best approach is to have a one-page role description with only the high-level, summary information. You'll also have a longer manual that outlines the ministry and any ministry-specific skills in more detail. All layer-specific information—such as what a team leader needs to be doing—can be found in the leadership pipeline material and doesn't need to be repeated. The downside of this is that the information is spread across three different documents, but the advantage is that it's in digestible chunks. People can get a handle on a role description that only takes up one page.

As well as clarifying *what* you want leaders to do, you also need to clarify *how long* you expect them to spend doing it. Your people may have very different ideas in their heads from those you have in yours! When the youth leaders prepare a game, how long are you envisaging they'll spend on that? An hour? Two? What if they plan on spending ten hours on game preparation? Do you expect team leaders to meet with each individual on their team for two hours every week? You probably don't, but what if one of your team leaders assumes that's the expectation? Maybe they'll do it for a couple of weeks, smashing themselves into the ground to make it happen, and then never do it again but feel a delicate mix of guilt and resentment for the rest of the year and quit at the end. All because of an expectation that you never had, said or wanted—but you're left to clean up the mess.

---

138 I recommend writing them down, but you don't even *have* to do that.

Here's what a one-page role description could look like:[139]

velocity

Leader role summary

Care for the students
- Pray for the students during the week
- Learn the students' names
- Prioritise your time to be with them
- Remember what you spoke about and develop ongoing conversations
- Join in activities with students at every opportunity
- Capitalise on opportunities to talk about Jesus

Care for the night
- Pray for the night during the week
- Actively help make the night happen
- Be trustworthy and reliable: being on time to meetings, being fully prepared, etc.
- Help with crowd control by getting the students around you to be quiet when needed

Care for the team
- Pray for the other leaders on the team
- Look for opportunities to be an encouragement to others on the team
- Share the load: organising the night, crowd control, etc.

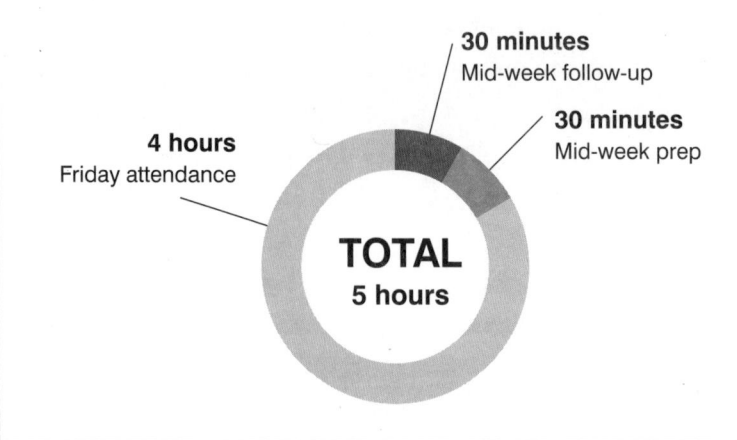

4 hours Friday attendance

30 minutes Mid-week follow-up

30 minutes Mid-week prep

TOTAL 5 hours

---

[139] For more example role descriptions and ministry manuals, visit revcraighamilton.com.

It's not that you *must* have a written role description, but writing one forces you to crystallize the swirling thoughts in your head. It also has the benefit of being an external object you can refer to and that people can refer to without needing you there to say it all again—which means you can extend the helpfulness of your presence even when you're not present.

Trust

The second element of effective ministry monitoring is trust. You should be entrusting ministry to your team and treating them with respect. This is just another outworking of loving those you lead the way you love yourself. Some leaders find it hard to trust others with ministry because they think it means trusting others not to make a mistake. That's impossible for them, of course; you're instead trusting them to both admit to and fix their mistakes. That's how you treat *you*.

There aren't many things I'm absolutely convinced about, but one of them is that in the near future I will make a mistake. I'll do or say something I shouldn't. The fact that my future failure is a certainty doesn't mean I disqualify myself from ministry. I trust that when I mess up, I will do everything I can to make it right. I'll apologize to anyone who needs an apology; I'll do whatever needs to be done to get us back on the right track. It's the same for the people I've entrusted ministry to. They will make mistakes, small and large—then they will do everything they can to fix things. And I'll be there to help when needed.

Now I'm not saying that you need to trust everyone indiscriminately and never be wary or discerning. Some people shouldn't be entrusted with a napkin. Trusting people is risky, and there's no guarantee that it will work out. But that uncertainty applies to you too. You'll be able to think of people in ministry who crashed and burned. Some failures were public and spectacular, others were quiet and pedestrian, but we all know those who disqualified themselves from ministry. Each of them trusted themselves with ministry until it became publicly clear that trust was misplaced.

You *must* use every ounce of wisdom that you can tap into as you entrust ministry to others. People should prove their faithfulness, and you should observe them handling responsibilities well as they are incrementally handed over. That's what the pipeline architecture itself is helping you build and what we discussed back in chapter 3 when laying out quadrants of responsibility and authority and gaining decision clarity. But you'll still need to *actually* trust people—not to be perfect but to be trustworthy. If you never trust anybody enough to hand over ministry to them, then you have seen the enemy and the enemy is you.

Do understand also that trusting people to fix their mistakes means *they* fix their mistakes. You don't solve their problems for them. The first thing you think when a blunder occurs amongst the ministry of those you lead should *not* be "What can I do to help?" but rather "Am I needed here at all?" We want to be caring and so we often think that means we need to help, but that's not always true. When a person brings you a problem they are facing, they may even want you to fix it, but that's not loving. Guide them, coach, advise, help them think it through, but don't do it for them. It doesn't help them grow and get stronger.[140]

Time

The final element of successful ministry monitoring is time. Back when we discussed pipeline architecture we covered leaders needing to view helping those they lead not as a distraction but as a key component of their ministry. A leader of leaders needs to give their time to their leaders.

This is done both formally and informally, proactively and reactively. When a leader sends you an email, gives you a call or grabs you during morning tea asking for help or advice, that's informal and reactive. These are important leadership moments. In this chapter, however, we'll look at a more formal and proactive mechanism for giving your time to your leaders: the one-to-one meeting.

When I say formal I don't have minute-taking in mind. You don't need to table a motion. I just mean these meetings aren't accidental. You might meet over a milkshake or a coffee, playing a game of pool or on the basketball court—wherever. The point is that you *organized* to meet up in

---

140 See Hamilton, 'There's no point having a dog and then barking yourself', pp. 311-316.

advance and the meeting is 'about' something. Regular meetings allow you to continually invest in the person and to show your care for them, and allow *them* to feel cared for. They also help you to catch issues before they mutate into their full-grown final form.

One of the keys to leadership development is talking with people. There's almost no problem on the planet that couldn't be solved with a simple and honest conversation. Wars have ended because two people sat in a room and talked. We call it diplomacy, but it's just conversation. The one-to-one meeting is the most crucial ongoing leadership tool in your toolbox. Once you're on the same page with your leaders as to what's happening, who is doing what and why it's being done, the one-to-one meeting is the centrepiece of your leadership arsenal. It's the main way you monitor the ministry.

What's the meeting for?

The meeting doesn't just exist for itself, however, and you don't have it just because it's in the calendar. The meeting is trying to *achieve* something. It's generally to care for, disciple and develop your leader, check in on the ministry and discuss any problems or opportunities. You're creating a regular and predictable forum so that they know, no matter how hectic things might get, they'll have this space to clarify, raise issues and ask advice.

The meeting is about them and the ministry, not about you. This is fundamental to leadership shaped by the gospel, an obvious point that gets forgotten more than it should. The meeting is a chance to display Christlike love and other-person-centredness. It is not about getting things off your chest, updating them on things you should have emailed them about or showing off by solving all their problems for them.

What do you do in the meeting?

There are two considerations: What should we do regularly? What else might be included occasionally? In other words, what does the base model include and what are some optional upgrades that I might add across the year?

The baseline model should be built around four simple topics that become the 'agenda' of the meeting. If you discuss these each time you meet, people will begin to learn and start to come prepared.

You'll always check in with the leader about their discipleship. Their relationship with Jesus matters because *they* matter to you, and because it will impact their ministry. This will not usually be the main topic of conversation, but it is an element. Presumably at your church there is an interconnected network of discipleship opportunities and some other piece of that ecosystem is playing the primary role in their discipleship. Your ministry monitoring meeting is a small piece of that puzzle but it's not the main thing.

And so, apart from discipleship, the first 'official' question I ask is just a broad, generic, "How're things?" This gives the leader a chance to bring up whatever is on their mind. They may talk about things happening in the ministry, in their personal life, issues with other leaders or other people more broadly—they might even bring up broader issues in the news that concern them. The point is that it allows them to take control of the meeting and talk about what they want to. This signals to them that this meeting is theirs.

If you discover that things have been badly falling apart, you may make the decision to jettison your plans for the rest of the meeting and spend your time there, listening, caring and praying for them. You'd tell them that what's been happening in their life feels much more important to talk about and that you'll find another time to catch up on the ministry things.

But assuming their life is its usual pace and within the bounds of typical pains, you would then move on to the second topic: "How was last week?" In particular cover how they went doing whatever specific thing they said they would at the previous meeting.

Next you talk about the ministry itself, which I signal with the elaborate question, "How's the ministry?" Here you're going to discuss: Are we achieving what we want to achieve? What's going well? What's not? What's the next thing on the horizon?

Again the question is open so that they can talk about what they think is important. Perhaps they have noticed things you haven't, since they are closer to the frontlines. It's important to give them this space and to help them think through what is happening and what they think they should do about it. As we'll discuss in the next chapter, these conversations are perfect opportunities for training and coaching. This means you won't necessarily be telling them what to do but will be asking, "What do you think the underlying issue is? What factors are in play?" But more on this in the next chapter.

Lastly, the final topic: what you wanted to talk about. From your perspective overseeing the whole team or ministry, you'll have noticed issues or opportunities they couldn't see. Or you might check in on the progress of something this leader was going to do that they haven't mentioned so far. Or perhaps there's something they need to change or that they've been doing really well that you want to point out.

There's no rule on how many items you can bring up here. It depends on the issues, your relationship with the leader and their general emotional state. If you are asking for updates you could cover quite a few, whereas if you are bringing up areas for them to improve, be careful about how many you raise in one go.

If you hammer them with ten areas where they are failing, they may leave that meeting exhausted from your complete evisceration. They may leave fuming and spend the next week simmering over what you've said. They might lose confidence and enthusiasm, the effects lingering beneath the surface and covertly impacting both them and the ministry for months. All ten areas may legitimately need to be dealt with, but that doesn't mean they all need to be dealt with *in one go*. Remember the meeting is about them and helping them improve, not about making complaints.

Consider the effectiveness of your feedback. You're telling them not so they have been told but so they grow and do better work. One or two things at a time will mean there's a much better chance that they'll actually hear, receive and work on what you've said. You also need to count the cost of your feedback. Is telling them everything you think is wrong with them worth the price of their emotions? Your criticism of them is much heavier for them to carry than it was for you, so be thoughtful in how much you place on them at once.

You'll ask these *same* questions in this *same* order *every* time because, firstly, this is *their* meeting for *them*. You want to minimize the power imbalance and help them to feel like they can speak and suggest. One way to do this is to allow them to speak first.

If you structure it this way, they may bring up some of the issues themselves that you had wanted to get to. Them raising the problems allows them to be proactive and it means you've learned something about their insight into the ministry. If they notice what you notice, then you know that their expertise and ministry maturity is developing and you can consider how to keep growing them.

Discussing the same topics in the same order also builds predictability into your meetings. The person you meet with can feel safe and comfortable because they know what's coming. It also means they'll be able to prepare, which means they'll bring more insightful things to talk about and reflections on the ministry.

With some people I have led, over the years we met together they would basically run the meeting themselves: they'd begin by talking about exercise, their pet bird and their Bible reading (along with whatever else was happening in their life), transition to talking about the ministry, and then finally ask me what items I had to discuss. It meant that our conversations could actually stray further away from these topics because we both knew where the meeting needed to get to.

This is the regular shape of the meeting, but every now and then you may want to deviate from this structure to discuss various other topics. Here are some of the extras that you could add into your usual structure or even completely replace it with.

GYR rating

Remember those fundamental operations? You divided up the processes the ministry needs to pay attention to and boiled them down so that your leaders have clarity on what needs to be done for the ministry to operate. Here's how you can keep them relevant and make them useful.

Running a ministry is often like spinning plates. Every aspect needs a regular injection of energy to keep going, but you need to keep watching every other aspect because another may start wobbling. Often problems in a ministry don't come out of nowhere; they build slowly over time and can be seen and solved long before they become crises so long as you can notice early enough to intervene. The issue is that we often can't keep an eye on everything at once. The fundamental operations help you avoid preventable calamities by enabling you to keep an eye on the whole.

Depending on how often you meet up, bring these fundamental operations along somewhere between twice a year and once a month. You both rate how you think each function is going: green for good (not necessarily perfect but more positive than negative), yellow for fine (neither good nor bad), and red for bad and needing attention. This is called a GYR rating, after the colours. You now have a conversation explaining your ratings, looking for where you agreed and disagreed. Suddenly you have clarity on whether any of your core processes need attention and it took just 15 minutes. Going to the effort to gain the clarity to create these fundamental operations earlier starts paying off.

The conversation then pivots to deciding what you need to do now. Any reds to deal with immediately? Any greens that you want to invest in to make even better? Perhaps you want to put energy into some yellows to keep them from turning red. Figure out a roadmap for action. Next time you meet and GYR rate, you can check to see whether your work helped that facet of the ministry. Maybe you'll discover that something else has fallen off the boil in the meantime.

1-2-3

A tool to help you have a conversation about actions and next steps with your leader is as simple as 1-2-3. You might use this at the end of every meeting, or only every now and then in broader discussions. It's a good tool to use after the GYR rating to help your leader work out what exactly needs to be done.

Firstly, ask them what one thing they could do before you meet again would have the most impact and most predictably make a difference. This one thing won't be the only thing they'll do, but it's the most important thing. If they don't get anything else done, they'll at least have accomplished this highest value, highest impact, most important thing.

They may come up with it themselves, you may guide them or you might just tell them what the one thing will be. This will depend on their experience in the role and their depth of insight into the ministry. Initially you'll be more directive, but as they gain confidence you'll input less and less until you are just agreeing with their genius ideas.[141]

Secondly, you ask what the two biggest hurdles or blockages they're facing right now are. They might be related to achieving the one thing from the previous question, or they could be blockages relating to leaders, systems, their personal life or their own lack of skills.

If you use this 1-2-3 set of questions in a whole team meeting, the subtext that you may want to make explicit is that we as a team may be able to help you with these two problems. Someone may be able to spare resources or make a tweak in their area that is negatively contributing to your issue, or may have experienced the same challenge and so can provide advice or comfort. This way, the team learns to rely on *each other* rather than on *you* as the sole source of help.

Thirdly, ask what the three next specific steps needed are. You want people to leave the meeting knowing *exactly* what they need to do now. It's not just "call someone who can help", "email someone to find out how it's done", "recruit five new leaders" or "make this thing better". These are not concrete enough. They need to be able to walk straight out of the meeting and take these steps without any more thinking: "call Gary about how the fire hose works for next time" or "email Jane to find out how much money is in the account".

Often people won't know the answers to any of these questions and won't think to ask them explicitly until after going through the process. Doing the process over and over helps them to do the thinking you'd like them to do. They'll do it themselves because you've been implicitly training them and it'll start to become as easy as 1-2-3.

Self-evaluations

If you are introducing a culture of development and coaching, it's a good idea to schedule in development conversations. These are where you can tell your leader something they're doing that you love and something that you want to see them grow in or stop doing. In your regular one-to-one

---

141 See Hamilton, 'Change your default style', pp. 105-110.

meetings, you should schedule in at least one self-evaluation meeting in the year.[142] Scheduling it will force you to think about it and will help both of you to prepare for it mentally.

Have the person complete their self-evaluation in their own time and then meet up to talk about it. You want to hear the thoughts behind their answers. You'll have your own ideas and opinions, and so you can have a genuine discussion. You may or may not agree with their evaluation, but them filling in the form is not the end of the story but the beginning of the conversation.

Pipeline development

To keep the leadership pipeline on the agenda and people growing and developing in their leadership layer, you'll need pipeline development conversations every 90 days or so. Schedule time in your meeting to discuss what the next layer-specific thing for them to learn is—they might choose, or you might assign one—and what you'll both do to see this happen. You could read and discuss something connected to that competency or introduce them to someone more proficient than them who can teach them. Make sure there are opportunities for them to practise and implement the new skill and to receive coaching on how it's going.

After 90 days, discuss how that new skill has gone, whether it still needs work or what the next thing to target might be. Will it be a new skill or going back to a previous one to sharpen it? Or you might begin training them in some of the things to learn from the layer *above* so they can test the waters and start getting ready should the opportunity arise.

Decision clarity

Don't neglect the decision-clarity quadrant for each leader (discussed in chapter 3). It's supposed to reflect reality; keep coming back to it periodically so that it doesn't calcify into irrelevance. Once a year, together re-evaluate which quadrant different decisions are in and whether some new issues have come up that need to be assigned.

---

142 At revcraighamilton.com you can download self-evaluation templates for various pipeline layers that you can adapt to suit your church and ministry.

This doesn't need to be a complicated process, just bring the quadrants and ask, "Is this still what reality looks like? If not, what happens now and which items need to be moved where?" It's also a chance to officially hand authority for a decision over. This will require talking together about what they need to know and how you see it working from now on.

Bonus questions

Along with the four standard topics—how're things, how was last week, how's the ministry and your things—throw in a bonus question once in a while. You can ask whatever you think would be useful and helpful in the moment. These are my favourites:

1. Is there anything I can do better to make your job easier?
2. What's preventing you from doing an even better job?
3. What are you spending time on that you don't feel you should be spending time on?
4. What's one thing you like about your role and one thing that frustrates you?
5. Is there something you've done at your company/job/last church that we should try here?
6. What are three things you think I should know about that I might not be aware of?
7. If you were me, what would you do differently?
8. Do you think we're a high-performing ministry? How do you know? What would us being a high-performing ministry look like?
9. If you had my job, what would be the first thing you'd do that isn't happening now?
10. What are three things you'd like to make sure we keep doing? What three things would you like to change?
11. The ministry is broken. How do we fix it?
12. What do you think are the five biggest mistakes we made in planning or execution this year?

Some of these questions require a bit of reflection, so tell them ahead of time what bonus question you'll ask so they can think in advance and come with prepared thoughts.

How frequently?

Now that you know what you're doing one-to-one, decide how frequently you'll meet. Three factors determine the cadence of your meetings.

The first and main factor is whether the person is a volunteer or a staff member. This isn't about pay but about how much of their time is devoted to the ministry and so how fast things change. Most volunteers have other things that take up the majority of their time—a job, tertiary education, running their household—and they give a handful of hours each week to serve in ministry. A staff member, while they may have those other things in their life too, are devoting a more substantial proportion of their time—days rather than hours each week. This means there will generally be more things happening, changing and needing to be done. For a full-time staff member, the amount that happens in a week might be the same amount that happens in three months for a volunteer. Meet more frequently with a staff member than with the average volunteer.

The second factor is the competence of the leader. The higher the competence, the less frequent your meetings can be. When a person has newly joined the ministry or team or pipeline layer, you may need to meet with them more to begin with. If you would typically meet once every three months, with a new person you might meet monthly for the first six months so you can onboard them, deal with their questions and provide a regular forum for them to check in with you and you with them.[143] As their learning curve flattens, lengthen the periods between meetings and adjust your role to ongoing coaching.

The final major factor is the degree of clarity their ministry role allows. The more clarity the role has or the more straightforward the ministry is, the less frequently you might need to meet. Increasing complexity or ambiguity principally happens higher in the pipeline as layers shift from being responsible for specific tasks and processes to being responsible for ministry areas and outcomes. Clarity decreases as you begin to more exclusively lead others, since people and their lives can become messy quickly.

---

143 See Hamilton, 'Change your default style', pp. 105-110.

Meeting frequency isn't one-size-fits-all, nor is it set-and-forget. As things change, change the frequency of your meetings. When a volunteer moves to the team leader layer for the first time, meet more frequently before you settle into meeting once a quarter. When your kids' minister is part-time, meet once every two weeks, but when their role changes to full-time, meet twice a week for the first two months and then settle into a weekly meeting as they become comfortable with their new responsibilities.

Here's a summary of the major factors that influence meeting frequency. There are no hard and fast rules, but rather rules of thumb and principles that need to be held in tension.

Factor	Frequent	Infrequent
Volunteer		X
Staff	X	
Less competent	X	
More competent		X
Clarity and order		X
Ambiguity and complexity	X	

Course corrections

Finally, what happens if the leader has met with you, discussed what needs to be done next, proposed a plan that you agreed with, gone off and begun to implement that plan—and then suddenly you realize you've changed your mind. You think another option would be better. What do you do then?

You cannot unilaterally declare a change of plan, not after they have discussed, formulated, presented and received your approval of it. You should only tell them their plan is changing if someone is going to die. If you sashay in and rip up the plan, you will pay a heavy price in morale, mental energy and emotional investment in literally everything they do for years to come. You just taught them, "Don't try too hard. Don't invest in a plan. Don't care too much. You never know when the boss will rip it out from underneath you." That kind of lesson is quickly learned and rarely forgotten. If you ever decide you need to do it, it had better be worth it.

Yes, maybe the plan you both agreed on wasn't the best it could be. But zoom out and think beyond this one moment. You need to balance the cost of this plan being sub-par with the cost of curbing the prospects of every subsequent activity for months and possibly years into the future. Remember, you approved it.

Now, this doesn't mean that you can't do anything. You can have a conversation about how you're re-thinking whether this is the best way forward. You can raise your concerns and see what they have to say. Perhaps they'll agree. Maybe they'll see a way to tweak the current plan so that they minimize the foreseen problems but with the thrust of the plan intact. Perhaps they'll remain convinced that the plan is good and should be stuck to.

This moment is critical: you need to let *them* make the decision.

For some of you, that sentence is ludicrous. But changing the plan needs to be their decision, otherwise you'll incur all of the costs we talked about already. If a mid-course correction is to happen, it must be their responsibility.

To the wise leader, nothing is ever a waste. Maybe they continue the plan as it was decided, against your further reflection, and it turns out great. They were right and you were wrong: fantastic! Now they have improved confidence, deeper investment and developed instincts. You need to resist being defensive or pouty and celebrate a good outcome. Maybe they continue the plan, ignore your wisdom, and it turns out badly, or at least not as well as it could or should have. Also fantastic! Now you have an opportunity to coach them and help them learn from their failure. Resist gloating and instead help them recalibrate their instincts and learn everything they can about why it didn't work. Which factors were relevant, and which only *appeared* important but were merely correlated? The goal is that next time they construct better plans and also listen to wise counsel regarding mid-game corrections. Either way, the loving leader will squeeze every last drop of leadership development benefit from the situation.

Ministries don't run themselves, and to stay on course takes constant energy and attention. Ministry monitoring is the art of keeping all the plates spinning through the overlooked and misunderstood—but never replaced—one-to-one meeting. When wielded skilfully, it's one of the most potent weapons in the arsenal of the effective leader.

Pipeline planning meeting 10

Before this meeting, the senior leader will have already held a three-month ministry evaluation with the ministry area leaders who report to them. In this meeting you'll create the first draft of a three-month evaluation and an end-of-year self-evaluation for each ministry area. If you have the team leader layer in your ministry, you'll create evaluations for the team and the frontline leader layers to complete. Start with the team leader layer since you'll launch this evaluation process with that layer first.

Each ministry area leader begins drafting the three-month ministry evaluation. If the units in your ministry area are quite different from each other then you may need to create a draft for each; otherwise re-use the work you can. Once you've done this for the team leader layer, move on to the frontline leader layer. If you have time, tackle the end-of-year evaluations as well while you have motivation.

The ministry area leaders now set up a time to talk about this new evaluation idea with the layer directly below them. Don't just send them the evaluation and tell them to fill it in. That would be efficient but ineffective, since generally people welcome evaluations with equal parts of disdain and cynicism. So, when you're face-to-face, explain how this isn't you evaluating them but them evaluating the ministry. Help them grow comfortable with the idea of evaluations in general and model your willingness to be on the receiving end.

Just like when the senior leader opened up, this is a big leadership moment that easily becomes a dog's breakfast. Ministry area leaders, your leaders won't be directly evaluating you—but it will probably feel otherwise. The ministry they're evaluating is the ministry you're responsible for. As with the senior leader, so it is with you. Be curious rather than defensive or combative. Create an environment where people tell you the truth because they feel as though they can. Don't punish your people when they do it; that's the fastest way to turn all of this into garbage and a complete waste of time. Truthful evaluations are a gift. Don't throw that away.

Once you've launched these three-month ministry evaluations with your team leaders you'll then launch them with your frontline leaders. Once everyone has evaluated the ministry and the end of a year draws close, launch the end-of-year self-evaluations with your teams.

25
Training and coaching

Leadership development framework

- Ministry grouping
- **Training and coaching**
- Pipeline architecture
- Leader development
- Ministry monitoring
- Leader recruitment
- Leader assessment

Leadership culture
Discipleship culture
Convictional culture

The whole leadership development framework is about developing leaders, but this final piece is firmly and explicitly about development. This piece is about intentionally doing things that help your leaders improve.

Training

When people think of training, they think of a conference or a seminar where you get people into a room with a handout and a whiteboard. At the end you might get a certificate to commemorate the fact that you are now officially 'trained'. Huzzah.

Classroom training has a place in the leadership development process—some things just need to be learned—but it's not the primary or first method we should think of. Instead, we should be thinking of on-the-job training and intentional conversations about how to improve: coaching. The winning formula is some classroom training and a lot of on-the-job training, supported and surrounded by care and coaching.

Classroom training

Here's an obvious thought: if your leaders don't know what to do or how to do it, then they won't get it done. Those things may happen by accident, but not intentionally or repeatedly. Your leaders need to conceptually understand what they need to do and then they also need to learn to actually do it in real life. These are two entirely different experiences, and we shouldn't think that because a person is doing one they are automatically doing the other.

This kind of distinction—between intellectual understanding and practical performance—is common. It's one thing to understand what a recipe says about mixing the ingredients together, but quite another to get a bowl and a spoon and do it yourself. You can know the rules of basketball and the steps to make a jump shot but not be able to play a game and shoot one on the court. Reading sheet music is not the same as actually playing the instrument.

Both types of learning are necessary—learning the rules of a game and practising the individual movements are important—but nothing compares to playing an actual game. It's the same with leadership. Reading this book is important (good job so far!), reading chapters of *Wisdom in Leadership* on the competencies you need to learn will be helpful, and getting resources from revcraighamilton.com will improve you as well. Sometimes there are frameworks you need to wrap your head around;

other times there are steps that you might accidentally be skipping or processes you weren't aware of. Understanding leadership principles or frameworks is a solid foundation, but that doesn't mean you're done and competent. Now you need to go practise them in real life.

On-the-job training

On-the-job training can be broken down into two types: trial and error, and intentional development. Both are helpful in their own way, and both should be used to train your leaders. However, sometimes when people say "on-the-job training" they only mean one of the options. This can mean trouble since each is a vastly different experience.

Trial and error

Trial and error is where people are left to do things they've never done before or that they don't know how to do. No-one helps or guides them; they just work it out themselves. If what they try doesn't work, they try something else. If it does work, they keep doing it until it stops working.

This form of training is looked down upon as inferior to intentional development, and in some ways it is, but it's nonetheless still valuable. People will learn and grow this way. The issue is that it can take a long time to reach proficiency because the person will inevitably walk down several dead ends and garden paths before they find the right road. It also requires the person to be highly reflective in order to diagnose and learn from their mistakes, while also needing a reasonable level of robustness to be able to endure the early stages of poor performance and constant mistakes—especially if those mistakes are public.

At the same time, mistakes and failures are a constant companion of any learner, and so as long as they are helped to process those mistakes to ensure they learn the lessons and so long as they aren't too catastrophic, frequent failures aren't a terrible drawback. It's also true that there will come a point in your leadership journey (you may be there already) when people will stop 'intentionally developing' you and everything you're learning will be through trial and error. Getting used to that when the stakes are lower gives you a long-term advantage.

Trial and error training is also realistic: no matter how planned and intentional you are, you'll never pre-empt every circumstance with training. You can prepare many competencies and experiences, but leadership doesn't always follow pre-programmed training stages. People are thrust into circumstances they are not trained or prepared for because life sometimes conspires against us, no matter how carefully planned and meticulously thought-through we are.

In other words, trial and error *will* be a part of your training regime, wanted or not. People will navigate circumstances you haven't prepared them for on a regular basis, and they'll need to use wisdom and guesswork. Debrief and discuss with them afterwards, helping them learn the lessons and backfilling anything that would help next time. This brings us back to the critical importance of your regular ministry monitoring one-to-one conversations.

People are going to encounter situations they aren't prepared for, and they'll need help to navigate and learn from them. There'll be a significant overlap between your *training* and your *coaching*.

Intentional development

The other form of on-the-job training is intentional development. You take a competency or activity and you gradually hand it over by incrementally building up a leader's competence. By the end of the process, the person is performing that activity with confidence. The hardest part is that it requires forethought and lead time. If you need someone to run the activity in the Sunday kids' program *next week* because you'll be away, it's too late for intentional development. You'll have to throw them in to sink or swim.

Intentional development is a four-step process. The first step is: I do, you watch. Model how it's supposed to work. "I'm going to run the activity in Sunday kids this week, and you're going to watch what I do and how I do it."

It's tempting to think, "Every week that I run the activity the other leaders are watching and learning how I do it. They're absorbing the things I'm saying and when I'm saying them." Sorry, but they're not. There may be some watching happening, but there'll be very little learning. But say to one of them, "Next week you're going to run the activity. I want you to watch what I do this week and then we can talk about what you noticed afterward and clarify any questions you have." Now I guarantee they really will be soaking up everything you say and do. Make sure you do talk afterwards with them about what they noticed, what you were doing and trying to achieve and why you made the decisions you made. This discussion is a vital part that you must not skip.

The second step is: I do, you help. "Next week we're going to run the activity together. I'm going to do it, and you're going to help me." You meet up or talk on the phone and plan out what is going to happen. When Sunday arrives, you run the activity and they help in some way—perhaps they run a particular piece or maybe they help you run the whole thing somehow. The point is, you're running it and they're helping you. Afterwards, again, you talk about how it went. How did they feel? What would they do differently if they were to do it again? What didn't go the way they expected it to? You discuss the parts that they did and what went well and any tweaks that will help them better run any activity in the future.

The third step is: you do, I help. "Next week, you run the activity and I'll help." You probably still plan together as they come up with the activity and how it'll work. You help them think it through and ferret out anything that won't work. On Sunday they run the activity and you have your discussed and designated responsibilities, but you will also assist as necessary—making sure catastrophes don't happen—without undermining the leader you are training. Talk later about how it went, what they would do differently and all the things they did well. You'll also tell them some of the things you did to help make it work and why.

The fourth and final step is: you do, I watch. "This week, let me know the plan you have for the activity. I'll ask questions to help you think through areas you may have overlooked." Then, when Sunday comes, they run the activity and you just observe. Afterwards, like every other week, you'll talk about how it went and what you both thought.

The advantage of this kind of training is that the new leader has incrementally shouldered the responsibility of running that Sunday activity in a way that has been stretching but not overwhelming. They have been set up to succeed. You provided them a safety net of help and expertise. They've learned through your interactions across a range of different activities so they understand not just the 'what' but also the 'why'. They are now at least *somewhat* confident, and their confidence is based on their experienced ability.

The downside is that it's time-intensive. It takes at least four iterations of the activity, but often it'll take longer than that. You'll do more of the "I do, you help" or the "you do, I help" steps, or you won't block out the four weeks just for them because you're using this training technique for more than one leader at a time.

It's also time-intensive for the trainer. It's far easier and quicker to just run the activity. But you won't, firstly because you've made the heart transition that sees developing your team as the actual job. Your objective is to develop your team, and there is no way that doing it yourself is the quickest and easiest way to achieve *that*. Secondly, in the medium-to-long term, once people have been trained, you will have more time to do the important work that only you can do while knowing that *this* vital work will also be competently covered.

Coaching

Coaching is a leadership relationship where you care for the members of your team and help them to maximize the effectiveness of their service for the kingdom. The keywords are *care* and *maximize*. You genuinely love and care for these people. You want the best for them and to do the right thing by them. And you want to maximize their ministry, to help them improve and get better. You want them to become increasingly effective for the kingdom. You want to help them play their part, as God has wired them, for the fame of his name in the spread of the gospel.

Lousy leadership minimizes people. They can do more and be better, but that leader constrains them, makes them lesser. And those people will be like that until the leader grows and changes or until one of them leaves. As a leader, you will either help people become more than they currently are or you will suppress them. The goal is to love and care for your team by training and coaching them so that they grow, get better and contribute all that God has gifted them with.

Now you could take this definition too far and push your team to spend more time in ministry until everyone is only doing ministry all the time to the exclusion of everything else. But this wouldn't maximize the effectiveness of their service, which is always shaped by their whole discipleship, not just the number of hours they serve. And if you genuinely care for a person you'd think about their whole life and the person that God has made them to be. So some internal constraints keep this definition from becoming silly.

The underlying assumption of coaching is, of course, that people can both get better and change. You need to really believe this is true—otherwise, what's the point? But if you believe that God has gifted everyone with a role to play in building God's church, and that they can also get better at these things, then it's your job as the leader to help people find the awesome that God has put in them and deploy that awesome for the sake of the kingdom and the glory of God.[144]

The other factor at play is that this person can get better only *if they actually want to*. It's almost impossible to effectively coach someone who doesn't want to be coached. You can love and encourage, teach and exhort, cast vision and inspire, schedule meetings and create systems. But if a person still doesn't want to grow, you can't *force* them to. You can lead a horse to water but you can't make it receive coaching.

Coaching HELPS

Coaching can be broken down into five discrete components that together spell what coaching does: helps. These are:

1. Helping them discover their own solutions
2. Encouraging strengths
3. Listening and asking questions
4. Providing feedback
5. Sowing care

---

144 See Hamilton, 'Find the awesome', pp. 295-301.

1. Helping them discover their own solutions

This piece is the most important. It's the heart of coaching: rather than telling them what to do, your objective is to help them discover the answer for themselves. What makes coaching different from training is that training is essentially about giving people the answers—here's how you do this thing—whereas coaching is about helping people to ask better questions and discover the answer themselves. It's a subtle, collaborative skill set.

2. Encouraging strengths

Your job as a coach is to discern people's strengths and point them out. This is not just their strengths in getting things done and achieving objectives but also in *how* they get things done.

The person I'm coaching may achieve what they need to in a very different way from how I would. I need to notice this difference and help the person to see it too. This will take discipline on my part because I probably think my way is the best way. I need to recognize that my approach has advantages and disadvantages. I need to look at the way this person has done it and determine whether the objective was still achieved.

Some strengths are obvious, others subtler. Some people's strengths are so subtle you might think that none exist. Some strengths are hidden beneath layers of incompetence, doubt, apathy, negativity—or all of the above. But even in these cases, strengths will still be present; you must figure out what they are and bring them to the surface, even if it strains your perceptions and insights to their limits.

This encouraging of strengths needs to be regular and repeated. After pointing their strengths out the first time, keep pointing them out as often as you can, at least to begin with. Their failures and weaknesses will be highlighted for them regularly by their own psyche and by external factors. While yes, you want them to be dealing with their weaknesses, you want them to be leaning into their strengths as much as possible too. It's where they have the most potential for growth and the ability to make the most impact.[145]

---

145 See Hamilton, 'Play to your strengths', pp. 99-104.

This constant recognition of strengths isn't to pump up their self-esteem or stroke their egos; it's to help them see reality. People are often better at pinpointing their deficiencies than they are at articulating their strengths. To help people see the world as it really is, you need to be more constant in facilitating people to recognize and remember their strengths than in pointing out their shortcomings.

3. Listening and asking questions

This is one of the central pieces that separates coaching from teaching. You're helping your leaders to discover solutions for themselves. They need to be thinking and talking; you need to get them reflecting on their situations. Guide them by the questions you ask towards the underlying cause, unifying issue or winning solution.

This kind of listening and questioning is not easy. There's a whole chapter on listening in *Wisdom in Leadership*, but its key point is the discipline of asking ten questions before even considering offering advice.[146] Their answers to these questions help you really understand what they're talking about so that you can help them reflect and think thoughts that might not have occurred to them otherwise. At the risk of seeming egotistical by quoting myself:

> What you might find is that, before you even get to the end of your ten questions, people will come up with the answer to their problem themselves and even convince themselves why they need to solve it in a particular way—which is a brilliant outcome. If this happens, you will have helped someone figure out the course of action to take and motivated them to go do it while also building their confidence and ability to solve their own problems.[147]

If your goal in coaching is to maximize the person you lead by genuinely caring for them, what is the best way to go about this? Just ask them:

---

146 Hamilton, 'Shut up and listen', pp. 229-234.
147 Hamilton, pp. 233-234.

- What are you finding frustrating?
- What's a roadblock that I might be able to move for you?
- What resources do you need?
- What experiences would you like?
- What skills would you like to learn?
- If you prayed tonight that God would fix this particular problem and then overnight while you slept he did, how would you tell the next morning that he had?

Learning to ask great questions will make you a good coach and so a terrific developer of leaders.

4. Providing feedback

To coach people, you cannot rely only on asking insightful questions and spotlighting people's strengths. You also need to give them feedback: tell them how they went and how they can improve.

Often when we think feedback, we think negative feedback, but that's only half the arsenal. Positive feedback is very powerful, maybe even more powerful than negative feedback. Negative feedback *feels* more impactful, and it often raises more heated emotions, but is it effective in producing more of the behaviour that you are after? In many situations, no.

Don't overlook giving positive feedback. People think it's empty platitudes and vapid clichés, but that's only when done poorly. Positive feedback isn't about mindlessly dispensing generic phrases; it's about carefully watching for the sometimes subtle behaviours that signal that people are effectively leading at their layer. If you specifically point them out, leaders will gain insight into themselves and their unique contribution as well as gain clarity as to what precisely they are supposed to be doing (compared to the somewhat abstract description on a page). Positive feedback is also easier to give, since you don't feel the need to craft it as carefully as negative feedback, so it can do its work more frequently.

This isn't to say that negative feedback is unimportant or unnecessary. Telling people what they are doing wrong and how they can improve is actually positive. It doesn't *feel* positive, and people often don't take it well, but it really is a good thing. Proverbs is full of praise for feedback. Seeing criticism as a gift is a sign of wisdom, while despising feedback is a sign of a fool. Here's a favourite of mine, Proverbs 9:8-9:

> Do not reprove [criticize, rebuke] a scoffer, or he will hate you;
> reprove a wise man, and he will love you.
> Give instruction to a wise man, and he will be still wiser...

The scoffer and the wise man might both be on your team; you may have reproved them and had them each react like this verse. But just because we gave negative feedback to a person once and they blew up at us doesn't mean we should never do it again. It probably means we need to grow in our skills and get better at giving negative feedback (that's always going to be true), but it also means we need to help our people grow in wisdom. Both of these are very hard tasks.[148]

5. Sowing care

The last component of effective coaching is sowing genuine care into the people you coach. Sow care like you sow seed: you're in it for the long haul. You're not expecting results immediately, but you provide support that helps growth over time.

Leader development isn't just a task or a job or a role or a responsibility; it's fundamentally a discipling relationship. Relationships are critical to high performance. Experience tells us this, the Bible tells us this and science tells us this.[149] The human brain needs oxygen, glucose and relationships. This isn't just rhetoric; this is true on a neurological level.[150]

As mentioned in the previous chapter, the person you lead will be in a web of discipling relationships at your church. There may be mutual, peer discipling relationships; one-to-one discipling relationships; small

---

[148] For more on giving feedback well, see Hamilton, 'People deserve to know the truth', pp. 281-293; and 'Public fans and private critics', pp. 235-238.

[149] One of the points of the book of Proverbs is that a key ingredient in a fruitful life is the wise management of relationships. More specifically, Paul's requirements for church overseers emphasize the interpersonal dimension of leadership (1 Tim 3:1-13; Titus 1:5-9). We can see this in characteristics like being respectable, hospitable, not violent but gentle, able to manage a household with dignity and so on. The doctrine of the Trinity also shows us the central importance of relationships in that relations existed between the Father, Son and Spirit before creation existed.

[150] See Hamilton, 'Two foundations of team-building', pp. 245-251.

group discipling relationships; pastoral discipling relationships; and the relationship that you have with them as their leader. Each relationship will help that person continue to follow Jesus and grow in faith in him—one doesn't need to do it all.

Some of these relationships have more authority and responsibility than others. You may not have primary responsibility for the discipleship of your leaders, but you aren't disconnected from their discipleship either. As we saw back in chapter 2, their discipleship will have a direct impact upon their leadership, but more importantly their discipleship will matter to you because *they* matter to you. You can't love and care for a person and be indifferent to their relationship with Jesus and their eternal trajectory. Their discipleship will always be in the background, informing everything you do as their leader developing them.

To be an effective coach, you need to care for the people you lead. You already know how to do this. You get to know them, spend time with them, treat them with compassion and understanding. You notice what they do and let them know that you noticed. You remember what you talked about and ask how those things are going. You help when and how you can, and tell them the truth even if it's hard. You pray for them, forgive them, ask for their forgiveness. You treat them with respect, look out for their interests, do what's beneficial for them even if it costs you—and a hundred other things. In other words, you seek to love them like Jesus loves you.

Revision

Since training and coaching is the final piece in the leadership development framework, let's recap one last time how the whole system fits together so you can check for any pieces you've missed.

All six pieces are cradled within the church's wider culture: the soil everything is planted in, grows out of and draws nutrients from. Getting that culture right makes your leadership development *faithfully healthy*.

The first two elements of the framework—ministry grouping and pipeline architecture—are about designing the space and structures that people will serve in. This is abstract and conceptual work, but it has an enormous impact on the practical and concrete ministry that people do. These elements help you create clarity and ensure intentionality. These two pieces make your leadership development *faithfully smart.*

The final four pieces—leader recruitment, leader assessment, ministry monitoring, and training and coaching—are squarely focused on people and leaders actually being involved in people's lives, speaking the word of God, making sure people are cared for and helped… doing ministry. These four elements make the system *faithfully effective.*

Recruitment brings people into your ministries, getting them out of the pews and into a team that serves. Assessment works out where your leaders are at and what they need next to keep growing and developing. Monitoring is about staying in touch with your team and having conversations about how they and the ministry are going. Finally, training and coaching helps your leaders improve and grow in their ability to minister effectively.

As we've seen, these elements are all interdependent and work together to create a system so that ministry can be done well and in a way that maximizes and multiplies the ministry that can be achieved. The leadership development framework is about ensuring that your leaders and ministries are faithfully healthy, smart and effective in the task of bringing God's word to bear in people's lives—those who follow Jesus and those who don't yet.

Pipeline planning meeting 11

This is the second-last mandated pipeline planning meeting and it focuses on training and recruitment. We could spend this meeting planning a training meeting or training course for your leaders and that would be a worthwhile use of time. However, training and coaching is at its most powerful when it becomes a mindset and an ongoing way of life. That's why the goals for this meeting are to intentionally prepare some on-the-job training, self-diagnose the recruitment levers and check back in on work you did a few pipeline planning meetings ago.

Individually, brainstorm a list of people you are *already* training and developing or whom you'd like to *start* developing. Pick two of these people and identify one skill or activity that you can begin on-the-job training together with using the 'I do, you watch/I do, you help' method. Go around the room sharing who you're going to begin training and what you'll train them in.

Next, reflect on your own personal recruiting practices. Take the three recruitment drivers—relational loyalty, displayed competence and vision—and consider your tendencies. Which driver comes most naturally or which do you lean on most heavily? Which one is most intuitive? Which takes more conscious thought? Rank them from strongest to weakest.

You might be very strong in all of them. You might be terrible at all of them! Everyone will have a range. If you're terrible at all of them, which one are you slightly the least terrible with? If you're legendary at all of them, in which one does your brilliance shine slightly brighter?

Once you've decided on your ranking, share it with the group and explain why you put them in that order.

Last of all, a few meetings ago you brainstormed the theology that undergirds your collective doctrine of serving and ministry and created a list of potential leaders. Share any further updates or additions that have come to you.

Core skills summary

	Core: foundations	Core: strategy	Core: development	Core: stewardship
Senior leader	Takes responsibility for creating, guarding and modelling the vision, values and culture of the church in line with the Bible.	Thinks strategically about and sets priorities for the church as a whole.	Wholly self-directed development.	Faithfully manages the allocation and prioritization of resources, funds the vision.
Ministry area leader	Translates church-wide vision for ministry area while carrying the values and culture into their ministry area.	Designs strategy for ministry area that feeds and fits within church-wide strategy, integrates this strategy with other ministry areas.	Largely self-directed development.	Faithfully effective in managing the church's resources.
Unit leader	Able to defend the vision and distinguish it from others and carries the values and culture into their unit.	Understands strategy and so is able to guard against 'strategy creep'.	Able to receive coaching from layers above and feedback from below.	Faithfully effective in managing allocated resources and understands resource parameters.
Team leader	Clearly articulates and implements vision and carries the values and culture into their team.	Leads team to unite around and execute the strategy.	Able to give and receive coaching.	Faithfully gets best results with allocated resources, helps team to understand their resource parameters.
Leader/ team member	Aware of and supports the vision while growing in the values and culture.	Knows the strategy and serves effectively in their role.	Able to receive coaching.	Faithfully manages personal resources, stays within allocated ministry resources.

26
Ongoing challenges

"I can imagine this has been a tough season—lots to do and implement and get your head around", said Luke as he finished his coffee.

"Yeah, it's been tough in some ways," agreed Phil, "but it's been valuable. I feel like I finally understand what's happening at my church, what I need to do and where we're heading for the next three or so years. I have a handle, for the first time ever, on what I'm supposed to be doing as the senior leader."

"And you've been implementing more than just the leadership pipeline, right? It's in the broader context of the leadership development framework?"

"Yep, exactly", said Phil. "When you first mentioned the pipeline, you said something like: the most common mistake leaders make when they need to implement the leadership pipeline is to immediately start implementing the pipeline."

"That sounds like something I would say."

"At the time I didn't understand, but it makes sense now. For us at St Phil's to do pipeline stuff, we first had to work out how our ministries were grouped, and that was harder than I'd thought."

"Yeah, it is, isn't it?" smiled Luke. "Was it the hardest part?"

"Oh, no way!" Phil exclaimed. "No, the hardest part was the culture—massaging our leadership culture. It wasn't *terrible*, but we definitely had a culture of helpers rather than leaders that was tricky to turn around. But you know what was the biggest revelation to me? As we grappled as a staff team trying to figure out what we had, someone said that we had an 'apologetic' leadership culture. She felt we often apologized for asking people to lead or gave off the vibe that we *thought* we were inconveniencing people, which meant people *saw it* as an inconvenience."

"This was news to me," Phil continued, "but she was right. We had to go back and re-examine what we really thought about service and ministry from the Scriptures. And *that* meant we had to change our minds and how we spoke."

"So how did you do it?" Luke asked, leaning slightly forward.

"Well, one thing we did was whenever a staff member talked about serving in a ministry as 'helping' or having an apologetic tone about it—during announcements or a sermon or whenever—they had to buy all the others donuts at the next staff meeting."

"And what happened?"

"Well, we ate a lot of donuts", Phil smirked. "But over time we ate less and less, until we went for a whole three months without eating any. At which point I took all the staff out to lunch to celebrate!"

"What a great idea!" grinned Luke.

"Let me ask you something", said Phil, draining his coffee. "You're way ahead of me in terms of implementing the framework and the pipeline. What's been the hardest thing in the ongoing maintenance of it all?"

"Good question", Luke replied, pondering for a moment. "I think it's been remembering to honour the structure. Even now I'm still tempted to come down the pipeline and do a leader's ministry or make decisions or solve problems for them. People come to me with something that's happening in a ministry, or I catch a whiff of it in a skip-layer meeting, and my instinct is to solve it then and there. It'd be quick and easy. It seems like a no-brainer."

"But it's actually a terrible idea", Phil said nodding.

"But it's actually a terrible idea!" Luke repeated. "It hurts those leaders: it disempowers and demotivates them and destroys their trust of me. Plus it trains their people that their leader isn't their leader, *I* am, which means the issues cascade on for months as they bring things to me that should've gone to their team leader. I made more work for myself—and for what? Some small problem that wasn't important or urgent. I could have left it for the actual leader to deal with and it would've gone fine. The pain and heartache was both unnecessary and my fault. And I still haven't learned; I keep doing it!

"But, now that I think about it, there's another thing I still haven't got under control, that I make a conscious effort about and fail in anyway: pride." Luke sat silently for a minute before continuing, "It never goes away, and you need to constantly be on the lookout because it keeps coming for you in ever-different ways. The shadow impulse is always waiting to take over."

"Wow, okay. That's good to be reminded of." Phil saw the time and gathered his things. "Well, as always, thanks for your time this morning—and over this last year with the leadership development framework and the pipeline and all your help. I've really appreciated it."

"Oh, you're welcome", said Luke as they stood to walk to the car park. "It helps me too, to keep thinking it through and realize new things. Just remember, for all the structure and frameworks and layers, the point isn't efficiency or building a hierarchy. The goal is to make disciples who make disciples; all the rest is just a means to that end. It just helps you do that better and more. You build leaders so that people can become and grow as disciples and find the place in church life where they can serve the best, loving the world like Jesus loves the world."

"Thanks Luke", said Phil. "That's exactly right."

Both men got into their cars and drove back to their churches to get on with the responsibility God had entrusted to them: to equip the saints for works of ministry.

Pipeline planning meeting 12

This is the final official pipeline planning meeting. Of course, you could continue meeting if they've been fun and productive times! This meeting is about catching up on things that were missed and/or identifying what's next.

If you followed along diligently through all the pipeline planning meetings in this book, you'll have accomplished an absolutely insane amount as a team. You might not have noticed, or it might not have occurred to you, but the things you've done and begun implementing are some of the most important and foundational for growing a church that develops leaders.

Here's a checklist of what you thought about, discussed, brainstormed, argued over and implemented. Some items you may not have completed as cleanly as you hoped, or you maybe skipped a few completely and you want to have another crack at them. Go for it! These meetings were just to help you get started. Now comes the challenge of maintaining what's good, fixing what's not working and continuously improving it all.

- [ ] why you exist
- [ ] the main thing you're seeking to achieve
- [ ] the overall plan
- [ ] words that describe your flavour
- [ ] initial 90-day priorities
- [ ] the fundamental operations of your ministry areas
- [ ] the decision-making authority for every member of the team
- [ ] your current culture
- [ ] aspects of your aspirational culture
- [ ] ministry grouping
- [ ] personalized pipeline
- [ ] the first ministry areas to receive the pipeline
- [ ] the timeline for your first pipeline rollout
- [ ] role descriptions for every ministry area with a common layout
- [ ] a theology of serving and ministry that undergirds recruitment
- [ ] a list of potential leaders for development and the next steps for many of them
- [ ] people who are ready for higher pipeline roles
- [ ] regular one-to-one meetings with your key leaders
- [ ] three-month and end-of-year evaluations for every layer
- [ ] specific on-the-job training with two people per ministry area
- [ ] recruitment driver preferences and tendencies

If you're reasonably happy with where you're up to with all these and you're wondering what to do now, here's an idea. One of the themes of this book has been how important clarity is to building a high-functioning team and to developing high-functioning leaders. Back in the ministry monitoring chapter we talked about GYR rating—rating things either green, yellow or red—and then 1-2-3 (one priority, two problems, three concrete next steps). Take the entire leadership development framework (culture, ministry grouping, pipeline architecture, leader recruitment, leader assessment, ministry monitoring, training and coaching) and GYR rate and 1-2-3 them to try and get a handle on where your church is at. Have a conversation about how to deal with your circumstances and where to focus your energies. Figure out what the reality is so you can figure out what needs to happen next.

Implementing the leadership development framework isn't a one-and-done proposition. It will take years to get it humming at top speed, and even then maintaining that pace is no easy task. GYR rating your whole church, a specific ministry area or the leadership development framework in your church is a good pattern for future pipeline planning meetings.

Appendix
Unit leader layer

Most churches will only need the three-layer pipeline: leader/team member, team leaders and senior leader. Some will need to add a fourth layer of ministry area leaders, while other larger churches and ministries may also need a layer between team leaders and ministry area leaders: the unit leader layer.

When a layer is added, there are no changes that need to be made to the layers below the new addition. However, some of the layer-specific things to learn from the layer *above* the new layer are brought down into it, and new responsibilities are created for the new layer due to the new pipeline architecture.

In this appendix we'll unravel what the pipeline looks like with the added unit leader layer, as well what the unit layer is doing and how that impacts the ministry area leader.

Here's the diagram:

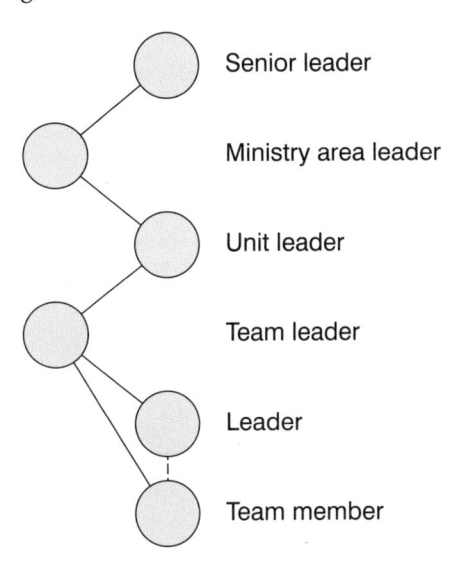

- Senior leader
- Ministry area leader
- Unit leader
- Team leader
- Leader
- Team member

Definition

The unit leader serves by leading a team of teams. A ministry unit is a discrete subset of a wider ministry area. For example, a kids' ministry might have the Sunday service ministry unit and a mid-week after school ministry unit. These ministries have separate teams and objectives but are both, obviously, a part of the kids' ministry area. In a basic leadership pipeline, the kids' minister will directly lead both of those units.

The unit leader layer becomes necessary when there are too many teams for that kids' minister to directly lead. Perhaps the Sunday ministry has three church services, and each service has a separate team for crèche, preschool, Kindergarten to Year 2, Years 3 and 4, and then Years 5 and 6. That's 15 teams across the Sunday. A unit leader would, depending on how the ministries were grouped, lead the team of teams responsible for kids' ministry at a single service.

Key distinction

The key distinction between the unit leader and the team leader below is that the team leader is focused on getting the individuals in their team working well together, while the unit leader is working towards getting teams working well together.

There is a noticeable increase in complexity at this layer. In our kids' ministry scenario above, the unit leader is leading a team of five team leaders. They still need to navigate all the issues and challenges of a team leader—doing ministry through others; seeing their fruit grow on other people's trees; helping the members of their team understand that this team of team leaders is their primary team—plus think both about how the five *individuals* on their team relate *and* about how the five *teams* relate. For example, there will be kids transitioning between groups—like crèche to preschool—and the unit leader will be responsible for helping these two teams to work together to manage this well.

The complexity continues, however, since the unit leader must also relate to the other unit leaders and ensure that the ministry is consistent across the whole Sunday while still being attentive to the uniqueness of their own service. Unit leaders must begin to think not just about their specific unit but beyond, and concern themselves with strategic issues that support the whole ministry area.

What makes this layer distinct from the ministry area leader layer is that they do not have the authority to craft a vision or decide on the strategy for the entire ministry area.

Heart focus

As we've said, the unit leader continues the posture developed at the team leader layer of leading *through others*. Their main job is to grow and develop team leaders. Instead of helping people grow as individual contributors, they need to help others make the difficult team leader transition. This means they need to deeply understand both the dynamics of that transition and the subtleties of that layer.

Unit leaders, in conversation with ministry area leaders, are also responsible for the selection of team leaders. They are developing the people who will become the church's key leaders! At the leader and team leader layer their recruitment efforts were provisional and subject to confirmation through another mechanism like the 101 meeting. Now they recruit directly, having conversations with leaders and asking them to become team leaders.

Time considerations

The role of the unit leader is further complicated by the fact that, while continuing their focus on leading *through* leaders—probably still a struggle—they also need to reincorporate being an individual contributor to a certain extent. This is because they now need to take responsibility for annual planning for their unit, things like budgets, projects and campaigns. The challenge is to ensure that the reintroduction of being an individual contributor doesn't bleed into the way they lead their teams and reverse the progress they made in learning to lead through others.

As well as thinking towards an annual time horizon, the unit leader will need to make time to communicate not just with their team of team leaders but also with the people who make up those teams two layers below them—without undermining the authority of their team leaders. This is the difficult art of leading the skip-layer.

Layer summary

The one-sentence summary of the unit leader layer is:

> I succeed when we succeed.

This layer is the move from learning to work through individuals to learning to work through teams of individuals, integrating the ministry of both. The *people* in the teams and the *teams themselves* need to work well together.

In this configuration, silos are easily created, either within the unit or when the whole unit walls itself off from the rest of the ministry area. It could be that the crèche team goes off and does a great job being the crèche but with very little thought or care about how what it's doing impacts the rest of the Sunday kids' teams at that service. Or the kids' ministry at the 10am service feels completely different to the kids' ministry at the 4pm service.

The unit leader needs to foster the mindset that success happens when all the teams they oversee are succeeding together as a unit *and* when all the other units are also succeeding and thriving. It's collective success *both* up and down the pipeline.

Why this matters

The consequences for a unit leader failing to make the transition to this layer are basically the same as when a ministry area leader fails to transition from being a team leader. I'll mention those issues again, but for detail return to chapter 18.

Clogging the pipeline

If unit leaders reward team leaders for ministry as individual contributors rather than *through their people*, they will clog the pipeline. Also, if they maintain and/or instil the wrong values through actions such as choosing the best or longest-serving contributors as team leaders rather than those with true potential, they will also clog the pipeline with people who shouldn't and can't function at their layer.

Disempowering team leaders

If the unit leader is thoughtless or clumsy in how they communicate with their frontline leaders, then they will be accidently training those leaders to bypass their team leaders and go directly to the unit leader to get their problems solved. The unit leader needs to foster open and honest communication between themselves and the frontline leaders while also empowering their team leaders to solve problems and deal with issues.

Drowning in details

If the unit leader disempowers their team leaders, the inevitable result will be the unit leader needing to do the ministry of the now-disillusioned team leaders. Creating competition between team leaders and frontline leaders, who all then seek the unit leader's input and approval, will leave little time for the unit leader to focus on their own responsibilities.

Whole church affected

The final consequence is that errors at this layer will reduce the whole ministry area's ability, and can leak into other ministry areas too. If poor team leader selection is happening, or team leaders are left undeveloped, this creates a leadership vacuum since team leaders are the source of key leaders across the church. The effects can potentially last for multiple years.

Signs of struggle

Leaders can struggle in almost infinite ways. To paraphrase Tolstoy, all effective leaders are alike; each ineffective leader is ineffective in their own way. These, however, are some of the most common ways that unit leaders can struggle.

Ministry distribution

This is another way of saying delegation: the handing over of authority and responsibility for a task or process. Ministry distribution is a hard skill to learn, but some leaders find it a hard skill to do at all and would rather keep doing things themselves. You can get away with it at the team leader layer without the effects being too catastrophic, but the unit leader *cannot* be doing the ministry of the team leader or the frontline leader.

Refusing to distribute the ministry to others is more of a problem now because more people are affected and ministry will be done slowly due to the unnecessary centralization. The unit leader won't have the time or space to focus on the task uniquely theirs: developing competent team leaders to lead the ministry.

Even when ministry distribution is happening it can still be done poorly, which will have a similar result. For example, if ministry is distributed without building in accountability, the unit leader will be creating team leaders who function as tyrants. This will also result in less ministry done at the frontlines.

Poor ministry monitoring

Unit leaders can forget or never realize that it takes a substantial investment of energy to keep the ministry plates spinning. This can result in them giving either poor or no feedback to their team leaders. It can also be expressed in a failure to be clear in communicating strategic direction, which means their direct reports will be unsure about what their specific goals are or should be.

Coaching

Overlapping with poor ministry monitoring, ministry area leaders need to focus on cultivating their unit leaders' ability to coach their team leaders. Unit leaders need to be coached in the discipline of asking the right questions of their team leaders to help those leaders solve their own problems. Unit leaders will need to be helped with how to give honest and helpful feedback. Again, these skills will need to be both taught and modelled. Ministry area leaders need to reward coaching ability in their unit leaders.

Creating a court

A more subtle sign of a struggling unit leader is when they consistently invite clones of themselves into their inner circle. This creates a leadership court where they are surrounded by people who are unwilling to challenge the unit leader or bring a fresh perspective. This is often a sign of an insecure leader. When a unit leader chooses for their team people like themselves, it causes the unit to closely reflect the unit leader's own weak areas, and the unit will lack some of the internal forces that would otherwise help it correct for and overcome those weaknesses.

The concrete layer

If the unit leader isn't being brought into the larger strategic discussions for the whole ministry area, they won't be able to deeply understand why things are being done the way they are, and why problems are being solved the way they're being solved. This will firstly result in the unit leader becoming a highly effective resistor to change, since they are the gateway to the vast majority of the leaders in the ministry. When they communicate the ministry area's—necessarily evolving—priorities and objectives, they will communicate in an uninspired and uninspiring way. They will become the concrete layer where communication gets blocked or reinterpreted. The second result of them not understanding and being on board with the plan is that they will likely disconnect their unit from the ministry area's or church's overall strategic direction and will instead work towards creating their own ministry fiefdom. This will require lots of energy to dismantle down the track.

One-page summary

**Ministry unit leader
(from leading other leaders to leading a team of team leaders)**

Serves by leading a team of teams.
Summary: I succeed when we succeed.
Key distinction: shift from 'individuals working well together' to 'teams working well together'.

Things to learn: layer-specific	**Things to learn:** core	**Things to learn:** ministry-specific
• planning projects, budget and personnel • recruiting people • relationship building for the ministry area's benefit • acquiring resources • holding team leaders accountable for managerial work • setting unit's priorities	*Vision:* able to defend the vision and distinguish it from others *Strategy:* understands strategy and is able to guard against 'strategy-creep' *Development:* able to receive coaching from above and feedback from below *Stewardship:* effectively manages allocated resources and understands resource parameters	• technical proficiency • using ministry tools, processes, procedures and reporting

Time considerations	**Heart focus**
• annual planning: budgets, projects, campaigns • communicating with other units within the ministry area • communicating with other teams within the unit	• growing team leaders • managing self • focusing on the success of the whole unit and understanding how it works • integrating the ministry of reporting teams • increasing comfort with assessing and differentiating people

Unit leader: layer-specific things to learn

Leading yourself
- Proficient in emotional intelligence
- Proficient in change management
- Balancing energy and efficiency[151]
- Sensitive to own power
- Avoiding intellectual biases

Building a team of teams
- Selecting team leaders
- Empowering recruitment at all layers

Running teams of teams
- Creating full unit clarity
- Fostering teamwork between teams
- Advanced decision-making: cost–benefit analysis
- Running post-mortems and pre-mortems
- Giving direction with freedom[152]
- Leading effective meetings[153]
- Negotiating
- Thinking from strategic first principles
- Thinking beyond the unit

Developing a team of teams
- Able to successfully onboard new team leaders
- Transition accountability
- Able to not solve people's problems
- Ministry distribution
- Basic coaching
- Having hard conversations
- Staying in touch with the skip-layer

---

151 Hamilton, 'Energy is more efficient than efficiency', pp. 191-195.
152 Hamilton, 'You're just the leader', pp. 175-177; and 'Get out of the way of good people', pp. 317-320.
153 Hamilton, 'Meetings are where real work is done', pp. 387-394; 'Ignore the org-chart', pp. 429-434; and 'Hellos and goodbyes matter', pp. 443-445.

Layer summary (with unit leader layer)

	Explanation	Summary	Key distinction	Layer-specific skills
Senior leader	Serves by leading the entire church.	I succeed when our ministries succeed together.	The buck stops here; how can our church bless a wider circle?	• self-directed ongoing growth as a disciple and helping your team grow • selection of key positions • willing to address ministry monitoring problems quickly with key staff • using the power of veto judiciously
Ministry area leader	Serves by leading an entire ministry area.	I succeed when we succeed differently.	Moving from 'doing it better' to "Should we do it?"	• ongoing growth as a disciple and helping your team grow • leading self • leading the ministry in teaching and structure • leading the ministry as a ministry area • designing roles • designing strategy • dealing with complexity • coping with high visibility, especially from below
Unit leader	Serves by leading a team of teams.	I succeed when we succeed.	Shift from 'individuals working well together' to 'teams working well together'.	• ongoing growth as a disciple and helping the team grow • selecting team leaders • developing team leaders • running teams of teams • leading effective meetings • being less dumb • advanced wisdom on dealing with people
Team leader	Serves by leading a team of leaders.	I succeed when you succeed.	Shift from doing the ministry to getting ministry done through others.	• ongoing growth as a disciple and helping your team grow • team dynamics • running a team • developing a team • entrance to higher-level leadership • recruitment
Leader/ team member	Serves by directly leading group members.	I succeed when I succeed.	Shift from doing ministry alone to doing ministry with others.	• ongoing character development • handling the Bible • tools to be an everyday evangelist • loving your team • developing a healthy mind • using a healthy mind

Time considerations	Focus and feelings
• spends significant time with ministry area leaders • spends increased time with external people and wider concerns	• focusing significant energy on only two or three key, long-cycle objectives • from immediate gratification to sustained progress • taking advice from parish council/elders • educating parish council/elders so they provide informed advice • asking questions and listening to a broad spectrum rather than a single trusted advisor
• three-to-five-year planning • setting priorities for area • spend less time solving tactical problems • leading by team meetings • financial management	• from valuing one unit to valuing all units appropriately • equally valuing the short-term and long-term • able to view own area in the context of the wider church and can make big-picture decisions (even at the expense of own area)
• annual planning—budgets, projects, campaigns • setting priorities for unit • communication time with other units within the entire ministry area • communication time with other teams within the unit	• main job is to grow team leaders • self as manager • focus is on the success of the whole unit and understanding how it works • integrating the ministry of the teams directly reporting • increasing comfort with differentiating people
• term planning • making time available for team members • setting priorities for team	• getting results through others • success of team members • accountability for the success of leaders • team success as personal success • visible integrity
• arrival and departure • meeting personal due dates for projects (usually short-term) • managing own time	• getting results through personal proficiency • high-quality work

Feedback on this resource

We really appreciate getting feedback about our resources—not just suggestions for how to improve them, but also positive feedback and ways they can be used. We especially love to hear that the resources may have helped someone in their Christian growth.

You can send feedback to us via the 'Feedback' menu in our online store, or write to us at info@matthiasmedia.com.au.

matthiasmedia

Matthias Media is an evangelical publishing ministry that seeks to persuade all Christians of the truth of God's purposes in Jesus Christ as revealed in the Bible, and equip them with high-quality resources, so that by the work of the Holy Spirit they will:

- abandon their lives to the honour and service of Christ in daily holiness and decision-making
- pray constantly in Christ's name for the fruitfulness and growth of his gospel
- speak the Bible's life-changing word whenever and however they can—in the home, in the world and in the fellowship of his people.

Our resources range from Bible studies and books through to training courses, audio sermons and children's Sunday School material. To find out more, and to access samples and free downloads, visit our website:

www.matthiasmedia.com

How to buy our resources

1. Direct from us over the internet:
   - in the US: www.matthiasmedia.com
   - in Australia: www.matthiasmedia.com.au

2. Direct from us by phone: please visit our website for current phone contact information.

3. Through a range of outlets in various parts of the world. Visit **www.matthiasmedia.com/contact** for details about recommended retailers in your part of the world.

4. Trade enquiries can be addressed to:
   - in the US and Canada: sales@matthiasmedia.com
   - in Australia and the rest of the world: sales@matthiasmedia.com.au

---

Register at our website for our **free** regular email update to receive information about the latest new resources, **exclusive special offers**, and free articles to help you grow in your Christian life and ministry.

Also by Craig Hamilton

Wisdom in Leadership

You're in Christian ministry—but are you a Bible-and-theology person or a leadership-and-management person?

Craig Hamilton is a Bible guy, but he also noticed that groups of people in God's world function in predictable ways that he could learn from and harness for their benefit. He realized that being a theology person also requires being a leadership person, and that leadership and management principles aren't necessarily godless pragmatism but can be about living with gospel-shaped wisdom and loving our neighbour.

With 78 chapters covering an extensive range of topics, this book is a goldmine of helpful insights for pastors and anyone else with leadership responsibilities in their church.

FOR MORE INFORMATION OR TO ORDER CONTACT:

Matthias Media
Email: sales@matthiasmedia.com.au
www.matthiasmedia.com.au

Matthias Media (USA)
Email: sales@matthiasmedia.com
www.matthiasmedia.com

Also by Craig Hamilton

Made Man

CRAIG HAMILTON

Made Man

Why God becoming human is so **shocking**, so **necessary** and so **life-changing**

We rely on Jesus for our salvation, but who is he? We say he is fully God and fully man… but what does that *actually* mean? How does it work? Why does he need to be both? Does it matter?

We miss a rich vein of gold when we mentally file the incarnation under 'too hard'. In his word, God beautifully expresses why the Word became flesh, and our Christian forebears worked long and hard to explain this mystery clearly. Now, in this warm and accessible book, Craig Hamilton takes us through the incarnation in a way that enables every Christian to understand what it means and why it matters that God became man.

FOR MORE INFORMATION OR TO ORDER CONTACT:

Matthias Media
Email: sales@matthiasmedia.com.au
www.matthiasmedia.com.au

Matthias Media (USA)
Email: sales@matthiasmedia.com
www.matthiasmedia.com

The Trellis and the Vine

All Christian ministry is a mixture of trellis and vine.

There is vine work: the prayerful preaching and teaching of the word of God to see people converted and grow to maturity as disciples of Christ. And there is trellis work: creating and maintaining the physical and organizational structures and programs that support vine work and its growth.

What's the state of the trellis and the vine in your part of the world? Has trellis work taken over, as it has a habit of doing? Is the vine work being done by very few (perhaps only the pastor and only on Sundays)? And is the vine starting to wilt as a result?

Colin Marshall and Tony Payne dig back into the Bible's view of Christian ministry, and argue that a major mind-shift is required if we are to fulfil the Great Commission of Christ, and see the vine flourish again.

FOR MORE INFORMATION OR TO ORDER CONTACT:

Matthias Media
Email: sales@matthiasmedia.com.au
www.matthiasmedia.com.au

Matthias Media (USA)
Email: sales@matthiasmedia.com
www.matthiasmedia.com